ROME AND THE EASTERN CHURCHES

Aidan Nichols, O.P.

ROME AND THE EASTERN CHURCHES

A Study in Schism

Revised edition

IGNATIUS PRESS   SAN FRANCISCO

Photograph by Stefano Spaziani
Pope Benedict XVI with Patriarch Bartholomew I
(Archbishop of Constantinople and Ecumenical Patriarch)

Cover design by Roxanne Mei Lum

To the honoured memory of
Adrian Fortescue
(1874–1923)
priest, Orientalist, liturgist
luminary of the English Catholic Church

*Now Bethsaida may rejoice
for in thee, as from a mystical pot,
flowered forth most sweet-smelling lilies,
Peter and Andrew.*

— *Greek Menologion for the Feast of Saint Andrew,
30 November*

Contents

Preface to the
First Edition (1992)

The present study of relations between the Papacy and the churches of the East appears at a crucial time for the fate of the "Great Church": historic Christendom. On the one hand, the internal difficulties of Western Catholicism are acutely apparent even to readers of the secular—never mind the religious—press, where reports of theological dissidence and revolt against the authority of Rome appear monthly if not weekly. Arising from a variety of immediate issues—liberation theology (the Americas, India, the Philippines), black theology and ecology (the United States), feminism and sexual ethics (the Anglo-Saxon world generally, Western Europe), "inculturation" and the possibilities of assimilating non-Christian religiosities (India, sub-Saharan Africa), and the use to be made of contemporary biblical exegesis (academe *überhaupt*)—such movements manifest themselves not only in continuing liturgical experimentation with the already mauled and suffering Roman rite, but, even more characteristically, in criticism of the *see* of Rome. Ranging in tenor from the courteous to the caterwaul, this criticism touches not only the policies and the power of the Papacy, but the context of those policies and the grounding of that power, namely, the fundamental position of Rome within the "communion of churches" which is Catholicism worldwide. It may be offered in the name of: a more effective co-governance of the Church by college of bishops and Pope; the rights of local, or national, churches; a "synodal" structure of Church government with rôles for laity and lower clergy as well as bishops; or a democratic populism of the "base church". Such critiques sometimes include reference to the doctrinal, and practical, posture taken up historically by the (separated) Eastern churches, insinuating or insisting, that the contemporary desire of Western Catholic liberals and radicals to cut the Papacy down to size is but the continuation of the (legitimate) fraternal correction offered by the Christian East to a Roman bishop tempted by the memory of his Petrine prerogatives to occupy the position of a super-pope.

On the other hand, those Orthodox (and other Oriental) Christians who are most *au fait* with the present situation of Western Catholicism are all too aware that, in the dynamic of forces now at play in the Latin church, assault on Rome becomes only too easily a sorcerer's apprentice, whose unstoppable sea of reform will wash away not only certain encrustations of papal practice but (humanly speaking) the apostolic tradition itself. For at the heart of many (but not all) of the centrifugal movements in modern Western Catholicism lies a common canker: the loss of a sense for the objective, supernatural Christian revelation given in history, and passed down by the apostolic Church, in the combined media of her liturgies, her doctrinal teaching, and her life. As Father Avery Dulles, of the Society of Jesus, recently wrote, divorced from this matrix, much contemporary theology runs the risk of turning into a rootless philosophy of religion, or into social commentary.[1] Observation of similar phenomena led such an experienced and widely read Orthodox theologian as Father John Meyendorff to assert that, where Rome loses, in present-day Western Catholicism, the gainer will be not so much episcopal collegiality as secularism and Modernism.[2] In recording the comments of these two writers, some allowance must be made for a North American standpoint; yet it will not do, as some voices in the Roman Curia seem occasionally to urge, to blame all the ills of the Catholic Church today on the deficiencies of American culture.

The present conjuncture necessarily lends a new ambivalence to any study of the relations of Rome with the Eastern churches—yet it also gives that study a new urgency. One strategy open to Rome is, evidently, to call up from the vasty deep the spirits of the Christian

---

[1] A. Dulles, S.J., "Intrepid Explorers out on Their Own", *Tablet*, 7 July 1990, 858.
[2] J. Meyendorff, "The Melkite Patriarchate: Paradoxes of a Vocation", *St. Vladimir's Seminary Quarterly* 30, no. 3 (1986): 250.

East—for in the struggle for the conservation of a classical understanding of doctrine, liturgy, spirituality, ethics, and (for the most
part) Church government, the East can stand with Rome over against
Neo-Modernist, or Neo-Protestant, tendencies in the West. The "Ori-
entalisation" of Rome is already apparent, indeed, in such diverse
media as the recent documents of the Roman Congregation for Catholic Education on the importance not only of a renewed study of
the fathers but, more specifically, of the Christian East itself, in seminary formation in the Latin church, and the ethos of the draft "Universal Catechism", many of whose citations are drawn from the Eastern
fathers and liturgies.

In this process, the ecumenical dialogue with the Orthodox (and,
to a lesser extent, the Oriental Orthodox) churches would seem an
obvious contender for the rôle of a major supporting part. However, the liberation of the Byzantine-rite Catholic churches of Eastern Europe, in the course of the dramatic events in the USSR and
elsewhere in 1989, and—to a less marked degree—the renaissance of
the Syrian-rite Catholic church in India has complicated the ecumenical aspect. The recognition by Rome of the Uniate churches of
the Ukraine and Romania (in particular) has dismayed, and even
angered, many Orthodox, and this at a time when the dialogue of
the (Chalcedonian) Eastern Orthodox with the (Non-Chalcedonian)
Oriental Orthodox ("Monophysite") churches is moving ahead with
great gusto. The high wire which the Holy See is dangerously trying to walk consists in, on the one hand, giving support and suste-
nance to the Oriental Catholic churches, while, on the other,
maintaining the full momentum of the dialogue with the separated
Eastern churches in whose eyes "Uniates" are, if not an abomina-
tion, then at least an obstacle. The suffering of the Uniates in the
cause of communion with Rome could be neglected by Rome only
at the cost of an undesirable reputation for supine ingratitude, as
well as a suspicion of failing confidence in her own special claims.
And yet the wider rewards of reunion with the Orthodox (and to a
lesser exter; Oriental Orthodox) East would be, if harvested, more
substantial—not only thanks to the presence of a large Orthodox
diaspora in those countries (North America, Australia, Western

Europe) where theological liberalism is at its most rife, but also given what could be expected of such self-confident churches as those of Greece and Russia in their contribution to a catholicity of which Rome would be the first see.

Yet it would not be unintelligible if the Orthodox, who share with the Non-Chalcedonian Orthodox a common Eastern ethos, should give the latter preference to Rome on the grounds of their greater closeness to both the historic patrimony and the present outlook of the Orthodox Church.[3] Such a reunion, perhaps made on the base of a revisionist understanding of the Council of Chalcedon which would exclude the Western, Leonine contribution to that Council's making, might leave Rome, as its only serious Eastern ecumenical partner, the tiny Assyrian (Nestorian) church whose leaders, according to a report in *Christian Newsworld* for May 1990, have already indicated their desire to move quickly towards unity with the Chaldaean-rite Catholic church of their traditional Middle-Eastern homelands.[4] Such a scenario would be richly symbolic in confirming, despite Rome, the tendency of Western Catholicism to a "low" Christology of the kind associated historically with the radical wing of the Antiochene school from under which the Nestorians came.

The other possibility—reunion with the Orthodox, and, perhaps via them, with the Non-Chalcedonian "Monophysite" East—also remains, for the Orthodox could usefully reflect that the troubles now afflicting Western Catholicism derive in large part from the inevitable tension between a secular, Western culture and the historic faith. Though the present crisis in the Western Catholic Church derives much of its force from acts of imprudence, based on a naive misunderstanding of the need for boundary and symbol in human culture, as well as a spirit of iconoclasm, which might have a more

[3] There are, in any case, enough contemporary Orthodox voices hostile to union with Rome: see, for instance, A. Kalomiros, *Against False Union* (Eng. trans., Boston, Mass., 1967); P. Sherrard, *Church, Papacy and Schism* (London, 1978); G. C. Zaphiris, *Der theologische Dialog zwischen den Orthodoxen und der Römisch-katholischen Kirchen* (Athens, 1982).

[4] "Assyrians Move to Heal Split", *Christian Newsworld*, May 1990.

devilish source, those factors were compounded by difficulties of adjustment and translation which the Orthodox too must face in the more fluid universe of democracy and the market economy to which the labours of Mr. Gorbachev have unwittingly committed them.

> *Aidan Nichols*
> *Blackfriars, Cambridge*
> *Feast of All Saints of the Order of Preachers, 1990*

Preface to the Second Edition

In the well nigh twenty years since this book has been written, much has happened in the world of Eastern Christianity, all of it—no doubt—monitored by Rome and some of it impacting the relations between "Rome and the Eastern Churches". The production of a second edition has made possible its updating in matters like the progress (or sometimes lack thereof) in ecumenical dialogues, some reference to the jurisdictional reconciliations (and new fragmentations) among the Orthodox, the implications of such pertinent political events as the coalition invasion of Iraq, and demography—though, as with the first edition, it is a problem that estimates of the numbers of adherents of the Eastern churches seem to vary very widely.[1] Some historical sections have been amplified. Bibliographies have been selectively expanded. References have been made more complete and of course errors, typographical and other, corrected where identified. Where (as rarely) questions of the sources and authorship of biblical texts are concerned, I have become somewhat more conservative—or quizzical—over the years.

I find no reason, however, to alter the principal lines of the book, though I have taken the opportunity to clarify my stance here and there, notably in removing an unnoticed ambiguity in the first edition. The defence offered there of the place of the famous *Filioque* clause in the Western confession of faith (the Holy Spirit "proceeds from the Father *and the Son*") was not intended to suggest that those words should be retained by, or introduced into the use of, the Eastern Catholic churches in recital of the Creed. Possibly some readers may have gained that mistaken impression. In the meanwhile, I

---

[1] In general, where possible, I have based estimates on figures given in D. B. Barrett, G. T. Kurian, and T. M. Johnson, eds., *World Christian Encyclopaedia: A Comparative Survey of Churches and Religions in the Modern World* (Oxford, 2001).

continued to look for theological enlightenment to the Christian East,[2] emboldened not least by the publication in 1995 of Pope John Paul II's letter *Orientale lumen*, which underlines the value of the enterprise represented by the present book. To quote from its opening section:

> Since, in fact, we believe that the venerable and ancient tradition of the Eastern Churches is an integral part of the heritage of Christ's Church, the first need for Catholics is *to be familiar with that tradition*, so as to be nourished by it and to encourage the process of unity in the best way possible for each. Our Eastern Catholic brothers and sisters are very conscious of being the living bearers of this tradition, together with our Orthodox brothers and sisters. The members of the Catholic Church of the Latin tradition must also be fully acquainted with this treasure and thus feel, with the Pope, a passionate longing that *the full manifestation of the Church's catholicity* be restored to the Church and to the world, expressed not by a single tradition, and still less by one community in opposition to the other; and that we too may all be granted a full taste of the divinely revealed and undivided heritage of the universal Church which is preserved and grows in the life of the Churches of the East as of the West.[3]

In this context it is encouraging to see how much Eastern Christian influence the 1992 *Catechism of the Catholic Church* manifests, much of it thanks to the input of a Melchite theologian, Jean Corbon.[4] Much remains to be done so as to complement what is best in the life and thought of Western Catholicism, not least in the realms of monasticism and theology.[5]

---

[2] As in *Byzantine Gospel: Maximus the Confessor in Modern Scholarship* (Edinburgh, 1993); *Light from the East: Authors and Themes in Orthodox Theology* (London, 1995); and *Wisdom from Above: A Primer in the Theology of Father Sergei Bulgakov* (Leominster, 2005).

[3] John Paul II, *Orientale lumen* (Vatican City, 1995), 1, 3–4.

[4] See A. Rojas, "Breathing with Both Lungs: A Brief Survey of Eastern Catholic Influence on *The Catechism of the Catholic Church*", *ECJ* 9, no. 3 (2002): 7–22.

[5] For monasticism: B. Luykx, *Eastern Monasticism and the Future of the Church* (Stamford, Conn., 2003); for theology: the survey in R. F. Taft, S.J., "Eastern Catholic

Insofar as I have modified my own view of the issues that this book (and the pope's letter) raises, it is in the direction of wanting to offer a more robust apologia for the existence of the—sometimes, but not always—distinctly minoritarian Oriental churches in union with Rome. I wish to use the remainder of this foreword to explain why.

Catholic participation in the ecumenical movement, by mandating maximum sympathy for other Christians, and notably in this case, the Eastern Orthodox, has sometimes given the impression that "Uniates" have become an embarrassment. This is an attitude that, when registered, naturally reduces Eastern Catholic morale. I note in passing here that the pejorative reading of the term "Uniate", which has led writers on Oriental Catholicism to avoid or even deplore it, is, in my opinion, without adequate foundation. Rightly understood, it is a beautiful word. The Liturgy of Saint John Chrysostom, the most frequently celebrated form of worship among Byzantine Christians, prays urgently in its litanies for the "peace of the holy churches of God and *the union of them all*". Orientals who have sought unity with the Petrine see have heard this prayer. The question remains, though: Even if a more lovely word than widely claimed, is Uniatism also a beautiful concept?

I propose that Uniatism should be reread as a term of Christian eschatology. After all, the transformation of a divided Christendom into a unitary communion is itself an eschatological aspiration. Even among the most optimistic ecumenists, who could ever suppose that the integration of all the baptised into a single communion is other than an "asymptotic" goal—an end that people take as an *ideal* reference point rather than a practical one? The movement for Christian unity strives in that somewhat Pickwickian sense to realize that end, namely by seeking endlessly to *approach* it. In and of itself—this is the lesson of both history and common sense—such a desired good can only be a gift of the Lord to his Church at the Parousia. We can call that a "metahistorical" gift.

Theology: Slow Birth after a Long and Difficult Gestation", *ECJ* 8, no. 2 (2001): 51–80.

But what, then, is a humanly realizable goal for the Church's ecumenical effort in the world on this side of "metahistory"? According to their own doctrine, Catholics have a special mission to guard the unity for which Christ prayed, since they hold that unity to endure in its essential (though not its plenary) form in their own Church. How can that unity be best exemplified "intrahistorically"— in other words, from *the human side* of the moment of the Parousia, when history will tremble into its own consummation at the turn of the Ages? In my proposal, on the supposition that a totally reunited Christendom is not, intrahistorically, a realistic hope, such unity will be seen most fully in the *representative gathering of apostolic churches and traditions* around the figure of Peter, represented in his vicar, the Roman bishop. On this view, Uniate churches are to be explained eschatologically. They are ordered to the manifestation of the unity of disciples on the human side of the Eschaton—granted that only on the divine side of that moment will there be (so far as a sane judgement can discern) the total and completely all-embracing unity for which Christ prayed. From the viewpoint of such "representative gathering", the fact that most Eastern Catholic churches are minoritarian, and some glaringly so, does not constitute a problem. The dignity of their eschatological significance is unaffected by the numbers game.

Such a view of "Uniatism" will have consequences. First, it should eliminate any suggestion that the Eastern Catholic churches are at worst a "mistake", or at best something of a halter round the neck of the Catholic Church when operating in ecumenical mode. I hope I am second to none among Latin-rite Catholics in my love for Eastern Orthodoxy. Nonetheless, I think it is high time Catholics ceased to be so preoccupied with apologizing for the Uniate churches that they fail to seek a recognition of the injustices done to those churches, notably in the twentieth century, from the Orthodox side.[6] Second, acknowledging the "protoeschatological" dignity of the Eastern Catholic

---

[6] See R. J. Taft, S.J., "The Problem of 'Uniatism' and the 'Healing of Memories': Anamnesis, Not Amnesia", *Logos: A Journal of Eastern Christian Studies* 41, no. 2 (2000–2001): 155–96.

churches should be a spur to the overdue recognition of their proper liberties within the *Catholica* as a whole. By "proper liberties" I refer to, principally, three points: their mode of governance, the extent of their jurisdiction, and their clerical discipline.

The normal *mode of governance* of an Eastern church of any magnitude (historical or demographic) has come to be a patriarch in synod. If we take the examples of the Byzantine-rite Ukrainian church and the East Syrian Malabar (Indian) church, we find these historically notable communities lack such governance, though each has some four million faithful. Assuming that these very large numbers translate into adequate spiritual and material resources, then their leadership surely merits the patriarchal dignity—if bishops and people wish it. It is reliably reported that, at the 1990 meeting of Pope John Paul II with the hierarchs of the Ukrainian church gathered in Rome, he promised them their long-desired patriarchate and assured them of the propriety, in the interval, of commemorating liturgically as patriarch their "major archbishop"—a title invented by Roman canonists under Pius XII. It is true that in Orthodoxy the primates of "autocephalous" (or "autonomous") churches may simply be archbishops, but, strange as it may seem, the modern *fontes* of Oriental canon law in the Catholic Church place more emphasis on the patriarchal principle in the East than do the Orthodox generally, rather than less. In any case, Catholics do not have "autocephalous" or "autonomous" churches: such concepts sit ill with their theology of hierarchical communion around Peter. All the more, then, is the patriarchal dignity desirable to give an Eastern Catholic church a voice that carries in the concert of the churches.

As to the *extent of jurisdiction*: most Eastern Catholic churches now have between a third and three-fifths of their faithful in diaspora. This is not altogether a new phenomenon, but it is an accelerating one. Going beyond (admittedly) the provisions of *Orientalium Ecclesiarum*, the Decree of the Second Vatican Council on the Eastern Catholic Churches,[7]

---

[7] On the canonical situation of those churches as envisaged by the conciliar document, there is much valuable information in *Les Eglises orientales catholiques: Décret "Orientalium Ecclesiarum", texte latin et traduction française, commentaire par Neophytos Edelby, métropolite d'Alep et Ignace Dick, du clergé d'Alep* (Paris, 1970).

the patriarchs need a worldwide extension of their authority—by which is meant beyond their historically traditional territories, although in the case of the Armenian Catholic patriarch it would need to include extension to the original Caucasian homeland as well. The claim that such an extension of patriarchal jurisdiction would conflict with the worldwide jurisdiction of the pope will not stand up to investigation. The "universality" of jurisdiction of the Petrine officeholder does not consist in his being the sole hierarch with a pastoral care for Catholics who may be anywhere on the earth's surface. Even the prelate of the Priestly Society of the Holy Cross, Opus Dei—a Latin-rite cleric—is another such bishop! In terms of the issue of universal jurisdiction, the uniqueness of the pope as supreme pastor is chiefly that he alone has care of the operation of the episcopal *taxis* in its entirety—something that could not be said of any Eastern patriarch, however far-flung his clergy and faithful. (Indeed, it pertains to the universal jurisdiction of the pope to resolve all interpatriarchal disputes that might arise from such extension of powers.) Perhaps the most plausible way to meet the need for a substantial qualification of the "principle of territoriality" is to redefine a patriarchal territory as including all erected eparchies of its "ritual church" (in the present Code of Canons for the Eastern Churches, that is more properly termed a "church *sui iuris*").

Finally, the Eastern *discipline of a married secular clergy*, working alongside a celibate monastic clergy, should not be affected by the circumstance of the settlement of Eastern faithful in the West—itself a development both irreversible and, with the geopolitical cards stacked against indigenous Christians in many parts of the world, likely to increase.[8] Of course, if pastors and faithful of an Eastern Catholic church *come to prefer* a wholly celibate priesthood, the situation is different again.

Eastern Catholic churches cannot function as "windows"—for Western Catholics onto Eastern Christianity, and for Eastern Christians onto the Catholic Church, unless they are able to live out their tradition. That is why, for instance, deterring the establishment of patriarchal governance favours ecumenism only in the short term.

---

[8] For an introduction to the principles of Oriental canonical ecclesiology from a Catholic perspective, see V. J. Pospishil, *Eastern Catholic Church Law* (Brooklyn, N.Y., 1993).

These changes are required in order to perfect the canonical organism and to allow the true strength of Roman obedience to stand forth, a strength which certainly exists when considered over against the jurisdictional arbitrariness and quarrelling—what the Jesuit Russianist Stanislas Tyskiewicz termed "canonicism"—so widely endemic in the separated East. Tyskiewicz wrote, as long ago as 1939, but his sentiments remain pertinent seventy years later:

A juridicocanonical system, organizationally perfect, healthy, and solid, is the best assurance against the penetration of *canonicism* into the interior life of the Church. We cannot too strongly insist on it: Catholicism, precisely in virtue of its strong canonical coordination, preserves the supernatural *sobornost'* against the untimely invasions of legalism. What the Orthodox theologians so deeply fear, the "Vatican", with all its precise judicial apparatus, is a solid dyke against the unchained floods of an undisciplined "legalism", such as arise when no authority exists able to put an end to the interminable polemics on the rights of such a particular church, or such-and-such a social element within the church: we know how prejudicial these polemics are to charity, to the *sobornost'*. What might be called "unilegalism" tempers the paralyzing action of centrifugal and dessicating multilegalisms. It is the lack of judicial precision that gives rise to most of the conflicts which bring disaster on the organic universality of Christian charity.[9]

Lastly, and on a very different note, it is my pleasure to thank Dr. O'Mahony for the gift of several helpful articles and also the editorial team of Ignatius Press, who lavished great care and patience on my book.

Aidan Nichols
Blackfriars, Cambridge
Solemnity of All Saints, 2009

[9] S. Tyskiewicz, S.J., "La théologie moehlérienne de l'unité et les théologiens pravoslaves", in *L'Eglise est une: Hommage à Moehler* (Paris, 1939): 281. That the writer in question was not always prudent in his own ecumenical relations does not annul the wisdom of these words.

Abbreviations

Conc.   *Concilium* (London, 1965–)

DC   *Documentation catholique* (Paris, 1919–1940, 1944–)

DOP   *Dumbarton Oaks Papers* (Cambridge, Mass., 1950–)

DS   *Enchiridion symbolorum*, ed. H. Denzinger and A. Schönmetzer, 33rd ed. (Freiburg, 1965)

DTC   *Dictionnaire de théologie catholique* (Paris, 1930–1950)

ECJ   Eastern Churches Journal (Maidenhead, and Fairfax, Va., 1993–)

ECQ   *Eastern Churches Quarterly* (Ramsgate, 1936–1964)

ECR   *Eastern Churches Review* (Oxford, 1966–1978)

EO   *Echos d'Orient* (Bucharest, 1897–1943)

Irén.   *Irénikon* (Chevetogne, 1926–1940, 1945–)

Ist.   *Istina* (Boulogne-sur-Seine, 1954–)

JEH   *Journal of Ecclesiastical History* (London, 1950–)

JTS   *Journal of Theological Studies* (Oxford, 1899–1949; n.s., 1950–)

Mansi   *Sacrorum conciliorum nova et amplissima collection*, ed. J. D. Mansi (Florence, 1759–1827)

NCE   *New Catholic Encyclopedia* (New York, 1967)

OR   *L'osservatore romano* (Vatican City, 1861–)

PG   Patrologia graeca, ed. J.-P. Migne (Paris, 1857–1866, 1928–1936)

PL   Patrologia latina, ed. J.-P. Migne (Paris, 1841–1849, 1850–1855, 1862–1864)

POC   *Proche Orient chrétien* (Jerusalem, 1951–)

REB   *Revue des études byzantines* (Paris, 1946–)

RHE   *Revue d'histoire ecclésiastique* (Louvain, 1900–)

RSR   *Recherches de science religieuse* (Paris, 1910–1940, 1946–)

Sob.   *Sobornost* (London, 1935–)

The Concept of Schism

Definition of "Schism"

Before entering the deep waters of the schism between Rome and the dissident Eastern churches, it seems reasonable to ask ourselves: Just what, exactly, *is* a schism? How has the concept of schism been understood in the Church's history? Can there be a schism *within* the Church, or is a schism always a matter of people cutting themselves off *from* the Church? What is the status of schismatics? Can there be degrees of schism? Must a schism be ratified by a formal act declaring that it has happened? I cannot expect to answer all of these questions adequately, yet it seems clear that many of them require an answer if we are to deal sensibly with the rupture between Rome and the East.

As a first attempt at defining the concept, it may be said that schism is the crystallisation of orthodox dissent. Schism is not in itself heresy. Although schismatics may come to believe heretical doctrines, and their partiality for these doctrines may originate in the circumstances of their schism, to be a schismatic is not in itself to be a heretic. And conversely, heresy is not itself schism. People holding heretical opinions are to be found very widely scattered through the Catholic Church. In general, Church authorities take the charitable view that the existence of heretical opinion is a result of misinformation. Those holding heretical opinions would abandon them if they realised that they were contrary to the faith of the Church. Even a pope may hold heretical opinions as a simple member of the Church—which is why such theologians as the "masters of the sacred palace" were employed at Rome to check his statements. Occasionally, the Church has to deal with someone who, though quite aware of the faith of the Church in some respect, nevertheless rejects the Church's judgement about faith and encourages others to do likewise. Historically, the usual reaction here of episcopate and papacy, as guardians of the common life of the Church, has been to excommunicate the person or persons involved. Excommunication can be defined as the deliberate placing of another in the state of schism. Yet heresy and schism remain formally distinct. While heresy is unorthodox dissent, schism is orthodox dissent, expressing itself in the organisation of a distinct ecclesial life by people who in all other respects share the faith of the Church.[1]

In terms of this preliminary definition, it may not be very clear why schism matters very much and why it has usually been held to entail an even more serious crime against the Church's life than heresy. Surely the important thing is to be orthodox, to have the true faith, and schismatics are not, by definition, unorthodox. But schism matters very much indeed if we regard the unity of the Church as a central feature of God's design for the world. And this is in fact how *Lumen gentium*, the dogmatic constitution *de Ecclesia* of the Second Vatican Council, sees it. In the words of its famous opening paragraph: "By her relationship with Christ, the Church is a kind of sacrament or sign of intimate union with God and of the unity of all mankind. She is also an instrument for the achievement of such union and unity."[2] On this view, a principal goal of the economy of salvation is the undoing of human divisions—divisions within the human family, and division between the human family and its Maker, these two types of division being seen as mutually implicated, one leading to the other. This affirmation of the Second Vatican Council is not an isolated flash in the pan but an attempt to articulate a deeply held conviction of Scripture and tradition. One "biblical theology", one

[1] Cf. the lucid statement of Jerome of Bethlehem: "[H]eresy comprises a perverse teaching; schism separates from the Church through dissent from bishops", *Epistola ad Titum* 3.10–11. Jerome goes on to remark, in this passage, that in practice, no schismatic separates from the Church without creating some heresy by which to justify his separation.

[2] *Lumen gentium* 1.

way of reading the unity of the whole Bible, would be in terms of this key motif. Various theologies found in different biblical writers could be seen here as subtheologies and integrated into a single architectonic theology of the whole biblical corpus. Thus, for instance, in the Old Testament, unity is a major preoccupation of the Book of Genesis (and notably for those who accept the late nineteenth-century literary analysis of the Pentateuch into four combined documents, in the element ascribed to the unnamed writer known as "the Yahwist"). In the prehistory of the book of Genesis, disunity is described in the story of the Tower of Babel, which leaves mankind estranged from God and divided among itself, speaking various tongues.[3] The term "tongues" here is not simply a reference to the plurality of human languages, something which in itself is neither good nor evil. It alludes, rather, to the condition of fragmentation and alienation that a breakdown in linguistic communication can symbolise. After the prehistory, for the Genesis writer, comes the beginning of the history of salvation, summed up in the call of Abram, and from there the entire biblical history unfolds, placed under the sign of remaking an original unity of the human family with itself and with God, undone by sin. Turning to the other end of the Bible: for the Johannine school, the unity of the disciples was a major preoccupation of Jesus on the night before his passion. This unity within the apostolic group is seen not simply as a good in itself but as a means to bring about a wider, indeed an indefinitely extensive, unity—the fellowship of the Church throughout all ages.

> I do not pray for these only, but also for those who believe in me through their word, that they may all be one; Even as thou, Father, art in me, and I am in thee, that they also may be in us, so that the world may believe that thou hast sent me.[4]

To see the full implications of this, we must bear in mind that for Saint John, the Church is the world insofar as it is capable of responding to the Logos made flesh, or the world to the degree

[3] Gen 11:1–9.
[4] Jn 17:20–22.

that it is not enslaved by this world's "prince" and so can recognise the truth.

In the Letter to the Ephesians, which may have doubled up as an introduction to the entire Pauline corpus, we have a clear indication that this high priestly prayer of Jesus at the Last Supper was not regarded by New Testament Christians as simply a pious wish. In Ephesians, the unity of the Church is spoken of as a supernatural reality given by God in and through Christ.

> For he has made known to us ... the mystery of his will, ... as a plan for the fulness of time, to unite all things in him, things in heaven and things on earth.[5]

Without necessarily using the word *ekklêsia*, Saint Paul envisages the Church as a family where all nations can be at home and which is the privileged means of bringing about unity in Christ. As he addresses his Gentile readers:

> So then you are no longer strangers and sojourners, but you are fellow citizens with the saints and members of the household of God ...[6]

and so sharers in a supernatural society that in principle embraces the whole world. The Church is the very body of Christ, and as such it is a single articulated whole: many members, playing their different parts, but within one organism, one body. Using, then, the Pauline writings to comment on the Johannine, we can say that the prayer of Jesus the night before he died was not ineffective. The unity of the Church was realised for all time as an essential aspect of the work of the Redeemer. By the outpouring of the Spirit, the Father gives this unity to the community of the Messiah. As a result, it is not simply that the Church ought to be one: it *is* one and cannot but be one. The question is how to maintain, manifest, and extend this unity so that the Church can truly be, in the words of *Lumen gentium*, the sacrament and sign of unity for the whole human

---

[5] Eph 1:9–10.
[6] Eph 2:19.

race. Clearly, therefore, any action or situation that retards or even reverses the divine thrust towards unity can be described only as terribly misguided and perverse.

So much for the theological gravity of schism. What of the history of the concept of schism? Etymologically, the word means "cleaving", "tearing", or "breaking". Aristotle, for instance, in his *Historia animalium*, talks about the "schismatised", cloven, foot of the camel.[7] In the New Testament, *schisma* means, broadly speaking, divergence or dissent. In the Fourth Gospel, at John 10:19, we find the word used for the divergent opinions of the Jews about Jesus.[8] But the specifically ecclesiological employment of the term comes from Paul's correspondence with the Church in Corinth. There Paul writes: "I appeal to you, brothers, for the sake of our Lord Jesus Christ, to make up the differences between you and instead of having schisms among yourselves, to be united again in your belief and practice."[9] What Paul is dealing with is not a schism in the modern sense but rather *partisanship*: the emergence of parties, cliques, private circles, exclusive movements, within the body of the Church. The unity of the local church is disturbed: Paul intervenes to proclaim in the name of the Lord of the Church that unity must come before group identity or private sentiment. From this text, the classical notion of the schism will take its rise.

From this point on, the development of the idea of schism turns on two things: first, on the *idea* of the unity of the Church held at a given time, for the concept of schism is only the reverse side of the concept of unity; and second, the *facts* about particular schisms, which made people think harder about what schism really was.[10]

The earliest Christian writer to have a concept of schism that might be called clear or technical is Ignatius of Antioch. For Ignatius, a major test of Christian discipleship is obedience to the bishop:

---

[7] *Historia animalium* 2.1.26.

[8] Jn 7:43; 9:16; 10:19.

[9] 1 Cor 1:10.

[10] Y. M.-J. Congar, O.P., "Schisme", *DTC*, vol. 14, pt. 1, col. 1288.

faithfulness to the doctrine he teaches and participation in the Eucharist he celebrates. A schismatic is someone who separates himself from the local bishop and raises up an altar against the altar of the bishop's Eucharist. Such a man, such a *schizón*, will not, according to Ignatius, inherit the Kingdom of God.

> Let no man be deceived: unless a man be within the sanctuary, he lacks the bread of God, for if the prayer of one or two has such might, how much more has that of the bishop and of the whole Church? So then he who does not join in the common assembly is already haughty and has separated himself. For it is written, "God resisteth the proud". Let us then be careful not to oppose the bishop that we may be subject to God.[11]

Ignatius' picture is reflected in the most ancient church canon known to us on this subject: the fifth canon of an Antiochene council held in 341.[12] In that canon precisely Ignatius' criteria are used: schism means, first, separation from the bishop, and second, the erection of an altar over against his. Moreover, as another canon of the same council points out, by rupturing communion with the local bishop, the schismatic also breaks communion with the universal Church, mediated to him through that bishop.[13]

A more developed form of the same idea is found in the East with Basil,[14] and (particularly) in the West with Cyprian. For Cyprian, the bishop's principal task is to symbolise and actualise the unity of the local church. The principal task of the bishops taken all together is to do the same thing for the universal Church. The episcopate for Cyprian is a single reality, a single body, and through the unity of this body the unity of the rest of the Church is created.

---

[11] *Philippians* 3; cf. *Philadelphians* 3–4, *Smyrnaeans* 7–8, and *Letter to Polycarp* 6 for further exhortations to peace through common obedience to the conditions of ecclesial unity.

[12] Mansi, 2:1309–10.

[13] Canon 6; cf. also canon 53 of Elvira (306); canon 16 of Arles (314), and canon 5 of Nicaea (325).

[14] *Letter* 188, to Amphilochius of Iconium.

The authority of the bishops forms a unity of which each holds his part in its completeness. And [so] the Church forms a unity, however far she spreads and multiplies ... just as the sun's rays are many, yet the light is one, and a tree's branches are many, yet the strength deriving from its sturdy root is one.[15]

Does anyone think then that this unity, which derives from the stability of God himself and is welded together after a heavenly pattern, can be sundered in the Church ... by the clash of [men's] discordant wills? If a man does not keep this unity, he is not keeping the law of God: he has broken faith with the Father and the Son, he is cut off from life and salvation.[16]

Cyprian's position is very clear-cut. If anyone—layman, presbyter, or bishop—break this *unitatis sacramentum*, this "mystery of unity", he ceases to share in the reality of the Church. The sacraments he receives or celebrates outside of visible unity are null and void. And because the sacraments express and realise the life of the Church, he is ecclesially dead.

What Cyprian had in mind was *either* a layman or priest breaking with his own bishop and so with the "concord" of the whole episcopate, *or* a single bishop breaking the unity of the episcopal body. He did not visualise the phenomenon of entire local churches, with great numbers of bishops, departing from Catholic unity. But this is what happened in North Africa, shortly after his death, in the Donatist schism, a schism so chronic and bitter that it produced a whole new literature about schism, associated chiefly with Augustine. The first theological response to Donatism came, however, from yet another African writer, Optatus of Milevis. He distinguished very sharply between heresy and schism, rather in the way I did myself in our preliminary definition. For Optatus, heretics—and here he has in view those who reject the fundamental Trinitarian and Christological doctrine of the Church—are quite outside the Church, having elected to reject the Church's faith. Schismatics, on the other hand, still have the Church (as he says) for their Mother: though they stray

[15] *De unitate Ecclesiae* 5.
[16] Ibid., 6.

from her and break her peace, they take with them the faith and sacraments that they received from her hands.[17]

This distinction is retained by Augustine up to about the year 405. In relevant writings before that date, Augustine argues, Optatus-like, that heresy is an act of contestation against the faith, while schism is simply a breakdown in brotherhood. But around 405 Augustine had a change of heart.[18] Having come to believe that the Donatists were not merely misguided but downright malicious, and that they would never be brought back to the peace of the Church by argument, he determined that the power of the (by now Christian) Roman Empire must be invoked against them. Since the legislation of the period, the Theodosian Code, contained penalties against heresy but not against schism, Augustine was obliged to make schism approximate to heresy. He argued that any rupture of brotherhood necessarily rests on some disagreement and that if division lasts it will inevitably turn into heresy.[19] Augustine kept, however, his moral analysis of the origins of schism. The ethical starting point of schism is *odium fraternum*, "hatred among brothers": in simple terms, disliking people.[20] But more deeply, Augustine suggests, schism comes from ascribing to ourselves what in reality belongs only to Christ, namely, the fulness of grace and truth. In concrete terms, we forget that we are only a part, needing other Christians and indeed Christ himself. Instead, we behave as though the part were the whole.[21]

But in a situation where numbers of local churches are at enmity, how can the true Church, the Church that still comports herself aright, be actually identified? Augustine's answer is to appeal to the criterion of the apostolic churches: the churches founded by the apostles or, as he puts it, in receipt of their letters. More especially, we must appeal to the judgement of the Roman church, where the chair

---

[17] *De schismate donatistarum ad Parmenianum* 1.10–11.

[18] Manifested in the *Contra Cresconium* of approximately that date.

[19] Congar, "Schisme", col. 1291.

[20] *De baptismo contra Donatistas* 1.11 (16).

[21] *In epistolam Joannis ad Parthos* 1.8.

of Peter is found.[22] Cyprian, in a second edition of his *De unitate
Ecclesiae*, had already realised that the single episcopate, in order to
bring about a single Church, needs a criterion of unity within itself.
Optatus too had made this very plain: "In the city of Rome, Peter
located his bishop's chair, in which he would sit as head, *caput*, of all
the apostles, so that through this one chair the unity of them all
might be preserved".[23] It is important to note, however, that for
Augustine the appeal to Rome is the supreme *example* of appeal to
the apostolic churches: it does not render the others superfluous.

Later on, when the West was increasingly cut off from the East
both culturally and politically, reference to the Roman see in this
context would become more exclusive. But this hardly happened
overnight. In the mid-sixth century, during the struggle of the papacy
and, more acutely, other sections of the Church in the West with
the emperor Justinian over the orthodoxy of the Antiochene doctors—
the so-called Three Chapters controversy—we find the pope of the
day, Pelagius I, declaring that schismatics are those who break communion with the apostolic *churches*, in the plural: "If anyone is divided
from the apostolic sees, it cannot be doubted that he is in schism
and is trying to raise up an altar against the universal Church." [24]
This text was reproduced in the influential collection of canons made
by Gratian in the twelfth century and so should have been well known
to the Latin theologians.

But reflection on these matters took a rather different turn in the
Western Church. The ecclesiastical centralisation consequent on the
Gregorian Reform turned the Roman see into the exclusive criterion and organ of unity in Latin eyes. Thus we find Pope Gregory
VII declaring in his posthumously published *Dictatus*: "The definition of what makes someone not a Catholic is that he is out of
concord with the Roman church." [25] In the first *Summa theologiae*,

[22] *Epistolae* 43.7; 52.3; *Contra litteras Petiliani* 2.51. See on this P. Batiffol, *Le cathol-
icisme de saint Augustin* (Paris, 1920), 1:177, 192–209.

[23] *De schismate donatistarum ad Parmenianum* 2.2.

[24] *Epistola* 2 (to Narses).

[25] *Dictatus papae* 26.

the work of the English Franciscan Alexander of Hales, we read that no rupture in the Church can strictly be called a schism unless it takes the form of sustained and systematic disobedience to the Roman see.[26] Such high notions of the Petrine ministry of the Roman bishop influenced the crop of treatises *de schismate* produced in the wake of the Great Schism from 1378 to 1417, when two or even three arguably legitimate pontiffs disputed the allegiance of Catholics among them.[27] It is curious that the Eastern Schism, which in historical perspective is so much more important than this painful pontifical squabble in the West, had almost no discernible effect on the theological literature about schism.[28] The last major contribution of the medieval West to the discussion comes from the inquisitors, who were mandated to investigate, among other things, schism and rumours of schism. As represented by, say, the *Directorium inquisitorum* of Nicholas Eymeric, their discussion was pithy. They put forward the idea—a revival of Optatus'—that "pure" schism consists entirely of orthodox dissent. This they distinguished from "mixed" schism, where heresy is intermingled.[29] But many held, with the later Augustine, that a pure schism is not especially likely. Every schism surely carries some disposition or other towards heresy, towards disobedience in matters of Christian believing.

That great internal crisis of the Western church, the sixteenth-century Reformation, added quantitatively to the literature on schism, but the authors read by Catholics offered no great originality of thought. Confirming the predominant insistence of the Latin Middle Ages on the rôle of the pope in the definition of schism, they continued to cite Cyprian but airily reinterpreted his references to the local bishop as the result of broad and impressionistic writing.[30]

---

[26] For references, see Congar, "Schisme", col. 1297.

[27] Usually embedded in wider works: a characteristic example is John of Turrecremata, *Summa de Ecclesia* 11–14. See more generally: H. E. Hall, "The Unity of the Church and the Forty Years of the Rival Popes", *Irish Theological Quarterly* 17 (1921): 331–44.

[28] Congar, "Schisme", col. 1294.

[29] *Directorium inquisitorum* (Rome, 1678), 2.48.

[30] Congar, "Schisme", col. 1296.

Better founded, historically, were the attempts by partisans and opponents of the Jansenists in the eighteenth-century church of France to exploit Cyprian's quarrel with Pope Stephen: here the question of the hour concerned whether bishops and theologians who rejected the bull *Unigenitus* (condemning Jansen's teaching on grace) should be considered schismatics or not.

In the Latin tradition, the classic account of schism is that provided by Saint Thomas Aquinas in his tiny treatise on the subject in the *secunda secundae* of his *Summa theologiae*.[31] The second part of volume 2 of this masterwork deals with man's return to God by faith, hope, and charity, and with the obstacles that impede this return. For Thomas, charity is a kind of friendship linking man to God, *amicitia quaedam hominis ad Deum*. This friendship is based on the communication to us of the Holy Spirit, who is personally the love of the Father and the Son. But this is not simply an affair between God and me, since I cannot love God without also loving those whom God loves, the other sharers of his life in grace. Towards my fellow-Christians, charity takes the form of fellowship, *consociatio*, founded on our common share in the divine life. Thomas then goes on to consider the results of such charity, and he finds that charity's principal or "proper" effect is *peace*. Peace is the order whereby we want what God wants and thus will in harmony with our neighbour. For this reason, charity can always overcome conflict: it is characteristic of friends that they choose in unison. Thomas then goes on to consider the vices that undermine peace, and it is here that he contextualises schism. Schism is the sin that leads people to separate themselves from the special unity that supernatural charity creates. As he writes: "Those are properly called 'schismatics' who freely and deliberately separate themselves from the Church's unity, which is the main kind of unity we know. For the particular unity that binds individuals to others in groups is ordered to the unity of the Church, just as the makeup of a particular human limb is ordered to the unity of the whole human body."[32]

---

[31] *Summa theologiae* IIa, IIae, 39.
[32] Ibid., q. 39, art. 1, *corpus*.

What, then, is, for Thomas, this "unity of the Church"? It may be of two distinct kinds. In the first place, it can lie in the connexion or interchange there is between the Church's members: *connexio membrorum Ecclesiae ad invicem*. At one level, the Church's life is made up of a network of mutual service. Each person with a special task in the community must care for others in the way proper to that task: the teacher by teaching, the preacher by preaching, the nurse by nursing. If we have no special job, we are still to devote ourselves to each other as brethren with whatever gifts and graces we have received. But second, the unity of the Church lies in the relation of the members to their Head, *ordo membrorum ad unum caput*. The Head of the Church is Christ, but acting for him in this respect is, says Saint Thomas, the supreme pontiff. Père Congar, in his restatement of the Thomist theology of schism in the *Dictionnaire de théologie catholique*, concerned not to omit here all mention of the episcopal college, says rather that the Head of the Church is invisibly Christ, but visibly (*sacramentally*) it is the hierarchy that Christ has established and that has as its criterion of unity the Roman bishop.[33]

A significant deepening of the classical account of schism was added by Aquinas' sixteenth-century disciple and namesake Thomas de Vio Cardinal Cajetan. Cajetan inquires: What creates the unity from which the faithful withdraw by schism? He considers three important ways in which the Church's unity might be said to be cemented: the unity of ecclesiastical government, the unity of the sacraments, and the unity of the theological virtues, faith, hope, and charity. But he decides to locate the Church's unity even deeper still: at the level of life in the Holy Spirit. It is the Spirit who impels people to act as parts of a single people. The charity that the Spirit pours into believers' hearts gives them a kind of gravitational pull towards mutual assistance and a heartfelt obedience to the Church's pastors.[34] Over against this, the law of schism is, as Augustine had long ago seen, the refusal to *agere ut pars*.

---

[33] Congar, "Schisme", col. 1300.
[34] *In IIam IIae*, q. 39, a. 1, n. 2.

The schismatic, then, attacks the unity of the Church. It is important that he actually has the *intention* of attacking that unity, or at least of acting in a way that he knows will lead to a break in unity. This means that he must refuse to act as part of the whole *in a way that touches the unity of the Church as such.* In effect, this means in some matter where a rule of faith or practice for communion with the Church has been duly expressed by the relevant authority. If, for example, I decide to invent a fresh gesture for the Mass liturgy and introduce it into my celebrations, I am refusing to observe the law of *agere ut pars.* But my lack of rubrical self-discipline hardly touches the unity of the Church as such and so could not lead to my being declared a schismatic. If, on the other hand, a particular church within the Western patriarchate chose to reorder its entire public prayer without reference to the rest of the Church, or to construct a new form of the Creed without the backing of the pope or a general council, then such an action could well be called schismatic, since the basic forms of Christian faith and action are to be determined by the whole Church, at least in the person of the pope. For one local church to redesign them "off its own bat" attacks the Church's unity in an essential way. However, it should be noted that in the classical theology of the subject, the effect of the schismatic's action is to destroy the Church's unity *only as that includes himself.*[35] He removes himself from the *connexio membrorum ad invicem* and the *ordo membrorum ad caput.*

The ways in which people can commit the sin of schism depend on whether we are thinking of the horizontal connexion of the members, or the vertical connexion with the head. Preserving for the moment the exclusive ministerial reference in the latter case to the Roman pope, we could cite as an example of a schism in the *first* case the *Petite église* of France in the nineteenth century. Having no direct quarrel with the Holy See, this body separated itself from the rest of the French church because of its detestation of the reordering of Church organisation demanded from Rome by successive revolutionary governments. In this first sense, a rupture of the *connexio*

---

[35] Ibid., n. 4; cf. Cyprian, *De unitate Ecclesiae* 4.

membrorum ad invicem, theologians have noted that *even the pope* could become a schismatic: for instance, by refusing to communicate with the Christian people, by ignoring the constitution of the Church as given by Christ, or by acting as the Church's temporal lord rather than as its spiritual head.[36] An example of the *second* kind of schism would be—as Thomas and his commentators suggest—the convoking of a Church council in defiance of a legitimate pope and with the aim of contesting his authority.[37]

Moreover, each of these two types of schism—horizontal and vertical—could itself be carried out in one of two ways, corresponding to the distinction made by the inquisitors between a "pure" and a "mixed" schism. A schism might simply be an affair of the will: in perfect orthodoxy of belief, I could simply refuse to submit to the unity of the Church, and to the pope as the criterion of that unity. More probably, however, there will always be an element of heresy mixed up with it: a schism will normally include some misjudgement on the part of the intellect. I go into schism, in all likelihood, because I refuse to believe that the Church is, and must be, one, or that the Roman see is its necessary centre of unity.

The Situation of Schismatics

Where does all this leave the schismatics themselves? For nearly all theologians until recent times, schismatics were simply *extra Ecclesiam*. A very rare exception is the seventeenth-century Jesuit Scholastic Francisco Suárez. Suárez argued that pure schismatics remain members of the Church since they preserve the faith of her visible

---

[36] Remarked by, for instance, Cardinal Suárez in his *De caritate*, disputatio 12, where he has in mind the case of a pope refusing to preserve union and "conjunction" with the rest of the Church by either trying to excommunicate the whole Church or attempting to root out all those "ecclesiastical ceremonies" (presumably, the sacraments) that the apostolic tradition carries. (In the ante-Nicene Church, the letter of Firmilian of Caesarea to Cyprian accusing Pope Stephen of making himself a schismatic by recognising the baptism of heretics constitutes a putative but, evidently, ill-grounded example of such a charge.)

[37] Congar's examples in "Schisme", cols. 1302–3.

head.[38] Suárez had no takers—understandably, since, for Catholicism, the Church is not only a communion in the same saving faith and sacraments. The Church is also that same communion expressed in a visible, corporate, and *social* way: *societas fidelium*. But we should note that in declaring schismatics to be wholly outside the Church, theological tradition had in mind formal schismatics, that is, persons who, knowing the true nature of the Church, have personally and deliberately committed the sin of schism. But most people who are empirically in schism, that is, non-(Roman) Catholic Christians, are not in this position. For them, the true nature of the Church is not *sufficienter nota*, "sufficiently known": they are not clear that the (Roman) Catholic Church *is* substantially the true Church founded by Jesus Christ. Hence, even before the more generous view of other Christian communities officially instated at the Second Vatican Council, Catholic theologians customarily spoke of such unknowing schismatics as members of the Church "imperfectly", "invisibly", "morally", or "by tendency", as distinct from those who were members in a fully visible fashion.[39] (By the same token, it may be added, Catholic divines were willing to speak of "occult schismatics": those who, though publicly members of the single Church, had, in point of interior fact, nullified the living principle of ecclesial communion and peace in their own hearts.)

These nuances applied to members of any and every non-Catholic Christian body, but a further refinement was invoked in the case of the separated Eastern churches and, especially, for the Eastern Orthodox. To preconciliar eyes, the status of the Orthodox churches did not appear to be in an unconditional sense one of schism from the Catholic Church. To begin with, it was noted that these churches, in departing from Catholic communion, have taken with them their entire constitution as particular churches within the one Church—faith, sacraments, and patristically originated church government. Concentrating on the last of this trio, they would appear

---

[38] *De fide*, disputatio 9, 1.14.
[39] Y. M.-J. Congar, O.P., *Chrétiens désunis: Principes d'un oecuménisme catholique* (Paris, 1957), chap. 7.

to occupy a different category from any other separated Christian community, even compared with those who have retained a valid sacramental system, like the Old Catholics of the Union of Utrecht. Numerous theologians and canonists considered the question of *marriage jurisdiction* to be interestingly symptomatic in this connexion. When separated Eastern bishops gave dispensations from the normal conditions of marriage so as to meet some pastoral need on the part of their faithful, such dispensations were accepted as authoritative by Rome should the individuals concerned be reconciled to the Catholic Church. This was held to indicate that the Eastern Orthodox have preserved not only valid sacraments but a true jurisdiction. And this in turn means that they must also have a continuing share in apostolic authority, and this they can have only if their hierarchs remain in some sense bishops of the Catholic Church. Catholic ecumenists in the interwar years noted this intriguing fact and produced a whole literature on the topic of whether the Orthodox clergy have true jurisdiction.[40]

Prior to the Second Vatican Council, those who considered that Orthodox bishops *do* possess apostolic authority frequently argued that they enjoy this authority through the tacit concession thereof by the Roman see. Thus even so enlightened an ecclesiologist as Père Congar was willing, writing in 1939, to use of dissident Orientals the curious phrase "tolerated excommunicates".[41] This linguistic oddity naturally suggested two important questions. May not one be a schismatic without being absolutely, unconditionally, totally, a schismatic? And furthermore, has not something gone awry in an ecclesiology that finds itself constrained to create so bizarre a notion as that of "tolerated excommunicates"?

It seems, indeed, that it *is* possible to be a schismatic in a certain sense, *secundum quid*, without being a schismatic *tout court*. Relevant here are some aspects of the practice of the early Church. As we have seen, Ignatius of Antioch and the early canons held that a

[40] J. Deslandes, "Les prêtres orthodoxes: Ont-ils la juridiction?" *EO* 26 (1927), 385–95; T.-H. Metz, "Le clergé orthodoxe a-t-il la juridiction?" *Irén.* 5 (1928): 142–46.
[41] Congar, "Schisme", col. 1309.

schismatic is someone who rejects the local bishop and raises up an altar against the bishop's altar. But there were occasions when, after the deposition of some bishop, many of his flock would still regard him as the true bishop and attend his Eucharist. Despite the canons, they were not regarded as having left the Catholic Church. A certain "economy" or prudence in the application of principle was used on their behalf. Again, according to Cyprian, the unity of the episcopate is necessary in order to express the unity of the Church. But there were times when large sections of the episcopate were only in a state of what has been called "mediate communion".[42] The bishop of Antioch might be in communion with his brother of Alexandria, but not with his brother of Rome. But as the bishop of Rome *was* in communion with Alexandria, Rome and Antioch were in mediate communion with each other. Should some great see be disputed between two candidates, the Roman bishop might support one but a bishop of the vicinity the other, so that bonds of communion were ruptured though not broken off. For reasons of this kind, Basil of Caesarea, at the end of his life, found himself in a state of impaired communion with Rome. This does not prevent his veneration as a saint and doctor of the Catholic Church.[43]

It is true that in none of these cases do we find an exact parallel to our contemporary situation, where rival Catholic and Orthodox bishops sit in the same cities all over the world: in New York, Paris, Beirut, Sydney. But on the other hand, these examples do indicate that the concept of schism may in certain circumstances have blurred edges. But here—and this is where Congar's concept of "tolerated excommunicates" becomes pressing—we cannot allow the concept of schism to become completely incoherent. Blurred edges are one thing; sheer self-contradiction is quite another. If we want to say that in one sense the Eastern Orthodox churches, because of their breach of Roman communion, are deprived of apostolic authority but that in another sense they still possess it, we must try to spell out—through our concept of schism—how this can be so.

[42] S. L. Greenslade, *Schism in the Early Church* (London, 1953).
[43] V. Grumel, "S. Basile et le siège apostolique", *EO* 21 (1922): 280–92.

The inherent difficulties that face the "classical" theology of schism when we are thinking of the Eastern churches become even more manifest if we consider the Decree on Ecumenism of the Second Vatican Council, the *Ecumenical Directory* of Pope Paul VI, and the speeches made by the Roman pontiffs to the patriarchs of the separated Oriental churches over the last forty or so years.

The Decree on Ecumenism places the dissident Oriental churches in a different category from the Reformed and Anglican tradition, in other words the communities flowing from the Reformation, whether radically or conservatively so. On the one hand, the Decree speaks about the breach in severe terms as a *scissio*, "cutting off", a *separatio*, "separation"; and a *solutio ecclesiasticae communionis*, "dissolution of ecclesial communion".[44] Although the term *schisma* is never used, it can hardly be doubted that the words I have cited, when taken together, are its equivalent. On the other hand, a great deal of a positive kind is said about the *consideratio peculiaris*, the "special position" of the Eastern churches. First, the word "churches" is used of them, in contrast to the phrase more normally invoked for other Christian bodies, *communitates ecclesiales*, "ecclesial communities". This need not, however, be terribly significant, since the term "churches" is also used by the Decree, apparently, for some non-Orthodox communities in the West, such as, for example, the Old Catholics of the Union of Utrecht. For the council, indeed, "churches" would seem to be groups of separated Christians whose ecclesial life includes the apostolic ministry, while the phrase "ecclesial communities" denotes groups of such Christians whose common life lacks that vital ministerial order. More important, therefore, is the fact that, in the second place, the council fathers declare: through the celebration of the Lord's Eucharist in each of these Eastern churches, *Ecclesia Dei aedificatur et crescit*, "the Church of God is built up and grows in stature".[45] In other words, while other Christian bodies have elements of the being of the one Church, some more and some less, in the Eucharist of the Eastern churches the one Church itself is present

[44] *Unitatis redintegratio*, 13.
[45] Ibid., 15.

and is edified. So the Church that the Catholic Church uniquely is—being that body in which the one, holy, catholic, and apostolic Church of Christ subsists—comes to be more fully precisely through the eucharistic life of these dissident churches.[46]

This exegesis is confirmed by a glance at what else the decree has to say about the East. First, there is a tendency for the council to speak of restoring *full* communion, *instauratio plenae communionis*, and the inclusion of the adjective *plena* here must surely have some force.[47] Second, the council accepts the patriarchal status of those Eastern churches that claim such a title: the local churches of Constantinople, Antioch, Alexandria, and so on.[48] It points out that not a few of these local patriarchal churches took their rise from the apostles themselves. In other words, the council does not simply say that certain dissident Eastern churches *call themselves* patriarchal but that they *are* patriarchal. And this is important, because to ascribe patriarchal status to a particular local church is to say that it rightly enjoins a special claim on the obedience of Christians living round about it. Finally, the decree says that a "certain degree of common worship", *quaedam communicatio in sacris*, with these churches is not only licit but is actively to be encouraged: *non solum possibilis est sed etiam suadetur*.[49] The practical implications of this are spelt out in the *Ecumenical Directory*, which speaks of a "very close communion" between Catholics and Orthodox in matters of faith, cites the remark of

---

[46] This teaching was by no means unknown, however, before the conciliar event. As early as 1926, the Jesuit Maurice de la Taille, of the Gregorian University, affirmed the same thing of the Eucharist of dissident Orientals—at least when their petitions at the Eucharistic sacrifice were "regulated by right intention, respectful of the bond of charity". Speaking of the fruitfulness of their eucharistic offering, de la Taille wrote: "It is for them that we rejoice, and in rejoicing we shall not be favouring dissidence, for we know that their sacrifice works against division and for unity. In the measure that it is pleasing to God, all [eucharistic] sacrifice, since it emanates from the one Church, pleads for the good of unity, exterminates the evil of division." Thus his *L'oecuménicité du fruit de la Messe: Intercession eucharistique et dissidence* (Rome, 1926), p. 135.

[47] *Unitatis redintegratio*, 14.

[48] Ibid.

[49] Ibid., 15.

the council fathers about the Church of God growing through the life of the Orthodox and concludes that in certain circumstances, Catholics and Orthodox may receive each other's ministrations of the sacraments of penance, Eucharist, and anointing. It also allows Catholics and Orthodox to act as godparents at the baptisms of each other's children.

Subsequent relations with the leaders of the Orthodox Church are set out conveniently in the collection of ecumenical documents *Doing the Truth in Charity* edited by T. F. Stransky and J. B. Sheerin, though for encounters subsequent to the date of publication of that volume (1982), one must turn to journals of record such as *L'osservatore romano* and *Documentation catholique*. For our purposes here, I note simply two significant moments. In 1967, in the Latin cathedral of Istanbul, Paul VI spoke of the "profound and mysterious communion which exists between us, participating in the gifts of God to his Church, [putting us] in communion with the Father, by Christ, in the Holy Spirit." He spoke also of the necessity of surmounting the obstacles that remain so that "we may bring to its fulness and perfection that unity—already so rich—which exists between us." [50] Again in 1979, Pope John Paul II spoke in the same place of the breach in communion as a "distance which the two Churches took in regard to each other". He referred to "misunderstandings and disagreements" existing "if not at the level of faith then at the level of theological formulation". He concluded: "It seems to me, in fact, that the question we must ask ourselves is ... whether we still have the right to remain separated." [51]

The phrase that seems to characterise most faithfully the present stance of the Roman see towards the Orthodox churches is that so often used in these addresses: *communio imperfecta*, "imperfect communion". An analogous situation appears to hold between the papacy and the hierarchs of the Non-Chalcedonian Orthodox: there too we find the same language about differences less in faith than in

---

[50] Cited in T. F. Stransky and J. B. Sheerin, *Doing the Truth in Charity* (New York, 1982), p. 187.

[51] Ibid., pp. 207–8.

faith's formulation, and the need to bring existing unity to its perfection.

The Need for a Revised Concept of Schism

What are we to make of all this in terms of the concept of schism? Three possibilities strike one. First, we could say that the classical theory of schism still holds but that we now know so much more about the historical circumstances of the division with the East that it has become unclear whether the classical concept applies to the Eastern schism(s) or not. After all, it was recognised by Scholastic theologians like Cajetan that in these matters facts are vital. If, for instance, I am unjustly excommunicated—because neither in the will nor in the intellect have I repudiated the unity of the Church or the necessity of regarding the Roman bishop as that unity's necessary organ—then I am *not* excommunicated, no matter what any pope or bishops may say. It may be that Rome and the Eastern churches blundered into a state of de facto breach of communion without there even being a true schism. But while the circumstances surrounding the Roman-Byzantine quarrel of 1054 might well be described in this way, it is harder to think that the "nonreception" of the Union Council of Florence by the Byzantine-Slav Orthodox in the course of the later fifteenth century was anything other than a conscious rejection of the claims of the Roman pontiff to be a necessary organ for the unity of the Church.

Second, it might be held that although there has been a full schism, the Roman bishops by use of their "plenary power" in the Church have implicitly granted and continue to grant a share in apostolic authority to churches that are otherwise cut off from the Catholic Church. This is the early Congar's position, but it is certainly a very odd one. It is difficult to credit that all that modern popes have embraced in embracing Orthodox patriarchs is the results of their own ecclesial generosity!

And so we are left with a third possibility. The classical concept of schism is not suited to the facts of the present situation and must be replaced by another. (This would be to apply to the "negative" concept of schism the theological development that has, since the council, enriched the "positive" concept of the ecclesial value of non-Catholic churches and communities.)[52] Crucial here is the fact that the "classical concept" was formed on the basis of an overwhelmingly *universalist* model of the Church. A theological model, especially when it is ecclesiological in nature, is adopted because of its theoretical and pragmatic fittingness to express the faith and practice of the Church. If a model is in some respect unilluminating, or unworkable when compared with the actual faith and practice of the Church, then it must be modified by bringing into play some other model that can complement it and make good its deficiencies.[53]

Giving formal priority to the concept of the *universal Church* is a fully justified proceeding that can appeal, among other things, to the witness of the Lucan account of Pentecost in the book of Acts. A single faith and life, born of the Spirit, is to include all languages and cultures. All particular churches are local concretisations of the single Church of Pentecost, centred as that was on the preaching of Peter. This approach is needed to make sense of a number of features of the Church's life, such as the existence of international papally mandated religious Orders of the type to which the present author belongs. Such an approach will stress elements in the Church's tradition that guard the principle of universality: the collegial symbolism at the ordination of a bishop, the references to a wider communion that are built into the local church's Eucharist, the intrinsic authority of ecumenical councils, and the unity of the episcopal order as safeguarded by the ministry of the Roman pontiff as successor of Peter. Here the particularities of local churches are seen as the explication or unfolding of a primordial unity.

But giving formal priority to the concept of the *local* church is also legitimate. Here a well-known passage of *Lumen gentium* is highly germane:

---

[52] Y. M.-J. Congar, O.P., "Le développement de l'évaluation des églises non-catholiques: Un bilan", in *Essais oecuméniques* (Paris, 1984): pp. 131–52.

[53] I am indebted here to the fine article by Père Jean Tillard, O.P., "Christian Communion"; *Tablet*, 14 January 1984, pp. 39–40.

The Church of Christ is truly present in all legitimate local congregations of the faithful which, united with their pastors, are themselves called "churches" in the New Testament. For in their own locality they are the new People called by God in the Holy Spirit and in full assurance. In them the preaching of the gospel of Christ gathers together the faithful, and the mystery of the Lord's Supper is celebrated so that by the flesh and blood of the Lord the whole brotherhood of his body may be joined together.

The council text continues:

Every community, gathered around the altar, under the sacred ministry of the bishop, is a symbol of the charity and of the unity of the Mystical Body without which there can be no salvation. In these communities, though frequently small and poor or living far from others, Christ is present. By virtue of him, the one, holy, catholic and apostolic Church gathers together.[54]

These statements are made about a legitimately constituted local congregation, which, in the context of this text, means one in peace and communion with the Roman church. Yet, as we have seen from the Decree on Ecumenism, something similar to these statements can be said of every Eucharist celebrated within the apostolic succession and in continuity with the apostolic mission. In some fashion, to some degree, every such Eucharist links a local church with the universal communion even when the bishop who presides in that church is not himself in full communion with the Roman bishop. On such an ecclesiology, the function of the Roman bishop is to bring to its fulness a universality already implicit in the local Eucharist at the bishop's chair and altar. Such full, visibly full, communion can never be simply an option in the life of a local church. It is not merely an additional adornment, lacking crucial ecclesial significance. Nevertheless, communities that preserve the apostolic tradition, its ministry and authority, may be said to remain the Church, even when they lack the bond of communion with the Roman bishop. Their participation in the life and being of the universal Church of

---

[54] *Lumen gentium*, 26.

Pentecost is defective, but still in them the one Church lives and acts.

On this view, therefore, there can be such a thing as "partial schism". To the extent that one preserves all the features of an authentic local church in the apostolic tradition, save the feature of communion with the chair of Peter, one is *not* in schism from the one true Church. To the extent that one breaks the bond of communion with the Roman bishop, one is in schism from the one true Church. One is, therefore, in "partial schism". In some such way, the theological problem of the *concept* of schism is easily solved: how much harder the spiritual, theological, and historical problem of the *actuality* of such partial schism between the First See and the ancient churches of the East.

Bibliography

Congar, Y. M.-J., O.P., "Le développement de l'évaluation des églises non-catholiques: Un bilan". In *Essais oecuméniques*, pp. 206–41. Paris, 1984.

———. *Divided Christendom*. Eng. trans. London, 1939.

———. *L'ecclésiologie du haut moyen-âge*. Paris, 1968.

———. *L'Eglise: De saint Augustin à l'époque moderne*. Paris, 1970.

———. "Quatre siècles de désunion et d'affrontement: Comment Grecs et Latins se sont appréciés réciproquement au point de vue ecclésiologique". *Ist.* 13 (1968): 131–52.

———. "Schisme". *DTC*. Vol. 14, pt. 1, cols. 1286–1312.

———. [with B. P. Dupuy], ed. *L'épiscopat et l'Eglise universelle*. Paris, 1961.

Greenslade, S. L. *Schism in the Early Church*. London, 1953.

Lubac, H. de. "Particular Churches in the Universal Church". In *The Motherhood of the Church*. Eng. trans. San Francisco, 1982.

Thomas Aquinas. *Summa theologiae*. Edited by T. Gilby. Vol. 35, *The Consequences of Charity*, edited by T. R. Heath, O.P. London, 1972.

Tillard, J., O.P. "Christian Communion". *Tablet*, 14 January 1984, pp. 39–40.

2

The Church of the Assyrian Christians

The main focus of interest in this book is the schism between Rome and the Chalcedonian Orthodox: the "Eastern Orthodox" of the overwhelming bulk of the Byzantine-Slav tradition in the Church—expressed historically, that means the Greek-speaking church of the Byzantine Empire, together with its later converts, the Slavs. But east and south of these Christians lie the ancient Non-Chalcedonian churches, whether "Monophysite" or "Nestorian". The Monophysites live principally in Egypt, Ethiopia, Syria, Armenia, and India; the Nestorians in Iraq and Iran, where Monophysite communities exist also. For a variety of political and economic reasons, many of the heirs of these ancient churches are now also to be found scattered through North and South America, as well as Australia and western Europe. Today, Monophysite Christians—also now called, with deliberate dulling of the cutting-edge, "Miaphysites"—are more courteously referred to in ecumenical contexts as the "Oriental Orthodox". Similarly, one supposes, the Nestorians should be described as the "Assyrian Orthodox". Alternatively, the Monophysites are allowed to scoop the title "Non-Chalcedonian Orthodox" (or "Pre-Chalcedonian Orthodox"), in which case, logically, the Nestorians should be dubbed "Non-Ephesian Orthodox" (or "Pre-Ephesian Orthodox") in their turn. In this study, though far from wishing to give offence to any Christian family, I usually prefer to use the names still customary in the West—without meaning to imply that these titles, "Monophysite" and "Nestorian", function by charging any present-day group of believers with formal heresy.

The Nestorian Crisis

Although the crisis that led to the departure of the Nestorians from the Great Church took place with the Council of Ephesus of 431, that crisis cannot be understood without a grasp of the Christological debate endemic in the Church of the fourth and early fifth centuries. Perhaps the best starting point for an understanding of what was going on is the Council of Nicaea of 325.[1] The bishops at Nicaea decided that for man's salvation to be guaranteed through Christ, Christ must be thought of as fully God and worshipped accordingly. In the celebrated phrase they adopted, he is *homoousios tô Patri*, "consubstantial" or "of one being with" the Father. It took fifty years before the council's teaching was generally received in the Church. Many people regarded Saint Athanasius' key formula as little better than Sabellianism, the dubious theology that saw the divine Word or Son as a temporary manifestation of the Godhead rather than as eternally distinct in his own right.[2] Saint Basil, in one of his letters, suggests, possibly rightly, that behind this way of looking at Christ was a basically Jewish doctrine of God, not yet modified by the New Testament experience.[3] Opponents of the Nicene doctrine feared that the formula would turn Christ's life into a mere epiphany of God on the earth, like the appearance of the glory of Yahweh to Moses in the book of Exodus. Eventually, however, the _homoousion_ was accepted: partly because it was found increasingly convincing by many thoughtful Christians; partly because the pagan reaction under

[1] F. Young, *From Nicaea to Chalcedon* (London, 1983); one major reason for regarding Nicaea as epoch-making must lie in its inextricable association with the work of Athanasius in clarifying the eternal preexistence and full divinity of God the Word: see here C. Kannengiesser, "Athanasius of Alexandria and the Foundation of Traditional Christology", *Theological Studies* 34 (1973): 103–13.

[2] W. H. C. Frend, *The Rise of the Monophysite Movement: Chapters in the History of the Church in the Fifth and Sixth Centuries* (Cambridge, 1972), p. 12.

[3] *Letter* 210; cf. *Letter* 265.

the emperor Julian made the Church close ranks; and partly, perhaps, because no one could think of anything better. By the 370s, it was being asserted virtually everywhere that the faith of Nicaea was "the rock of orthodoxy".[4] Once a council is received in this way, it becomes of course an integral part of the Church's tradition. So none of the people I shall mention in the rest of this chapter thought for a moment of questioning the faith of Nicaea.

Unfortunately, the Nicene Creed left a number of issues unresolved. The *homoousion* posed a problem: if Christ were fully God, then how was his divinity related to his humanity? In about 372 a theologian in the Athanasian tradition thought he had the answer. This was Apollinarius, bishop of Laodicea in Syria.[5] Sadly, his answer was not at all satisfactory. Apollinarius asserted that in Christ the divine Word is directly enfleshed in a human body. There is no human mind or soul in Christ; the functions carried out by the rational soul in us were carried out in him by the Logos itself. Christ is literally the "Word made flesh", and as such he is one *hypostasis, one individual* substance.[6] Apollinarius did not work out clearly whether by "one *hypostasis*" he meant that Christ was one person or that he had one nature. In the philosophical language of the time, the word could serve for either, depending on which philosophical tradition you belonged to. Apollinarius' contention was simply that Christ is one single reality, the Logos enfleshed.[7] Soon enough, theologians in the Athanasian line of inheritance realised that Apollinarius had been wrong to deny the presence of a human mind in Christ. After all, as one of them, Gregory of Nazianzus, put it: "What the Word has not assumed, it has not redeemed."[8] Nevertheless, it remained characteristic of Alexandrian theologians that they held Christ to be

---

[4] Basil, *Letter* 258: "the cliff against which heretical waves dispersed into foam".

[5] H. Lietzmann, *Apollinaris von Laodicea und seine Schule* (Tübingen, 1904), remains the standard study.

[6] For the appearance on the scene of this term—complex and controverted yet destined for a glorious future—see M. Richard, "L'introduction du mot *hypostase* dans la théologie de l'Incarnation", *Mélanges de Science Religieuse* 2 (1944–1945): 5–32, 247–70.

[7] Apollinarius, *De fide et incarnatione* 6.

[8] Gregory Nazianzen, *Letter* 101.

one single reality. In time, they came to prefer the term *phusis* to *hypostasis*, though whether they saw any great difference there is debatable. Their slogan was "one incarnate nature (that is, reality) of the Logos". In other words, Christ is God, and he is one being, God-made-human. This Christology became thoroughly identified with the church of Alexandria. And so it also became identified in people's minds with the claims of Alexandria to be an apostolic church, a church with a right to teach the ecumenical Church, the Church at large.[9] By tradition, indeed, Alexandria claimed to be the first among churches after Rome, since she had been founded by the evangelist Mark, the co-worker of Peter. The more-or-less official adoption of the "one incarnate nature" Christology at Alexandria inevitably meant polarisation among the patriarchal sees. People now had two reasons for fighting: suspicion of this Christology, and dislike of the pretentions of Alexandria.

The polarisation became immediately evident at Antioch, and it is from there that the Nestorian schism would take its rise.[10] The founders of the Antiochene school of theology were Diodore of Tarsus, the city of Saint Paul, and Theodore of Mopsuestia, a neighbouring town in what is now southwest Turkey.[11] The basic assertion

[9] On the idea of "apostolic succession" in the ancient Church at large, see A. M. Javierre Ortas, *El temo literario de la sucesión: Prolégomenos para el estudio de la Sucesión Apostólica* (Zurich, 1963).

[10] Cf. the words of Adrian Fortescue in *The Lesser Eastern Churches* (London, 1913), p. 59: "It seems that the remote origin of Nestorianism is to be found in anti-Apollinarian zeal in Syria."

[11] Diodore of Tarsus was, during the Arian troubles, a celebrated defender of Nicene orthodoxy. But in his account of the union between the Word and the man Jesus, he speaks of the Son of David as the temple of the Son of God—or so fragments embedded in the work of Marius Mercator and Leontius of Byzantium suggest. The unfortunate imagery recurs in Theodore, himself the faithful friend of Chrysostom. For Theodore's teaching, see E. Amann, "La doctrine christologique de Théodore de Mopsueste", *RSR* 14 (1934): 161–90; idem, "Théodore de Mopsueste", *DTC*, vol. 15, pt. 1, cols. 235–79; R. Galtier, "Théodore de Mopsueste: Sa vraie pensée sur l'Incarnation", *RSR* 45 (1957): 161–86, 338–60; R. A. Norris, *Manhood and Christ: A Study in the Christology of Theodore of Mopsuestia* (Oxford, 1963); and F. A. Sullivan, "Theodore of Mopsuestia", *NCE* 14:18–19.

of Antiochene Christology, aimed chiefly at Apollinarianism, is that
even after the Incarnation the divinity and humanity in Christ remain
as different as chalk and cheese. More precisely, they remain as different as the Uncreated and the created. Between them there lies, as
Sören Kierkegaard would have written, an "infinite qualitative difference". And yet, despite this enormous ontological fact, the Godhead and the manhood are united by the grace of God to form a
common expression that acts through Jesus, the man assumed by the
Logos. There is one *prosôpon*, one personal self-expression, but two
phuseis, two natures. The opponents of Antioch claimed that this
made Jesus into no more than another prophet or saint. But the
Antiochenes counterargued that this is not so because the association of the Logos with the man Jesus is definitive, complete, and
unbreakable from the moment of the Incarnation onwards. In virtue
of it, what Jesus does, the Logos may always be said to do as well.

We can sum up the differences between the two schools by saying
that for Alexandria, if we are truly to be saved by Christ, then Christ
must be God. For Antioch, if we are truly to be saved by Christ,
then he must be one of us. For Alexandria, the attempt to show that
Christ is God is more important than the attempt to show that he is
man. For Antioch, it is just the other way round. For Alexandria,
the humanity of Jesus yields to the divinity of the Word and is deci-
sively transformed by it, if need be at the expense of Christ's consubstantiality with us as man. For Antioch, the humanity of Jesus is
maintained in its full integrity precisely by *not* being transformed by
its union with the Word. Instead, it is definitively associated with
the Word in a common expression.

All this might have remained at the level of erudite debate had it
not been for the fact that the Antiochene view fell foul of the rise
of Marian piety in the great cities of the Eastern empire. Devotion
to Mary as the God-bearer, *Theotokos*, had been on the increase for
some time, especially in the East. But the title *Theotokos* was more
or less nonsense in terms of Antiochene Christology.[12] What Mary

---

[12] However, after the Council of Ephesus, an Antiochene theologian such as Theodoret of Cyr could accept it in the sense that the Virgin was the instrument by

bore was the man Jesus, who was united to the Logos by a common *prosôpon*: she did not bear the Word itself. As Nestorius himself roundly put it, "He who says that God was born of Mary makes the Christian teaching ridiculous in the eyes of pagans." [13] Mary is the Christ-bearer, *Christotokos*, but not *Theotokos*. Here an issue that was immediately intelligible to the mass of people and that Alexandria could use to mobilise support for her policies. The ideal opportunity was presented in 428 when an Antiochene theologian, Nestorius, became archbishop of Constantinople. This appointment gave Alexandria the chance to scupper two rival sees in one single blow. The rise of Constantinople to preeminence was based essentially on its position as the imperial capital, though some attempt was made to find and rehouse the relics of the apostle Andrew in this connexion. [14] According to legend, Andrew had preached to "Scythians", tribes in the Black Sea region. By claiming Andrew as its founder, Constantinople identified itself with the brother of Peter, a brother who moreover had "brought Simon Peter to Jesus". In 381 the emperor Theodosius had called a council at Constantinople to seal the ending of the Arian crisis and to condemn Apollinarianism. At this council, later regarded as the Second Ecumenical Council, a canon was enacted declaring the bishop of Constantinople to "have the primacy of honour after the bishop of Rome, for Constantinople is New Rome." The idea here was that Rome's primacy derived chiefly from its status as capital of the Christian empire, an empire seen since the days of Constantine the Great as God-willed and providential: the God-given means to convert the world. By becoming

---

which the divine form of the Word was united to the form of a servant, thus his *Letter 83*. Theodore, as cited by Severus of Antioch in the latter's *Liber contra impium grammaticum* 1.134–35 apparently allowed Mary her title *Theotokos* in the sense that "God was in the man that was born": thus Frend, *Rise of Monophysite Movement*, p. 14.

[13] Cited in Frend, *Rise of Monophysite Movement*, from the fragment of Nestorius' homiletic material found in Marius Mercator at PL 48:775. But Frend warns against placing too much reliance on Marius' verbal accuracy here.

[14] F. Dvornik, *The Idea of Apostolicity in Byzantium and the Legend of the Apostle Andrew* (Cambridge, Mass., 1959).

New Rome, Constantinople had inherited the moral identity of Old Rome. Therefore it was only right that the bishop of Constantinople should inherit, or at least share in, the ecclesial identity of the bishop of Rome. There was a sort of ecclesiastical "communication of the idioms", to take an analogy from Christology, between the two local churches, Old and New. Not surprisingly, this canon was studiously ignored at Rome, since it posed a clear threat to Rome's authority. But it caused even more alarm in the other patriarchal sees, Alexandria and Antioch, who saw themselves pushed down the league table by an upstart. Nestorius' preaching against the cultus of the Blessed Virgin as God-bearer was a perfect chance for Alexandria to strike a decisive blow both at the Antiochene Christology and at the ambitions of this *nouvel-arrivé*, the see of Constantinople.[15]

The resultant uproar forced the emperor, Theodosius II, to summon a new council at Ephesus on the Aegean coast of Asia Minor. The dexterous and slightly ruthless Alexandrian patriarch Cyril managed to become papal spokesman for the occasion. And in this capacity, being an adroit politician, he opened the council before the arrival of the bishops of Syria, many of whom would have been sympathetic to Nestorius, and before the arrival too of the actual papal legates, who would have been relatively neutral. Rome tended to support Alexandria ecclesiastically, but its own Christology, as the East would later discover, was if anything closer in spirit to that of Antioch. Nestorius wrote in his apologia: "Cyril presided. Cyril was accuser. Cyril was judge. Cyril was bishop of Rome. Cyril was everything."[16] After his inevitable condemnation, Nestorius was at first confined in an Antiochene monastery and then exiled to the Upper Nile, where he died in obscurity. Even the date of his death is unknown. It is probable, then, that the judicial process that condemned Nestorius left much to be desired. But what of the actual issues themselves?

---

[15] N. H. Baynes, "Alexandria and Constantinople: A Study in Ecclesiastical Diplomacy", *Journal of Egyptian Archaeology* 12 (1926): 145–56; also published in *Byzantine Studies and Other Essays* (London, 1955), pp. 97–115.

[16] *Le Livre d'Héraclide*, trans. F. Nau (Paris, 1910), p. 117.

Opinion is divided, partly as a result of the discovery (1895) and publication (1909) of a hitherto unknown text, Nestorius' *Book* (or, more colourfully, *Bazaar*) *of Heracleides*, found in the library of the Nestorian patriarch at Kotchanes, in Turkish Kurdestan, whence the patriarchs, there established after 1662, believing the local water-course, the Greater Zab, to be the Pison—one of the streams of Eden—wrote their official letters "From my Cell on the River of the Garden of Eden".[17] This text represents almost all that we know of his writings, apart from fragments embedded in the polemical works of his opponents: the frequent fate of the literary efforts of heresiarchs, or those held to be so, in the ancient Church.[18] It has often been asserted that Nestorius ascribed to Christ a dual personality in the strictest sense. Not only was he in two natures, he was also two persons. The matter admits of no simple check, for Nestorius at times uses the term *hypostasis* in its (for his day) novel sense of person, coined by the Cappadocian fathers in the previous century, but more frequently he employs it in a rather older sense, in which it is largely indistinguishable from *ousia*, "being". But in his zeal for upholding the two-natures doctrine that was Antioch's hallmark, he spoke with particular vigour of Christ's oneness as the unity of the *will* of the Logos with the *will* of the man assumed. The divine Word and the son of Mary are one reality because their wills are united. The union is *kath' eudokian*, "by good pleasure", not, as Cyril wished to say, *kath' hypostasin*, "in the substrate of the self". It was held at the time, and has been held with less conviction since, that Nestorius therefore denied a *metaphysical* union between God and man in Jesus Christ, confining their unity to the purely *moral* level.[19]

---

[17] C. Dauphin, "The Rediscovery of the Nestorian Churches of the Hakkari", *ECR* 8 (1976): 56; for modern scholars' investigation of Nestorius' memoir, L. Abramowski, *Unterschungen zum Liber Heraclidis des Nestorius*, Corpus scriptorum christianorum orientalium 242, subsidia 22 (Louvain, 1963).

[18] Collected in F. Loofs, *Nestoriana* (Halle, 1905); additionally, three homilies found by F. Nau are appended to his translation *Le Livre d'Héraclide*, cited above (note 16).

[19] This is the position, thus, of F. Loofs in his *Nestorius and His Place in the History of Christian Doctrine* (Eng. trans., Cambridge, 1914).

Not long after the first, negative evaluation of the newly discovered *Nestoriana* by their editor Friedrich Loofs, the English scholar Leonard Hodgson pointed out, in Nestorius' defence, that one could imagine a metaphysic in which will was the ultimate reality.[20] The philosophical world view of Arthur Schopenhauer (1788–1860), as expounded in his *Die Welt als Wille und Vorstellung*, fertile source of the "voluntarisms" of *fin-de-siècle* Europe, held just this to be the case. In patristic terms, this would mean identifying *thelêma*, "will", with *ousia*, "being", and saying that, since the will of the Logos and the will of the man assumed coincided totally, they were ontologically united in the deepest sense. However, there is little reason to think that Nestorius, or any other writer in the patristic Church, took such a Schopenhauerian view of will.

A defence of Nestorius could also be constructed, so Hodgson insisted, by following a second tack. For the union of wills—the union of "good pleasure"—is not, for Nestorius, the *only* union of divine and human in Christ. He also spoke, following Theodore of Mopsuestia, of a "prosopic" union in Christ. As mentioned above, for Theodore, the Incarnation means the formation of a single personal self-expression or *prosôpon* for divinity and humanity alike. Nestorius has a similar picture, though he may have watered down an already somewhat thin account of the Incarnation—the word means, after all, the "enfleshment" of the divine Son—in Theodore. At first sight, to locate the unity of Christ in a *prosôpon* seems a distinctly unpromising proceeding. The fundamental meaning of *prosôpon* in Antiochene thought is "appearance": a philosophical metaphor, for originally *prosôpon* signified "mask". (Even today, we still preserve something of this usage when we go to the theatre and look at who is playing whom. The *dramatis personae* are the actors who wear the masks—*personae*, *prosôpa*—of the characters whom they are playing.) But what, in a Christological context, did Nestorius mean by "appearance"? Ancient thought, it is suggested, knew nothing of a *counterposing* of appearance and reality. So when Nestorius claims that, in Jesus Christ, as well as the twofold divine and human *ousia* or *phusis*,

[20] L. Hodgson, "The Metaphysic of Nestorius", *JTS* 19 (1917): 46–55.

there is also a single shared appearance, he must be making an ontological claim. An element of being (whether Uncreated or created), found in God and man, "appearance", is now, in Christ, common to both thanks to the Incarnation.[21] And indeed, Nestorius himself wrote: "In virtue of the union, the one nature makes use of the *prosôpon* of the other, so that there is only one *prosôpon* for the two natures. The man [Jesus] is not adored in his own *prosôpon* but in the *prosôpon* that is united to him and that as a result of the union is one."[22] If someone's *prosôpon* is the self-manifestation of his being or nature, then we should expect there to be as many *prosôpa* as there are beings or natures. But in Christ this is not so, and it is precisely here that the mystery of the Incarnation lies.

And yet the fact that so many of Nestorius' Antiochene friends abandoned him at the last may suggest that, in their view, better informed as this was than ours, he had compromised the Christology of Antioch in his very effort to defend it.

The Nestorian schism itself was not organised by Nestorius who, being exiled to a monastery, could do little about it. His teachings were spontaneously espoused by a large proportion of Christians in Eastern Syria, thus splitting the Antiochene patriarchate down the middle.[23] At the time, the main see of Eastern Syria was Edessa, famous for its theological academy. Its bishop Ibas had translated into Syriac the works of Nestorius' master, Theodore of Mopsuestia, for whom he had a great admiration. Though never formally professing Nestorianism, Ibas showed himself in sympathy with the exiled archbishop. On his death in 457 he was succeeded by an open Nestorian, the Syriac poet-theologian Narsai. Under pressure from both imperial and church authorities, Narsai fled from Edessa, crossing the nearby Persian border to Nisibis. There he organised a new

[21] Ibid., p. 48.

[22] Nau, *Livre d'Héraclide*, p. 194.

[23] A. Fortescue asked after the special attraction of Nestorianism for East Syrians: "Is there any inherent tendency towards 'dividing Christ' in the Edessene mind? Hardly", *Lesser Eastern Churches*, p. 54. He ascribed the general acceptance of Nestorianism in Eastern Syria and Persia to (a) its rejection by the empire, and (b) a vehement denial of Monophysitism, which, after all, began at virtually the same time.

and even larger centre of Christian scholarship to rival Edessa. Angered by this, the Roman imperial authority dismantled what remained of the school of Edessa, which was Antiochene in tendency, and ordered the expulsion of all Nestorians from the territories of the Roman state. Although Nestorianism thus quickly became an entirely Persian affair, based in what is now Iraq and Iran, the Nestorians continued to beam propaganda to the rest of the old Antiochene patriarchate, in Western or Roman Syria. In 553, the emperor Justinian, hoping thereby to conciliate the Monophysites, who were protesting that Chalcedon itself was quasi-Nestorian, persuaded the Second Council of Constantinople, i.e., the Fifth Ecumenical Council, to condemn three "chapters" or subjects: the person and works of Theodore of Mopsuestia; the writings of a second Antiochene doctor, Theodoret, against Cyril; and a letter of Ibas of Edessa ("to Maris") defending Diodore and Theodore, but not Nestorius. The Roman church agreed to this step with the greatest reluctance, protesting that it had never been the Church's custom to condemn posthumously those who had died in her peace.

Given the circumstances, it is hardly surprising if the crystallisation of the Nestorian schism took some while. About fifty years elapsed before the Nestorian church got onto its feet. It was greatly assisted by the fact that the church in Persia, under pressure from the Sassanid monarchy there, already showed a strong tendency to independence—and particularly after the Roman Empire, the natural enemy of Sassanid Persia, became officially Christian.[24] Thus in 424, that is, seven years before Ephesus, a synod of thirty-six bishops, under the presidency of the bishop of the royal capital, Seleucia-Ctesiphon, declared that the Persian catholicos was subject only to the tribunal of Christ. That raises the possibility, evidently, that the first Oriental schism would have taken place anyway, even had there

---

[24] Tradition ascribes the origins of the church in Mesopotamia-Persia to the activities of one of the seventy disciples, Mari, who came to Seleucia-Ctesiphon at some point between 79 and 116. Its growth was assisted, apparently, by converts among the Jewish diaspora in Babylonia, merchants, and migrant monks in the mountains of the Tur 'Abdin: thus H. de Mauroy, "Contribution à la connaissance des Assyro-Chaldéens ... en Iran" (dissertation, University of Paris IV, 1973, I).

been no Nestorian crisis on the eastern shores of the Mediterranean. The central figure in forging a common policy, and common church structure, for the Persian and East Syrian churches was perhaps the Syrian bishop Babowi or Baboe, who died in 484. During the latter part of the fifth century, Baboe organised the church's common life on the basis of a patriarchal-episcopal system modelled, presumably, on that of Antioch. The senior bishop bore the title "Patriarch of the East" and was responsible for convening episcopal synods to deal with matters affecting the faith, worship, and life of the people. Interestingly, and perhaps indicating, once again, a political dimension to the schism, the patriarchal see was located in the Persian capital, Seleucia, though in due course the normal residence of the patriarch became Baghdad, the capital of present-day Iraq, and situated a few miles up the Tigris river.

Under Baboe, however, there appears to have been no clear official statement of adhesion to Nestorian or radically Antiochene Christology. That came later—according to some, under his successor Acacius, or again, according to others, not till over a century later, with the work of the influential abbot-theologian Babai the Great, of whom more anon. One Catholic student has remarked of the Christological formula found in Babai's work that it is the first produced in the Nestorian church which "can in no sense be interpreted in a way that would make it harmonise with the decrees of Chalcedon"—Chalcedon being, of course, the Fourth Ecumenical Council, 451, called to put an end to the Christological ferment left by Ephesus, something which it signally failed to do.[25] However, a more optimistic assessment of Babai's work has been offered more recently by—remarkably—a writer from the Syro-Malankar tradition, the Indian Uniate church, whose theological ethos stems ultimately, via the Monophysites, from the Alexandrian school and who here confronts, therefore, an author who is the opposing Antiochene tradition's Syriac theologian par excellence.[26]

[25] M. J. Costelloe, "Nestorian Church", NCE 10:343–46.
[26] G. Chediath, The Christology of Mar Babai the Great (Kottayam, 1982).

The Subsequent Story of the Nestorian Church

The Nestorian church achieved a decent organisational structure, then, around the turn of the fifth century. It was unique for Christendom at the time in possessing its own university—founded or, more strictly speaking, re-founded at Nisibis in 457, by Barsumas, a pupil of Ibas. The school's dominant characteristics were Aristotelianism in philosophy, and in theology and exegesis faithfulness to the school of Antioch.[27] At its largest extent, this theological centre was perhaps about the same size as the Angelicum university in Rome—where these words were largely written—that is, one thousand or so students. For the first hundred years of its existence, the rôle of Thomas Aquinas as principal intellectual patron in that Roman institution was played at Nisibis by Theodore of Mopsuestia, now officially excoriated in the Great Church. But in the seventh century, an attempt was made to substitute for Theodore's influence that of another Antiochene, John Chrysostom, whose orthodoxy had never been questioned. This shift of direction in the school of Nisibis naturally had the effect of reducing the heretical or dubious elements in Nestorian Christology.[28]

As already mentioned, the chief theologian produced by the Nestorians was an abbot, Babai the Great, who lived from 569 to 628. His

[27] A. Vööbus, *History of the School of Nisibis*, Corpus scriptorum christianorum orientalium 266, subsidia 26 (Louvain, 1965). For the wider church history of the see of Nisibis, see J.-M. Fiey, *Nisibe: Métropole syriaque orientale et ses suffragants des origines à nos jours* (Louvain, 1977).

[28] Fortescue wrote in his *Lesser Eastern Churches*, op. cit: "Of Nestorius himself, the theologians of Edessa and Nisibis knew little; nor did they care much about him. But in the movement against him, in the decrees of Ephesus, they saw an attack against their revered masters, Diodore and Theodore; they were (rightly) conscious of defending these. Often in later ages, the Nestorians have protested that they are not the school of Nestorius, they are the school of Diodore and Theodore, of which Nestorius was also a pupil. They stand for the old school of Antioch; it is a mere coincidence that one disciple of that school once became Patriarch of Constantinople, and there got into trouble with Cyril of Alexandria and his council at Ephesus. Still, among the Nestorians 'Theodore the Interpreter' is the honoured master against whom they will allow no accusation", p. 61.

Book of Union became the *Summa theologiae* of the Nestorians, extracts from it being incorporated into their divine Office. A passage claimed to be characteristic reads: "One is Christ, the Son of God, worshipped by all in two natures. In his Godhead, begotten of the Father without beginning from all time. In his manhood born of Mary, in the fulness of time, in a united body.... The natures are preserved in their individuality, in the one person of a single sonship." [29] While it is not, of course, possible to reach a judgement on Babai's Christological orthodoxy on the basis of a single brief passage (eighty-three dogmatic works are ascribed to him, though only three are known[30]), the only defect in this formulation, when compared with the classic patristic Christology of the Roman tradition, the *Tome* of Leo the Great, lies in its omission of any reference to the interrelations of the natures, the "communication of idioms"—itself, indeed, only implicit in Leo's text. This principle states that, while the divine and human natures in Christ are distinct, the attributes of the one may be ascribed to the other on the grounds of their union in the single person of the Saviour. It is germane to investigation of the *kind* of personhood Babai proposes for the incarnate Son, which, to escape the charge of heterodoxy, cannot be that, simply, of a moral reality, nor, a fortiori, the type of judicial fiction by which we call the political state a "person".

In a younger contemporary of Babai's, Išoyahb II of Gdala, who ministered to the East Syrian church as its patriarch from 628 to 646, the communication of idioms is, by contrast, "totally admitted".[31] His *Christological Letter* bears out the confession of faith of Babai's *Book of Union*: Jesus Christ is at once true God and true man, consubstantial with the Father, and also, by virtue of the Incarnation,

[29] Ed. A. A. Vaschalde, in Corpus scriptorum christianorum orientalium (second series) 61. For Babai's theology at large, see V. Grumel, "Un théologien nestorien, Babai le Grand", *EO* 22 (1923): 153–81, 257–80; 23 (1924): 9–33, 162–77, 257–74, 395–99.

[30] L. Abramowski and A. E. Goodman, eds., *A Nestorian Collection of Christological Texts: Cambridge University Library Ms. Oriental 1319* (Cambridge, 1972), 2:xlviii–xlix. Aside from the *De unione*, the other two pieces mentioned are very brief.

[31] L. R. M. Sako, *Lettre christologique du patriarche syro-oriental Išoyahb II de Gdala, 628–646* (Rome, 1983), introduction.

with ourselves. That Incarnation brings with it neither change of the natures nor confusion between them: they preserve their properties but are united in the single person of the Son. Study of this letter by a modern Chaldaean scholar, Father (now Archbishop) Louis Sako, throws light on the Syriac terms used, and notably on the disconcerting fact (for Cyrillians, and for Chalcedonians more widely) that Išoyahb II ascribes to the incarnate Lord two *hypostaseis*— translated innocently in the extract from the *Book of Union* cited above as "individualities". United in the single person, *parsôpâ* (*prosôpon*), of the Son are not simply two natures, *kyânê* (*phuseis*), but also two hypostases, *qnômê*. But according to Sako, it seems that *qnôma* here does not signify "personal subject", as *hypostasis* came to mean in Greek, but rather "concrete nature". *Kyâna* or *usia* in contemporary Syriac stood for a nature in the abstract—catness, humanity—while *qnôma* referred to a nature's concrete being and self-manifestation. Applied to Christ, the term *qnôma*, which we might be tempted to translate "person", apparently denotes the concrete existence and self-manifestation of the divinity and humanity of the Lord: in other words, the *particularities* of the two natures in their self-expression. Moreover, for Sako, the concept of person, used in the *Christological Letter* for that in which the concrete divinity and concrete humanity are united, is fully ontological, belonging in the most complete sense to the order of reality. As Išoyahb himself puts it: "[The meaning of] person [*parsôpâ*] is a form [*schêmâ*], well established by the wise divine Economy in view of the revelation of the divinity by the humanity, and the humanity by the divinity. Thus the person binds, and unites, the two forms [*dmûtâ*]—that of Lord and that of slave—in an inseparable manner." [32] The same notion of person as *schêmâ* or mode of existing (Sako's paraphrase—influenced, surely, by the favoured phrase of the Cappadocians and Maximus the Confessor, *tropos tês huparxeôs*) occurs in a Syriac Christology at the opposite pole, ecclesiologically speaking, from Išoyahb's: the Monophysite James of Sarug. [33] But more important is Išoyahb's attribution

[32] Ibid., pp. 150–51.
[33] R. Chesnut, *Three Monophysite Christologies* (Oxford, 1976), pp. 133–41.

of such "personhood" not only, Theodore-like, to the union between the Word and the man assumed (the "prosopic union" of Nestorius), but to God the Word in and of himself.[34]

The question naturally arises, How representative is the *Christological Letter* of later Nestorian teaching? Sako, understandably concerned to make the best case for the Assyrian tradition, from which his own Catholic mother church, the Chaldaeans, arose (more of this soon), is anxious to stress that—with the exception of Išoyahb's commitment to the *communicatio idiomatum*, it is no fluke or sport but faithfully echoes numerous pronouncements from the late sixth century onwards. And indeed, the profession of faith made by the first Uniate Assyrian patriarch, John Sulaka, to Pope Julius II in 1553, recognisably in this tradition, was accepted by the Roman see as an adequate statement of the faith of the Church in the person of the Redeemer.

From the standpoint of Chalcedonian orthodoxy, it is, in terms of our present knowledge, somewhat premature to present the Assyrians so blithely with a clean bill of health. Significant is the fact, mentioned by Sako, that Išoyahb II never refers to Nestorius, or even to Theodore of Mopsuestia, and that he is silent on the "impiety" or "inanity" of calling the Virgin "Mother of God".[35] It is known that, in the period of Babai and Išoyahb, East Syrian theology was much divided. Isaiah of Tahal certainly, and Henana of Adiabene possibly, rallied to the Neo-Chalcedonian Christology of the "composite hypostasis" of the Redeemer as a successful exposition, within the faith of Nicaea, of Christ's integral humanity.[36] On the other hand, most of the authors studied by L. Abramowski and A. E. Goodman in their edition of an important Nestorian *florilegium* (from the thirteenth to fourteenth century, but including an older collection dating from the seventh century) argue against the "one composite hypostasis" idea. As the latter scholars commented: "The texts of our collection witness to the Nestorian dogmatical war on two or three fronts *within their own church* and against the neighbouring

---

[34] Sako, *Lettre christologique*, pp. 119–22.

[35] Sako, *Lettre christologique*, p. 124.

[36] Abramowski and Goodman, *Nestorian Collection*, p. xlv.

churches." [37] Unlike Išoyahb, their texts—in the making, evidently, until the High Middle Ages and in use until far beyond—do not shrink from attack on Mary's title, *Theotokos*; they extol (less unreasonably) Theodore the Exegete and, in the case of an extract from Shahdost of Tarihan, acclaim Nestorius as "the righteous martyr and *christophoros* ('Christ-bearer')". [38] It may be, then, that Išoyahb II occupies a distinctly "right-wing" position on the doctrinal spectrum of the Assyrian Christianity of his day.

And yet two, possibly three, mitigating factors may be adduced. In the first place, the suggestion that, in many East Syrian texts, the value of "ultimate personhood" carried in post-Cappadocian Greek patrology by the term *hypostasis* attaches to the term *prosôpon*—*hypostasis* or its Syriac equivalent doing service here for, rather, "nature in its concreteness"—still carries conviction. Second, a certain number of the later Nestorian Christological writings avoid the word *hypostasis* altogether (probably because, for the writers concerned, it is fully acclimatised only in *Trinitarian* theology)—and thus the question of their conformity to Chalcedon is not posed with sufficient clarity to be capable of answer. [39] And third, those texts, hostile to the "single composite hypostasis", which some scholars would interpret as a deliberate distancing of the writers concerned from Neo-Chalcedonianism and so from the authoritative interpretation of Chalcedon offered in the Great Church by the Second Council of Constantinople, may be, rather, attacks on the Christology of Severus of Antioch, the most plausible—because the most moderate—of the Monophysite theologians of the epoch. [40]

All in all, then, we cannot entirely eliminate the thesis which has it that the Nestorian church gradually came to identify itself not with the extreme Antiochenism of Nestorius but with a more restrained Antiochenism, along the lines of Theodore, or even, perhaps, Chrysostom: stressing the distinctness of the natures but not

---

[37] Ibid., p. xix, emphasis added.
[38] Ibid., p. 19. Shahdost was patriarchal vicar for Aba II (died 751).
[39] Ibid., pp. xl–xli.
[40] Frend, *Rise of Monophysite Movement*, p. 211.

without defending the unity of the person. Although today the church of the Assyrian Christians has no theologians to speak of, its theologians in the past came to adopt a position not unlike that of Chalcedon and at no great remove, indeed, from the more moderate statements of Cyril. That the Nestorians were proscribed in the Byzantine Empire is perhaps enough to account for the fact that nobody in the Great Church at the time realised the character of the internal evolution in Nestorian teaching.

What, then, happened to the community whose theological orientation we have glimpsed at one crucial point? The Nestorians were at first fortunate in their banishment from the East Roman Empire. Though they no longer lived under the protection of Christian rulers, they no longer had to tolerate—by the same token—emperors who considered they had a right to govern the Church as they saw fit. The Nestorians were for the most part left in peace by the Persian monarchy, whose own religion was Zoroastrianism, though there were occasional brief periods of persecution, sometimes severe. (The "great" or "forty-year" persecution, under the fourth-century shah Shapur II, with its thousands of martyrs, antedates the Nestorian schism.) Persia itself was fundamentally an eastward-looking country, the meeting point of trade routes from Arabia, central Asia, India, and China. This fact of economic geography enabled the Nestorians to carry out a truly extraordinary programme of missionary activity.[41]

Nestorian Christianity established itself in four far-flung regions of the planet. First, Nestorians evangelised in *Arabia* from the sixth to the ninth centuries. Around 600 a Yemeni king, ruling, however, in northern Arabia, was a Nestorian Christian as was the city-state of Najran in Yemen proper. It is possible that Muhammad received his first lessons in Christianity from Nestorian missionaries about this time.[42] If so, they may well be responsible for his decision to give Christians a favoured status as "people of

---

[41] Surveyed in J. Stewart, *Nestorian Missionary Enterprise: The Story of a Church on Fire* (Edinburgh, 1928).

[42] T. Andreae, *Mohammed: The Man and His Faith* (Eng. trans., New York, 1936), p. 92.

protection" (*ahl al dhimma*), their religious freedom theoretically guaranteed in return for the payment of a poll tax. In *central Asia*, there were Nestorian bishoprics in at least two Turkestani cities, Bokhara and Tashkent, as well as Samarkand. In the course of the tenth and eleventh centuries, Nestorian missionaries pushed up to Lake Baikal in southern Siberia, an area where even today, after seventy years of Communism, many people remain animists. And the occasional western envoy on a visit in the mid-thirteenth century to the Great Khan, the leader of the Mongol Horde, was astonished to find a Nestorian church in his capital, Karakorum.[43] In *China*, when the Jesuits arrived in 1635, they were equally or more amazed to be shown a stone tablet recording the arrival of the Nestorians in 631.[44] This tablet describes a meeting between the Nestorian envoys and the Chinese emperor, summarises the teachings of the Bible and the Creed, and reports that the emperor, having read the Scriptures, has decreed that they should be made known throughout his realm. The text is written in Chinese characters by a Chinese hand and records the names of the Nestorian patriarch together with a suffragan bishop, Adam, described as "bishop and pope" of China. Nestorian Christianity flourished in China for two centuries, suffering setbacks only in the ninth century, when the last emperors of the Tang dynasty began a campaign against all foreign religions. Nevertheless, the Nestorian church hung on, and a Chinese man held its supreme post of patriarch of the East from 1283 to 1317.[45] Under the Mongol or Yuan dynasty in approximately this period, though the court was officially Buddhist, the Nestorian clergy were in great demand as doctors, scribes, and occasionally as envoys to the West. The end came, however, with

[43] F. Nau, *L'expansion nestorienne en Asie* (Paris, 1914); J. Dauvillier, "L'expansion de l'Eglise syrienne en Asie centrale et en Extrême-Orient", *L'Orient syrien* 1 (1956).

[44] C. E. Couling, *The Luminous Religion: A Study of Nestorian Christianity in China with a Translation of the Inscriptions upon the Nestorian Tablet* (London, 1935).

[45] Possibly a Mongolian, Yabhalaha III sent to Rome, in 1304, a profession of faith by the hands of a Dominican returning to Italy, an initiative frustrated by his coreligionists. For such contacts, see S. Giamil, *Genuinae relationes inter Sedem apostolicam et Assyriorum orientalium seu Chaldaeorum ecclesiam* (Rome, 1902).

the rise to power in the late fourteenth century of the Ming dynasty, part of a general movement against all things non-Chinese popular with peasant masses. Thus the destruction of the Nestorian church in many ways anticipates what happened to the Catholic Church there under Mao Tse-tung. Finally, in *India*, the Nestorians had their most enduring conquest, when groups of Thomas Christians in the south of the subcontinent were hierarchically integrated into the Church of the East.[46] But by an irony of history, the Nestorian church in India, where it was not forced into Roman union by the Portuguese, switched its ecclesiastical allegiance and joined forces with the great historic foe of Nestorians, the Monophysites: only in the twentieth century, in confused circumstances, did a tiny Indian Nestorian community revive at Trichur. But the failure of the Nestorian missions was mainly a matter of politics. Their success derived from the imaginative nature of their missionary work. Wherever they set up a bishopric, they also created a library and a hospital. In addition, the Nestorians had a great pool of potential missionaries in the monks of Syria and Persia, who were willing to "go apostolic", rather as the early Franciscans and Dominicans took to the roads of western Europe in the early thirteenth century.

What, then, of the Nestorian church in its homeland, Persia—that is, Mesopotania-Iran?[47] Along with the rest of the country, the church there had to suffer three major military invasions. First, the *Arabs* invaded Persia, incorporating it into an empire, the Abbasid caliphate, centred on Baghdad. To begin with, the Nestorians were well treated by the Arabs, who used them as administrators, doctors, and interpreters. It was through the Nestorians that the Arabs read the Greek philosophers and scientists. But though Christian disabilities increased, the Nestorian church survived the collapse of the caliphate in the ninth century and went on to achieve great things under the

[46] Pahlavi inscriptions on sixth- and seventh-century stone crosses at Madras and Travancore record the Nestorian presence. For the little-known history of the Nestorian church in India, see especially E. Tisserant, "Nestorienne, L'Eglise", in *DTC*, vol. 11, pt. 1, cols. 265–88.

[47] J.-M. Fiey, O.P., *Assyrie chrétienne* (Beirut, 1965–1968).

caliphs' successors, the *Mongols*. It was, in fact, the enormous extent of the Mongol dominions, the so-called *pax tartarica*, from Hungary in the West to China in the East, that made most of the Nestorian missionary work possible. In 1295, however, the Mongol khan of Persia accepted Islam, a conversion used by Muslims to get even with Nestorian Christians, whose privileges they resented. However, the real undoing of the Nestorian church was the third and last of the military invasions: that of *Turkic tribes* under the famous (or infamous) Timur the Great in 1400. Under Timburlaine, whose name became a byword for cruelty in the West, the Nestorians were decimated and fled from the cities to the mountains of Kurdistan. In the wild and barren countryside lying between two great lakes, Lake Urmia and Lake Van, they retreated to an almost Stone Age lifestyle, becoming chiefly herdsmen and hunters. A symptom of their decadence was the fact that they confined the patriarchate to members of a single family. The post of head of the church passed from uncle to nephew or, occasionally, younger brother in a system that died out only in the 1970s. Unwittingly, this peculiar arrangement also opened up the Nestorians to the influence of the church of Rome.

During the Crusades, Latin churchmen came into contact with Non-Chalcedonian Christians for the first time since the schism. Nothing much came of these early ecumenical contacts, however, until the sixteenth century.[48] In 1551 a Nestorian patriarch died, and a number of his flock determined to abolish the method of succession that had brought them so many unsuitable candidates. Under pressure, the bishops elected a monk from outside the patriarchal family, John Sulaka. Shortly before, Franciscans had arrived in Kurdistan by way of Jerusalem. They managed to convince the patriarch-elect that his position would be strengthened if he accepted

[48] G. Beltrami, *La Chiesa caldea nel secolo dell'Unione* (Rome, 1933). An interesting harbinger of the union was the signature appended to the bull of union with Orientals at the Council of Florence by an East Syrian bishop from Cyprus. (The Arab conquest of the Middle East had the unexpected consequence of permitting the Nestorians to return, if not in large numbers, to the Byzantine regions west of the Euphrates, including, even, Greek-speaking ones.) This is perhaps the earliest recorded use of the adjective "Chaldaean" for Catholic Assyrians.

confirmation by the pope. So, armed with a letter from the Franciscan *custos* of the Holy Land, he travelled to Rome and was duly consecrated by Pope Julius III. On his return, however, accompanied by two Maltese Dominicans, the patriarch who took the name of John VIII was intercepted by the Turkish authorities and executed. But for a hundred years his successors continued to offer canonical obedience to the Roman see. Thus the breach between Rome and the church of the Assyrian Christians appeared mended.

But owing to the problems of communication over distance, and the complexities of power relations in the Nestorian church, a very odd situation proceeded to develop. Parallel to the Uniate succession of John Sulaka, a non-Roman succession had also continued among the Nestorians, through a certain Shimun (Simon) Denkha, the nephew of the last pre-Sulaka patriarch. In the course of the seventeenth century, the patriarchs of this continuing schismatic line, which was based at Mosul further south in Iraq, tried to disarm their Uniate rivals, who were still living up in the mountains of Kurdistan or in the valleys west of Lake Urmia, by themselves entering into union with Rome. Inexplicably, the popes sought to recognise their claims as well, so that two Uniate Assyrian Churches of the East were in the offing simultaneously. And when the Sulaka union collapsed and the negotiation attempts of their rivals foundered in the mid-eighteenth century, there still remained, at Diyarbakir in the upper Tigris valley, a line of bishops in Petrine communion to whom the title of Catholicos-patriarch was (as things turned out) temporarily conceded also.

What, then, is the origin of the present Uniate Assyrian church, better known as the Catholic Chaldaean rite? In 1826 a patriarch in Mosul returned to Catholic unity and in 1830 was confirmed in office as "Patriarch of Babylon of the Chaldaeans" by Pope Pius VIII. Paradoxically, therefore, the present Uniate Chaldaean patriarch derives his succession from the original Nestorian line—albeit in Baghdad, to where the patriarchal seat was transferred in 1950 owing to the considerable migration of Chaldaean Catholics from northern Iraq to the modern capital. It is the heirs of Sulaka's Uniate line who have become the representatives of resistance to Rome.

This line itself adopted the dynastic principle for the patriarchal succession, which it had, of course, originally come into existence in order to avoid! However, the dynasty came to an end in 1975 with the murder in California of the patriarch Shimun XXIII, who had been living in the United States as an exile since 1939. His successor, the present patriarch Denkha IV, was consecrated in London in 1976. At once he had to face the fact that the Iraqi government was not enthusiastic about letting an Assyrian patriarch return to the country. Why this should be so may become clearer if I say that *one* motive for the assassination of Shimun XXIII was his refusal to recognise a movement called the "Assyrian Universal Alliance", whose aim is to create an Assyrian "homeland" within the borders of present-day Iraq, rather as the state of Israel was formed out of Arab Palestine.[49]

The political situation of the Nestorian church has been extremely unhappy in modern times, something which accounts for many of the conversions to the Uniate church, which now numbers some quarter of a million practising members in a community of perhaps 600,000.[50] Under the Ottoman Empire, the Catholic Assyrians were protected subjects, while the Nestorian patriarch himself exercised his functions only at the whim of the local emir of Kurdestan.[51] In the vain hope that they might get political self-government, the Nestorians chose to help the Allied forces in the First World War by revolting against the Turks. As a result, thousands had to abandon their homes and moved south with the British army in an exodus that has been compared to the Mormon exodus of 1846. During the years

[49] For the murder of the patriarch Shimun XXIII and its background, see *POC* 26 (1976): 165–74.

[50] Now a more significant "player" in its homeland than is its separated sibling, its recent history is the focus of A. O'Mahony, "The Chaldaean Catholic Church: The Politics of Church-State Relations in Modern Iraq", *Heythrop Journal* 45 (2004): 435–50.

[51] This contrast is a recurrent factor in the large number of conversions to Catholicism in the Ottoman Empire on the part of Oriental Christians of all traditions—duly chronicled in C. A. Frazee, *Catholics and Sultans: The Church in the Ottoman Empire* (Cambridge, 1983). In the Nestorian case, it prompted the decision of the patriarch Shimun XIX, early in 1914, to open negotiations for corporate union with the Russian Orthodox church, which was protected by the tsars.

after the First World War, the Nestorians were greatly assisted by the Church of England, whose authorities considered them, given their low doctrine of the Blessed Virgin, to be the Protestants of the East.[52] The relative absence of images in Assyrian churches was also a draw to Reformed Christians, but its explanation is likely to be fear of iconoclastic attacks by Muslims from the later fourteenth century onwards, not a theologically based iconophobia.

Since in 1917, the patriarch-elect was a boy of eleven, he was taken to England and brought up as a ward of the archbishop of Canterbury. His predecessors' sister (actually an aunt) took over the government of the community but totally failed to make it adjust to the new world of Arab states after 1919. At one point, the Iraqi government even considered transporting the Nestorians en bloc to Canada. The situation became especially serious in 1933. In that year, the patriarch, after failing to meet the requests of the Iraqi government (reports of deliberate Iraqi decimation, assisted by elements in the Kurdish population, of Assyrian villages are variously credited by Western commentators),[53] was deported to Cyprus, from whence he went to the United States, only to die as I have described. Not surprisingly, a recent study of the Nestorian church by one of its members is entitled *Death of a Nation*. Assyrian Christians in the world today number some 400,000 people, of whom perhaps half are practising their faith.

In the past few years, however, there have been some signs of a revival among the Nestorians. There is a great thirst among their

[52] Set forth in *The Archbishop of Canterbury's Mission to the Assyrian Christians* (London, 1891). A full narrative of this impressive, if ill-fated, venture will be found in J. F. Coakley, *The Church of the East and the Church of England: A History of the Archbishop of Canterbury's Assyrian Mission* (Oxford, 1992). A detailed account of the various missionary visitations that the Nestorians received, or suffered, from the mid-nineteenth century onward is offered in J. Joseph, *The Nestorians and Their Muslim Neighbors: A Study of Western Influence on Their Relations* (Princeton, 1961). A revised edition of this book has been published as *The Modern Assyrians of the Middle East: Encounters with Western Christian Missions, Archaeologists, and Colonial Powers* (Leiden, 2000).

[53] For literature, see A. O'Mahony, "Eastern Christianity in Modern Iraq", in *Eastern Christianity: Studies in Modern History, Religion and Politics*, ed. A. O'Mahony (London, 2004), pp. 11–43, at note 44.

young members for a knowledge of their church and its certainly glorious history. The Assyrian clergy, however, are ill-educated and parochial in outlook. One cannot easily imagine them providing members for a theological commission to discuss reunion with Rome. (A notable exception was a bishop of the Church of the East domiciled in the United States, Mar Bawai Soro, but at Pentecost 2008, along with six priests, thirty deacons and some three thousand laity, Mar Bawai was received into the Catholic Chaldean diocese of Saints Peter and Paul.) However, the patriarch Denkha IV, then resident in Tehran, paid a formal visit to Pope John Paul II in early November 1984. In his speech of welcome, the pope said: "The treasures of faith that we have in common are such that what unites us is stronger and greater than that which still separates us. But it is necessary to clarify the misunderstandings and ultimately the divergences which may still remain between us. In doing so, we shall be able to arrive at full communion." The patriarch in his reply drew attention to the common faith of Nicaea: "We too believe today in one only God, the Father of all, and in the mystery of the Holy Trinity: Father, Son and Holy Spirit, and in one only Lord, Jesus Christ, the Son of God." And he concluded in words that were, perhaps, easier for him to say than to achieve, given the limited resources of his church: "We shall be able to arrive at peace and love between us through frequent meetings and reunions, especially when they are desired as dialogues and consultations." [54] It would remain to be seen what substance, if any, could be given to those words. [55]

It might be thought that, given the relatively minuscule dimensions of the Assyrian church today (and an internal schism which broke out in 1968 on Shimun XXIII's adoption of the Gregorian calendar has weakened it further), an effort to solve the outstanding problems between Rome and the self-styled "patriarchate of the East" is hardly worth the trouble involved. On the other hand, it is part of being human and being Christian to have an historical memory, to

[54] *OR*, 9 November 1981.

[55] In 1989 a renewal of commitment by the Assyrians to reunion with the Chaldaeans, and so with Rome, was recorded in *Orthodox Outlook* 4, no. 3 (1989): 7.

feel the glory and the tragedy of the past that has made us what we are. The poet Wordsworth wrote in his sonnet "On the Extinction of the Venetian Republic":

> Men are we, and must grieve when even the Shade
> Of that which once was great is passed away.

The shade of the Nestorian church has not passed away but is still with us.

The heart of any dialogue with the Assyrians would necessarily be the Christological issue. Some texts with a classical status in their tradition, such as the *Christological Letter* of Išoyahb II, might be taken as the basis for such discussion. It may be possible to show that the letter's dogmatic intention is the same as that of the Christological definition of Chalcedon. If, then, Chalcedon is compatible with Ephesus, why should not the *Christological Letter* be, and thus much, at least, of the subsequent Assyrian tradition, which preserved it as a significant monument of faith? In this way, a path would open up to a common Assyrian-Catholic re-reception of Ephesus, the council that was the occasion of the schism. I shall say more about this, and about the difficulties that such a Christological adjustment could create for dialogue not only with the Oriental Orthodox but with the Eastern Orthodox themselves, later on.

With fewer learned preliminaries than the above remarks suggest, in 1994 Denkha IV and Pope John Paul II signed their historic "Common Christological Declaration", which, so they maintained, would enable them henceforth to "proclaim together before the world their common faith in the mystery of the Incarnation".[56] From the starting point of the Creed of Nicaea, they confess that the eternal Word "became incarnate by the power of the Holy Spirit in assuming from the holy Virgin Mary a body animated by a rational soul, with which he was indissolubly united from the moment of his conception." In the twofold consubstantiality that binds him with the Father, on the one hand, and with human beings on the other, his "divinity and

[56] "Common Christological Declaration between the Catholic Church and the Assyrian Church of the East", *Ecumenical Trends* 24, no. 11 (1995): 3–4.

humanity are united in one person, without confusion or change, without division or separation." There we hear an echo of the Chalcedonian definition. The pope and patriarch emphasise the difference of the natures (with all their properties, faculties, and operations), but they immediately go on to add, in the spirit of the Second Council of Constantinople—and indeed, of Saint Cyril—that the unique person who is the subject of these natures is "the object of a single adoration". The Logos who was begotten of the Father from before all ages was, at the Incarnation, born of a human mother "without a [human] father ... in the last times". The declaration reports that the Assyrian Church of the East, while acclaiming the Blessed Virgin by its own formula—"Mother of Christ our God and Saviour"—recognises the legitimacy of her title "Mother of God". Indeed, as the statement points out, Catholic Christians too call Mary "Mother of Christ". Evidently, they do not think they are impugning the councils after Nicaea in so doing.[57]

From the Trinitarian communion named in such doctrine, there issues the communion of the Church with her sacramental life, and the 1994 declaration warms to that subject too by affirming a great commonality of teaching and practice in regard to the sacraments of initiation, orders, and the Holy Eucharist. Cooperation was considered in evangelisation, catechesis, and the formation of priests, and a "mixed commission" for theological dialogue between the Catholic Church and the Assyrian Church of the East established, at any rate in principle.

In 1996 the Chaldaean Catholic patriarch, Raphael I, who had been enthroned at Baghdad in 1989, signed with Denkha IV a series of common proposals for the restoration of unity, and these were approved in the following year by their respective synods. High on the list was the possibility of a degree of eucharistic hospitality, at any rate in particular circumstances (namely, the inaccessibility of priestly celebrations for faithful of one or the other tradition), despite the merely partial nature of the ecclesial communion between the two bodies. One

---

[57] For a discussion of this text against the historical background, see G. Thumpanirappel, *Christ in the East Syriac Tradition: A Study of the Christology of the Assyrian Church of the East and the Common Christological Declaration of 1994* (Satna, 2003).

difficulty had been the primitive—not only historically but doctrinally—character of the Assyrian Eucharistic Prayer, the "Anaphora of Addai and Mari", which, to the dismay of Catholic scholars of an earlier generation (and some contemporary ones), lacked an institution narrative with the words of consecration. The "mixed commission" gave it their attention. In 2001, after considerable consultation and careful thought, the Holy See accepted the argument that in that prayer "the words of eucharistic institution are indeed present ... , not in a coherent narrative way and *ad litteram*, but rather in a dispersed euchological way, that is, integrated in successive prayers of thanksgiving, praise, and intercession." [58] This conclusion did not please all Catholic theologians, though its formulation was indebted to excellent historical scholarship. [59] Rome made it clear it would still prefer the Assyrians to align their Eucharistic Prayer more fully with the Canons of the Mass in the West and non-Assyrian East. Some were willing, but not all.

In the early twenty-first century, it became plain that attitudes within the Church of the East to a *rapprochement* with the Catholic Church varied widely. A wider document on sacramental life more generally was ready but not endorsed. In June 2007 a new pope, Benedict XVI, welcomed Denkha IV once again to the papal city and expressed his appreciation of what had been hitherto achieved as well as his sadness at the fresh troubles in which the coalition invasion of Iraq had unwittingly involved separated Assyrians and Catholic Chaldaeans alike. War, emigration, sanctions, social breakdown, and now "regime change" that has made Christians more free but less secure: it was hardly surprising that survival, especially in the ancient homelands (the situation in Iran, with its Islamic theocracy, is scarcely more encouraging), had become their overwhelming priority. [60]

[58] "Orientamenti per l'ammissione all'Eucaristia fra la Chiesa Calda e la Chiesa Assira dell'Oriente", *OR*, 26 October 2001.

[59] See, for example, A. Gelston, *The Eucharistic Prayer of Addai and Mari* (Oxford, 1992).

[60] For the (generally bleak) outlook for Christianity in the Arab world, see the essays gathered together in A. Pacini, ed., *Christian Communities in the Arab Middle East: The Challenge of the Future* (Oxford, 1998).

Meanwhile, as the further ecumenical dialogue awaits, we can note here the additional problem that the Assyrian Christians, like the Non-Chalcedonian Orthodox, have taken from their experience of conciliar history an alternative patrology in which the "blessed Nestorius", as they call him, is extolled and called upon in prayer, while the "wicked Cyril", Cyril of Alexandria, is excoriated. Of some importance in their liturgy is the feast of the "Greek doctors", who turn out to be the trio of Diodore of Tarsus, Theodore of Mopsuestia, and Nestorius himself. For the Great Church, in which faith is not only acceptance of a set of dogmata but a life of faith in communion with the living and the dead, this is a complication. At the same time, the seriousness with which the Church of the East takes its desire for reconciliation was signalled in 1997 when its governing synod decided to remove from the liturgical books all condemnations of both Cyril of Alexandria and Severus of Antioch—hitherto excoriated as Monophysite heretics.

Naturally, the topic of Christology, and the Christological divines of the ancient Church, does not constitute the whole of the story. In addition, there is all the doctrine confessed by subsequent general councils, and notably those held in the West since the early Middle Ages. Once again, I believe that the idea of re-reception is the key but would rather defer what I have to say on this subject until we have looked at the other two great communions to which it is relevant: those of the Oriental, and of the Eastern, or Chalcedonian, Orthodox.

Bibliography

Background

Duchesne, L. *The Early History of the Christian Church from Its Foundation to the End of the Fifth Century*. Eng. trans. London, 1950–1951.

Grillmeier, A. *Christ in Christian Tradition*. London, 1964, 1975.

Labourt, J. *Le christianisme dans l'empire perse sous la dynastie sassanide, 224–632*. Paris, 1904.

Meyendorff, J. *Imperial Unity and Christian Divisions: The Church 450–680 A.D.* Crestwood, N.Y., 1989.

Young, F. *From Nicaea to Chalcedon: A Guide to the Literature and Its Background*. London, 1983.

Nestorius and Nestorianism

Amann, E. "Nestorius". *DTC*. Vol. 11, pt. 1, cols. 76–157.

Bethune-Baker, J. F. *Nestorius and His Teaching*. Cambridge, 1908.

Braaten, C. E. "Modern Interpretation of Nestorius". *Church History* 32 (1963).

Chadwick, H. "Eucharist and Christology in the Nestorian Controversy". *JTS*, n.s., 2 (1951).

Galtier, P. "Nestorius mal compris, mal traduit". *Gregorianum* 34 (1953).

Hodgson, L. "The Metaphysic of Nestorius". *JTS* 19 (1917).

Loofs, F. *Nestorius and His Place in the History of Christian Doctrine*. Eng. trans. Cambridge, 1914.

McGuckin, J. A. "The Christology of Nestorius of Constantinople". *Patristic and Byzantine Review* 7 (1988): 93–129.

Vine, A. R. *Approach to Christology: An Interpretation and Development of Some Elements in the Metaphysic and Christology of Nestorius*. London, 1948.

The Development of Nestorian Christology

Abramowski, L. and A. Goodman, eds., *A Nestorian Collection of Christological Texts*. Cambridge, 1972.

Chediath, G. *The Christology of Mar Babai the Great*. Kottayam, 1982.

Sako, L. R. M. *Lettre christologique du patriarche syro-oriental Išoyahb II de Gdala, 628–646*. Rome, 1983.

The Assyrian Church in Later History

Baum, W., and D. W. Winkler. *The Church of the East: A Concise History*. London, 2003.

Baumer, C. *The Church of the East: An Illustrated History of Assyrian Christianity*. London, 2008.

Couling, C. E. *The Luminous Religion: A Study of Nestorian Christianity in China with a Translation of the Inscriptions upon the Nestorian Tablet*. London, 1935.

Dauvillier, J. "L'expansion de l'Eglise syrienne en Asie centrale et en Extrême-Orient". *L'Orient syrien* 1 (1956).

Fiey, J.-M., O.P. *Assyrie chrétienne*. Beirut, 1965–1968.

———. *Jalons pour une histoire de l'Eglise en Iraq*. Louvain, 1970.

Le Coz, R., O.P. *Histoire de l'Eglise d'Orient: Chrétiens d'Irak, d'Iran et de Turquie*. Paris, 1995.

Malek, R. ed., *Jingjiao: The Church of the East in China and Central Asia*. Sankt Augustin, 2006.

Nau, F. *L'expansion nestorienne en Asie*. Paris, 1914.

Stewart, J. *Nestorian Missionary Enterprise: The Story of a Church on Fire*. Edinburgh, 1928.

Tisserant, E. "Nestorienne, L'Eglise", *DTC*. Vol. 11, pt. 1, cols. 157–323.

Vine, A. B. *The Nestorian Churches: A Concise History of Nestorian Christianity in Asia from the Persian Schism to the Modern Assyrians*. London, 1937.

Wigram, W. A. *An Introduction to the History of the Assyrian Church, 100–640 A.D.* London, 1910.

Life and Liturgy

Badger, G. P. *The Nestorians and Their Rituals.* London, 1852; reprinted 1987.

Costelloe, M. J. "Nestorian Church". *NCE* 10: 343–46.

Fortescue, A. *The Lesser Eastern Churches.* Chapters 3–5. London, 1913.

3

The Churches of the Oriental Orthodox

I turn now to the story of the second of the Eastern schisms, that between the Great Church and the bodies known colloquially as "Monophysites" or more politely as the "Oriental Orthodox". As we have seen, the Council of Ephesus in condemning Nestorius by no means won an absolute victory for Alexandria and Saint Cyril. First, so many of the faithful and clergy in Syria and Persia defected. But second, all was not smooth sailing afterwards for the relations between the quartet of major sees: Alexandria itself, Antioch, Constantinople, and Rome. To see how this was so, we can go back to the months immediately prior to the meeting of the council in June 431. During the preceding eighteen months, Cyril was engaged in defining the theological standpoint of Alexandria. For this purpose, he wrote three letters.[1] Despite their violent language, the first two of these letters proved acceptable to all but the Nestorians. The first letter simply asked that Nestorius should accept Mary's title: the "God-bearer". The second criticised him for regarding the union of divine and human in Christ as simply a result of "will", *thelêma*, or "good pleasure", *eudokia*. Cyril pointed out that, if we are to speak of Christ as "he" and not "they", the Logos *and* the man assumed, then divinity and humanity must be fully joined in one Lord, the single concrete being of the Saviour. The stress is to be placed on the essential unity of Christ's person, something Cyril felt to be endangered by the Antiochene approach and undermined completely in that of

[1] For an analysis of the three letters *ad Nestorium*, see W. H. C. Frend, *The Rise of the Monophysite Movement: Chapters in the History of the Church in the Fifth and Sixth Centuries* (Cambridge, 1972), pp. 18–19.

Nestorius. The third letter, however, proved more controversial. In it Cyril spoke of the "single hypostasis of the Word incarnate", using the term "hypostasis" not so much, it would seem, for "individual person" as for "nature" or "concrete being".

Although Cyril hastened to add that he did not mean that the Godhead was actually changed by the Incarnation, it was not immediately obvious how it could escape change if Cyril were right about the "single nature". In any event, Cyril attached to this letter twelve propositions which he called on Nestorius to renounce—the so-called *Twelve Anathemas*.[2] The bishop of Antioch, John, saw at once that some at least of the *Twelve Anathemas* were highly debatable. This was especially true of number 2 and number 12, which spoke of the Word as "suffering in the flesh". This was not a statement with New Testament backing, and indeed, so far as John could see, it was lifted from the writings of Apollinarius of Laodicea, who had been condemned at the First Council of Constantinople some fifty years previously. As we saw in the last chapter, when the bishop of Antioch arrived at Ephesus, he found the council already convened and three-quarters of the way to a condemnation of Nestorius. With the support of forty-three bishops, John proceeded to excommunicate Cyril and all bishops who accepted the *Twelve Anathemas*. At first the imperial government gave John its support, but the combination of popular pressure in favour of Cyril and the huge bribes sent by the church of Alexandria to the Byzantine court proved too much for the imperial will. It was decided to let the teaching of Ephesus stand and to veil the *Twelve Anathemas* in a decent obscurity. But, as it proved, this would not make them go away. The Monophysite churches derive from the determination to go all the way with the *Twelve Anathemas*, while the Dyophysites, on the other hand, accepted the central core of Cyrilline theology on Christ's essential unity of person but would go no further with him than Ephesus itself.

In 433 Antioch and Alexandria came to some sort of compromise settlement, though there was deep distrust between them. In exchange

---

[2] It was important for the future that an Egyptian council had confirmed Cyril's anathemas: "the church in Egypt was henceforth committed to them", ibid., p. 19.

for Antioch's acquiescence in Nestorius' downfall, Cyril agreed to sign a document called the *Formula of Reunion*.[3] In this, Christ was said to be "of two natures", the preposition "of" proving to be of decisive importance for the whole affair. Christ is *ek*, "of", "out of", or "from", two natures in a "union without confusion". Anticipating phrases of the later Chalcedonian definition, he is said to be "consubstantial with the Father as touching his divinity, and with us as touching his humanity". Antioch and Alexandria also agreed that "as regards the language of the Gospels and the apostolic writings about Christ, we know that theologians apply them to him in different ways. One class of words referring to his single person they apply to both the natures; the other they distinguish as applying to one nature or the other." The *Formula of Reunion* was the furthest Cyril was willing to go in recognising two natures in Christ. As time would show, it went a good deal further than many of his supporters cared for. The formula safeguarded the claim that, in the Incarnation, Godhead and manhood were inseparably united, but it did not use what had become Cyril's favourite phrase for this: *mia phusis*, "one nature" or (better) "one concrete reality". Instead, it used the Antiochene phrase *hen prosôpon*, "one person". While there was no mention of *hypostatic* union, the statement that Christ's being was formed from the "union of two natures", *duo phuseis henôsis*, satisfied the Alexandrians for the moment.

The *Formula of Reunion* was the first of a long series of attempted compromises between differing views of Christ that were to continue down to the seventh-century Arab invasions of the East Roman Empire and beyond. One result of Cyril's concessions to the Antiochenes was that it became possible to interpret his theology in both a Dyophysite and a Monophysite sense. But Cyril's long-term aim, apart from spreading the truth as he saw it, was to establish the supremacy of the see of Alexandria over that of Antioch, and of the theology

---

[3] Ibid., pp. 21–23. It has been suggested that the 433 Formula of Reunion was the inspiration for the terms of the Common Christological Declaration signed in 1994 by John Paul II and the Assyrian patriarch Denkha IV: thus C. Baumer, *The Church of the East: An Illustrated History of Assyrian Christianity* (London, 2008), p. 281.

of the school of Alexandria over that of the school of Antioch. To do this once and for all, he needed to secure the posthumous condemnation of the two principal Antiochene doctors, Diodore of Tarsus and Theodore of Mopsuestia. Within a year of Ephesus, Cyril's supporters began a campaign to that end. But Nestorius' successor at Constantinople, though highly favourable to the Cyrilline Christology, was unwilling to condemn its Antiochene rival outright. John of Antioch stood firm as well, pointing out that both the great Antiochene doctors had died in the peace of the Church.

The Monophysite issue had now reached the boiling point. The two men responsible for turning up the heat were, on the Antiochene side, Theodoret of Cyr and, on the Alexandrian side, Cyril's successor at Alexandria, Dioscorus. Theodoret, one of the most all-round men of the patristic Church—missionary, historian, theologian, patron of the monastic movement—was bitterly hostile to Cyrilline thought, which he denounced as Apollinarian.[4] The intensity of his feeling is well captured in the letter he wrote on Cyril's death: "At last, at last, he is dead, that wicked man.... His departure gives joy to those who survive, but it will bring grief to the dead. We must cover his tomb with a heavy stone so that we may never see him again."[5]

On the other hand, Dioscorus, the newly elected Alexandrian bishop, was equally determined to root out the Antiochene Christology, the two-natures doctrine now being proclaimed from the housetops by Theodoret and his collaborators. He was also set on securing the absolute primacy of his see in the East over against Constantinople and Antioch.[6] Rejecting a canon of the First Council of Constantinople forbidding bishops from interfering with sees not their own, he allowed

---

[4] P. Canivet, "Theodoret of Cyr", *NCE* 14: 20–22, who argues, in his survey of the literature, that it is now clear that Theodoret's Christological views showed marked development up to the point that, while rejecting the *communicatio idiomatum*, he nevertheless affirmed the Word's assumption of human nature and operations so as to guarantee man's salvation.

[5] *Letter* 180.

[6] Possibly also against Rome: the Coptic *Vita* ascribes to Dioscorus the claim that Mark was superior to Peter: thus F. Haase, "Patriarch Dioskur I. nach monophysitischen Quellen", in M. Sdralek, ed., *Kirchengeschichtliche Abhandlungen* 6 (1908): 204.

his devotees to address him as "ecumenical patriarch". Meanwhile, in Constantinople, out-and-out Cyrillianism was now represented by a Greek monk, Eutyches, who enjoyed the enviable position of god-father to the chief civil servant of the empire. Eutyches accepted the whole doctrine of the *Twelve Anathemas* and added to it his own inter-pretation of Cyril's formula about the one incarnate nature of the Logos. According to Eutyches, when we say that "the Word became flesh", we cannot really mean our flesh. Flesh would not remain flesh if the Word himself had been changed into it. Whatever the body of Jesus was, it was not of our substance. So, despite the *Formula of Reunion*, Christ is not, it would appear, consubstantial with us in his humanity.[7] Eutyches' reading of Cyril was calculated to infuriate the Antiochenes, in which it succeeded very well. Theodoret immedi-ately dashed off his treatise *Eranistes*, "The Beggarman", in which he insists on the principal theological premises of the Antiochene Christology. First, because of his own ontological perfection, God can-not undergo change or suffering. Second, the divinity and humanity in Christ must remain distinct after the union since the example of Christ as the perfect man is essential for our salvation. Were he not fully human, he could not be our model and our inspiration.

Although the Byzantine court supported Eutyches, the Byzantine patriarch, Flavian, would not follow them and had the offending monk stripped of his priestly status. At this juncture, the Eastern churches might have held together on the basis of the moderate Cyrillianism of the *Formula of Reunion* had not Ibas of Edessa, whose sympathies, as we have seen, lay with Nestorius, chosen just this moment to deliver an attack on the memory of Cyril. As at Ephesus itself, the anti-Alexandrian bishops failed to read public opinion, which in most of the empire veered as naturally towards the highest possible Christology as in the recent West it has veered contrariwise towards the lowest.[8] The emperor, Theodosius II, more sensitive to

---

[7] R. Draguet, "La christologie d'Eutychès, d'après les actes du Synode de Flavien, 448", *Byzantion* 6 (1951): 441–57.

[8] For the popular agitation against Ibas of Edessa, see Frend, *Rise of Monophysite Movement*, p. 37.

this than the episcopate, invited Dioscorus to summon another council at Ephesus, this time to determine the status of Eutyches' opinions as well as to vindicate the holiness and orthodoxy of Cyril. Meeting in 449, this council is regarded by Monophysites as a general council of the Church, "Ephesus II". To the rest of the Church, however, it soon became known as the *Latrocinium*, the "Robbers' Synod". The manipulation of the council by Alexandria vastly exceeded that of 431. However, it was noteworthy for the fact that at it the Roman church began to play a major part in these debates for the first time.

What had the Roman church been doing during these years? Basically, it had been too preoccupied with the Pelagian crisis over the doctrine of grace in the West to have much energy to spare for the Christological problems of the East. Moreover, the Roman popes of the period were not especially well endowed as theologians and lacked, of course, a Congregation for the Doctrine of the Faith or even a pontifical university to help them out. All this changed with the accession of Pope Leo I in 440. In a letter to Flavian of Constantinople, this energetic and brilliant pope gave the Western response to extreme Cyrillianism by, on the one hand, affirming with the Antiochenes the abiding distinction of the two natures, but, on the other hand, with Cyril affirming their unity through the *communicatio idiomatum*, the mutual sharing of properties.[9] However, Dioscorus managed to ensure that Leo's *Tome*, as it became called, was pushed so far down the agenda that it was never reached. What *was* produced was a document castigating the two-natures doctrine, which, through the fury it aroused among the people, was rendering ungovernable the great cities of the Eastern empire. Dioscorus asked the assembled bishops the rhetorical question:

[9] E. H. Blakeney, ed., *The Tome of Pope Leo the Great* (London, 1923). For the context of Leo's work as a whole, see T. G. Jalland, *The Life and Times of St. Leo the Great* (London, 1941). Dom Bernard Green, monk of Ampleforth, has argued that in an attempt to criticize simultaneously both Eutyches and Nestorius (understood, with the early Cyril, as a quasi-Adoptionist) Leo in effect downplayed his customary emphasis on the single *persona* of Christ as true source of his unity. Leo's subsequent explanatory letter to the monks of Palestine is more typical: thus B. Green, *The Soteriology of Leo the Great* (Oxford, 2008), pp. 188–247.

"Two natures before the union, one nature afterwards: is not that what we all believe?" [10] The papal legates made a formal protest from the safety of the sanctuary, but as it was in Latin, no one understood them. The imperial proconsul of Asia then entered with a body of soldiery to encourage second thoughts in any bishop who might disagree. Finally, the council deposed the Antiochene bishops throughout Syria, as well as the patriarchs of Antioch and Constantinople and closed by formally accepting the *Twelve Anathemas*.

Despite the ruthlessness shown at the Robbers' Synod, its decisions represented the beliefs of a great number of the faithful in the East. So long as the emperor lived, indeed, the triumph of the extreme Cyrilline party was intact. But it was difficult even for an emperor to impose on the East as a whole any theological system that was openly rejected by the papacy. The authority of the papacy at this time was chiefly a negative one. That is, the popes could veto someone else's theology, but they could not always manage to impose a theological doctrine of their own. At first, Pope Leo could do nothing, but with the death of Theodosius II and the accession of the emperor Marcian, the situation became fluid once again. Eutyches was exiled, and steps were taken to convoke a new council. While the decisions of the *Latrocinium* remained part of the law of the empire, the *Tome* of Leo had not been condemned and so could serve as a basis for negotiation. Chalcedon's task was, in the words of the imperial edict of convocation, to "settle the true faith more clearly and for all time". On arrival, Dioscorus declared Pope Leo excommunicate for departing from the faith of "Ephesus II",[11] but confronted with a pro-Western emperor, most of the bishops rallied to the *Tome*. "We believe as Leo does", they cried, "Peter has spoken through Leo." Dioscorus was deposed not as a heretic but for his attempt to excommunicate Leo. Theodoret and Ibas were restored to their sees, though with some reluctance. Doctrinally, the council accepted an

---

[10] Mansi, 6:744.

[11] And more specifically by teaching a form of the two-natures doctrine, declared in 449 to be an infringement of Ephesus I's veto on "any other faith" than that taught at Nicaea.

amalgam of Cyril's *Formula of Reunion* and Leo's *Tome*. It taught that the two natures were inseparably joined in one person, each nature retaining its own properties yet "coming together" in the single person. The bishops acclaimed the Chalcedonian definition with the words "Cyril and Leo taught alike." [12] Whether they did or not was a question that would occupy theologians for the next hundred years. [13] Worrying over this bone of contention brought the Monophysite churches into existence.

The doctrinal issue was, evidently, delicate and complex. Equally problematic, however, was the status of the Chalcedonian decrees. Most of those present did not see the Chalcedonian formula as the equivalent of a creed. When the imperial commissioners, indeed, invited the conciliar fathers to compose a new creed, many of them were indignant. There was no call for any other creed, they said, than that taught by the fathers: the Creed of Nicaea-Constantinople. For many Eastern bishops, the definition was simply a legal instrument for the elimination of the "left-wing" heresy of Nestorius and the "right-wing" heresy of Eutyches. For Leo, on the other hand, it was a solemn definition of faith, truly comparable to the Creed, and so nonnegotiable. [14] This was another cause of trouble in store, to add to the inherent difficulty of the Christological question.

The Attempt to Maintain the Chalcedonian Settlement

The story of the next century and more is mainly the story of an increasingly desperate imperial attempt to maintain the Chalcedonian

[12] Mansi, 6:972. Chadwick suggests that Leonine influence is apparent in the affirmation that Christ is "in" (not "from") two natures; otherwise, the Chalcedonian definition "exploited concessive clauses found in Cyril": thus his *East and West: The Making of a Rift in the Church; From Apostolic Times until the Council of Florence* (Oxford, 2003), p. 42.

[13] For a closely argued case that they did not, see A. Baxter, "Chalcedon, and the Subject in Christ", *Downside Review* 107, no. 366 (January 1989): 1–21.

[14] Thus in his *Letter* 145 to his imperial namesake he speaks of Chalcedon as gathered in the Holy Spirit and its definition as so full and perfect that it must be ascribed to divine inspiration, admitting, consequently, neither of addition nor diminution.

settlement in the face of opposition. The emperors were faced with three major problems. First, they had to bear in mind the conflicting religious outlook of Latin and Greek Christendom. The Latins were practical people whose chief concerns centred on the Christian society and the Christian life, reflected theologically in talk about the Church and about grace in freedom. The Greeks, on the other hand, were incorrigible speculators about the mystery of the Godhead and its saving incarnation. Second, the imperial authorities were obliged to grapple with the intransigence (as they saw it) of the Roman popes in regard to the status of Chalcedon. Third, they had to contend with the forces of popular religion in Egypt and Syria, hostile as these so often were to the council and its celebrated definition.

Very soon, party lines began to form throughout the Church. In the capital, a trio of groups could be made out. There were those who continued to accept Eutyches as orthodox; then there were the Chalcedonians; finally, there were those who rejected Eutyches, Nestorius, *and* the *Tome* of Leo. These people, known as the "Hesitants", *diakrinomenoi*, are the true doctrinal forerunners of the Monophysites. In Egypt, on the other hand, the overwhelming majority were anti-Chalcedonian without necessarily being Eutychist. In Syria, the eastern part of the region tended towards Monophysitism—perhaps by reaction against the Nestorians, now exiled in Persia—while the coastal area, including Antioch, was Chalcedonian.[15] In Rome there was complete satisfaction with the definition, and anyone who questioned its truly definitive nature was branded as heretical. What a contrast with the popular verdict in Egypt and Syria as summed up by a contemporary: "Under the pretext of suppressing the heresy of Eutyches, Chalcedon has established and exacerbated that of Nestorius. And by substituting one heresy for another, it has divided and confused the entire Christian world."[16] The council was popularly represented as teaching that Christ was man and not God, and the Jews were reported to be highly satisfied with its outcome. Monks

[15] Frend, *Rise of Monophysite Movement*, pp. 144–45.

[16] Zacharias of Mitylene, *Historia ecclesiastica* 3.1, cited in Frend, *Rise of Monophysite Movement*, p. 148.

saw visions of Christ cursing Chalcedon, or of Satan, who inquired why they did not worship him since, after all, their bishops did. Riots broke out in Alexandria and Jerusalem. Large numbers of the faithful refused the ministrations of Chalcedonian clerics, saying, "We wish to stay in communion with our fathers." [17]

The geographical spread of the later Monophysite churches derives from the tendency of the provinces to become more anti-Chalcedonian as the capital became more pro-Chalcedonian. The Greeks, in other words, swung round more and more to the council as the rest, the Semitic and Hamitic peoples of the empire, turned ever more against it. This pattern has suggested to modern historians that incipient nationalism lay behind the Monophysite revolt. In Egypt, the pro-Chalcedonian patriarch appealed in vain to Rome for a more flexible presentation of the definition: some way of avoiding the statement that the difference of natures would never be abolished by their union. The formula "two natures after the union" was, he claimed, incapable of bearing an orthodox interpretation in Alexandria. Lynched by the mob, his place was taken by a firm anti-Chalcedonian, Timothy Aelurus, "the Cat".[18] The imperial government then approached the principal bishops throughout the East, asking them to convoke local synods to offer an opinion on both Chalcedon and the candidature of Timothy. The replies, contained in something called the *Codex encyclius*, represented the views of about sixteen hundred bishops. They show overwhelming support for Chalcedon and constituted in the eyes of the papacy solid evidence for the claim that the council had indeed been "received" by the Church. However, a careful reading of the *Codex encyclius* has suggested some caveats to scholars. First, many bishops tried to equate Chalcedon's "two natures inseparably united" with Cyril's "one incarnate nature". Second, there is a tendency to stress the disciplinary aspect of the council's decrees,

[17] Ibid., pp. 148–51.

[18] Ibid., p. 155: for Timothy's Christology, see J. Lebon, "La Christologie de Timothée Aelure", *RHE* 9 (1908): 677–702. A characteristically Monophysite reading of Cyril, Timothy's doctrine stresses the full divinity of Jesus, maintains that his "nature" resides in his divinity even after the Incarnation, and regards his humanity, though real, as assumed merely by way of dispensation for the purpose of saving man.

to see them as an instrument for the doctrinal pacification of the Church.[19] Be this as it may, Pope Leo was delighted with the result and sent to the emperor, his namesake, the masterly *Letter 165*, which, in the words of George Every, "succeeded in stating his doctrine of the person of Christ in Alexandrian terms":

> Although then in the one Lord Jesus Christ, the true Son of God and of man, the person of the Word and flesh is one, who without separation or division takes actions common to both of them, nevertheless we must understand the qualities of the same acts, and discern with the contemplation of a sincere faith, where it is that the humility of the flesh is raised up, and where it is that the majesty of the divinity is lowered; what it is that the flesh without the Word does not do, and what it is that the Word without the flesh does not effect. For without the power of the Word the Virgin would neither conceive nor bear, and without the true reality of the flesh his infancy would not have lain, wrapped in swaddling bands.[20]

But Leo would die in 461 without gaining the adhesion of Egypt to the definition.

In Syria too, many voices were raised against the council. Alongside the dominant Antiochene school, there had always been a strong Apollinarian party, Apollinarius having been himself a Syrian. In 469 this body managed to have a priest of their tendency, Peter the Fuller, elected patriarch of Antioch. Although Peter survived for only a year, this was long enough for him to introduce important changes into the Antiochene liturgy. Well aware that liturgies are vital sources and criteria for doctrine, Peter revised the Antiochene doxology, adding the words, addressed to God: "you who were crucified for us": "Holy God, holy and mighty, holy and immortal, you who were crucified for us, have mercy on us." [21] This prayer would be perfectly orthodox if it referred to the single person of Christ who,

[19] Frend, *Rise of Monophysite Movement*, p. 162.

[20] *Letter* 165.6. Cited in G. Every, S.S.M., "The Monophysite Question, Ancient and Modern", *ECR* 3, no. 4 (1971): 408–9.

[21] Evagrius, *Historia ecclesiastica* 3.44.

being God, died as man.[22] But Peter's sympathisers interpreted it otherwise. One of the Holy Trinity suffered for us in his one incarnate nature. This "theopaschite" formula became and remained the touchstone of Monophysite belief. What made Peter's gambit especially significant was his friendship with the East Roman emperor Zeno, who was now also the civil overlord of the pope, the Western Roman Empire having come to an inglorious end in 476.

Zeno's Henotikon *(482)*

Zeno's attempts to repair the breaches in communion appearing everywhere throughout his provinces took the form of a document called the *Henotikon*, or "Proposal for Unity". Unlike previous imperial interventions, this text did not claim to represent the voice of any see but to be a personal imperial recognition of the majority religious sentiment in the Church. It was a kind of attempt to identify the *sensus fidelium*, but at the same time it constituted the highwater mark of imperial claims to order doctrine. The preamble of the *Henotikon* states its purpose. Because of disagreements in the Church, baptism and Eucharist are not being administered, and countless citizens have died by violence. What is to be done? The *Henotikon* advises the reception of the councils of Nicaea, Constantinople I, and Ephesus I. It maintains that both Nestorius and Eutyches were justly condemned. It accepts the *Twelve Anathemas* as true doctrine. It declares that Jesus Christ is consubstantial with both God and us: "incarnate from the Holy Spirit and from the Virgin Mary, the Godbearer; one and not two, for both his miracles and the sufferings which he willingly underwent in the flesh are of one person." And it concludes: "Every person who has thought or thinks anything else either now or at any time, either in Chalcedon or in any synod whatever we anathematise." [23] On this basis, all were invited to reunite themselves to the Church. It should be noted that Chalcedon was

---

[22] Cf. J. Chéné, "Unus de Trinitate passus est", *RSR* 53 (1965): 545–88.

[23] For the text, and notes, see P. R. Coleman-Norton, *Roman State and Christian Church* (London, 1966), 3:924–53.

not expressly repudiated. It was still seen as authoritative insofar as it was the necessary legal instrument for the proscription of Eutyches. But the adoption of the *Twelve Anathemas* in preference to the *Tome* of Leo changed the perspective in which Chalcedon was reviewed. It entailed the acceptance of full-blooded Cyrillianism rather than the moderate Cyrillianism acceptable to Rome.

The *Henotikon* enjoyed a real if limited success. For a while it restored communion between Alexandria and Constantinople. But the Egyptian church was in no mood for compromise. Its members forced their patriarch into seeking an outright condemnation of Chalcedon. In Antioch, the patriarch Peter accepted the *Henotikon* on behalf of the Syrian church. In Rome, Pope Felix III was informed of its promulgation by pro-Western Chalcedonians in Constantinople and at once broke off relations with the Byzantine patriarch Acacius, resulting in the so-called Acacian schism, which lasted for thirty-five years. In effect, the *Henotikon* united the four Eastern patriarchates (Jerusalem having received patriarchal status at Chalcedon) at the cost of a breach with the West. But underneath the superficial unity in the East, feelings still ran high in various directions. A new generation of hardliners was emerging among the anti-Chalcedonians. Foremost among them were Philoxenus of Mabboug,[24] representing the Syriac-speakers in the Antiochene patriarchate, and Severus of Antioch representing the Greek-speakers.[25] The patriarch Peter banished every cleric suspected of Nestorianising tendencies, a move that prompted the Persian church to come to a clearer confession of Nestorian and separatist principles. During these years, negotiations between the popes and the East were carried on somewhat halfheartedly. At one point Pope Anastasius II declared himself willing to sign the *Henotikon* if its implication that the substantive doctrine of Chalcedon might be erroneous could be removed.[26] But

[24] A. de Halleux, *Philoxène de Mabboug, sa vie, ses écrits et sa théologie* (Louvain, 1965).
[25] J. Lebon, *Le Monophysisme sévérien* (Louvain, 1909).
[26] According to J. N. D. Kelly, indeed, Anastasius' election itself "reflected dissatisfaction in influential circles with the hard-line attitude of Felix III and Gelasius I to the Acacian schism", *The Oxford Dictionary of Popes* (Oxford, 1986), p. 49. Dante

on the whole, the Roman church was moving rapidly towards a systematic rejection of the idea that the Roman emperor, as the Church's senior layman, had a part to play in the definition of doctrine. This was the so-called Gelasian viewpoint that in all matters ecclesiastical the emperor was entirely subordinate to the episcopate.[27]

As yet there was only a schism of minds, not two distinct churches. Within the Monophysite, or ultra-Cyrilline, movement, two parties were in process of formation. The smaller and more clearly heretical was that of Julian of Halicarnassus, who taught that the flesh of Christ was emancipated from death and decay from the moment of the Incarnation onwards.[28] The Resurrection was, as it were, ontologically entailed by the Incarnation, rather than a fresh gracious act of God. The other party, larger and less heterodox in Chalcedonian terms, was that of Severus of Antioch, a philosopher and lawyer turned priest. Severus was definitely a Cyrillian, not a Eutychian. He taught that through the Incarnation, the divinity and humanity formed a synthesis, but a synthesis without confusion of properties. What he could not stomach was the idea that the Word became *diplos*, "double", both God and man. Severus accepted in remarkably explicit terms the primacy of the Roman church, arguing that the *Tome* of Leo represented the erroneous remarks of a pope speaking as a private theologian. He did not regard Leo's account of the unity of the natures as amounting to hypostatic union, or of their interrelations as an implicit version of the communication of idioms. Leo taught merely a "relative communion of forms".[29] Severus' accession as Antiochene patriarch led to the mutual anathematising of Chalcedonians and anti-Chalcedonians in Syria. To Severus,

---

evidently thought more tolerantly of rigour, since in canto 11 of the *Inferno* he offers a description of Pope Anastasius' tomb in Hell.

[27] Expressed in, above all, Gelasius' *Letter* 12. The new factor lies in the confident, legislative tone: so W. Ullmann, *The Growth of Papal Government in the Middle Ages* (London, 1955), p. 12.

[28] R. Draguet, "Julien d'Halicarnasse et sa controverse avec Sévère d'Antioche sur l'incorruptibilité du corps du Christ" (dissertation, Louvain, 1924).

[29] Severus, *Liber contra impium grammaticum* 3.1.5.

Chalcedonians were not brothers suffering under a misapprehension about Christology. They were Dyophysite heretics to be converted to Orthodoxy. To the Chalcedonians, the Monophysites appeared increasingly as Manichaeans who should be punished or expelled from the Church.[30]

Severus' ruthlessness towards Chalcedonians in the Syrian East brought about his downfall, but it led at the same time to the creation of a distinctively Monophysite church structure. The treatment of Chalcedonians in Syria enraged the Byzantine capital. The emperor, Justin, was a Latin-speaking Byzantine who believed strongly in the importance of the West and the desirability of good relations with the see of Rome. Justin was able to capitalise on a change of feeling in the Church. Many were scandalised by the rigour of Severus. Some began to say that they were tired of the whole debate, which was nothing more than senseless argument over words.[31] Justin persuaded the Byzantine patriarch to sign a *libellus* condemning those who had accepted the *Henotikon*. The Severan bishops in Syria were exiled, occasionally amid violent scenes. Severus himself fled to Egypt, so solidly Monophysite that the government's writ hardly ran. The Monophysites outside Egypt now saw that their only hope lay in the creation of a rival hierarchy, and this they began to do in the next reign, that of Justinian. This meant, of course, true schism for the first time.

Justinian and the Emergence of the Monophysite Church

Justinian's aims were to restore the Roman Empire to its fullest geographical extent. The decline of the barbarian kingdoms in North Africa, Spain, and Italy seemed to make this possible. For a Byzantine emperor to be accepted in the West, however, he was obliged to arrange ecclesiastical matters in the East in a way that won the approval of the Roman church. Justinian's task, therefore, was to find a formula acceptable both to Severan Monophysites and to Chalcedonians. He put forward the principle that, to remain within the

[30] Frend, *Rise of Monophysite Movement*, pp. 221–22.
[31] Ibid., pp. 239–40.

law of the empire, one must accept the four councils of Nicaea, Constantinople I, Ephesus I, and Chalcedon, but with the Chalcedonian definition interpreted in terms of the theopaschite formula: "One of the Holy Trinity suffered for us." [32] Time was of the essence, because the longer the breach lasted, the stronger an independent Severan hierarchy would become. At one period, if a contemporary account may be trusted, over one hundred men a day were coming forward for priestly ordination, producing an estimated total of 170,000 Severan clergy by the middle years of Justinian's reign. [33] In 533 Justinian took his greatest step toward the Monophysite cause—to which in some degree by personal spirituality, and the influence of his wife, he inclined, though maintaining in doctrine the faith of Chalcedon. He offered, as terms for a new peace of the Church, the theopaschite formula, the Cyrilline principle of the unity of the two natures *kath' hypostasin*, the four councils (without the *Tome* of Leo), and a special condemnation for Nestorius' "evil and Jewish doctrines". [34] Meanwhile, his wife Theodora, herself a scarcely concealed Monophysite, did all she could to advance Monophysite-leaning bishops throughout the empire. The Severans were given safe conducts to enable them to hold discussions with the Chalcedonian bishops, but they simply used the opportunity to make converts. In 536 Justinian, exasperated by the Severan nonresponse, issued an edict condemning Severus and his supporters and ordering the burning of his writings, which, he said, "from now on shall be considered as profane and contrary to the Catholic Church". [35] The imperial police hunted down a good many Severans, and the future Monophysite church began to grow through the blood of its martyrs.

Despite the persecution, the theological gap between Severans and Chalcedonians narrowed in midcentury. This was the result of

[32] Chéné, "Unus de trinitate passus est", art. cit.

[33] Elias, *Vita Joannis episcopi Tellae*, ed. and trans. E. W. Brooks, Corpus scriptorum christianorum orientalium, Scriptores syri, ser. 3, 25 (Paris, 1907), p. 39, cited in Frend, *Rise of Monophysite Movement*, p. 261.

[34] Justinian's new *henotikon* is contained in a letter to Pope John II incorporated into the *Codex Justinianus* at 1.1.8.

[35] *Novel* 42.

the rise of the "Neo-Chalcedonian" school, associated with three theologians: Leontius of Byzantium, Leontius of Jerusalem, and Cyril of Scythopolis. Neo-Chalcedonianism taught that the humanity of Jesus was "enhypostatised" in the Logos. It had no independent ontological centre or foundation of its own but was a perfect human individuality operating from within the being of the Logos himself. By combining this idea with the doctrine of two natures after the union, the Neo-Chalcedonians hoped to prove that Chalcedon and the *Tome* were compatible with Cyril, that the bishops' cry in 451, "Leo and Cyril taught alike", was correct after all. But most Monophysites stayed unconvinced. Justinian made one final effort in 553 when he secured the exceedingly reluctant consent of the papacy at the Second Council of Constantinople, later recognised as the Fifth Ecumenical Council, to a symbolic condemnation of three Antiochene doctors—Theodore, Theodoret, and Ibas—originally promulgated as an imperial edict in 544. More specifically, the attainted objects were: Theodore's writings en bloc, Theodoret's expostulations against the *Twelve Anathemas*, and Ibas' letter to Maris criticising Cyril's activities and theology in the years after 431. Cordially detested as the Antiochene doctors were by Monophysites, Chalcedon had failed to mention Theodore (who died over twenty years before the council's convocation), and it had explicitly vindicated Theodoret and Ibas, whose very letter to Maris had been defended both by the papal legates and by the Antiochene patriarch Maximus. Although in the immediate aftermath of becoming pope, Vigilius of Rome had written confidentially to Theodora expressing doubts over the language of "in two natures" used by Leo, the consequences of signing the condemnation of the Three Chapters for his own patriarchate could not but fill him with trepidation. Africa in particular was deeply attached to the memory of the Antiochene divines. As W. H. C. Frend wrote: "At a moment when the papacy seemed disposed to accept the will of the emperor so long as Chalcedon remained inviolate, the Africans produced in Facundus of Hermiana and the archdeacon of Carthage, Liveratus, active, able and well-informed defenders of the Three Chapters."[36] Vigilius attempted, accordingly, to nuance the decree, for example by limiting the anathematisation of Theodoret's work to a *prout sonant* ("as quoted") condemnation, which would leave the author's good faith intact—but to no avail. His signature caused major rifts in the Roman patriarchate, both (North) Africa and northern Italy breaking off, for a while, communion with Rome. In the long dogmatic view, more important, however, than the condemnation of the Antiochene doctors (which involves factors of textual and contextual evaluation going beyond the ambit of conciliar infallibility and rendering the judgements on persons of Constantinople II, unlike its doctrinal determinations, revisable) are the council's eleven *capitula* on Christology, and especially the seventh and eighth.

> If anyone saying "in two natures" does not confess that our one Lord Jesus Christ has been revealed in godhead and manhood, in order to indicate by the use of this expression the difference between the natures, of whom an ineffable union has been made without any confusion, in which neither is the nature of the Word changed into that of the flesh, nor that of the flesh transformed into the nature of the Word— for each remained what it naturally is by nature, and the union took place according to *hypostasis*—but shall take the expression with regard to the mystery of Christ in a sense that makes for division ... not content to take the difference as in theory only ... let him be anathema.

Here the Chalcedonian "in two natures" is more exactly defined, while in the succeeding section, the formula "of two natures" is also permitted.

> If anyone confessing the union of two natures, of godhead and manhood, to have taken place, or saying "one nature of God the Word made flesh", does not understand these expressions as the holy fathers have taught, that of the divine and human natures, according to the hypostatic union that took place, one Christ resulted, but from such expressions shall deduce one nature or *ousia* of godhead and manhood in Christ, let such a man be anathema.[37]

[36] Frend, *Rise of Monophysite Movement*, p. 257.
[37] Translation taken from Every, "Monophysite Question", p. 413. Vigilius' rough handling (physically, not least) at Constantinople, and his subsequent absenting of

But neither the council's thunderings against the Antiochenes nor the nuances of its Christological presentation *in propria voce* entailed, of course, the rejection of Chalcedon—by this juncture the only thing that the Monophysites cared about. Meanwhile, the creation of a parallel church proceeded at a cracking pace.

The principal organiser of the separate Monophysite communion was a Syrian bishop, James Baradai ("Of the Horsecloth", his favoured garment): from him the Monophysites get their nickname "Jacobites".[38] In his effort to organise a worldwide church parallel to the Great Church, Baradai covered enormous stretches of Syria, Armenia, Asia Minor, and the Greek islands. To elude the imperial police, he often travelled in disguise, sometimes dressed as a tramp. By the time of his death in 578, the Jacobite church had some thirty archbishoprics, ranging from the Caucasus Mountains in the north to the valley of the Upper Nile in the south, from the Tigris valley in the east to Greece in the west. The Monophysites claimed the patriarchal sees of both Alexandria and Antioch, and so far as numbers were concerned their claim may well have been better founded than that of the Chalcedonian bishops alongside them. But though Monophysite bishops took the titles of the traditional sees, they rarely lived in the cities themselves. For one thing, they were generally banned from entering them, and for another, the strength of Monophysitism lay in the countryside, not in the towns. The towns were too dependent on the institutions and trade of the empire for them to risk a final break with Constantinople. The typical Monophysite base was a village combined with a monastery where a bishop lived as a monk. The language of its liturgy was Syriac or Coptic rather than Greek. Though the early *Life* of James

---

himself from the proceedings, were a source of embarrassment in the Greek East. Significantly, the acts of the council survive in full only in Latin: see Chadwick, *East and West*, p. 57.

[38] E. Honigmann, 'La hiérarchie monophysite au temps de Jacques Baradée, 542–578", Corpus scriptorum christianorum orientalium, subsidia 2 (Louvain, 1951); A. van Roey, "Les débuts de l'église jacobite", in *Das Konzil von Chalkedon: Geschichte und Gegenwart*, ed. A. Grillmeier and H. Bacht (Würzburg, 1953–1962), 2:339–60.

Baradai, by John of Ephesus, does not imply a concern for ethnicity, the new church came to organise itself on a regional basis and has maintained this sharply regional or national character to the present day.

The association of the empire with Chalcedonian orthodoxy meant in the long run the loss of the Monophysite provinces. At no time was it suggested that both the Great Church and the Monophysite church might coexist within the boundaries of the same state. To Byzantines, the emperor was the Church's guardian: he could not be simultaneously guardian of two opposing bodies, any more than a man might have two heads. Thus when enemy states invaded, the Monophysites, alienated from the Byzantine civil order, tended to surrender without a blow. The Persians were astute enough to capitalise on this by replacing Chalcedonian bishops with Monophysites in any city they captured during their campaign in the early seventh century. Although they were thrown back, the Arabs were not. In the course of the later seventh century, Egypt and Syria passed under Islamic domination, which they still enjoy or endure today. By force or persuasion the great majority of the Christian population, whether Monophysite or Chalcedonian ("Melchite"), eventually embraced Islam.

It remains, then, to outline the story of the five principal regional or national Monophysite churches: those of Egypt, Ethiopia, Syria, Armenia, and South India.

The Church of Egypt

The Arab invasion of Egypt in 640 enabled the Monophysite church to complete the independent reorganisation begun as early as the reign of Justinian and Theodora. Despite some civil disabilities and intermittent pressure for not only Arabisation but Islamisation too, the Egyptian church flourished greatly during the first three centuries and more of Muslim rule, up to about the year 1000.[39] To profit

---

[39] See J. Tagher, *Christians in Muslim Egypt: An Historical Study of the Relations between the Copts and Muslims from 640 to 1922* (Altenberge, 1998).

by government favour, the patriarchal residence was transferred to the secular capital of the Fatimid caliphate, Cairo. However, the brutal persecution of Christians by the (probably mad) caliph al-Hakim, which erupted in the opening years of the eleventh century, was a blow to Coptic confidence from which the church never fully recovered. The arrival of the Crusaders in the eastern Mediterranean brought about a general deterioration in the condition of Oriental Christians in the Arab East, and Egypt was no exception. After the fall of the Latin kingdom of Jerusalem at the end of the twelfth century, government became more tolerant towards Coptic Christians (they were in high demand as financial advisors, and this would continue to be so under the Ottomans, whose rule began in 1517), but its change in attitude was not shared by the masses. From the Crusading period onwards, the situation of the Copts has been insecure because of the enmity of the Muslim populace. Only under Napoleon, and then the British protectorate over the Egyptian Khedives, were they really exempt from background menace.[40]

At the Council of Florence, representatives of the Coptic church accepted the reunion with the Roman see offered in the so-called Decree for the Jacobites. A certain John, describing himself as abbot of the monastery of Saint Anthony, signed in the church's name. For well over a hundred years, the Holy See attempted to get this reunion put into effect, but while a number of patriarchs appeared to toy with reunion, their genuineness of intent may for ever remain a mystery.[41] In 1741, the reconciliation to Rome of the Coptic bishop of Jerusalem, Athanasius, made possible the beginnings of a Uniate parallel to the official Coptic church.[42] Both before and after that date,

[40] See the pseudonymously authored *The Decline of Eastern Christianity under Islam: From Jihad to Dhimmitude; Seventh–Twentieth Century* (Eng. trans., Madison, N.J., 1996), by "Bat Ye'or", an Egyptian Jewess and specialist in the history of Coptic Orthodoxy who in this wide-ranging work furnishes evidence that the treatment of Christians in Islamic countries was historically poorer than is often claimed.

[41] A. Hamilton, *The Copts and the West, 1439–1822: The European Discovery of the Egyptian Church* (Oxford, 2006), p. 73.

[42] A. Colombo, *Le origini della gerarchia della Chiesa copta cattolica nel secolo XVIII* (Rome, 1953); G. Giamberardini, O.F.M, *I primi Copti cattolici* (Cairo, 1958).

the Roman Congregation Propaganda fide had encouraged the Franciscans—whose "custody of the Holy Land" included not only Palestine but Lower Egypt, from Alexandria to Cairo—to pursue the possibility of reconciling Copts with the Holy See. The Turco-Egyptian government of Mehmet Ali made no difficulty about the extension to Upper Egypt of such missions (generally entrusted to Friars of the Reformed observance) though it considered irksome the attempts of Austro-Hungary, generous patron of these Uniates, to secure an official position as "procurators" of Catholic Copts. In the later nineteenth century, by which time the Egyptian Khedives had themselves been taken in charge by a British protectorate, the Uniate Coptic body was placed on a full organisational footing under a Coptic-rite patriarch, appointed in 1899. This church numbers today perhaps some 120,000 practising members from an estimated total of 200,000.

The Coptic mother church, though intensely hostile to the Coptic Uniates, has no historical animus towards the Latin church or towards the Roman see, with which, indeed, the church of Alexandria had historically been allied. The most outstanding of its nineteenth-century patriarchs, Cyril IV—as well as reforming the theological education of the clergy, instituting schooling for women, and revising the liturgy—had dreams of Christian unity. His relations with the Greek Catholic (Melchite) patriarch, whose title incorporated "Antioch and the East, Alexandria and Jerusalem", were so good that when the latter was outside Egypt the Coptic patriarch took responsibility for the welfare of Melchites in the country. Unfortunately, Cyril IV's interest in contacts with Moscow and Canterbury aroused the suspicion of the Egyptian Khedive, and he may well have been poisoned when he died in 1861.[43] Under his successor, Demetrius II, a Coptic Community Council was formed to help the patriarch in his governance of the Church. The council enabled the Coptic church to survive some mediocre patriarchs in the interwar years, but in 1981 this modification of the traditional patriarchal

---

[43] A charmingly naïf account of this figure is offered in T. Y. Malaty, *Introduction to the Coptic Orthodox Church* (Ottawa, 1987), pp. 145–46.

structure encouraged the Egyptian government to remove the patriarch Shenouda III and place him under (effective) house arrest in
the monastery of Anba Bishoi.[44] The church passed thereby under
the joint control of the patriarchal synod and the Community Council. Church-state relations in Egypt remain delicate, despite the release
of Shenouda III at Christmas 1984, because of the volatile quality of
Arab Muslim feeling, which any government ignores at its peril.
The officially admitted size of the Coptic community has generally
been a deliberate underestimate, and in any case, owing to social
pressures, Egypt has many crypto-Christians. In a national population of some 76 million, the number of Orthodox Copts may be as
high as 10 million, of whom maybe 5.5 million are practising. The
diaspora contains several hundred thousand. The calculated moder-
ation, both internally and externally, of the Egyptian government
since the fall of Colonel G. A. Nasser depends on the state's ability
to fend off Islamic fundamentalism, and from this point of view a
renaissance of the Coptic church, under way through the inspiration
of the highly charismatic Shenouda, is the last thing it wishes to
see.[45] It is a revival profoundly inspired by the continuing vitality of
monasticism in the church—an ever more marked phenomenon since
the election of Cyril VI, a renowned anchorite and spiritual father,
in 1959. What is most typical of the long reign of Shenouda III
(patriarch from 1971) is the shift of identity among the Coptic laity,
by which they now tend to identify themselves in their distinctive
ecclesial rôle—here the "Sunday schools movement" has been
vital—and not as a Westernising or even secularising element in the
wider Islamic society.

Less controversial than the interaction of the Copts with civil society and state is the relationship between the Egyptian church and the

---

[44] This revealing church-state struggle is described and analysed in J. Watson, *Prisoner of Conscience: Christian Patriarch* (London, 1984).

[45] Some indications in W. Andrawiss, "Le renouveau dans l'Eglise copte", *Le Monde
Copte* (1977): 47–50. A fuller account, including the sociopolitical context, is A.
O'Mahony, "The Politics of Religious Renewal: Coptic Christianity in Egypt", in
Eastern Christianity: Studies in Modern History, Religion and Politics, ed. A. O'Mahony
(London, 2004), pp. 66–111.

papacy. In September 1971, Catholic theologians met with representatives of the Non-Chalcedonian Orthodox in Vienna, their first meeting since Chalcedon itself.[46] The success of the occasion—and notably its production of an agreed statement on Christology, later called the "Vienna Christological formula"—was a contributory factor to the warmth of the encounter between Paul VI and Shenouda III in 1973: Shenouda had taken part in the Vienna meeting, prior to his elevation to the patriarchal throne. Referring to the Nestorian crisis, Paul VI remarked in his address to the patriarch in Saint Peter's: "The churches of Alexandria and Rome ... [served] as beacons of light when faith in the God-man Jesus Christ was obscured by those who refused to render to the holy Mother of God her glorious title of *Theotokos*." And the pope went on: "In the history of our churches, we have experienced fierce disputes over doctrinal formulae by which our substantial agreement in the reality they were trying to express was overlooked. ... Reasons of a cultural and political order as well as theological ones have been used to justify and even extend a division that should never have taken place." Recognising Shenouda III as "father and head of your church" (his official title is pope of Alexandria and patriarch of the see of Saint Mark),[47] the two went on to make a "common declaration" that owed much to the Vienna colloquy of two years previously. In the crucial portion of their statement, they said: "In Christ are preserved all the properties of the divinity and all the properties of the humanity. [They exist] together in a real, perfect, indivisible, and inseparable union."[48]

[46] For an overview of the conversations between the Oriental Orthodox and the Catholic Church, from 1971 on, see R. G. Roberson, C.S.P., "The Modern Roman Catholic—Oriental Orthodox Dialogue", *One in Christ* 21 (1985): 238–54; on the Vienna consultation and subsequent repeats of the same, see Pro oriente, *Five Vienna Consultations between Theologians of the Oriental Orthodox Churches and the Roman Catholic Church: Selected Papers* (Vienna, 1993).

[47] For the emergence of high claims to apostolic authority based on the founder evangelist, see S. J. Davis, *The Early Coptic Papacy: The Egyptian Church and Its Leadership in Late Antiquity* (Cairo and New York, 2004), especially pp. 2–14.

[48] For the meeting between the two popes, see *DC* 70, no. 1635, 3 July 1973, pp. 510–16.

A commission then established by both popes, Roman and Alexandrian, reported after four meetings that the Christological question was, in effect, resolved. Both sides agreed on the affirmation that the properties of Godhead and manhood in Christ are preserved intact after the union. The Catholics recognised that affirming the continued existence of the two sets of properties after the union accurately reflects the intention of the Council of Chalcedon and also that the phrase "in two natures" or "two natures after the union" is for the Copts too bound up with memories of Nestorianism to be acceptable. So far so good. What the Catholic-Coptic commission also reported, however, was that in matters of ecclesiology the two traditions were still far apart. Basically, this comes down to the development of doctrine in the West over the nature of the primacy of the Roman bishop. Paul VI, on a famous occasion in Geneva, had made the admission that "we are ourselves the gravest obstacle to the restoration of unity". But John Paul II made a similar declaration, at once less dramatic and more self-confident, when he spoke to a Coptic delegation in 1979. The central problem, the pope said, lay in "the nature of that full communion we are seeking with each other, and the rôle that the bishop of Rome has to play, by God's design, in serving that communion of faith and spiritual life that is nourished by the sacraments and expressed in fraternal charity." [49]

In this dialogue, as in others, the fundamental problem of East-West reunion has thus been identified as being the authority of the church and bishop of the city of Rome. Meanwhile, relations have hardly been improved, to say the least of it, by the way that, in recent years, the Alexandrian pope has encouraged the rebaptism of Catholics who pass over to the Coptic Orthodox church.

The Church of Ethiopia

The Ethiopian church is by far the largest Monophysite church today, having an estimated thirty-eight million adherents, of whom about

---

[49] *DC* 76, no. 1768, 15 July 1979, pp. 662–63. For the wider context of the Coptic church's ecumenical outreach and its limitations, see D. W. Winkler, *Koptischer Kirche und Reichskirche: Altes Schisma und neuer Dialog* (Innsbruck, 1997).

a half are reckoned to be practising. The evangelisation of Ethiopia appears to have been carried out from the Red Sea ports at some time in the fourth century.[50] Athanasius consecrated a bishop for the Ethiopians, and a tradition was thereby established that the Ethiopian metropolitan would be an Egyptian, ordained in Egypt but resident in Ethiopia: originally in Axum, but in modern times in Addis Ababa. He bore the title *abuna*: "father" or "pope". In the fifth century, the Ethiopian church was (arguably) much influenced by the Severan movement, whose missionaries—the celebrated "Nine Saints"—certainly came to them from Syria. Since Syrian Christianity, being Semitic, remained closer in ethos to Judaism than other parts of the Church, this influence may account for the marked quantity of Old Testament and even later Jewish elements in the practice of the Ethiopian Christians. (Other explanations are Jewish proselytism among the Ethio-semitic tribes of the highland zone in the pre-Christian period, or desire, on a vulnerable Christian "island", to claim the privileges of Israel, and an unwise zeal to reproduce all possible rules: Ethiopian poets praise the early kings for their adherence not only to the Gospel but also to the Law of Moses!)

The combination of the Alexandrian connexion and the Severan influence ensured that Ethiopia would become Monophysite, though opinion is divided on just when. Some scholars put the acceptance of full Monophysitism as early as the sixth century; others hold that the Ethiopian schools stuck to a line of their own until as late as the thirteenth.[51] The eventual importance of the issue is reflected in the church's official name, which includes the term "Tewahedo", or "Union": this is a church that defines itself by professing the unification of natures in Christ.

The postpatristic history of the Ethiopian church in the Middle Ages is not well known. It must have been then, however, that the

[50] Rufinus, *Historia ecclesiastica* I.9.
[51] For obvious reasons, Catholic writers with Ethiopian enthusiasms are disposed to set the date later rather than earlier. See, for example, J.B. Coulbeaux, *Vers la Lumière: Un martyr abyssin, Ghebre Michael, prêtre de la Mission martyrisé en Ethiopie* (Paris, 1926).

Church developed into a community with a pronounced ascetical and liturgical character, in which, moreover, the *neghuse neghest* ("king of kings")—the emperor—played a major part as "Lion of Judah", claiming descent from the marriage of Solomon to the Queen of Sheba.[52] As may be imagined, with changes of dynasty that brought a variety of Amharic- and Tigrinya-speaking rulers to the throne, the bloodlines could be controversial, but the claims were always made, if more enthusiastically by some emperors than by others.[53] It was, and remained, a church rich in mysticism, iconography, poetry, despite serious pagan and Islamic depredations on its patrimony.

Though Latin envoys reached Ethiopia in the early fourteenth century, the Ethiopian church had no significant relations with Westerners—unless one counts the presence at the Council of Florence (1438–1445) of Ethiopian monks from Jerusalem—until the arrival of the Portuguese, in the wake of the great movement of seafaring exploration and discovery that had gripped Portugal since the late fifteenth century. The 1490 mission of the lay explorer Pedro Cavilham led a number of Ethiopians to visit Rome, where, as a consequence, the printing of the Ethiopic Bible was undertaken for the first time. The Psalter saw the light of printed day in 1513; the New Testament, in 1548–1549. A book for the celebration of the Ge'ez liturgy—the wide-ranging Ethiopian expansion of the Alexandrian rite—was published at the same time. The Ethiopian monarchy tended to encourage the Portuguese in the hope of gaining Portugal's political and military support for its own attempts to deal with the unruly Muslim elements in the population—the Somalis of Harar, where the Ottoman Turks lurked menacingly in the background. In the 1530s, indeed, the emperor Lebna Danghel went so far as to petition the pope for a Roman-consecrated bishop to replace the Egyptian-consecrated *abuna*. The Fethat Neghest, or "Code of Kings", the official law-book of the Ethiopian monarchy, contained, after all, a clear affirmation of Roman primacy. Twenty

---

[52] On the relation between Church and monarchy in the high to late mediaeval period, see T. Tamrat, *Church and State in Ethiopia, 1250–1527* (Oxford, 1972).

[53] A simplified diagram of their interrelation is provided by R. Greenfield, *Ethiopia: A New Political History* (London, 1965), p. 127.

years later, no less a figure in contemporary Latin Christendom than Saint Ignatius Loyola sought papal permission to go to Ethiopia himself but was refused. Nonetheless, the pope did create three Jesuit bishops for Ethiopia, one with the title of patriarch. This mission failed abysmally, as did a second, much more substantial, attempt in 1624, when the emperor Susneos determined on union with Rome and accepted yet another Jesuit as *abuna*. But with the emperor's abdication and subsequent death, the Ethiopians, outraged by the Latinising proclivities of their Western father-in-God, forced him to flee for his life.[54] The weakening of imperial authority in the course of the eighteenth century produced a situation where the subsequent anti-Catholic decrees ceased to be enforced.

A Lazarist mission in the early nineteenth century proved more successful and led to the creation of a Catholic "prefecture apostolic" which in the years 1846 to 1847 developed into two vicariates—one for historic Abyssinia and the other for the Oromo people largely settled further south. The mission's original aim had been purely unionist and therefore ecumenical, but the hostility of the Alexandria-appointed *abuna* and the appeals from local communities somewhat pastorally neglected by the Orthodox led to a change of policy.[55] The Italian occupation of 1936 favoured, evidently, Catholic expansion. But in 1945 the numerous ecclesiastical circumscriptions so ambitiously created in the 1930s were cut back to two: an apostolic exarchate for Eritrea, and another, for Ethiopia proper, centred on Addis Ababa, which latter was raised in 1961 to the standing of a metropolitan see. Subsequently, it would expand again, so that in 2007 the Ge'ez-rite Catholic church has eparchies for Tigray, based at Adigrat, and the Gurage region, with a bishop at Emdibir, as well

[54] G. B. A. N. W. Aregay, *The Question of the Union of the Churches in Luso-Ethiopian Relations, 1500–1632* (Lisbon, 1964); for the rôle of the Society of Jesus, see P. Caraman, S.J., *The Lost Empire: The Story of the Jesuits in Ethiopia, 1555–1634* (Notre Dame, Ind., 1985).

[55] "The Orthodox Church was initially taken by both Catholics and Protestants as the cornerstone of their strategy. A revitalized Ethiopian Christianity was seen to be the key to the conversion of the 'pagans of Africa'": D. Crummey, *Priests and Politicians: Protestant and Catholic Missions in Orthodox Ethiopia, 1830–1868* (Oxford, 1972), p. 5.

as the archeparchy in the capital, while its Latin-rite sister has a variety of juridical circumscriptions closer to the borders with Somalia, Kenya, and the Sudan.

The Italian occupation (1936–1941)—though an act of unprovoked aggression by a power that, pursuing a policy of *divide et impera* in a diverse country, often favoured Muslims rather than Christians— was not without use to the Ethiopian Orthodox themselves.[56] In 1929, the future emperor Haile Selassie, still only regent, had managed to secure from a new Egyptian *abuna*, Cyril, the consecration for the first time of five Ethiopian bishops. This was a first step towards achieving autonomy for the Ethiopian church. Since for reasons of their own the Italians also wished to separate the church from Alexandria, which lay outside their political control, they saw fit to continue this policy. In 1937 *abuna* Cyril, who, despite a degree of collaboration with the Italian viceroy, refused to countenance the rupture, returned to Egypt, and an assembly of the Ethiopian church elected as his successor a bishop of Ethiopian birth, by name Abraham, taking the opportunity also of augmenting the *abuna*'s auxiliaries. All these bishops were then excommunicated by Yohannes IV of Alexandria acting in concert with his patriarchal synod. Nor was *abuna* Abraham universally recognised by the clergy and people back home, owing not least to his excommunication in turn of the leaders of the Patriot resistance. It was with such leaders that British military agents sought contact as soon as Italy entered World War II on the German side. That explains how, with the arrival of British troops in 1941, the Ethiopian *abuna* came to be deposed and Cyril reinstated. Moreover, provincial separatists, for instance in Tigray, could claim that Showa, Haile Selassie's home territory, was "opposed to the Alexandrian connection of the Ethiopian Christian Church".[57] That proved a difficulty in reestablishing Haile Selassie's authority. Not till 1959 did the church of Ethiopia obtain one of the chief benefits that it had earlier sought from the West. In that year, it acquired its full independence from the Coptic church with a patriarch of its own, *abuna* Basilios.

[56] See G. Mojoli, *La Chiesa in Etiopia: Note e recordi di un nunzio* (Rome, 1975).
[57] Greenfield, *Ethiopia*, p. 283.

In 1976, two years after the Marxist revolution, the overthrow of the monarchy, and the establishment of the military dictatorship known as the Derg, the first genuinely Ethiopian patriarch to enjoy an undisputed legitimacy, Tewofilos, was removed from office by a state now officially committed to "scientific socialism". His successor, Tekle Haimanot, suffered considerable restraints on his freedom of action in governing his church. (Incidentally, his name is confusingly common in Ethiopian Christianity. Meaning "Tree of the Faith", it derives from the national saint of that name, the thirteenth-century founder of the monastery of Debra Libanos, whose head was, in the absence of native born bishops, the premier monk of Ethiopia as well as, traditionally, confessor and adviser to the emperor.) The need for pragmatism, given the depth of popular attachment to Orthodoxy and the precarious character of the regime's hold on power, coincided with a will to propagate atheism—for instance, by removing from Amharic usage the customary polite expressions referring to God and replacing them with neutral terms.[58] In 1991, the overthrow of the Derg by a broad antigovernment coalition (the Ethiopian People's Revolutionary Democratic Front) would make possible a new beginning.

The arrival of the Latin missionaries caused internal dissensions in Ethiopia whose effects continue today. The most obvious of those effects is the formation of the Uniate church, which came into formal existence in 1839 and now numbers some 140,000 members with possibly 80,000 practising regularly. Though its leadership is indigenous, missionaries from the Catholic countries of Mediterranean Europe remain numerous: despite the brutalities of Fascism, Italians are popular in Ethiopia, and not only through gratitude for their provision of magnificent roads. Catholicism's contributions to education, health care, and the promotion of women in Ethiopia today would be hard to replace, as the request of the post-Derg government of Meles Zenawi for the foundation of a Catholic university serves to show. That is not to say the Catholic presence is

[58] J. Persoon, "Between Ancient Axum and Revolutionary Moscow: The Ethiopian Church in the 20th Century", in O'Mahony, *Eastern Christianity*, pp. 160–214.

generally appreciated by the Orthodox, though on the author's (third) visit in 2009, he found signs that the anxiety generated by the political renaissance of Islam is bringing the two churches together.

More importantly for theology, as distinct from pastoral care: in the wake of doctrinal controversy with the Latins, from the seventeenth to the nineteenth centuries, the Ethiopian Orthodox church became internally divided on the crucial subject of Christology. A bitter argument arose, still lively in recent memory, despite the imperial attempt to silence all parties to the dispute in the late nineteenth century.[59] The controversy turns on the meaning of those biblical passages that speak of Jesus as *ho Christos*, the "Anointed One". The Latins maintained that the title *Christos* must mean that the humanity of Jesus was sanctified by the Holy Spirit. And this in turn must mean that the humanity survived the union as a distinct reality. In other words, Chalcedon was right: two natures after the union. The strict Monophysite reaction was to say that God the Son is at once the Anointing, the Anointed, and the Unction. In this way, they would avoid having to concede that the Spirit anointed Jesus' humanity. This rigorist view has become known by the slogan *Weld-qeb*, "the Son is Unction", and holds that the humanity assumed is so transformed by the Word that only the divine nature fully remains. But other Ethiopian theologians accepted the Roman argument, and in doing so moved a long way towards the Chalcedonian position. This group and their successors are known as the "Son by Grace" school. It appears that the Monophysite response did not become fully dominant until the late eighteenth or even the nineteenth century. In the late eighteenth century, the superiors of forty-four monasteries wrote to Alexandria asking for the ratification of the *Weld-qeb* formula, which would be formally confirmed by a synod of the Ethiopian church in 1878. However, Catholic missionaries in the country noted the continuance of the alternative, more Chalcedonian tradition, which received the name of the "Union" school. In the 1950s, a study of Ethiopian Christology by a Uniate scholar, Ayele Tekle Haimanot, led to a fresh

---

[59] Coulbeaux, *Vers la Lumière*, pp. 43–83.

outburst of controversy.[60] Some writers, anxious to distance them-selves as fully as possible from Chalcedon, took up positions far exceeding traditional Monophysitism, teaching, for example, that Christ is equal to the Father and the Spirit even in his humanity, that his flesh *became* the Logos, and so forth.[61] On the other hand, the *abuna* Tewofilos on his enthronement in 1971 made a defi-nitely unionist profession of faith, affirming that both divine and human properties were fully present in Jesus Christ.[62] A major dif-ficulty in the whole business is the finding of adequate Amharic equivalents for the various patristic or technical terms.

Representatives of the Ethiopian church took part in the collo-quies between Catholic and Oriental Orthodox theologians orga-nised by the institute Pro oriente under the patronage of the archbishop of Vienna, and in October 1982 the *abuna* Tekle Haimanot, making use of a rare travel concession by the hardline Marxist regime of the Derg, travelled to Rome to meet Pope John Paul II. In his speech of welcome, the pope attributed the centuries-old "living apart" of the two churches to lack of knowledge of the necessary languages, as well as differences in historic circumstance, in culture, and in thought. But, touching on the Christological issue, he showed a circumspection

---

[60] Originally published as *La dottrina della Chiesa etiopica dissidente sull'unione ipo-statica* (Rome, 1956), it appeared in Amharic at Asmara in 1959 (Ethopian calendar: 1951) and in English at Addis in 1982 under the title *The Ethiopian Church and Its Christological Doctrine*.

[61] For an account of the controversy, see T. Uqbit, *Current Christological Positions of Ethiopian Orthodox Theologians* (Rome, 1973), and R. H. Cowley, "The Ethiopian Church and the Council of Chalcedon", *Sob*. 6, no. 1 (1976): 33–38. Cowley concludes: "The Ethiopian church does not accept the application of Cappadocian Trinitarian catego-ries to the doctrine of the Incarnation, nor the use of any term to express duality in the incarnate Logos. These two appear to be the essential differences between the Ethio-pian and Chalcedonian traditions", p. 38. Uqbit, after pointing out the "abundant" Dyo-physite statements in the Ethiopian liturgy, reports that, while the recent controversialists generally concede that Chalcedon's decisions are based on Scripture and the fathers, they nevertheless "discard from the same Council's dogmatic formula the phrase 'in two natures', defining it as Nestorian in origin and as having no basis in the Scriptures or the com-mon teaching of the Church Fathers", ibid., p. 181.

[62] Given in full ibid., pp. 183–86.

reflecting awareness of the controversies mentioned above. Referring to the separation, the pope concluded: "That has led, equally, to different liturgical, disciplinary and theological expressions: in themselves, and *as long as this variety is complementary rather than contradictory*, these diverse expressions are an enrichment for the life and mission of the Church among the nations."[63] In 1993 Pope John Paul II was able to resume this courteous but clear-sighted conversation in the more relaxed circumstances, for Ethiopians, of the post-Marxist era. Receiving at Rome the *abuna* Paulos, the pope declared: "We share the faith handed down from the apostles, as also the same sacraments and the same ministry, rooted in the apostolic succession.... Today, moreover, we can affirm that we have the one faith in Christ, even though for a long time this was a source of division between us."[64]

A Note on the Church of Eritrea

The overthrow of the Derg in 1991 led to the independence of the former Ethiopian province of Eritrea, with marked consequences for church life. Eritrea's Christian highlands are linked by language and ethnicity to Tigray (before 1890 they had been Ethiopian), though the coastal lowlands are Muslim and were formerly under Ottoman or Egyptian rule. From 1890 to 1941 Eritrea was an Italian colony; during World War II it came under British military administration; and in 1952 it was federated by the United Nations with Ethiopia, an arrangement converted into outright union ten years later. The Coptic patriarch, Shenouda III, seized the opportunity of Eritrea's new statehood—officially declared in 1993—to nudge the by-no-means-unwilling Eritreans towards ecclesial autocephaly. In 1994 he consecrated five Eritrean abbots as diocesan bishops. Then in 1998 he enthroned the first patriarch of Eritrea, Philipos, at a ceremony in the capital, Asmara. The two first patriarchs died soon after attaining office, and in 2007 the Eritrean government replaced

---

[63] *OR*, 18 October 1981; *DC* 79, no. 1821, 3 January 1982.
[64] *OR*, 11–12 June 1993.

the third patriarch, Antonios, who had criticized its repressive policy towards Orthodox Christianity, with Dioskoros, who was more docile. Eritrean Orthodox number some 1.75 million. Owing not least to the bellicose political stance of Eritrea towards Ethiopia, with whom it has seemingly intractable border disputes (these flamed into war in the years 1998–2000), relations between the church of Eritrea and the church of Ethiopia are somewhat strained. The sealing of the borders has also made life difficult for the Uniates: the Catholic archbishop in Addis is the metropolitan of three Eritrean eparchies: Asmara, Barentu, and Keren.

The Church of Syria

As we have noted, it was a Syrian bishop whose career gave the Monophysites their nickname of "Jacobites", a name at one time effectively official in Catholic usage, as we can see from the title of the reunion decree of Florence: *Decretum pro Jacobitis*. By the end of the sixth century an independent Syrian Orthodox church of "Antioch and all the East" had come into existence, though Antioch itself was abandoned *qua* center of leadership in 518. Sassanid (and subsequently Abbasid) Persia was a more attractive option than coastal Syria, where Chalcedon was law. But the Syrian Monophysites came to decline disastrously in the same way as their Nestorian neighbours and for much the same political reasons. Like the Nestorians, the Jacobites under Islam enjoyed an alternation of state patronage and state suspicion. Muslims found themselves increasingly able to dispense with the services of Christian inhabitants of areas they had conquered. The Jacobite golden age was the thirteenth century, when they achieved a remarkably high level of culture, theological and otherwise. In the mediaeval heyday of the church, three figures are outstanding: the patriarch Michael the Syrian, an historian; the bishop Dionysius, a systematic theologian who also commented the Bible and the fathers; and the bishop Gregory bar Hebraeus, who has been acclaimed as a forerunner of the *uomo universale* of the Western Renaissance, equally at home in philosophy, mathematics, astronomy, history, and biblical studies. Bishop Gregory, by the way, bore the

important title of *maphrian*—literally, "the fructifier"—acting as patriarchal vicar for the "East", the country across the Tigris: the missionary dioceses of the maphrianate stretched as far as the Oxus river.
As with the Nestorians, the Jacobites were defeated by two political
developments: the conversion of the Mongols to Islam, which produced a new hardline Muhammadan stance, and the Turkestani invasion under Timburlaine. By the nineteenth century, Jacobite numbers
were down to about 150,000, mainly concentrated around Mosul in
Iraq and Homs in Syria. The patriarch, still keeping the title "of
Antioch", in 1924 left his fortress-like residence near Mardin in the
mountains of southeast Turkey to reside first at Homs—at that time,
by authority of the League of Nations, under the protection of
France—and now at Damascus, the Syrian capital. The recent revival
of a classically liturgical and learned monasticism has been a source
of encouragement to their diaspora, spread as this is through western Europe, the Americas and Australia. There are today an estimated one million Syrian Orthodox worldwide, of whom half are
reported as practising.

Uniatism has also played a part in the fortunes of the Syrian Jacobites. Until the sixteenth century, this was on their own initiative.[65]
After that time, it was on the initiative of Rome, usually mediated
through the French diplomatic service, which wanted the Catholici-
sation of Christians in the Near East for its own ends. In the 1660s a
Catholicising element in the Jacobite community of Aleppo was sufficiently strong to carry to the episcopal throne a Catholic candidate,
Andrew Akigian, trained theologically at the Roman college of Propaganda fide. Consecrated by the Maronite patriarch, he was himself
elected Syrian patriarch of Antioch in 1662 and sent to Rome his profession of faith. Although this "personal union" endured only until the
death of his successor in 1701, a lasting Uniate body was fashioned

---

[65] Cf. the texts collected in C. B. Benni, *The Tradition of the Syriac Church of Antioch concerning the Primacy and the Prerogatives of St. Peter and of His Successors, the Roman
Pontiffs* (Eng. trans., London, 1871). Also relevant to the Syrian church's interest in
Rome is P. Sfeir, "La promessa del Primato nei commentari siriaci", *Bessarione* 20
(1916): 83–109; 21 (1917): 14–35.

towards the end of the eighteenth century. In a doublet of the earlier history, the Jacobite archbishop of Aleppo, Michael Giarveh, entering Catholic communion in 1774, was elected and enthroned as patriarch in 1782. Forced to flee, he established the monastery of Saint Mary the Liberator on a spur of Mount Lebanon, the first of a permanent Catholic succession that has included some notable scholars and administrators.[66] Much of the work of these men was, however, destroyed by Turkish persecution of Eastern Christians during the years 1915–1917. The furies were unleashed not only against Armenians (as is often erroneously thought) but found numerous victims among the Syrian Jacobites, whether schismatic or Catholic, and the Nestorians and Chaldaeans as well. Following this disaster, the patriarch of the Syrian Catholic Church moved from Mardin, where considerable numbers of Syrian Catholics resided, to Beirut, to be among the friendly Maronites, in the (then) secure world of the Christian Lebanon under the French mandate. This was something of a golden age for the community, which at that time drew many Syrian Orthodox to itself. Catholic Jacobites today amount to about one hundred thousand persons, of whom perhaps sixty thousand are active in their faith. The pattern of their distribution, in the homelands as in the diaspora, reflects that of their Orthodox counterparts.

The Jacobite Monophysite patriarch Ignatius Jacob III—the see, which is officially, of course, "of Antioch", is now based in Damascus—visited Paul VI in 1971. Referring to the Vienna meeting of Catholic and Non-Chalcedonian theologians organised that spring, pope and patriarch said in their common declaration: "Progress has already been made, and Pope Paul VI and the patriarch Mar Ignatius Jacob III are in agreement that there is no difference in the faith they profess concerning the mystery of the Word of God made flesh and become really man, even if over the centuries difficulties have arisen out of the different theological expressions by which this faith was expressed."[67] Pope John Paul II confirmed the terms of

---

[66] W. de Vries, S.J., "Dreihundert Jahre syrisch-katholisch Hierarchie", *Ostkirchliche Studien* 5 (1956): 137–57.

[67] DC 69, no. 1600 (1972), p. 48.

this declaration in an address to the same Syrian patriarch at their meeting in May 1980. Some four weeks after his return to Damascus, the patriarch died, leaving in his will a request for a new Christological formula that could reestablish full communion between the Catholic and Monophysite churches. His successor, Mar Ignatius Zakka I Iwas, signed a common declaration with Pope John Paul II in June 1984 that also provided for limited intercommunion and shared priestly training. Its Christological section followed lines by now familiar. Confessing the mystery of the Incarnation in the (highly Cyrilline) words, "He who is eternally and indivisibly God became visible in the flesh and took the form of a servant", pope and patriarch went on to say: "In him, humanity and divinity are united in a real, perfect, indivisible, and inseparable fashion, with all their properties present in him, and active."[68]

The Church of Armenia

The Church of Armenia—a substantial body with an estimated membership of more than 6 million, with perhaps 350,000 practising—has a very complex story. Reduced to its essentials: at the time of Chalcedon, we find the Armenians engaged in a struggle to maintain the Christian faith in any form against the Persians. Persia won the war but not the peace. She gave up the attempt to eliminate Armenian Christianity and returned to her older policy of encouraging solidarity with Persian Christians, who by now were Nestorians. As luck would have it, the writings of the anti-Chalcedonian Alexandrian patriarch Timothy the Cat were translated into Armenian about this time and of course presented the *Tome* of Leo, and the Chalcedonian definition, as Nestorian. Because the Armenians were anti-Persian, they were anti-Nestorian. Because they believed Timothy Aelurus, they rejected Chalcedon. (Tension between the Persian monarchy and the East Roman state had inhibited Armenian bishops from attending the Second, Third, and Fourth Ecumenical Councils, so firsthand knowledge of the conciliar development of

[68] *OR*, 24 June 1984; *DC* 31, no. 1990, 2 September 1984.

doctrine was not possible for them.) At the Synod of Vagharšapat (506), the Armenians accepted the *Henotikon* of Zeno. At the successor Synod of Dvin (525–527), they anathematised Chalcedon as tainted with Nestorius' heresy.[69] From this period is dated the ecclesial independence of Armenia, which had formerly depended on the see of Caesarea Mazacha in Cilicia, whence had come in the late third century the apostle of Armenia, Gregory the Illuminator. From the moment of their rejection of Chalcedonianism, the bishop of the principal Armenian see, Etchmiadzin, became the catholicos, or primate, of Armenia.

The Arab invasions produced the by-now-familiar pattern: freedom from the Byzantine government's religious interventionism but at the cost of occasional persecution. After the collapse of the Christian monarchy, the catholicos wandered from place to place without any fixed see. But a branch of the Armenian dynasty, the Bagratids, managed to create a new state, often called "Lesser Armenia" in Cilicia, a kingdom carved out of the dwindling Byzantine Empire towards the end of the eleventh century. The Armenian princes and bishops in Cilicia enjoyed excellent relations with the Crusaders and the Latin church, sharing a common dislike of the Greeks.[70] In 1160, under the catholicos Constantine I, the Armenians of Lesser Armenia were reconciled to the Roman see, and for three hundred years after this a catholicos in Roman communion sat at Sis in Cilicia while a rival catholicos, not in Roman communion, operated in Greater Armenia itself, from the city of Aghthamar on Lake Van. At the reunion council of Florence, pressure was put on the Armenians to enact a formal union of their entire church with Rome. But the pressure proved unfortunately counterproductive, and by 1450 both patriarchal lines, Aghthamar and Sis, were out of union with Rome.

Until 1919, the organisation of the Armenian church—in the full dignity of its title, the "Armenian Apostolic Church" (there is a tradition that the Caucasus witnessed the apostolic endeavours of Saint

---

[69] K. Sarkissian, *The Council of Chalcedon and the Armenian Church* (London, 1965).
[70] B. Hamilton, "The Armenian Church and the Papacy at the Time of the Crusades", *ECR* 10 (1978): 61–87.

Bartholomew)—was extremely confusing. To all appearances, there were five patriarchs, or one may rationalise the situation and say that there was one patriarch with four coadjutors residing at, respectively, Etchmiadzin, Agthamar, Sis, Jerusalem, and Constantinople. As the Jews of the Christian world, the Armenians were scattered here, there, and everywhere. The principal patriarch was the one who happened to have the chief relic of Armenian Christianity, the *atsh*, or right arm, of Saint Gregory the Illuminator, which was ceremonially held over his head at his consecration. Since 1919, however, the archbishop of Etchmiadzin has been recognised as "supreme catholicos" of his church, while his brothers of Jerusalem and Constantinople, though bearing the title of patriarchs, are regarded, in contradiction to Eastern usage at large, as his subordinates. The catholicate of Cilicia, on the other hand, is effectively autonomous. Since its holder has the freedom of movement denied to the supreme catholicos, a Soviet citizen until 1991, the jurisdiction of his church—once confined to the Lebanon, Syria, and Cyprus—now extends to many lands, as entire eparchies and individual parishes have transferred themselves to his care.

The creation of an enduring Armenian Uniate church occurred in the eighteenth century via the French. The story opens in 1712, when a distinguished Armenian scholar-bishop, Mekhitar of Sebastia, became a Catholic and tried to persuade his fellow Armenians to follow him. When they declined, he left for Venice, where he founded a flourishing Armenian Catholic centre on the island of San Lazzaro in the Lagoon of Venice. The rôle of Mekhitaristine monastic clergy in preserving and transmitting Armenian culture and scholarship, there and at Vienna, became justly celebrated. Encouraged by this development, and with French diplomatic help, the remaining Armenian-rite Catholics in Cilicia set up a Catholic patriarchate in 1740, a *fait accompli* accepted by Pope Benedict XIV in 1742.[71] The first primate, Abraham Ardzivian, took the additional throne name of Peter, in honour of Roman communion, and this

---

[71] J. M. Terzian, *Le patriarcat de Cilicie et les Arméniens catholiques 1740–1812* (Beirut, 1955); cf. G. A. Frazee, "The Formation of the Armenian Catholic Community in the Ottoman Empire", *ECR* (1975): 149–63.

practice continues to the present day. The office holder's self-description is "patriarch of the Catholic Armenians and catholicos of Cilicia", and, after many wanderings, his seat was fixed in 1928 at Bzommar near Beirut. In the sufferings that befell the Armenian community during the First World War, the numbers of Armenian Catholics in the Ottoman Empire declined dramatically—a not-unknown effect of massacre. The number of Uniate Armenians today is estimated at 150,000, of whom two-thirds are said to be practising. It should be added that some of these groups derive from local unions with the Catholic Church of Armenian settlers in Poland and Transylvania during the seventeenth century.[72] It is a point of contention among Catholic Armenians that the jurisdiction of their patriarch is currently restricted by Rome to the territory of the former Ottoman Empire. Perhaps through concern for sensitivities in the Armenian Apostolic Church, when, with the independence of the Caucasian countries in 1991, it became possible to appoint Eastern-rite bishops for Catholics there (they were numerous in the Panik region of northern Armenia), Pope John Paul II nominated personally a Mekhitaristine monk as "Ordinary for Armenian Catholics in Eastern Europe"—taken to include the entire area up to the Caspian Sea.[73] That nerve endings are exposed became apparent in 2004 when the heads of the Oriental Orthodox churches in the Middle East at their annual meeting issued a communiqué that sought the withdrawal by the Armenian Catholic patriarch of his title of "catholicos".

The meeting of Pope Paul VI with the supreme catholicos Vasken I in 1970 was the first encounter of a pope with a Monophysite patriarch. At it the pope pioneered the line he would take with the Syrian and Coptic patriarchs later. We have one faith, expressed in alternative formulae. He quoted some eirenic words of an earlier

[72] C. Lukácsi, *Historia Armeniorum Transilvaniae a primordiis gentis usque nostram memoriam* (Vienna, 1859); G. Petrowicz, *L'unione degli Armeni di Polonia con la Santa Sede, 1626–1686* (Rome, 1950).

[73] J. Whooley, "The Armenian Catholic Church: A Study in History and Ecclesiology", *Heythrop Journal* 45 (2004): 427.

Armenian catholicos, spoken during a rare ecumenical encounter with the Byzantines in the twelfth century. There the Armenian had explained to the Chalcedonians:

> In no way do we introduce confusion, change, or alteration into the union of Christ, as do the heretics. We affirm one single nature to signify the hypostasis that you also acknowledge in Christ: this we admit to be legitimate, and it has just the same meaning as our formula "one single nature".... We do not refuse to say "two natures" as long as this is not by way of confusion, as Nestorius held, but rather to indicate the absence of confusion, against Eutyches and Apollinarius.[74]

The 1983 meeting of Pope John Paul II with the Orthodox catholicos of Cilicia—based, like his Catholic counterpart, in the vicinity of Beirut—went on to produce a common declaration, somewhat meagre in doctrinal content because overshadowed by a more immediately practical concern for the fate of the Armenian community in the Middle East, and notably in the war-torn Lebanon. However, the text ended beautifully, calling the "paschaltide encounter" of pope and catholicos a "communing at the source of prayer, light, and love, [which] participates in the day without sunset of the Resurrection of their Lord", and so a meeting that "opens out on other beginnings", beginnings, doubtless, not only social and political but also, and above all, ecclesial in character.[75]

In 1995, Karekin II of Cilicia ("the Great House"), who had progressed from coadjutor to catholicos in the year the above words were spoken, 1983, was elected catholicos at Etchmiadzin and thus supreme catholicos, assuming there the style—confusingly, but logically—of Karekin I. Karekin considered his 1996 encounter with the same pope a major triumph of his ministry. A new joint declaration, signed in the presence of Armenian bishops from several continents, formed a satisfactory conclusion to the ancient Christological dispute—though his gesture was not universally welcomed in Armenia itself (understandably, in reaction to decades of Soviet

[74] *DC* 47, no. 1564, 7 June 1970, pp. 513–16.
[75] *OR*, 17 April 1983.

hegemony, a less open society than much of its diaspora), nor for that matter by all the Armenian bishops present at the Roman ceremony, some of whom saw the text only on their flights home.

The Church of India

The Christian Church may well have existed in India in apostolic or at least subapostolic times.[76] Trade routes between the Roman Empire and the west coast of India were easy and well patronised. But by the time the Indian church emerges into the light of recorded history, it is already Nestorian: the longest surviving missionary achievement of the Assyrians. It had its own metropolitan see at Angamale in Travancore, but the bishops always travelled to Mesopotamia, where they were directly consecrated by the Nestorian patriarch at Seleucia.[77] With the arrival of the Portuguese in the sixteenth century, this church was brought into union with Rome, or, as *Oriente cattolico*, the Vatican handbook on the Eastern Catholic churches, prefers to put it, a communion never formally interrupted arose spontaneously.[78] The aftermath, alas, was far from happy. In 1553, when Pope Julius III recognised John Sulaka as Assyrian patriarch, he also recognised his traditional jurisdiction over Indian Christians. In 1556 Joseph Sulaka, the patriarch's brother, reached Malabar as bishop but at once encountered opposition from the Portuguese. The latter, firm in their regalian view of Church patronage, the *padroado*, would not admit into their Indian possessions any other prelates than those appointed by Portugal's king. His case unresolved, Joseph died at Rome in 1569. His successor, Abraham, proved the last Catholic bishop canonically dispatched to the Indian church by the Assyrian patriarch. His career, stormy but protracted, lasted till 1597. Immediately afterwards, the Latin archbishop of Goa (later to

---

[76] P. Podipara, C.M.I., "The South Indian Apostolate of St. Thomas", *Orientalia christiana periodica* 18 (1952): 229–45.

[77] For the little that is known of the pre-Portuguese period, see C. V. Chevian, *A History of Christianity in Kerala* (Kottayam, 1975).

[78] G. Schurhammer, *The Malabar Church and Rome* (Trichinoppilly, 1934); Sacra congregazione per le Chiese orientali, *Oriente cattolico* (Vatican City, 1974), p. 400.

claim for his see a titular patriarchate that still survives) had the primatial church of Angamale reduced to the level of a suffragan see of Goa and, to add insult to injury, found for it a candidate pleasing to his heart in the shape of a Spanish Jesuit. In 1599 Archbishop Menezes convoked the notorious Synod of Diamper (Udayamperur) that suppressed numerous Malabarese customary rights and usages, destroyed liturgical and archival materials on the grounds of their tainting by Nestorianism, and introduced Latinisations into both rite and discipline.[79] No doubt some doctrinal purification of liturgy and creed was necessary, and the meeting with the West could have been an opportunity for the enhancement of an Oriental tradition by the sharing of the Latin patrimony. But the new broom swept away wheat with chaff to the point that, by the early seventeenth century, the Eastern Christians of South India were thoroughly disaffected and preferred an Oriental bishop of any persuasion to a Latin. So it was that in 1652 the Coptic patriarch of Alexandria sent a Syrian Jacobite bishop to India. When a popular uprising failed to rescue this unfortunate cleric, who had been sentenced to death by the Inquisition, an assembly of Oriental Christians at Cochin swore to cast off the Roman obedience, expel the Society of Jesus, and find another chief pastor from an Eastern church. In the interim, they took a priest-leader of the secessionist movement, Thomas Parampil, and attempted to raise him presbyterally to the episcopate as Mar Thoma I. Unintentionally, the Dutch conquest of the Malabar coast in 1663 aided the Catholic cause. Released from the burden of the *padroado*, the Carmelite Joseph Sebastiani, made vicar-apostolic by Pope Alexander VII, consecrated for the Christians of Saint Thomas one of their own presbyters, Alexander Parampil, cousin of the schismatic, whose energetic efforts recovered for the Roman communion the greater part of the Malabar community. In 1665, a second Syrian Jacobite bishop reached India and (it is assumed) supplied the deficiencies of Thomas Parampil's consecration by the laying on of hands. However, the episcopal succession in the Indian Orthodox church hardly depends on this dubium, as further Syrian bishops were sent out on a fairly regular basis.

[79] J. Thaliat, C.M.I., *The Synod of Diamper* (Rome, 1958).

But the poor quality of many of these leaders led to a variety of splits within the Indian Orthodox. Some returned to communion with the Nestorians, for the Patriarch of the East made feeble attempts periodically to get in touch with his former flock.[80] Others entered into union with Rome. Still others in the British period made common cause with Anglicanism. Within the rump of the Indian Orthodox, some 1.5 million strong, there is a long-standing jurisdictional dispute between the Syrian patriarch in Damascus and the metropolitan of Malankar. Around 1912 the then Syrian patriarch gave the Indian church autonomous status by granting the Malankara primate the ancient title of maphrian, or "catholicos of the East": head of all Monophysites east of the Tigris. Later patriarchs tried to revoke this grant, but in 1958 the Indian Supreme Court recognised the primate of Malankar, resident at Kottayam, as head of the Indian Orthodox church. Congregations directly dependent on the Syrian patriarch are now probably somewhat fewer than those attached to the Malankar primate. Each body has a million or so adherents, with a practising total of maybe 1.4 million.

An interesting testimony to the paradoxical history of the Indian church is found in the two quite distinct Catholic Uniate bodies.

The Syro-Malabar church, a highly flourishing and missionary-minded body, with metropolitan sees at Ernakulam (a "major archbishopric") and Changanacherry, consists of descendants of Oriental Christians who chose to remain in Roman communion after 1653.[81] Although the worship of the Syro-Malabarese is somewhat Latinised, they preserve in essentials the East Syrian liturgy used by the

---

[80] The Nestorian patriarch sent a Mar Gabriel as bishop in the period 1708–1730; in 1952 Shimun XXIII, from his American base, created a Nestorian bishop of "Malabar and India". A modern metropolitan of the Church of the East in India, Mar Aphrem (Dr. George Mooken), is an indefatigable exponent of his church's glories, as in his *The Nestorian Fathers* (Trichur, 1976); *Nestorian Missions* (Trichur, 1976); *The Chaldaean Syrian Church in India* (Trichur, 1977); *The Council of Ephesus of 431* (Trichur, 1978), and *Nestorian Theology* (Trichur, 1980). The church is small and mainly confined to the neighbourhood of Trichur, the place of publication of these books.

[81] P.J. Podipara, *The Hierarchy of the Syro-Malabar Church* (Alleppey, 1976); V.J. Vithayathil, *The Origin and Progress of the Syro-Malabar Hierarchy* (Kottayam, 1980).

Nestorians (and Catholics of the Chaldaean rite).[82] This church, conscious of its strength in priestly and religious vocations, is currently seeking to acquire an "all-India jurisdiction", parallel to that of the Latin hierarchy, in place of the eight mission dioceses, ultimately responsible to the Latin bishops, which it has so far managed to create in the north.[83] In May 1988, Pope John Paul II went some considerable way to meet these requests by changing the status of the Indian bishops' conference to that of an "assembly" for general issues transcending the different rites, granting equal rights and responsibilities to all the churches in evangelisation, and erecting a Syrian eparchy in Bombay as the first instalment of a true double hierarchy wherever this seems pastorally necessitated.[84] That meant the canonical liberation of the missionary energies of the (highly dynamic) Syro-Malabar church.[85]

The other Uniate community, the Syro-Malankar church, with its main metropolitan see at Trivandrum, is much smaller—some 320,000 faithful (possibly 190,000 practising), compared with the Syro-Malabarese total of over 3 million (nearly 2 million active). This younger brother originated in a breakaway movement from the Indian Orthodox, whose members were reconciled with Rome in 1930. Being an offshoot of the Indian church in its Monophysite phase, this community uses the West Syrian liturgy, the liturgy used

[82] For the contemporary disagreements over the reshaping of Syro-Malabar liturgical practice, see the somewhat intemperate plea of K. T. Kathanar, "The Liturgical Crisis in the Syro-Malabar Church", *ECJ* 5, no. 2 (1998): 143–72, which includes Roman documents of 1998 as an appendix. The "crisis" consists in having to decide between a more consistently Syrian liturgical form and "Neo-Latinisation": following the principles for revision of the Latin rite in the Constitution on the Sacred Liturgy of the Second Vatican Council.

[83] [Mar Thoma Yogam] [a fellowship of Syro-Malabar and Syro-Malankar priests in Rome], *The Oriental Churches in India Twenty Years after the Second Vatican Council: An Evaluation on the Occasion of the Extraordinary Synod of Bishops, Rome, November 25–December 8, 1985* (Rome, 1985).

[84] G. Valente, "The Restless Sons of St. Thomas", *Thirty Days in the Church and in the World* (September–October 1990): 26–27.

[85] G. Mifsud, "Missionary Activity in the Syro-Malabar Church", *ECJ* 3, no. 1 (1996): 91.

by the Syrian Jacobites dependent on Antioch.[86] In 2005, Pope John Paul II gave the see of Trivandrum the status of a major archbishopric, thus recognising the Syro-Malankar church's growth and distinctiveness of patrimony.

The Malankar Orthodox catholicos, Mar Thoma Mathews I, had paid an official visit to Pope John Paul II in June 1983, describing the purpose of his visit in these terms: "to pray at the tombs of saint Peter and saint Paul, first among the apostles, to receive the grace of earth sanctified by the blood of so many martyrs, especially saint Ignatius of Antioch and saint Clement of Rome, and to venerate the holy relics of our Lord's passion." And with a certain assertiveness, he described his own community, born from the preaching of Thomas, as "a church which gives place to none in terms of antiquity, which is as faithful to tradition as any other, as proud of its heritage, and as autonomous as any other." [87] The apostle Thomas, he went on, meets again the apostles Peter and Paul in their respective successors. The pope did not spurn these descriptive terms and, in a nice touch, introduced his own references to the shared Christological faith, based on the first three councils, by recalling Thomas' cry, "My Lord and my God!" as a proclamation of Christ's divinity, his saving Lordship, and his bodily Resurrection. For once, however, the more theological address was that of the Oriental, perhaps reflecting the contribution of Father Paul Verghese, a noted theologian with strong ecumenical interests who, as Mar Gregorios, was the Malankarese primate's coadjutor with right of succession. Striking an unusual note for such dialogues, the catholicos sought not only a "common understanding of our separate histories" but also the coordinating of social engagement, in the service of India's poor.

---

[86] Under the editorial title "The Reunion Movement in Malabar, 1930–1955", see the entire issue of *ECQ* 11, no. 3 (1955); A. Raes, S.J., "L'unione dei Malankaresi con la Chiesa cattolica", *Unitas* (1956): 142–50. In view of the marked fragmentation of the Syrian tradition in India, it is encouraging to see that in 1985, under the influence of the late Mar Isaac Youhanon, bishop of the Syro-Malankara diocese of Tiravalla, a St. Ephrem Ecumenical Research Centre was created, with the aim of drawing together the various churches in the study of their common Syriac heritage.

[87] *OR*, 3–4 June 1983; *DC* 80, no. 1858, 4–18 September 1983.

Ecumenical Assessment

The Catholic Church has engaged in bilateral dialogue with the Monophysite churches since 1971, whereas only since 1995 has there been official exchange with the Nestorians.[88] Ampler discussion makes it easier to identify the basic points at issue.

First of all, there is the search for a generally acceptable Christological formula, or what is sometimes called a *formula concordiae*, a "formula of concord". It will be remembered that, in the wake of Ephesus (431), the churches of Antioch and Alexandria were in virtual schism from each other until John and Cyril managed to agree on the *Formula of Reunion* (432), which permitted both sides to accept Ephesus. Today, Catholics and Monophysites may be thought of as in a "452 situation" with regard to Chalcedon (451). The council has happened, but there is need of an explanatory formula before everyone can accept it. The *formula concordiae* needed will, in all probability, affirm two sets of distinct properties after the union in the Word incarnate, those of the Godhead and those of the manhood—but without an explicit affirmation of the two natures. On the Catholic side, this can be regarded as faithful to Chalcedon, since the council's intention was to affirm that everything which God has, Christ has, and that everything which we have, Christ has—the twofold consubstantiality of the single person, our Lord Jesus Christ. On the Monophysite side, the preservation of two sets of properties after the union has been defended with a fair degree of consistency. Those extremists who denied it, like Julian of Halicarnassus with his insistence that the flesh assumed is immortal, have been combatted, and even anathematised, from within the Monophysite churches themselves. In such a formula, the Monophysites will be able to avoid the "two natures" language, which for them has been spoiled by its inextricable association (in their eyes) with Nestorianism. Alternatively,

---

[88] Technically, the consultations with the Oriental Orthodox, as distinct from the more recent dealings with the Church of the East, have been officially "Non-Official" (capitalised letters are original to those consulting and consulted). In practice, this appears to be a distinction without a difference, but see Roberson, "Modern Roman Catholic—Oriental Orthodox Dialogue".

a *formula concordiae* could take the form of a common affirmation of Cyril's *mia phusis tou Logou sesarkomenê*, "one reality of the Word incarnate", with the added statement that the word *phusis* here is equivalent to *hypostasis* or *persona*.

It is relatively easy to find a formula. More difficult is the providing of a mutually satisfactory interpretation of the events and documents of Chalcedon as a whole in terms of such a *formula concordiae*. Although the great majority of the bishops at Chalcedon were Cyrilline, they accepted the *Tome* of Leo, which is, in Eastern terms, a compromise between Cyrilline and Antiochene theology. The *Tome* of Leo is greatly displeasing to Monophysites because of its assertion that the natures in Christ are true subjects of action, even though the ultimate subject of action is the Word incarnate's single person. As Leo put it: "Each of the natures does what is proper to it in communion with the other, the Word doing what pertains to the Word, and the flesh doing what pertains to the flesh." [89] In following the dialogue between the Eastern Orthodox (the non-Roman Chalcedonian Orthodox) and the Monophysites, one soon realises that a number of Eastern Chalcedonians are now willing to abandon the *Tome*.[90] It is open to them to argue that Chalcedon is essentially a Cyrilline council; that the *Tome* was accepted only on the grounds that it was compatible with Cyril; that this was, in point of fact, a mistake of judgement—something which, in such matters of documentary evaluation, can happen at even an ecumenical council.[91] The temptation to ditch the *Tome* has two aspects. First, such an

[89] Leo, *Tome* 4.

[90] P. Gregorios, W. H. Lazareth, and N. A. Nissiotis, eds., *Does Chalcedon Divide or Unite? Towards Convergence in Orthodox Christology* (Geneva, 1981); cf. B. Dupuy, "Où en est le dialogue entre l'Orthodoxie et les églises dites monophysites?" *Ist.* 31, no. 4 (1986): 357–70. Official dialogue—prepared by technically "Non-Official" consultations since 1964 (Aarhus, 1964; Bristol, 1967; Geneva, 1970; Addis Ababa, 1971)—was opened at Chambésy in December 1985. Two common declarations followed in 1989 and 1990.

[91] Many Western patrologists today would indeed regard the Chalcedonian definition as largely Eastern, and even Cyrilline, in expression but with a Leonine twist. See A. de Halleux, "La définition christologique de Chalcédoine", *Revue théologique de Louvain* 7 (1976): 5–25, 155–70.

action could reunite the Monophysites with the Chalcedonian East (the Uniate churches excepted). Second, it could rebut the Roman claim that the acclamation of the fathers of Chalcedon, "Peter has spoken through Leo", was an effective acceptance of papal authority to determine doctrine on the basis of the Petrine succession in the Roman see. However, perusal of the discussions between these two communions suggests that this temptation is more strongly felt by the church of Greece than in other quarters. (One should note, even there, the negative reaction in 1995 of the monastic council on Mount Athos to what it considered excessive pro-Monophysite eirenicism.[92]) Theologians in the Russian tradition, in particular, are wary of it. They can point out, first, that, when all is said and done, one can hardly gainsay the acceptance of the *Tome* not only at Chalcedon but at subsequent Christological councils; second, that it is impossibly narrowing of the scope of tradition to maintain that only Cyrilline Christology can represent the faith of the Church; and third, that Leo's attempt to safeguard the integrity of the manhood is in fact more successful than Cyril's.[93]

This brings us to the *second* issue in relations with the Monophysites: the ecclesiological question. Professor (now Bishop) John Zizioulas has questioned the thesis that an agreed statement of doctrine would suffice to restore Christendom's unity. This thesis originates, he points out, in the confessional "model" of the Church found in classical Protestantism.[94] For the Great Church, by contrast, belonging to the Church is not just a matter of what you believe. It is a matter, also, of who you are in communion with. At Chalcedonian councils, and notably the Sixth Ecumenical Council, Constantinople III, in 681, Monophysite doctors and bishops were anathematised and declared to belong no more to the Church of all the ages. Similarly, at Monophysite synods, the same has been done in regard to

[92] "Chronique des Eglises: Athos", *Irén.* 68, no. 3 (1995): pp. 400–404.

[93] See the contributions of the late Father George Florovsky in Gregorios et al., *Does Chalcedon Divide or Unite?* p. 48, and of the archpriest Vitaly Borovoy, ibid., pp. 74–75.

[94] J. Zizioulas, "Ecclesiological Issues Inherent in the Relations between Eastern Chalcedonian and Oriental Non-Chalcedonian Churches", ibid., pp. 138–56.

Chalcedonians. The problem of rehabilitating those long dead to whom the Church's communion was denied is a properly ecclesiological problem—and not simply a disciplinary one following on the conclusion of an agreed doctrinal statement. (Its difficulties figured prominently in the Athonite rebuff to the Oriental Orthodox cited above.) In 1989 a response to this problem was made by another Chalcedonian Orthodox theologian, Father John Meyendorff.[95] Pointing out that, in the Orthodox Church, there are occasional examples of the veneration of non-Orthodox saints, such as the Nestorian Isaac of Nineveh or the anti-Chalcedonian Peter the Iberian (a Georgian bishop of Gaza in Palestine), as well as instances of the Non-Chalcedonian veneration of specifically Chalcedonian saints, such as the Alexandrian patriarch John the Merciful, Meyendorff argued that there could be regional veneration of the Monophysite doctors. This veneration, he wrote, would "acknowledge their merits, not their faults, which are left to the judgment of God". The issue is highly pertinent to the 1990 recommendation of the Third Official Meeting of the Oriental Orthodox–Eastern Orthodox Dialogue, renewed at the successor meeting of 1993, that mutual anathemas should be lifted. As yet there is no sign of this proposal being carried out.

The Catholic Church has a considerably fuller experience of the problem of the anathematised than do the Orthodox, owing to the existence of the Uniate churches.[96] My impression is that, in Catholic practice, a distinction is drawn between those heretical doctors who were partly responsible for schism, although their lives and teaching may have been admirable in other respects, and the rest of the holy dead, esteemed as saints by a particular schismatic tradition. Thus, in the Syrian liturgy used by those Jacobites who have returned to Roman communion, Severus of Antioch is not called on as a saint, though his name is mentioned with respect during the liturgical action—as a visit to the procuratorial church of the Syrian

[95] J. Meyendorff, "Chalcedonians and Non-Chalcedonians: The Last Steps to Unity", *St. Vladimir's Theological Quarterly* 33, no. 4 (1989): 319–30.

[96] Cf. Y. M.-J. Congar, O.P., "A propos des saints canonisés dans les Eglises orthodoxes", *RSR* 82 (1940): 240–59.

Catholic patriarch in Rome, Santa Maria in Campo Marzio, will confirm. Again, Catholics of the Byzantine rite do, I believe, commemorate saints canonized by the Orthodox during the period of schism, and even dedicate parish churches to them, like the one recently erected under the patronage of Seraphim of Sarov (a nineteenth-century Russian hermit) in Toronto, Canada, but I have not heard of Uniate veneration of an Orthodox saint instrumental in the making or continuance of schism, such as the fifteenth-century Greek bishop Mark of Ephesus. If Eastern Catholic practice is consistent in these respects, then a significant distinction is being drawn that could help us to resolve the difficulty identified by Zizioulas. Schismatic saints are acceptable; saints who caused schisms are a contradiction in terms. However, even those partly responsible for the creation or conservation of schismatic situations may be deemed worthy of respect, and that in a liturgical setting, at the climax of the Church's life. If Catholic practice is not homogeneous here, it might be helpful to make it so.

The ecclesiological problem does not, however, end there. More: are the Monophysites to be asked to accept explicitly all the subsequent general councils of the Church—the three others after Chalcedon accepted by both Catholics and Orthodox, and the fourteen beyond that accepted by the Catholic Church alone? Three approaches are possible here. First, one could simply invite the Monophysites to subscribe to the dogmatic definitions of all these councils in turn. Second, one could say that, so long as they do not deny what these councils affirm, they need not be pressed so to subscribe, on the grounds that they are not in a situation of rebellion against councils to which, historically, they were (with the exception of Florence) never summoned. Third, one could maintain that the return of these historic particular churches to Catholic communion should bring with it a re-reception of the councils in question, namely, the producing of a common interpretation of these councils in which the bishops who participated in them, the divines who influenced them, and the popes who ratified them would become the venerated "fathers" of the (erstwhile) Monophysites also. This is certainly the most satisfactory of the three "solutions", and I shall return to the idea of conciliar re-reception, in the context, more specifically, of the Chalcedonian Orthodox, at the end of this study.

But since these councils are, in Catholicism, defined in terms of, if not convocation, then at least ratification by the Holy See, we come next, on the ecclesiological side, to the matter of the bishop of Rome. Since the time of Chalcedon, the Latin church has witnessed a massive development in the theology of the Petrine ministry of the Roman bishop, coming to its climax in the dogmatic constitution *Pastor aeternus* of the First Vatican Council. Of course, one must distinguish between the rôle of the Roman bishop in the Latin church proper as its patriarch (even if, since 2006, this title does not belong to his official style) and his claims to a more generalised authority operating as need demands (and therefore occasionally) in the wider Church. Yet many Orientals seem to see no need for a centre of unity for the episcopate at all, holding that the Holy Spirit gives the episcopate the only unity it needs when actualising the sacrament of orders, whereby all become bishops in a single Church, no matter what conflicts of jurisdiction history may throw up. However, it is surely clear that in practice, under the pressure of such conflicts, all sense of solidarity seeps away. It will be interesting to see what tendencies manifest themselves in the proposed document "The Nature, the Constitution and the Mission of the Church" of which a draft revision was discussed early in 2008 at the meeting of the commission for theological dialogue between the Catholic Church and the Oriental Orthodox churches that was held at the monastery of St. Ephrem at Ma'arrat Saydnaya in Syria.

The rôle of the Roman bishop as centre of unity cannot be separated, historically, from the periodically recurring unionist movements in, and from, Oriental churches in schism from the papal church. Here we touch the delicate issue of the Uniate communities, considered not so much as helpful examples of reintegrated traditions—as in the matter of what to do with heretically minded saints—but, rather, in the way in which many non-Catholic Orientals see them still, namely as stumbling blocks. The whole purpose of the Uniate churches in Ethiopia, Egypt, Syria, Armenia, and India was to provide bridges to unity. The aim was to show that everything worthwhile in the tradition of the Orientals could survive in Roman communion. But the way in which this aim was actualised left, in many cases, a good deal to be desired. One thinks, for instance, of the union synod of Diamper in 1599, which determined on the destruction of all the records of the preunion Syrian church lest they be continuing sources of Nestorian influence. Unwittingly, the synod completed the work of the Turkic invasions in the Mesopotamian homeland of the Assyrian Christians, which, circa 1400, put paid to the archival remains of the mother community. On the other hand, not every onslaught against "Latinisation" can be justified. One important aspect of inclusion within Catholic communion is precisely openness to what other traditions within the Church can offer. If Westerners can learn from the riches of the East, should Orientals reject everything that originates in the treasury of the Christian West?

Finally, there is the question of the current tendency towards a low Christology in the contemporary Western Catholic church. Even leaving aside those writings that are manifestly abusive in their failure to meet the standard set by Nicene orthodoxy, namely, in affirming the full Godhead of Jesus Christ, some of the most respected Christological treatises in the Latin church today are heavily Antiochene in approach. Thus, for example, Walter Kasper's *Jesus der Christus* maintains that there are two persons within the total reality of the Word incarnate, though it regards the human person as heteronomous, that is, as non-autonomous, vis-à-vis the divine person. If carefully handled—that is, where human personhood is treated as personality in the sense, effectively, of individualized soul—such an approach need not be heterodox (as already suggested in relation to the Christology of Išoyahb II) but (as this historical comparison itself indicates) the general Christological approach that it exemplifies in the end produced Nestorianism. Of course, one could also argue that the alternative "anhypostatic" Christology, in which there is no human person in Christ, exemplifies the general Christological approach that in the end produced Eutychianism. But the conversations between the Chalcedonian

and Non-Chalcedonian Orthodox sometimes throw up the suggestion that Western Catholic Christology is increasingly Nestorian
and that this is the dead end to which the *Tome* of Leo leads. It
can be argued that the measures taken by the Congregation for the
Doctrine of the Faith, in matters Christological, against such Western theologians as Hans Küng and Edward Schillebeeckx derive in
part from the papal sense that relations with the separated East will
deteriorate even further unless the Latin church silences its own
neo-Nestorians and so puts its own house in order.[97] Of course,
the prevailing thinking in John Paul II's pontificate was not so much
in terms of the Monophysites as in that of the Eastern Orthodox,
and above all of the church of Russia, which must play a vital part
in any overall ecclesial strategy for the future of Europe, and not
of Europe only. But a secondary strand may be to draw in the
churches of the East so as to redress the effects of theological liberalism, and of Neo-Protestantism, in the Latin church since the
Second Vatican Council.

In all this, one must be careful to have a strategy rather than simply a tactic. Tactically, a move towards the Monophysites is a move
away from the Nestorians, and vice versa. One cannot on Monday
try to win over the Monophysites by cursing Nestorius, and on Tues-
day try to win over the Nestorians by doing the same to Dioscorus![98] But strategically, it should be possible to work out what are
the limits of an acceptable Christological pluralism in a Church that
is not simply a Cyrilline Church, or a Leonine Church, or an Antiochene Church either. The *pax dogmatica* that we seek must be true
peace, based on a justice and coherence that stem from the ethos

[97] For an overview of the difficulties that recent Western Christologians have felt
in regard to Chalcedon, see W. Kasper, *Jesus der Christus* (Mainz, 1974), pp. 16–26.

[98] Thus while the Catholic Church may be in officially recognised dialogue with
both the Church of Egypt and the Church of the East, the proposal that the latter
should be admitted to the Middle East Council of Churches was blocked in 1999 by
the former. The Coptic Orthodox synod has also refused to consider a draft of a
common declaration on Christology produced by theologians of the two churches
involved in 1995. See S. Brock, "The Syriac Churches in Ecumenical Dialogue on
Christology", in O'Mahony, *Eastern Christianity*, pp. 44–65.

and logic of Christology itself.[99] In practice, this means asking: To what degree can we permit Christians in actual or prospective union with the see of Rome to speak of a twofold personality in our Lord on the one hand and, on the other, allow them to speak of his single theandric or divine-human nature after the Incarnation? In other words, what degree of linguistic or conceptual divergence from Chalcedon can be regarded as compatible with the dogmatic intention of Chalcedon—which was to affirm the ultimate oneness of Christ's personal reality and the authenticity of both its divine and its human expression?

[99] Stimulated by Patriarch Denkha IV's visit to Rome in 1984, the Vienna foundation Pro oriente launched just such an enterprise in 1994—albeit limited, partly as a result of Coptic objections, to the Syriac-speaking churches: Chalcedonian (Catholic), non-Ephesian, and Non-Chalcedonian. See S. Brock, "The Syriac Churches and Dialogue with the Catholic Church", *Heythrop Journal* 45 (2004): 466–76, and for a fuller theological analysis, A. Olmi, *Il consenso cristologico tra le chiese calcedonesi e non calcedonesi (1964–1996)* (Rome, 2003). In 1998, a meeting of Oriental Orthodox patriarchs convened by Pope Shenouda decided that in the future, dialogue with other Christian bodies would have to be by common decision of all the Oriental Orthodox churches together.

Bibliography

General

Chaillot C., and A. Belopovsky. *Towards Unity: The Theological Dialogue between the Orthodox Church and the Oriental Orthodox Churches.* Geneva, 1998.

Frend, W. H. C. *The Rise of the Monophysite Movement: Chapters in the History of the Church in the Fifth and Sixth Centuries.* Cambridge, 1972.

Girgis, W. A. *The Christological Teaching of the Non-Chalcedonian Churches.* Cairo, 1962. (In English and Arabic.)

Gregorios, P., W. H. Lazareth, and N. A. Nissiotis, eds. *Does Chalcedon Divide or Unite? Towards Convergence in Orthodox Christology.* Geneva, 1981. (This volume contains the four Eastern Orthodox–Oriental Orthodox agreed statements from the "Non-Official consultations" of Aarhus [1964], Bristol [1967], Geneva [1970], and Addis Ababa [1971], together with some supplementary essays.)

Grillmeier, A., S.J. *Christ in Christian Tradition.* Vol. 2, *From the Council of Chalcedon (451) to Gregory the Great (590–604).* Part 1, *Reception and Contradiction: The Development of the Discussion about Chalcedon from 451 to the Beginning of the Reign of Justinian.* Eng. trans. London, 1987.

Jugie, M. "La primauté romaine d'après les premiers théologiens monophysites". *EO* 33 (1934): 181–83.

Lebon, J. "La Christologie du monophysisme syrien". In *Das Konzil von Chalkedon* I. Edited by H. Grillmeier and A. Bacht. Würzburg, 1951.

———. *Le Monophysisme sévérien: Étude historique littéraire et théologique sur la résistance monophysite au Concile de Chalcédoine jusqu'à la constitution de l'Eglise jacobite.* Louvain, 1909; reprinted New York, 1978.

Luce, A. A. *Monophysitism, Past and Present: A Study in Christology.* London, 1913.

McGuckin, J. A. *St. Cyril of Alexandria: The Christological Controversy, Its History, Theology, and Texts.* Leiden, 1994.

Meyendorff, J. *Imperial Unity and Christian Divisions: The Church 450–680 A.D.* Crestwood, N.Y., 1989.

Pro oriente. *Five Vienna Consultations between Theologians in the Oriental Orthodox and the Roman Catholic Church: Selected Papers.* Vienna, 1993.

Sellers, R. V. *The Council of Chalcedon: A Historical and Doctrinal Survey.* London, 1961.

Vries, W. de. "La conception de l'Eglise chez les Syriens séparés de Rome". *L'Orient syrien* 2 (1957): 111–24.

Wigram, W. A. *The Separation of the Monophysites.* London, 1923.

Egypt

Atiya, A. S. *The Coptic Encyclopedia.* 8 vols. New York, 1991.

Bell, H. I. *Egypt from Alexander the Great to the Arab Conquests.* Oxford, 1948.

Cannuyer, C. *Les Coptes.* Turnhout, 1990.

Chauleur, S. *Histoire des Coptes.* Paris, 1960.

Cramer, M. *Das christlich-koptische Ägypten einst und heute: Eine Orientierung.* Wiesbaden, 1959.

El-'Itr, F. *The Coptic Nation and Its Orthodox Church.* Cairo, 1953.

Hamilton, A. *The Copts and the West 1439–1922: The European Discovery of the Egyptian Church.* Oxford, 2006.

Hardy, E. R. *Christian Egypt: Church and People.* New York, 1952.

Malaty, T. *Introduction to the Coptic Orthodox Church.* Toronto, 1986.

Wakin, E. *A Lonely Minority: The Modern History of Egypt's Copts.* New York, 1963.

Watson, J. H. *Among the Copts.* Brighton, 2000.

Watterson, B. *Coptic Egypt.* Edinburgh, 1989.

Westermann, W. L. et al. *Coptic Egypt.* New York, 1944.

Worrell, W. H. *A Short Account of the Copts.* Ann Arbor, Mich., 1945.

Ethiopia

Coulbeaux, J.-B. *Histoire politique et religieuse d'Abyssinie: depuis les temps les plus reculés jusqu'à l'avènement de Ménélick II.* Paris, 1929.

Harden, J. M. *An Introduction to Ethiopic Christian Literature.* London, 1926.

Hyatt, H. M. *The Church of Abyssinia.* London, 1928.

O'Leary, De Lacy. *The Ethiopian Church.* London, 1936.

Paulos, A. *The Ethiopian Orthodox Tewahedo Church: Faith, Order of Worship and Ecumenical Relations.* Addis Ababa, 1995.

Uqbit, T. *Current Christological Positions of Ethiopian Orthodox Theologians.* Rome, 1973.

Syria

Baumstark, A. *Geschichte der syrischen Literatur.* Bonn, 1932.

Devreesse, R. *Le patriarcat d'Antioche depuis la paix de l'Eglise jusqu'à la conquête arabe.* Paris, 1945.

Graf, G. *Geschichte der christlichen arabischen Literatur.* Vatican City, 1947.

Kaweran, P. *Die jakobitische Kirche im Zeitalter der syrischen Renaissance.* Berlin, 1955.

Mounager, J. *Les synodes syriens jacobites.* Beirut, 1963.

Ortiz de Urbina, J. *Patrologia syriaca.* Rome, 1958.

Sélis, C. *Les Syriens orthodoxes et catholiques.* Tournai, 1988.

Ziade, I. "Syrienne (Eglise)." In *DTC.* Vol. 14, pt. 2, cols. 3017–88.

Armenia

Arpee, L. *History of Armenian Christianity, from the Beginning to Our Own Time.* New York, 1946.

Dédéyan, G., ed., *Les Arméniens: Histoire d'une chrétienté.* Toulouse, 1990.

Ormanian, M. *The Church of Armenia.* London, 1955.

Sarkissian, K. *A Brief Introduction to Armenian Literature.* London, 1960.

India

Brown, L. W. *The Indian Christians of St. Thomas.* Cambridge, 1956.

Menachery, G., ed. *The Saint Thomas Christian Encyclopaedia of India.* Trichur, 1973.

Navakatesh, J. T. *Die syrisch-orthodoxe Kirche der südindischen Thomas-Christen.* Würzburg, 1967.

Perumatil, H. E., C.M.I., and E. R. Hambye, S.J., eds. *Christianity in India: A History in Ecumenical Perspective.* Allepey, 1972.

Tisserant, E. *Eastern Christianity in India.* Eng. trans. London, 1957.

4

The Estrangement between Rome and Constantinople, I: General Trends

The rest of this book will be concerned with the schism between Rome and the Chalcedonian Orthodox—the bulk of Eastern Christians, and all those who remain once the Assyrian and Non-Chalcedonian Orthodox churches have been surveyed. The rupture between Rome and Orthodoxy may not unfairly be called a separation between Rome and *Constantinople* for two reasons. First, Constantinople is, for Chalcedonians, the Rome of the East—though this bald statement will be, in a moment, considerably qualified. Second, in its historical development the schism between Rome and the Chalcedonian East was, above all, a sundering of the West from the Byzantine church, of which the see and court of Constantinople formed the energising centre. It was, to a large degree, a quarrel between Latins and Greeks, even though the other churches of the Orthodox world followed the suit played by Constantinople and (from the Catholic viewpoint) entered into schism—not necessarily but by a "domino effect" of an historically explicable kind.

The Structure of Orthodoxy

From these brief opening remarks, two correct inferences may at once be drawn. First, the Orthodox Church is not a unitary church. It is a communion of sister churches joined by sharing the same faith and the same sacraments. Second, the position of the patriarch of Constantinople is by no means fully analogous to that of the Roman pope in Catholicism, despite his title of "ecumenical" or "universal" patriarch. The origins of that title are a grey area, connected, most probably, with the desire of the early fifth-century imperial court to boost the prestige of the church of the capital city. While eventually all other Orthodox churches ratified the title implicitly by their own epistolatory usage, the canonical and theological weight to be accorded it remains very much in dispute among them.[1] We cannot define the Eastern Orthodox Church as all those in communion with Constantinople, in the way that we may legitimately define the Catholic Church as all those in communion with Rome. So far as the Orthodox are concerned, it is perfectly possible that the church of Constantinople could lapse from Orthodox communion tomorrow. In that case, the church of Alexandria would, presumably, become the first see in the ecclesiastical *taxis*, being next in honour after Constantinople itself.

That the Orthodox Church is not a unitary church and has no permanent centre of communion and authority renders it a prey to difficulties over jurisdiction. These jurisdictional disputes can lead, and have in fact led, to ruptures in eucharistic communion among the Orthodox themselves. Thus for instance, until 2006 the Russian Church in Exile—sometimes called the "Synodal Church" since it originated at the 1921 Karlovtsy Synod, in Serbia, and more recently the "Russian Orthodox Church Abroad"—was not in communion with the patriarchate of Moscow. In, for example, the United States of America, two sets of Orthodox lived side by side but without intercommunion: namely, those who belonged to the metropolia of the Russian Church in Exile, and those whose allegiance was to the "Orthodox Church of [North] America", given self-government by the Moscow patriarchate in 1970.[2] Nevertheless, both jurisdictions

---

[1] For a Russian perspective, see e.g., S. Troitsky, "The Limits of Authority of the Constantinopolitan Patriarchate over the Diaspora", *Journal of the Moscow Patriarchate* 11 (1947): 34–45. For Troitsky, the canonicoecclesiological theory currently held by the ecumenical throne is the creation of patriarch Meletios (Mataxakis) in 1922!

[2] These grave anomalies do not go unnoticed by all Orthodox. At a 1968 consultation at the institute of the ecumenical patriarchate at Chambésy, near Geneva, speakers painted "a sad picture of nationalistic divisions, political struggle and canonical disorder": K. T. Ware, "A Conference on the Problems of the Orthodox Diaspora", *ECR* 2 (1968–1969): 185–89.

would be found in the very useful handbook *Orthodoxia* published biennially by the Ostkirchliches Institut at Regensburg, providing comprehensive coverage of the different Orthodox (and also Oriental Orthodox) churches throughout the world. Nor indeed have all the clergy and lay faithful of the Synodal church rallied to the recent reconciliation, whose own terms imply a certain degree of provisionality. Again, in Ukraine since the 1990s, Orthodoxy is found in three competing jurisdictions: the Moscow patriarchate church, inherited from the tsardom and the Communist period; the 1921 breakaway body calling itself the "Ukrainian Autocephalous Church", whose origins are disfigured by an attempted presbyteral ordination of its first bishop, Basil Lypkivsky, and which was accepted into communion by Constantinople in 1995; and finally, the church body arising from the rupture whereby the Moscow patriarchate metropolitan of Kiev, Philaret Denisenko, established in 1991 a "Ukrainian Orthodox Church—Kievan Patriarchate" against the will of his own mother church. Patriarch Bartholomew I of Constantinople also entered into communion with this grouping, declaring at the Phanar in the spring of 1995 that these actions would serve the beginning of a "great healing" of the Church in Ukraine—a claim hotly disputed by his brother of Moscow. (It needs to be remembered that in its prepatriarchal period, Moscow achieved ecclesial eminence when in 1326 the metropolitan Peter of Kiev and All Russia took up residence there: autonomy for the Kievan church naturally worries Muscovites.) Temporary or local schisms are regarded by many Orthodox as a regrettable but virtually inevitable fact of life, something which the Church can and must take in her stride. There is truth, therefore, in the suggestion that the Orthodox regard heresy as far graver than schism, whereas Catholics reverse this order of priorities, tolerating heretical opinions (often) for the sake of unity. For the student of Orthodoxy, however, the jurisdictional confusion often regnant among the Orthodox churches can make life difficult.

There are generally reckoned to be sixteen fully self-governing churches within the Orthodox family today: the technical term is "autocephalous", meaning able to provide themselves with their own head.[3] Orthodox canonists accept that the term "autocephaly" is not found in the ancient Church but argue that the reality intended by the word was well known in the patristic epoch. Early councils do refer to groups of local churches empowered to resolve internal problems on their own authority. These circumscriptions, when stabilised, coincided with the civil dioceses of the Roman Empire, the five great jurisdictions or patriarchates, the "Pentarchy". (More anciently, they were, rather, the smaller units of provinces.)[4] However, these did not constitute, evidently, *national* entities—whereas, for modern Orthodox canon law, the daughter church of a region located outside the state boundaries where its mother church operates has the right to ecclesiastical independence, provided that it has enough bishops to continue the apostolic succession (namely, according to the fourth canon of the Council of Nicaea, three), and provided

[3] Namely: Constantinople, Alexandria, Antioch, Jerusalem (i.e., the four remaining patriarchates of the Pentarchy, Rome being lapsed), Cyprus (431), Russia (1448? 1589), Sinai (1575? 1782), Greece (1833? 1850), Romania (1865? 1885), Bulgaria (1870? 1955), Serbia (1879), Georgia (1917? 1943*), Czechoslovakia (1920?–1946, 1951), Albania (1922? 1937), Poland (1924?–1948, 1951*), and North America (1970*). To these must be added two other groups: those churches, technically termed "autonomous", who have limited autocephaly, and a collection of mavericks: (i) Autonomous churches: Finland (1921*–1939, 1957*), Japan (1947?), China (1957*), Macedonia (1960?), and Hungary (situation confused); (ii) Alia: Russian Church in Exile, Ukrainian Church in Exile, Byelorussian Church in Exile, and Ruthenian Church in Exile. Sigla: ?—Claim to autocephaly by local church; *—Autocephaly/autonomy granted or regranted or revised terms by Moscow rather than by Constantinople. Cf. T. Ware, *The Orthodox Church* (Harmondsworth, 1963, 1967), pp. 13–15, who maintains, however, that, thanks to the presence of such nonnational bodies as the church of Sinai (effectively, the monastery of Saint Catherine there), the principle of modern Orthodoxy cannot *strictly* be called national. Canonical realignments rapidly produce changes in such listings, and these may be controversial. A regularly updated account, which also includes reference to such irregular bodies as Old Ritualists and Old Calendarists, has been provided in the last quarter of the twentieth century by Ronald Roberson, C.S.P., under the title *The Eastern Christian Churches: A Brief Survey*, 6th ed. (Rome, 1999). He finds four categories: autocephalous churches, autonomous churches, canonical churches under Constantinople, and churches of irregular status; thus *The Eastern Christian Churches*, pp. 43–138.

[4] P. Duprey, P.B., "La structure synodale de l'Eglise dans la théologie orientale", *POC* 20 (1970): 152–82.

also that it originated in a canonically proper way from a mother church that was itself autocephalous.

In other words, modern Orthodoxy has accepted, not without some misgivings, the idea of the national church. In the ancient Church, by contrast, it would be juster to regard autocephaly as rather territorially based than nationally based, though the manner of implantation of the Gospel (frequently through the good offices of local rulers) sometimes produced anticipations of the later national church idea. Technically, the present constitution of Orthodoxy turns on a misunderstanding of an early canon: canon 34 in the "Apostolic Collection", a book of rules for Church life and governance, drawn eclectically from early sources and standing first in all Oriental canonical collections.[5] According to this canon: "The bishops of every *ethnos* must acknowledge him who is first among them." However, as the Orthodox canonist A. A. Bogolepov has pointed out, *ethnos* here does not signify nation in the later sense.[6] The 341 Council of Antioch, of great legislative if less dogmatic importance, explains "nation" here as a Roman imperial eparchy, or province: in other words, the main subdivision of the civil diocese. *Ethnos* in this context, and at this date, certainly does not mean a body of people bonded together by blood, language, and custom. Yet this later sense of nationhood crept into the affairs of the Eastern churches comparatively early. Already in the tenth century, in its premodern dress it affected the attitudes of such newly christianised peoples as the Bulgars and Serbs toward the authority of the patriarch of Constantinople.

The Orthodox Church as we have it, then, is built upon a combination of the ancient idea of a *taxis*, or hierarchical ordering, of patriarchal or metropolitical sees, with the mediaeval and modern notion of a national church. The first church to be permanently formed in this way was the church of Russia, which declared its independence in 1448, using as pretext the acceptance of the Council

---

[5] C. Kirch, *Enchiridion fontium historiae ecclesiasticae antiquae* (Barcelona, 1947), no. 697.
[6] A. Bogolepov, *Toward an American Orthodox Church: The Establishment of an Autocephalous Orthodox Church* (New York, 1965).

of Florence by the Byzantines in 1439. With the steady disintegration of the Ottoman Empire in the course of the nineteenth century, the churches of Greece, Serbia, Bulgaria, and Romania also broke away from the church of Constantinople and became self-governing. After the First World War, further grants of autocephaly were allowed, chiefly at the expense of the church of Russia. Sometimes, however, this did not amount to full autocephaly but only what was termed "autonomy"—a situation where the chief bishop of a church must be confirmed by its former mother church prior to taking office. On occasion, grants of autocephaly were controverted, so that a newly autocephalous church was obliged to return to its mother church.[7] Needless to say, political considerations bulked large here. Thus, in the wake of the Second World War, the government of the USSR, succeeding to the ambitions of the tsardom, forced the church of Poland to accept reincorporation into the Moscow patriarchate. Both world wars swelled the rate of emigration from traditionally Orthodox lands and produced a new complication: the problem of the Orthodox diaspora. This was especially acute in America where a variety of European and Asian churches had established missions, parishes, and dioceses without reciprocal reference since the end of the eighteenth century. The organisational chaos of the North American Orthodox led in 1970 to the formation of a new autocephalous church, the Church of [North] America, from which, however, the Russian Church in Exile, as already mentioned, stayed aloof, as did the Greek communities, which remain under an exarch of the ecumenical patriarch.

The structure of the Orthodox Church constitutes the gravest problem facing the Orthodox today, and not just the knottiest problem facing the student of Orthodoxy. We may say that, if the rejection of the Council of Florence marks, from the Catholic standpoint, the definitive entry of the Orthodox churches into (partial) schism, then, from the beginning of its (partly) separate life until the nineteenth

[7] For an example of the problems involved in such disputes, see S. K. Pavlowitch, "The Church of Macedonia: 'Limited Autocephaly' or Schism?", *Sob.* 9, no. 1 (1987): 42–59.

century, Orthodoxy's own vision of itself as a unity-in-plurality has largely disappeared in practice. Essentially, what we find between 1453 and, say, 1800 are two megachurches, that of Russia, protected by the tsardom, and that of Constantinople, upon which the Ottoman Porte conferred rights of superintendence over all Orthodox congregations within the Turkish Empire. The church of Russia dominated all the Orthodox that the tsardom could swallow—and that was not a few, since tsarist Russia had been an expansionist power from the time of Peter the Great onwards. The church of Constantinople dominated the rest, and, with the support of the Ottoman government, made and unmade the patriarchs of the other ancient sees, Alexandria, Antioch, and Jerusalem. Had this situation continued through the nineteenth and twentieth centuries—had the political history of Europe and the Near East been different—there would be only two significant variants on Orthodox church life today.

What actually happened, however, was that each of these two great churches used political events to break up the ecclesiastical empire of the other. At first, in the nineteenth century, this meant the Russian church encouraging rebellion against Constantinople. Through Russian pressure on the Turkish government, Jerusalem (1845), Alexandria (1899), and Antioch (1899) regained their independence. Through Russian influence, the Greeks and the other Balkan peoples won a self-government both political and ecclesiastical. Thus the church of Greece became autocephalous in 1850, Romania in 1865 (confirmed in 1885), Bulgaria in 1870 (not confirmed till 1953!), and Serbia in 1879. In the twentieth century, however, the boot was on the other foot. The church of Constantinople took advantage of the weakness of Russia after the Bolshevik Revolution, and of Russia's international isolation, to carve off huge chunks of the old patriarchate of Moscow, creating autocephalous churches in Georgia (1917), Czechoslovakia (1920), and Poland (1924). As already observed, some of these developments were unravelled by the emergence of the Soviet Union as a great power after the Second World War. Nevertheless, it is the rivalry of Constantinople and Moscow, the Second and Third Romes, which has produced the present multiplicity of Orthodox churches. Thus in 1996 Moscow and Constantinople suspended for a while their relations (including eucharistic communion) after Constantinople had created an autonomous metropolitanate in Estonia, an act Moscow considered an invasion of its prerogatives. The Russian Orthodox church is by far the most numerically potent of the churches of the Orthodox family, with some 81 million members, of whom 51 million are described as practising. (Compare 20 million in Romania, of which 14 million are active; 15.5 million in Greece, with maybe 11 million active adherents; 7.5 million in the patriarchate of Serbia, with 4 million practising; and in Bulgaria some 6 million formal adherents, of whom a little over 3.5 million are said to practise.) If one adds to the total numbers in the Moscow patriarchate in the Russian Federation, those Orthodox in Ukraine who either are or, in the opinion of the patriarch of Moscow, ought to be under his *omophorion* (jurisdiction), one would arrive at the huge total of 109 million faithful, with an estimated 70 million active worshippers. Even when one factors in the diasporas over whom the patriarch of Constantinople, from his highly marginalised position in Turkey, claims canonical oversight, these figures render the church of Russia, in comparison with the church of Constantinople, truly a "megachurch". I shall return to these political and—above all—*national* issues in the conclusion to this book. Meanwhile, having established who the modern Orthodox are, it is time to turn to the origins of the division between Rome and (in the first place) the *Byzantine East*.

Differences in Culture

The matrix of the schism between the Catholic and Orthodox churches must be sought, in the first place, in the phenomenon of cultural estrangement between Latin West and Byzantine East.[8] The idea that the Church's life and faith are always embodied in a culture is a pervasive one in the later twentieth century. Two of the most influential pastoral concepts at work in modern Catholicism, for instance, are those of *aggiornamento*, "bringing up to date", and indigenisation, or "going native". The subject of such *aggiornamento* and

[8] G. Every, *Misunderstandings between East and West* (London, 1965), pp. 26–29.

indigenisation is not the faith of the Church but, rather, the expression or embodiment of that faith in culture. A culture is that tangle of ideas, images, and institutions within whose interweaving strands we live, move, and have our being. The Word of God, becoming man in Jesus of Nazareth, accepted, among the limitations that involved, the need to express himself in terms of the ideas, images, and institutions of the culture of first-century Palestine. The Church of that Word incarnate is affected by the same necessity. Whether willingly or unwillingly, she has to make her way by means of the normal methods of human life and intercourse in this world. When we study Church history, we are studying the manifold ways in which the Church has incarnated her faith in culture. Some cultures, or so we may feel in retrospect, have been more open to the expression of one aspect of that faith, others to the expression of another. Part of the intellectual excitement of Church history consists in seeing how the Church, with greater or less success, manages to communicate her message in very different human environments. These differences in culture are not always an enrichment for the Church. They can also be a problem, a handicap. When different local churches are habituated to markedly different ideas, images, and institutions in the embodying of faith, this may threaten their communion one with another. As we know from our experience of human relationships at the ordinary level, difficulties in communication generate misunderstandings; misunderstandings produce hostility, hostility leads to the total breakdown of communication. This is a perfectly possible analysis of what transpired in the relations between the Roman Church and the churches of the Byzantine-Slav East.

By enumerating some important factors in the cultural engagement between East and West, we shall be considering, in effect, the disparity in the overall contexts in which doctrine was understood theologically by Greek East and Latin West during the centuries that produced the schism.

The first and most obvious difference between Rome and Byzantium was *language*. In the first two centuries of the Christian era, educated people in the cities of the West could understand and write Greek. Similarly, in the East, officials and soldiers knew Latin. But the diffusion of the two languages followed very different patterns. Latin was essentially the language of the imperial administration, on the one hand, and of the Western cities on the other. Greek, on the other hand, was the language of culture throughout the Mediterranean world. Because of the link between Greek and cultural sophistication, the Greek language in its written form developed in an increasingly specialised way. Unlike New Testament Greek, which is simple, almost proleterian, the Greek of the lower classes, and, perhaps, most notably of the ports, patristic and Byzantine Greek is a marriage between this common tongue, the *koinê*, and the classical literary language often referred to as Attic. Owing to this "elevation" of linguistic quality, users of Byzantine Greek came to identify their speech with civilised standards of discourse at large and to hold in contempt, accordingly, those who could neither read nor speak it. When in the West the knowledge of Greek failed, not only did this impede communication, it also made Eastern snobbery a compulsive habit.[9] Only in scattered periods were there men available in the West to turn the Greek fathers into Latin, particularly in the fourth, ninth, and twelfth centuries. After the twelfth century, Latin wariness of Greek theology was such that, while technically the Byzantine theologians could have been translated (as people translated the ancient philosophers and Church fathers), no one cared to do the work.

At the same time, it was becoming harder for the Greeks to grasp Latin. The Greeks might call themselves *rômaioi*, "Romans", but the use of the Latin language was not considered an essential feature of such *romanità*. On the contrary, at the very moment of the Christianisation of the Roman Empire, when Providence gave it the task

[9] Cf. D. M. Nicol's description of Byzantine intellectuals as "the perfected products of an intensive training in 'Byzantinism'. They were the members of an exclusive club in which the rules were determined by cultured manners and sophisticated language, by the initiation into a style." *Church and Society in the Last Centuries of Byzantium* (Cambridge, 1979), p. 61. Nicol makes it clear that his comments are not restricted to the fourteenth and fifteenth centuries. With regard to the period up to Photius and slightly beyond, he draws the reader's attention to the comments of P. Lemerle, *Le premier humanisme byzantin: Notes et remarques sur l'enseignement et culture à Byzance des origines au Xe siècle* (Paris, 1971), pp. 300–307.

of bringing peace and the Gospel to the entire inhabited world, its capital had been transferred from the old Rome on the Tiber to Constantinople, the new Rome on the Bosphorus. The Greeks retained an interest, both civil and religious, in Old Rome, realising that the New Rome was historically dependent on its predecessor. But they had no desire to keep up its language.[10] Or rather, the only people interested in so doing were those members of the imperial circle who believed in following a Western policy: recovering, when the time was ripe, those Western provinces of the empire that had passed under barbarian rule. After Justinian I (483–565), this was never feasible politics again.

As a result, little Latin Christian literature was turned into Greek. Hardly any Augustine was translated until the fourteenth century,[11] and in the same period "Latinophrone", Latin-tending, theologians with "unionist" convictions began to take an interest in the thought of Thomas Aquinas. When Westerners went east, the possibilities of communication were limited. Admittedly, this situation changed with the Latin conquest of Constantinople during the Fourth Crusade of 1204. Large parts of the Byzantine Empire fell under Latin occupation; some areas, like the Ionian Islands, did not return to Greek government until the nineteenth century. In such places, Byzantines were obliged to learn Latin, or, more probably, such Latin-derived languages as Italian, for the sake of a lingua franca. But this was precisely so as to correspond, or converse, with those generally regarded as enemies—or whose position, at any rate, was widely resented.

From the disparity of language a number of more specific consequences arose, of fateful significance for the divergence of doctrine in the two traditions. For instance, in ecclesiology Greek had no equivalent for the Latin *infallibilitas* or for the term *vicarius*, both crucial to the elucidation of Western claims for the Petrine office. Again, the Greek term for "cause", *aitia*, suggested the idea of a primary principle or

[10] On the knowledge of Latin in the Greek East, see B. Rochette, *Le latin dans le monde grec* (Brussels, 1997).

[11] See A. Nichols, O.P., "The Reception of St. Augustine and His Work in the Byzantine-Slav Tradition", *Angelicum* 64 (1987): 437–52.

source, and this accident of lexicography muddied the waters of discussion about the *Filioque*, the Spirit's procession from the Son. If the Latins were maintaining that the Son played a causal rôle in the coming to be of the Spirit, this could only mean for the Greeks that they were overthrowing the "monarchy" of the Father, his status as unique source of the Trinitarian life. Yet again, the Latin decision to translate the Greek *metanoia*, "repentance", by *poenitentia*, "penitence", itself closely related to the word *poena* (compare such English derivatives as "pain" and "penalty"), forms parts of the background for the emergence of the doctrine of Purgatory in the Western church. And this was to become yet another disputed question.

This lack of adequate communication, both popular and technical, underlay the parting of the ways between Latin and Greek theological method, which preceded by centuries any notion of a schism between the Latin and Greek churches. The development of theology as a discipline followed a different path in East and West. In the East, where the language of theology, Greek, was also that of lay education, theology was not the preserve of clerics as it largely became in the West. Theological study formed part of the higher education of the Byzantine civil service: one of the principal theologians of the later Byzantine period was a lay state official, Nicholas Cabasilas (born c. 1322). Carried by this culture of continuity, indeed of conservation, Greek theology developed in a fundamentally gradual fashion, maintaining its patristic base but elaborating certain features of the fathers' thought with the help of Greek philosophy, the tradition of whose study was unbroken. There was no revolution in theological method comparable to that which occurred in the West with the rise of Scholasticism.[12] This is not to say, however, that the Greek East knew nothing of the Scholastic method.[13] There existed a Byzantine Aristotelian tradition, with a concern for definition, internal

[12] The indispensable survey is H. G. Beck, *Kirche und theologische Literatur im byzantinischen Reich* (Munich, 1959).

[13] Concentrating on the late Byzantine period, but with much material on its predecessors, is G. Podskalsky, *Theologie und Philosophie in Byzanz: Der Streit um die theologische Methodik in der spät-byzantinischen Geistesgeschichte, 14/15. Jahrhunderte, seine systematische Grundlagen und seine historische Entwicklung* (Munich, 1977).

coherence of thought, and logical demonstration. This philosophical tradition could itself appeal to the example of the Greek fathers, who had called on reason to refute heresies and expose errors of interpretation. In such ways, writers like Athanasius, Basil the Great, and the two Gregories (Nyssene and Nazianzen) made considerable use of rational tools within theology, as did the Iconophile doctors of the ninth century who drew on Aristotle's *Categories* in order to express the relation of holy images to the realities that they represent or evoke. The same is true of the mid-Byzantine figure Photius, a crucial agent in the making of the schism. The later Byzantines, especially in the fourteenth century, were much exercised by questions of theological method and by what would later be called in the West the nature of theological "conclusions". In this, the Byzantines were stimulated by the first substantial translation project for Western theological writing, which occupied the Latinophrone school between the first reunion council, Lyons II, in 1274 and the second, Florence, in 1439. But any tendency to theological rationalism was checked by the continuing influence of the monastic vision of theology, all the easier since many of the Byzantine monastic communities were situated in the great cities, unlike their Latin counterparts. It was characteristic of such monastic theologians as Gregory Palamas (c. 1296–1359) to insist that all theology must be "apophatic"; that is, it must recognise the limits of human thought confronted with the great mysteries of God, man, Christ, the Spirit, the Church.[14] Monastic theology, combining study of the fathers with Christian experience in a contemplative and liturgical setting, was actively influencing a more rational and argumentative theology well after it had ceased to do so for the mainstream of the scholastic tradition in the West.

In the West, indeed, one can speak of a constant succession of theological movements, whereas in the East the main elements characteristic of each of these phases tend to be found simultaneously.

---

[14] A pervasive theme of the writings on this subject of Father John Meyendorff: especially *Introduction à l'étude de Grégoire Palamas* (Paris, 1959); *St. Grégoire Palamas et la mystique orthodoxe* (Paris, 1959); *Le Christ dans la théologie byzantine* (Paris, 1969), pp. 278–86; and *Byzantine Theology: Historical Trends and Doctrinal Themes* (London and Oxford, 1975), pp. 75–77.

After the patristic age, one can think of Latin theology as passing through three principal stages. First, in the last centuries of the first millenium, theology consists essentially in the rearrangement and harmonisation of the thoughts of the fathers. Second, for the first few centuries of the second millenium, a Latin monastic theology tries to restructure patristic teaching, as well as its own fundamental experience of the Christian life, by centering theological reflection on a small number of basic themes from Christian anthropology and soteriology. Finally, with the thirteenth century, the nascent Scholastic movement attempts to systematise patristic teaching (and its monastic extension) in order to make the *sacra doctrina* of Bible and Creed into a single rationally coherent unity. The dominant feature of each of these phases can be encapsulated in a phrase: for the first, faithfulness to tradition; for the second, spiritual experience; for the third, rational coherence. To the extent that these three stages are distinct chronological phases, Latin theology can be described as more disjointed in its development, and hence less balanced, than Greek theology even though, taken as a whole, the Latin tradition is by no means necessarily poorer than the Greek.

Painting with such broad brushstrokes is simplistic, but we have somehow to convey the difference in atmosphere of the theological enterprise in East and West, since this difference was noted by contemporaries themselves. As one of the Orientals at Florence remarked in a moment of exasperation: "St. Peter, St. Paul, St. Basil, St. Gregory the Theologian; a fig for your Aristotle, Aristotle!" [15] Rather earlier, Symeon of Thessalonica (died 1429), in his *Dialogues against the Heresies*, had been more expansive in his rejection of Latin Scholasticism: "I too, if I wanted, could have sophistical arguments with syllogisms better than yours. But I do not want. I ask my proof from the fathers and their writings. You will oppose to me Aristotle and Plato, or perhaps your recent doctors: against them I put the sinners [of Galilee] with their frank speech, their wisdom and seeming madness." [16]

[15] Cited in J. Gill, S.J., *The Council of Florence* (Cambridge, 1959), p. 227.

[16] Symeon of Thessalonica, *Dialogue against the Heresies* 29, PG 155:140, cited in M. Viller, "La question de l'union des églises entre grecs et latins depuis le Concile de Lyon

Some Latins shared this aversion to Scholasticism—from various perspectives, not only that of the monks. One thinks of the example of Petrarch.[17] Naturally, diversity in theological method is not equivalent to divergence in doctrine. But the disparity explains how it was, at Florence and elsewhere, that the Latins believed they had won the argument, whereas the Greeks considered they had come nowhere near the heart of the matter. What, on the other hand, Byzantine spokesmen could universally admire was the patristic erudition of such Latin representatives at Florence as the Dominican John of Montenero. The Scholastic expertise, which was more frequently the complement to that scholarship than it was its alternative, reminded them too painfully of certain bitter controversies in their own tradition. It generated the extremely serious charge that the Latins had (in Symeon's words) "changed the meaning of Holy Scripture and of the fathers" and left a lasting conviction among many Orientals that Scholasticism—despite its recurring use in the Russian and Greek schools of the seventeenth, eighteenth, nineteenth, and twentieth centuries—was essentially incompatible with the spirit of Orthodoxy.[18]

A third cultural difference lies in the liturgical sources of the greater theological literacy of the Byzantine laity. Because the Greek language

---

jusqu'à celui de Florence", *RHE* 17 (1921): 526; see also 17 (1921): 260–305, 515–32; 18 (1922): 20–60.

[17] K. Foster [O.P.], *Petrarch: Poet and Humanist* (Edinburgh, 1984), pp. 15–17, 151–56.

[18] The rejection of Scholasticism as "un-Orthodox" is a key feature of the neo-patristic theological programme of the late Father George Florovsky and governs his history of Russian theology, *The Ways of Russian Theology*, vol. 1 (Eng. trans., Belmont, Mass., 1979) and vol. 2 (Eng. trans., Vaduz and Belmont, Mass., 1987). A tendency to blame Latin Scholasticism for all the succeeding woes of Western culture is manifested, in the modern church of Greece, by the lay theologian Christos Yannaras—the rape of nature in idem, "Scholasticism and Technology", *ECR* 6 (1974): 162–69, and individualistic moralism in his *Alêtheia kai henotita tês Ekklêsias* (Athens, 1977). Neither author mentions the weaknesses of the "controversial theology" that (rather than Scholasticism) was the dominant force in Greek theology in the period of the *Tourkokrateia*, as shown by G. Podskalsky, *Griechische Theologie in der Zeit der Türkenherrschaft, 1453–1821: Die Orthodoxie im Spannungsfeld der nachreformatorischen Konfessionen des Westens* (Munich, 1988).

survived as both a liturgical language and the language of ordinary life, the Byzantine liturgy was more fully comprehensible to laity and clergy alike than was its counterpart in the West.

The language of the Latin liturgy with its fine rhetorical cadences represents a unique point in the history of Christian Latinity: that moment when a large portion of the senatorial aristocracy of Rome sought baptism, in the course of the fourth and fifth centuries, bringing with them into the Roman Christian community their own high standards of purity of diction. One reason why the responses of the people in the Roman rite are so brief is that it was hard to find an ordinary congregation able to make longer responses in correct Latin. The gap between the classical Christian Latin of the liturgy and the vulgarised Latin of the common man grew wider in the succeeding centuries. The new Romance languages—Italian, French, Spanish, and so forth—did not grant an immediate understanding of their own original Latin base, and so the worshipping assemblies of the Western church withdrew into a degree of outward passivity, and silence.[19] One major source of theological enlightenment was thus to some extent closed off.

In the Greek East, the preservation of the vernacular liturgy was, for the Byzantine church, both an advantage and a disadvantage. It was an advantage insofar as that church could draw upon a liturgically instructed laity, a disadvantage insofar as the laity, jealous of their traditional confessional inheritance, provided the bishops with a continual challenge to the conciliar reinterpretation of faith. The reunion councils of the later Middle Ages failed chiefly because the decisions of such gatherings could not be "sold" to the educated—or even the not-so-educated—layman and laywoman back home.

Moreover, the Byzantines exported this same state of affairs by way of their missionary endeavours. Although the Greek church

---

[19] "A degree": for evidence of how a lay devotional culture, in an offshore island of the European continent, continued to appropriate the Mass liturgy, at least in its essentials, see E. Duffy, *The Stripping of the Altars: Traditional Religion in England, 1400–1580* (New Haven and London, 1992), pp. 109–30.

came to insist on a single rite for all those enjoying its communion, gradually extinguishing what remained of the Syrian and Alexandrian liturgical inheritance in the communities beneath its sway,
it never required unity of liturgical language. The prevalence of
the vernacular within the Byzantine sphere had originally stemmed
from the circumstance that much of the countryside of the East
was altogether non-Hellenic, being Syrian, Coptic, or Armenian.
When, in the ninth century, the Byzantine church went missionary and undertook the conversion of the Slavs, it simply assumed
that it must translate its liturgy into their vernaculars. So the same
ecumenically mixed blessing of a theologically articulate yet dog-
matically conservative laity was eventually brought to be in the
Balkans and Russia also. On, above all, the "Sunday of Orthodoxy", anathemas on heretics and schismatics form a part of the
public worship of the Byzantine-Slav rite.[20] In this sense, the liturgy can become a vehicle of "antiecumenical" passion (as well as
of passion for the truth).

It is true that the texts of the Sunday of Orthodoxy contain no
fulmination against the Latin church. Yet daily, at the Commemoration of the Living, the same liturgy mentions by name the chief
hierarchs with whom the congregation is in communion—an
expanded version of the naming of the bishop and the pope in the
Roman rite. A community would at once know if a pope's name
were omitted from the diptychs and could speedily learn the reason
why.[21] In practice, most Greek Christian dislike of the papacy is
based on popular history—rather like the antipapalism of Northern
Irish Protestants in the West. But the folk history has been nourished by elements of genuine history, and of genuine theology. For
that, the liturgical and theological consciousness of the Byzantine
laity is chiefly responsible.

---

[20] J. Gouillard, *Le synodikon de l'Orthodoxie: Edition et commentaire* (Paris, 1967).

[21] In the remoter parts of the Byzantine East, and above all in the non-Greek-
speaking East, the cause was often doctrinally innocuous: for lack of the most basic
communication, no one knew what the pope was called.

Differences in Fundamental Ecclesiology

Apart from differences in culture, both general and Christian, the
most important factor making for disharmony between the Latin
and Greek churches in the mediaeval period was what may be termed
a divergence in fundamental ecclesiology—in the primordial sense
of what the Church is, and is for. The Latin church, we can say, has
a customary view, which is historically conditioned and distinctive,
of what it is to be the Church; this is both a mentality and, at times,
an explicit theology. The Eastern churches also have a customary
view, a distinctive mentality, and, on occasion, an explicit theology
of what the Church is. These two fundamental ecclesiologies may
not conflict, strictly speaking, yet they are not the same. This broad
and abstract statement must be narrowed and made concrete. Following a cue from Congar, we can make use here of a scheme that
distinguishes the Church's "inside" from her "outside".[22] The "inside"
of the Church consists of those theological realities that make of her
what she is in the saving economy of God. As the continuance of
the Incarnation and of Pentecost, the Church is the body of Christ
living with his Spirit and so able to bring human beings to the Father,
who is the source of both Spirit and Son. Because she has this "inside",
the Church is a sacramental mystery. The human behaviour, the signs
and gestures, that make up her distinctive life do not simply tell us
about the beliefs and values of the people who form the Church.
They actually bring us into the presence of the Church's Lord, the
God of salvation. On the other hand, the Church also has an "outside": she has a public, social existence as one body among many in
human history. The sacramental mystery that forms her "outside"
must find expression in ways liturgical, canonical, and cultural, for
all of these—worship, government, making, thinking, doing—are necessary features of any human society here below, while we are *in
statu peregrinationis*, in the condition of pilgrims.

[22] Y. M.-J. Congar, O.P., "Conscience ecclésiastique en Orient et en Occident",
Ist. (1959): 189–201, translated into English as "Ecclesiological Awareness in the East
and in the West from the Sixth to the Eleventh Century", in P. Sherwood, O.S.B.,
ed., *The Unity of the Churches of God* (Baltimore, 1965), pp. 127–84.

Between the "inside" and the "outside" there will never be a perfect correspondence. Instead, there is the promise of Christ that the reality of salvation will always be communicated through the Church no matter what human frailties afflict her in her earthly course. This does not mean, however, that attention to the outward aspect of the Church is so much wasted time—that such things as liturgical forms, canonical structure, sacred and spiritual art, theological life, and—in the widest sense—ecclesiastical practice are so ecclesiologically trivial as to be beneath our doctrinal notice. On the contrary, the way we fashion these things is most important from two points of view coincident, more or less, with the needs of two groups of people.

First, from the perspective of those outside the Church, her social, public side is, to begin with, all they see. If this outward side is seriously distorted, then the inward sacramental side will be obstructed in its outworking. To perceive this inwardness of the Church always requires grace; now it will need a special grace. Second, from the perspective of the Church's members, imbalances or corruptions in the Church's self-expression in time and space will tend to affect adversely the way the faithful think of the theological glory within. If the Church as an empirical body is too ghastly, it becomes harder to maintain our dogmatic faith that she is, nevertheless, Christ's own Body, and, in the complementary metaphor, his Bride.

On the Church as mystery, there is in East and West basic agreement, yet no total coincidence of emphasis. As Congar points out, to acquire a sense of how the Western and Eastern traditions have thought, historically, about the Church, we cannot—paradoxically—get much help from their theology. Neither in West nor in East was the study of the nature of the Church (ecclesiology) a recognised branch of theology in patristic and mediaeval times. Even the post-mediaeval Schoolmen, with their tendency to treat the various regions of Christian believing under separate headings—the treatises *De Deo*, *De Christo*, *De sacramentis*, and so on—came late to a *De ecclesia*. Congar holds this absence of conscious reflection on the Church's nature to be yet more marked in the East. At least the West knew scattered *loci* where reflection on the Church was made explicit:

commentaries on the liturgy (the *expositiones Missae*), for example, or on certain biblical books such as the Apocalypse of John.

Yet this reticence of theological tradition on the Church as mystery should not be misconstrued. So far from deriving from a low doctrine of the Church, a disregard for the place of the Church in the economy of salvation, virtually the opposite is the case: because the Church was taken for granted as the necessary medium and environment of all meeting with God in Christ, it was not felt to be a problem; indeed, it was hardly felt to be an object, since it was the *milieu* within whose embrace all theological objects were seen. Nonetheless, there are indications of what a Byzantine treatise on the Church's inner reality would have contained: following up those indications, in Congar's company, we find, comparing notes from the likewise limited sources in the West, not a divergence so much as a difference of emphasis.

Congar's sketch of the inner dimension of Byzantine ecclesiology begins with some words of the second-century father Clement of Alexandria, in his *Paedagogus*: "Just as the will of God is an act and is called the world, so also his intention is the salvation of men and is called the Church."[23] The Church constitutes, in other words, the concrete form in which the divine outreach to human beings, for their salvation, achieves its actuality. The seventh-century Byzantine theologian Maximus the Confessor develops this insight, in a more metaphysical key, in his *Mystagogia*, or initiation into the Christian life.[24] For Maximus, the Church is the image of God as Source and End of all things. As God brings the world into unity, into harmony with itself and with its Creator, so the Church mirrors the divine unifying activity. God so acts in her that the various races and generations that make up mankind are brought into unity with each other and with their Maker. The Church is *catholic*: she brings the fragmentary experience of the human race into a unity that is willed by God and—above all—is in God. According to Congar, the key to the Oriental sense of the Church is to be found in the concept of

[23] *Paedagogus* 1.6.
[24] *Mystagogia* 1.

deification or divinisation, a concept familiar to the West but not exploited there to the same degree.[25] The notion of deification in Christian use carries two charges. First, nature or creation has a certain God-given capacity to receive God, with man placed at the crucial point where the material order is open to a transcendent domain: an idea classically expressed in Saint Basil's *Hexaemeron* (commentary on the six days of creation) and in the *De opificio hominis* of his fourth-century contemporary Saint Gregory of Nyssa. Second, this primordial "openness" to God is turned into the actual reception of the divine life by the agency of the Holy Spirit: a major theme of Saint Cyril of Alexandria's writing, and notably of his *Commentary on John*, as of the more disparate lucubrations of Saint Maximus. The Byzantines regarded the Church as the locus of this divinising activity whereby human beings may be filled with the very life of God. The Church is the arena where all of this takes place, the theological space in which God acts to make us godlike in the image of his Son. With the assumption of human nature by the Word, that nature has been restored, in the depths of its being, to a state of likeness to God. It is able now to live with the "immortality", or sharing in the endless divine life, for which it was made. The Church's task is to realise divinisation for the same human nature as personalised in individual human beings. Whereas nature has been restored by the Incarnation—by all the mysteries of the Saviour's life from his conception to the sending of his Spirit—the appropriation of that restoration in human persons is done by the Spirit of Christ through the Church. So clear a statement is rare in the Greek tradition and owes much to such contemporary systematisers of Orthodox thought as the French-domiciled Russian theologian Vladimir Lossky. Yet Congar (and Lossky) have surely identified aright the tacit distinction with which Byzantine theology often operated.[26]

The Church carries on her task, so defined, in two main ways: through the sacraments, which the Greeks call (precisely) "the

---

[25] Congar, "Ecclesiological Awareness", pp. 132–33.

[26] For Lossky, see his *Mystical Theology of the Eastern Church* (Eng. trans., London, 1957), pp. 181–86.

mysteries", and by asceticism, ideally realised in the monastic life. This explains why the principal Byzantine writings on the Christian life are either spiritual-ascetic treatises, or explanations of the liturgies of the main sacraments. Into the first category would fall the texts that make up the *Philokalia*, a spiritual anthology originally created for monastic use but now widely spread, and widely translated into western as well as eastern European languages. Into the second category would come such works as Cabasilas' *Life in Christ* and his *Commentary on the Divine Liturgy*. The authors presuppose, rather than state, that the Church is an institution filled with interior mystery, since she it is who can place men in touch with the living God. Her life, interior and mystical, is expressed in the celebration of the sacraments, above all the Eucharist, and in ascetical effort. While the Byzantine church certainly carried out much charitable, philanthropic activity (what we would now think of as the "social ministry" of the Church),[27] and missionised extensively,[28] especially among her Slav neighbours, these works of love were not, it seems, central to the way in which Byzantine people saw their church. A less practical, more theoretical (in the original sense *contemplative*) view of the Church is well expressed in a piece of poetic prose ascribed to the eighth-century Byzantine patriarch Germanus:

> The Church is the sanctuary of God, a holy place, a house of prayer, the assembly of the people, the body of Christ. Its very name, "Bride of Christ", calls us to penance and to prayer, purified by the waters of baptism and washed by the precious blood of Christ, adorned with the splendid robes of a bride, sealed with the anointing of the Holy Spirit.... The Church is an earthly heaven where the more-than-heavenly God lives and moves.... She is a divine house wherein is

[27] D. J. Constantelos, *Byzantine Philosophy and Social Welfare* (Rutgers, N.J., 1968).

[28] F. Dvornik, *Byzantine Missions among the Slavs: SS. Constantine-Cyril and Methodius* (New Brunswick, 1970). For contemporary Orthodox comment on the Church as missionary, see the documents gathered together in I. Bria, *Martyria/Mission: The Witness of the Orthodox Churches Today* (Geneva, 1980). It is notable that of the five concluding sections, pp. 224–48, which attempt to summarise the concrete content of mission, three are concerned with liturgical life and monasticism as forms of witness (the other two deal with evangelism and struggle for justice).

celebrated the mystic and living sacrifice ... whose precious stones are the divine doctrines taught by the Saviour to his disciples.[29]

Though similar texts in praise of the Church could be found in the West—for example, in the liturgical prefaces for the feast of the dedication of a church building—we might expect to find reference to mission, and to works of mercy, among the defining activities mentioned. D. M. Nicol has captured something of importance, commenting on the widespread fear of "Latinisation" in the last Byzantine centuries, when he writes: "Byzantinism was a psychosomatic condition, revealed at its highest spiritual level in the sanctity of an anchorite or the mystical-corporeal vision of a hesychast, revealed more commonly in the daily mysteries or sacraments of the Church, revealed above all in lasting form for all to see and wonder at in Byzantine art." [30]

A more theologically refined account is offered, as we might expect in turning from cultural historian to ecclesiologist, by Père Congar. According to Congar, the tendency to focus the sense of the Church on those aspects of her life relevant to our divinisation by grace is entirely characteristic of the general theological bias of the Greek church after its traumatic loss of the Non-Chalcedonian communities in the fifth century.[31] Imperial pressure, allied with some genuine conviction, encouraged a Cyrillianism *à l'outrance*. As we have seen, Greek theology would interpret Chalcedon more in terms of Cyril than of Leo. Its typical Christology was that of the Neo-Chalcedonian movement: an attempt to combine the teaching of Chalcedon on the unity of Christ in his two natures, divine and human, with some of the texts of Saint Cyril on which historic Monophysitism had made its stand. Its habit was to stress the asymmetry (as an Orthodox scholar contemporaneous with Congar, George Florovsky, termed it) of the relation of divine and human in Christ. We are not to regard the unity of Christ as that of a divine person in two natures, each of which is, so to speak, an equal contributor

---

[29] *Historia ecclesiastica et mystica contemplatio* 1.

[30] Nicol, *Church and Society*, pp. 129–30.

[31] Congar, "Ecclesiological Awareness", pp. 133–38.

to his total reality. Rather, the divine nature is always primary since, with the hypostatic union between the Word of God and the human nature of Jesus, the divine nature at once begins to penetrate and transfigure the human. Since the whole purpose of the Incarnation is our divinisation, that divinisation must have its model and proto-type in the person of Christ. Though the humanity of Jesus is not swallowed up by the divinity (as in full-blown Monophysitism), it is wholly penetrated and transformed by it. This interpretation of Chal-cedon has been favoured at certain times in the Catholic West—notably in the wake of the Modernist crisis and, above all, during the pontificate of Pius XII. Yet, historically regarded, it cannot really count as the common voice of the Latin tradition, as the continued vigour of a *homo assumptus* Christology bears witness.[32]

The later Greek fathers and the Byzantine doctors continued this line of reflection into ecclesiology.[33] The human reality of the Church is not denied—how could it be?—but the divine side of the Church's life is given greater stress. Here the Church is not so much a perfect society (a favoured phrase of the later Latin tradition), the perfect form of a human, creaturely reality; rather is she a colony of Heaven, an outpost of the divine world of the Trinity and their angels. Vis-itors to the Byzantine liturgy have come away with the impression that its aim is to create the sense of Heaven on earth, and their number began early. The twelfth-century *Russian Primary Chronicle*, in describing the conversion of the early Russian state to Orthodox Christianity, has it that, on the return of the Russian envoys from their first experience of the patriarchal liturgy at Hagia Sophia in Constantinople, they declared: "We no longer knew whether we were in heaven or on earth, but this we do know, that there God lives among men, and we shall never forget that beauty."[34] Congar has made a little collection of jewellike Orthodox texts on the Church's

---

[32] See, for example, F. T. Harris, "*Homo assumptus* at St. Victor: Reconsidering the relationship between Victorine Christology and Peter Lombard's First Opinion", *The Thomist* 77 (2008): 595–624.

[33] F. Dvornik, *Byzance et la primauté romaine* (Paris, 1965), p. 17.

[34] Cited in T. Ware, *The Orthodox Church* (Harmondsworth, 1963, 1967), p. 269.

essence, all bearing witness to this same emphasis. Paul Evdokimov wrote, "The essence of the Church is the divine life unveiling itself in creatures; it is the deification of the creature in the strength of the Incarnation and Pentecost."[35] George Florovsky opined, "The Church is the living image of eternity within time".[36] Vladimir Lossky has it that "the Church is an image of the Holy Trinity."[37]

There is nothing here, of course, with which a Catholic Christian might wish to disagree. Yet awareness of the human side of the Church somewhat inhibits Christians of the Latin tradition from using such warm, heightened language, except on special liturgical occasions. On the other hand, the more customary Western ways of expressing the Church's sacramental mystery are not themselves unknown to the East. For the East too the Church is, in the Pauline and Augustinian phrase, the "body of Christ": an organic body, made up of different members with differing rôles who are yet in union with each other through receiving their common inspiration from Christ as the body's Head. In dependence on this Head, the same life and faith are common to all. The unity of the body is achieved for one and for all through, in the first place, baptism, but supremely is it won in the Eucharist, whose heavenly Bread by uniting the faithful to their Lord brings them into unity with each other.

Differences multiply, however, when we turn to the "outside" of the Church: the manifestation of this sacramental reality in terms of a society where human beings interact in ways defined by custom and canon. We can tabulate a number of respects in which the fundamental ecclesiological awareness of the Eastern churches differs here from that of Rome's Latin family.

First, in the East the local church—the local community of a bishop, with his presbyters, deacons, and people—is often seen as the most fundamental expression of the Church's life. If one thinks of the universal Church at all, one thinks of her as primarily a communion

[35] P. Evdokimov, *L'orthodoxie* (Paris, 1932), p. 5.
[36] G. Florovsky, "The Catholicity of the Church", in E. L. Mascall, ed., *The Church of God: An Anglo-Russian Symposium* (London, 1934), p. 65.
[37] V. Lossky, *Mystical Theology of the Eastern Church*, p. 176.

of local churches.[38] So testifies the Liturgy of Saint John Chrysostom in its prayer for "the peace of the holy churches of God" and "the union of them all". Or again, as the Eastern Orthodox ecclesiology of the twentieth century, and notably its Russian representatives, will insist, the local churches are not parts of the whole. They do not, theologically, gain anything by being added together. In a comparison found more than once in the writing of Nicholas Afanas'ev (1893–1966), each is the total church, just as the Holy Gifts are Christ's real presence in such a way that two celebrations do not make him more fully present, nor is he found in more plenary form when the consecrated elements are quantitatively extended.[39]

The natural consequence of this way of thinking is that the rupture of communion between two local churches is taken less seriously in the East than in the West. The number of local schisms in the early Church of the East can be bewildering and their character confusing. As we have seen, some churches were in mediate communion with others—via third parties, not directly. To reiterate a point made at the start of this study, the East abhors heresy far more than it does schism. The Western church is more liable to tolerate heretical opinions on the ground of the need to preserve the unity of the body, at least so long as such opinions are not too publicly canvassed. In the East, ruptures of communion are seen as a sickness of the body of Christ, not a life-and-death affair. The West spontaneously thinks of the Church as, first and foremost, the whole Church spread throughout the world. Of this whole, the local churches are but parts, dioceses. They are the way the whole expresses itself in a given place, but by themselves they are fragments. To be connected with the whole is, for them, life; to be sundered from it, death.

The Eastern stress on the fulness of the particular local church was, naturally, generative of tension when it encountered the universal

---

[38] Congar, "Ecclesiological Awareness", p. 139.

[39] A. Nichols, O.P., *Theology in the Russian Diaspora: Church, Fathers, Eucharist in Nikolai Afanas'ev, 1893–1966* (Cambridge, 1989). The fullest Catholic account of this theme is (interestingly) by a senior official of the Roman curia: F. López-Illana, *"Ecclesia unum et plura": Riflessione teologico-canonica sull'autonomia delle Chiese locali* (Vatican City, 1991).

claims of the Roman bishops. So long as the difference between West and East in fundamental ecclesiology was simply a matter of nuance in general outlook, the two attitudes could coexist without too much difficulty. The problem began in earnest when the Roman church—the church of the city of Rome—started to act on her own sense that she has special responsibility for defending and extending (among other things) this feeling for the single universal Church of Christ. Believing herself to be endowed with the rôle of guarding Christian unity, the Roman church could have conceived that unity on the (predominant) Eastern model: the unity of a communion of local churches, all of which are sisters. But, as a Western community, it was, perhaps, historically inevitable that the Roman church should conceive its service of unity in (primarily) universalist terms, and so try to put forward institutional forms and procedures that would render the whole Church a governmental unity.[40] (And yet, for much of the patristic period, the interventions of the popes in the East are much concerned with defending the proper *presbeia*, seniority, of local churches disregarded by more predatory Eastern neighbours.)

Despite what has just been said, however, the local churches of the Byzantine world were certainly not the autonomous congregations that the theory might suggest. The rôle of the synodical principle must not be overlooked. That the bishops of local churches should come together in council, *sunodos*, and legislate together for the churches under their care was accepted on all sides. Such synods, however, were not infrequently impeded by a variety of adverse circumstances. Nor could the problems they took as their agenda always be resolved on a regional level alone. Yet the general, "ecumenical", form of the synod was a rarity—understandably so, given the formidable demands of its organisation. What about, then, the ordinary, year-by-year, day-by-day life of the Church? What authority was involved to regulate the local churches of the Christian world?

If the Western answer to these questions soon became clear—namely, that the apostolic see of Rome, as mother and mistress of all

---

[40] Y. M.-J. Congar, *L'Eglise: De saint Augustin à l'époque moderne* (Paris, 1970), pp. 30–31.

Christians, alone has ecumenical authority to coordinate the thought and actions of the churches of God, the Eastern answer was also soon forthcoming. From the time of the first Christian Roman emperor until the destruction of the Byzantine polity in 1453, responsibility for the "outside", the social and public configuration of the Church, was deemed to devolve upon the Roman-Byzantine emperor, whose God-given task it was to be protector and guardian of the churches. Our next step, then, must be to investigate the antecedents and nature of this "imperial theology" and the character of the "papal theology" that was, eventually, its conscious rival.[41] These will constitute, after cultural difference and divergence of fundamental ecclesiology, the (more particularised) third and fourth chronic factors in the growing estrangement.

[41] The alternatives of pope and emperor are taken as crucial to understanding the distinctive development of the Western church in W. Ullmann, *A Short History of the Papacy in the Middle Ages* (London, 1972). The author noted of his own book: "The axis, so to speak, on which the papacy is seen to develop was Rome-Constantinople, a viewpoint which has not been so distinctly highlighted before." Cited in E. Ullmann, *Walter Ullmann: A Tale of Two Cultures* (Cambridge, 1990), p. 65.

Bibliography

Congar, Y. M.-J., O.P. "Ecclesiological Awareness in the East and in the West from the Sixth to the Eleventh Centuries". In *The Unity of the Churches of God*, edited by P. Sherwood. Baltimore, 1963.

Every, G. *Misunderstandings between East and West*. London, 1965.

Geanakoplos, D. J. *Byzantine East and Latin West: Two Worlds of Christendom in Middle Ages and Renaissance*. Oxford, 1966.

———. *Constantinople and the West: Essays on the Late Byzantine (Palaeologan) and Italian Renaissances and the Byzantine and Roman Churches*. Madison, Wisconsin, 1989.

———. *Interactions of the "Sibling" Byzantine and Western Cultures in the Middle Ages and Italian Renaissance*. New Haven and London, 1976.

Lossky, V. "Two Aspects of the Church". In *The Mystical Theology of the Eastern Church*, pp. 174–75. Eng. trans. London, 1957.

Sherrard, P. *The Greek East and the Latin West*. London, 1959.

Spácil, T. *Conceptus et doctrina de Ecclesia iuxta theologiam Orientis separati*. Rome, 1923.

5

The Estrangement between Rome and
Constantinople, II: The Rôle of the Emperor

The move of the Roman imperial court to the banks of the Bosphorus may seem to us a theological irrelevance. But it was not felt
to be so by late antique Christians. We must remember that the
conversion of Constantine was at once interpreted as an act of God
in a very strong sense.[1] The *pax romana* whose existence had enabled
the original Gospel message to circulate freely around the Mediterranean world and beyond had now itself accepted that same Gospel
and become its guardian and spokesman. The Roman imperial government was now an instrument of the Christian apostolate. Constantine received a title, *episkopos tôn ektos*, which may mean either
"overseer of the Church's public life" (in Congar's term, the Church's
extérieur), or, alternatively, "overseer for those outside the Church"—
that is, the principal agent of her missionary expansion.[2] More than
this, Constantine could also be hailed as *isapostolos*, the equal of the
apostles themselves. While not all Christians accepted such a theology of the imperial office, many did, not least among those being
members of the intelligentsia and aristocracy who were beginning,
in considerable numbers, to seek out baptism.[3] As recent converts

---

[1] *Vita Constantini* 1.44; 4.24.

[2] The question is whether the key words, *tôn ektos*, should be regarded as in the
neuter or in the masculine gender. See J. A. Straub, "Kaiser Konstantin als *episkopos
tôn ektos*", *Studia patristica* (Berlin, 1957), 1:678–95; idem, "Constantine as *koinos episkopos*: Tradition and Innovation in the Representation of the First Christian Emperor's
Majesty", *DOP* 21 (1967): 39–55.

[3] V. Twomey warns against treating Eusebius of Caesarea, preeminent source for
early "imperial theology", as "the adequate representative of the general fourth century

from Hellenism, they would regard it as wholly natural that the emperor, whom Greco-Roman paganism saw as quasi-divine, should take up a position of religious moment within the Christian dispensation. As for the emperor himself, he soon made it crystal clear that, in his own eyes, his responsibilities did indeed extend to securing the peace of the Church—the good order of the Church, her unity in faith and discipline—for what was this save an aspect of the good order of the empire he ruled? The first of the ecumenical councils, Nicaea I, was an imperial initiative to settle the problems raised by the theological conundrum of Arianism: a foretaste of the Church policies of East Roman emperors in subsequent centuries. As the Old Rome became ever more marginal, geographically and politically, to the emperors' policies, so the New Rome, Constantinople, became ever more central to them. Along with the institution of councils, the bishop of New Rome was to be the principal means of expressing the imperial mind in matters religious. While it would be wrong to give the impression that the see of Constantinople was simply a running dog of the Byzantine emperors, nevertheless no Byzantine patriarch could escape the proximity of the court, the imperial civil service, and the emperor himself. Moreover, the patriarchal church, despite its later claims to apostolicity through the preaching, in Scythia, of the apostle Andrew, had in fact come to prominence by clinging to the coattails of the Christian emperors. It was hard for it not to follow the imperial line, as it is for anyone to resist the wishes of his patron.

Pagan Foundations of the Imperial Ideology

Let us look rather more closely at attitudes to the emperor in antiquity by way of explanatory background to the customary outlook of Constantinople.[4] Throughout the ancient Near East, society was

---

Christian attitude to the emperor". *Apostolikos Thronos: The Primacy of Rome as Reflected in the "Church History" of Eusebius and the Historico-Apologetic Writings of St. Athanasius the Great* (Münster, 1982), p. 162.

[4] My guide to this subject at large is F. Dvornik, *Early Christian and Byzantine Political Philosophy: Origins and Background* 2 vols. (Washington, D.C., 1966).

monarchical in form, and in each case the king was conceived as a religious as well as a political figure. In some regions, such as Mesopotamia, the king was seen as the representative (simply) of the gods, united to them in a (merely) moral way. In others, such as Egypt, a definite metaphysical relationship bound the king to the gods, or to God. But, whether the union were moral or metaphysical, the king was thought of as a saviour and as a mediator between the divine world and mankind. (There may be a connexion here with the Christologies of Antioch and Alexandria. The Syrian mind was predisposed towards the notion of a mediator morally united to the Godhead; the Egyptian mind, to that of a metaphysical mediation.) The high view of monarchy prevalent in the valley of the Nile was not confined to its native place, for Egypt became in time the first polity to acquire imperial authority over the lion's share of the ancient Near East—under its eighteenth dynasty, in the course of the second millennium before Christ. According to the Egyptian royal ideology, the king was chosen by the sun god, Re, and given a share of the divine spirit to become his own spirit, *ka*. The ruler could thus be portrayed as worshipping his own divine spirit as something distinct from himself; he could also be shown as himself being worshipped since, after all, his share of the divine spirit really was his. Because of his possession of the divine *ka*, Pharoah was described as the only rightful lord and owner of the earth, the unique source of property and honours. At the same time, he was high priest of the religion of the sun and was charged with bringing all men to a knowledge of the divine.[5]

Under and after Alexander of Macedon, the Greeks conquered the entire area, which shared this theocratic concept of kingship, from Egypt to Persia. From the Greek conquest of western Asia and the Nile Valley there sprang the Hellenistic civilisation, at one and the same time really Greek yet so enriched by other cultural traditions that its appeal transcended local frontiers. The Hellenistic civilisation was, of course, the civilisation in which the early Church took shape. Alexander himself had been convinced of his own divine

[5] Ibid., 1:4–20.

mission to conquer, and in conquering civilise, the earth. Probably he knew of Aristotle's statement that government might be conferred on the best man, who, by his life and achievements, would be like a god on earth.[6] By degrees, the successors of Alexander introduced the Oriental concept of an absolute monarchy, ruled by a divinised king—if also tempered by custom and limited technological ability. To some extent, this was good politics, yet to a degree it went against the grain of the general intellectual trend of the centuries immediately before and after the birth of Jesus. The tendency at the time was rationalistic, setting a distance between the intellectuals, at any rate, and traditional religion. Still, the intellectuals might accept the ruler cult on their own terms, regarding the king as the animate form of the law, *empsychos nomos*, the "law personified".[7] Just as God harmonises the universe by the natural law, and by his Providence, so the king can harmonise the kingdom by his positive law and by bringing welfare to his subjects. The heart of the Hellenistic royal ideology in its mature form was the notion that the state is a mirror of the divine world. In this mirror, the king's rôle is all-important.[8] He above all must imitate God, promulgating laws which bring the divine plan into play on earth. Thus, in the first century after Christ, Plutarch remarks that kings must possess the divine Logos itself, since they are the incarnation of the law that comes from God. But Plutarch, as a pure Hellene from mainland Greece, drew the line at offering divine cultus to rulers, a practice to which Christians also were objecting at the same time.

---

[6] Ibid., 1:215. See also H. Kelsen, "The Philosophy of Aristotle and the Hellenic-Macedonian Policy", *Ethics* 48, no. 1 (1937): 1–64; cf. Alasdair MacIntyre's underlining of the paradox that Aristotle, who saw the forms of social life of the city-state as normative for essential human nature, was himself a servant of that Macedonian royal power that destroyed the city-state as a free society (*After Virtue: A Study in Ethical Theory* [London, 1981], p. 149). His explanation is that, owing to Aristotle's weak grasp of historicity, he did not appreciate the possible transience of the *polis*.

[7] F. Dvornik, *Early Christian and Byzantine Political Philosophy*, 1:245–47.

[8] Cited from Diotogenes, in ibid., 1:249; cf. also 1:252–65 for the similar notions of the Pseudo-Ecphantus and the Pseudo-Aristeas.

Turning, then, to the Christians: the teaching of Paul echoes a celebrated *logion* whereby Jesus granted authority, in different respects, to both God and Caesar. In the Letter to the Romans, Paul adjured the Roman Christians: "Let every person be subject to the governing authorities. For there is no authority except from God, and those that exist have been instituted by God. Therefore he who resists the authorities resists what God has appointed, and those who resist will incur judgment.... He [the ruler] is God's servant for your good." [9] And, again, in First Timothy, the apostle, whether *in propria persona* or through a disciple confident of being of one mind with him, has this to say: "First of all, then, I urge that supplications, prayers, intercessions, and thanksgivings be made for all men, for kings and all who are in high positions." [10] Similarly, in Peter's first epistle, we read: "Be subject for the Lord's sake to every human institution, whether it be to the emperor as supreme, or to governors as sent by him to punish those who do wrong and to praise those who do right." [11] The earliest recorded prayer of the local Roman church, in the *Prima Clementis*, reflects both Peter and Paul:

> You, O Lord, have given our rulers the power of sovereignty through your own excellent and indescribable might, so that we, knowing your glory and the honour which you have given them, may submit ourselves in all things to them, in nothing resisting your will. Grant them health, peace, concord, security, so that they may not fail in administering the government you have given them. [12]

The emperor in First Peter, the ruler in Paul and Clement, is, naturally, the *Roman* emperor. The Roman political tradition was essentially republican, but in the first century before Christ, owing to the class warfare and faction endemic in the republic as well as to admiration for the Greek mind, the Romans began to look with more favour on the monarchical idea. With the conquest of Syria and Egypt, completed by 30 B.C., they were virtually obliged to borrow

---

[9] Rom 13:1–2, 4; cf. vv. 3–7.
[10] 1 Tim 2:1–2; cf. vv. 3–6.
[11] 1 Pet 2:13–14; cf. vv. 15–17.
[12] 1 Clem 96.

the clothes of Hellenistic ideology, for, deprived of their vesture, government would have been that much less attractive to the indigenous population. In effect, the Romans adopted the idea that the emperor is the animate law but combined this with their own tradition that the ruler is subject to the law. Characteristically, they maintained that the emperor must be the first to keep the law, which he embodies. This double-sided principle accounts for the fundamental concern with legality and rationality in Roman government to the close of the Byzantine period—at any rate if one omits periods when rogues or madmen occupied the throne.

Christian attitudes to the imperial ideology were complicated by the fact that, in the first two centuries of the Church's existence, emperors or imperial officials indulged in sporadic persecution of her members, some of it extremely serious. In the Johannine Apocalypse, the dragon (Satan) takes control of the beast (the Roman Empire) and uses it for his own wicked ends, giving it power and making it utter blasphemies. At the time when the Apocalypse was written, towards the end of the first century, the emperor cult (as distinct from the imperial ideology) was not very advanced. But in the second century, the gesture of offering incense to the *numen* or divine spirit of the emperor would become a life-and-death affair. The writings of the early Apologists suggest that, while Christians can never worship the emperor, they can honour him as the first man on earth after God. In their *acta*, the martyrs protest their loyalty to the emperor but simultaneously insist that there is a greater *dominus*, Jesus Christ, whose sovereignty over all things in Heaven and on earth, received from the Father, transcends that of kings. Clement of Alexandria, encouraged by the precedent of Philo Judaeus, tried to marry the imperial ideology with Christian doctrine as far as he could. The emperor, as expounder of God's commands, stands in a relation to the Logos of God, and therefore to Christ himself, though he be ignorant of it. But the failure of any other ante-Nicene theologian after Clement to take up this theme shows that its hour had not yet come. So long as the emperors remained pagans, it was unlikely to arouse enthusiasm. Origen, however, contributed an argument that became standard, namely, that without the general peace secured for the Mediterranean basin by the Roman emperors, the *pax augusta*, the Gospel could hardly have been preached to the ends, virtually, of the known world. "God prepared the nations for his teaching by seeing to it that they would be under one prince, the king of the Romans. Thus there would not be strife among the nations, which would have made it more difficult for the apostles of Jesus to fulfil the task that he gave them when he said, 'Go, make disciples of all nations'." [13]

The Rôle of the Emperor in the East

The theory of divine monarchy among Christians came into its own with the conversion of Constantine. As soon as Constantine revealed his sympathies for the Christian religion in the 313 Edict of Milan, Christians proved ready to recognise him as an image of the Logos on earth. The Christian emperor reflects the divine monarchy: as God brings the universe to an unity through his Providence, so the emperor brings the world to unity in God through his pious rule. The influence of a widespread *Weltanschauung*, relief at the removal of state pressure, and the personal confidence of the episcopate in the good intentions of Constantine: these factors suffice to explain the painless initial acceptance of the imperial philosophy. The principal theologian of the imperial office was Eusebius of Caesarea, who happens to be the early Church's main historian as well. [14] In his

---

[13] *Contra Celsum* 2:30; cf. A. Grillmeier, *Christ in Christian Tradition*, 2nd ed. (London and Oxford, 1975), pp. 250–51.

[14] Special factors pertinent to Eusebius' case were his belief that the emperors had acted as God's instruments in purging the Church (by persecution) and then establishing it, and also the disarray of the great sees in the 320s (for various reasons—the controversy over the *lapsi* at Rome, the Meletian schism at Alexandria, the Paschal dispute, and other matters at Antioch). Hence the tenor of the final revision of the *Historia ecclesiastica*, the *Vita Constantini*, and the *Laus Constantini*. Thus Twomey, *Apostolikos Thronos*, pp. 156–70, who comments, p. 183: "Whatever truth there may be in the contention that the bishop of Rome stepped into the political vacuum left in the West by the emperor when he moved his capital and court to Byzantium it is as true to say, if not more so, that the emperor in the East stepped into the ecclesiastical vacuum in Eusebius' thought which resulted from the inadequacy of his theology, his

oration *The Praise of Constantine*, Eusebius considers the reign of the emperor on earth to be a replica of the reign of God in Heaven. Like Christ, Constantine is a saviour and a word of God to his people. He is the friend of the Logos. Called to mirror the divine perfection, he will not achieve this happy condition until he has brought both peace and the true faith to all the nations. In the Western portion of the Church, however, where the imperial idea had shallower roots, more scepticism could be expected, yet the popes, the Western patriarchs, by and large accepted the utility and congruity of the imperial rôle until at least the eighth century.

The emperor's chief task in the mind of the East Roman church was to order the life of the Church in its public aspect, by securing for it disciplinary unity and doctrinal peace. As already mentioned, the First Council of Nicaea was the classic moment in the cooperation of emperor and episcopate, and to it all later ecumenical councils of the "undivided" Church would look for their model. The emperor convoked the bishops using the same procedure employed for the convocation of senators. Legally, it can be argued, the early councils were meetings of the Senate in its ecclesiastical aspect—something attested procedurally in the way the bishops added their names to a council's acts in the order of precedence laid down by the civil authority for the various provinces of the empire.[15] What, in the Providence of God, saved the independence of the bishops was that, for Roman law, the emperor could neither vote in the Senate nor in any other way intervene in its proceedings: the last vestige of the ethos of the old Roman republic. The emperor confined himself to confirming the decisions of the bishops, granting

disillusionment with the Petrine and Apostolic Succession, and the effects on his person of the Synods of Antioch and Nicaea."

[15] F. Dvornik, "Emperors, Popes, and General Councils", *DOP* 6 (1951): 1–23. So far as the Church's territorial divisions are concerned, the parallel appears to have been first noted by K. Lübeck, *Reichseinteilung und kirchliche Hierarchie des Orients bis zum Ausgang des vierten Jahrhunderts* (Münster, 1901), pp. 75–98. For the analogy with the Senate, see another scholar of Wilhelmine Germany, H. Gelzer, *Ausgewählte kleine Schriften* (Leipzig, 1907), pp. 142–55.

them validity thereby in the civil law. Most probably, Constantine aimed at a compromise between his own claims as *basileus* in the Hellenistic tradition and his awareness that the bishops were, sacramentally, the chief authorities of the Church. As for the see of Rome, it accepted the right of the emperor to call councils up to and including the Second Council of Nicaea of 787, though it did not regard imperial convocation and confirmation as rendering a council definitively binding. Only the reception of its teaching or edicts by the Roman bishop could effect that.[16]

At the same time, the Church allowed Constantine a semisacerdotal status of a somewhat vague variety. Using biblical typology, churchmen portrayed Constantine as a new Moses, a new David, a new Solomon. He had the privilege of entering the sanctuary, otherwise denied to the laity. He could kiss the altar ceremonially during the liturgy, bless the congregation, present the offerings to the bishop, receive communion in the same fashion as the clergy, read the Gospel, and preach on certain feast days. It is already indicative of a certain distance from all this in the West that as early as Ambrose we find a Western bishop querying the practice of letting the emperor stand in the sanctuary with the celebrants at the Eucharist. Ambrose made this objection in person to Theodosius the Great, who apologised with grace and made his way back into the nave of the basilica.[17] The only Eastern bishop of so early a date to manifest a comparable distrust of such imperial prerogatives appears to be John Chrysostom.[18]

---

[16] On the theological significance and ecclesial reception of Constantine's synodal rôle, see A. Kartaschow, "Die Entstehung der kaiserlichen Synodengewalt unter Konstantin dem Grossen, ihre theologische Begrundung und ihre kirchliche Rezeption", in Kirchliche Aussenamt der Evangelischen Kirche Deutschlands, *Kirche und Kosmos: Orthodoxie und evangelisches Christentum* (Witten, 1950), pp. 137–53.

[17] Note also Ambrose's refusal to admit Theodosius I to communion after the massacre of citizens in Thessalonica and his affirmation that the emperor is "the son of the Church, ... for the emperor is within the Church, not above it", *Against Auxentius*, PL 16:1018B.

[18] But M. Azkoul, "*Sacerdotium et imperium*: The Constantinian *renovatio* according to the Greek Fathers", *Theological Studies* 52 (1971): 431–64, considers that the

How, then, did Church and state relate to each other in the East Roman Empire? The basic principle was laid down in the Code of Justinian: between the emperor and the Church there is *symphonia*, "harmony". In this music, the complementary voices have each their own part. The emperor realises in the public forum the dogmatic faith determined by the bishops. He summons synods and actualises their decisions, but he does not define the Symbol, the faith of the Church. This was the fundamental theory, transgressed on numerous occasions but never abandoned. To some extent, it is possible to sympathise with the emperors' position. On the whole, they *did* adhere to the judgements of episcopal synods; the trouble began when they had to adjudicate between the claims of competing synods. An emperor might follow a synod later rejected by the wider Church as heretical, even though it might boast a more numerous attendance of bishops than some other synod whose teaching was later regarded as orthodox. When spiritual (and not only spiritual) warfare broke out between the emperor and the orthodox bishops, the Eastern church made efforts to restrict the ecclesial ambit of imperial authority without, however, ever surrendering the principle of *symphonia*.

A classic example from the early Byzantine period concerns the Church policies of Constantine's son, Constantius, whose attempt to whitewash the Arian party eventually gained him the implacable ill will of Athanasius. In the latter's *Historia Arianorum*, we read that when, at the 355 synod at Milan, Constantius sought Athanasius' condemnation, the bishops demurred on the grounds that it was uncanonical to condemn a bishop who had been officially exonerated from ecclesiastical censure. To this (according to Athanasius), Constantius made the reply, "My will is a canon. . . . Obey, or go

---

majority of the Greek fathers implicitly combatted the Eusebian synthesis of Church and empire in expressing their understanding of both entities on the basis of the Chalcedonian confession and the model of Hebrew kingship. In Azkoul's interpretation, *sacerdotium* and *imperium* interrelate on the analogy of the two natures, with priesthood superior to imperial authority by virtue of its spiritual function within the *oikoumenê*.

into exile." [19] But by no means do all historians regard these words as
ipsissima verba, or even the *ipsissima vox* of the emperor. [20] Constantius'
real attitude is better conveyed, perhaps, by a passage in Theodoret's
Church History that reports a conversation between Pope Liberius and
the emperor on the same topic. Athanasius had been condemned in
335 by the semi-Nicene, homoi-ousian, or "Eusebian" bishops who
would later embark upon the reconciliation of Arius. The pope sought
a fresh examination of Athanasius with a view to clearing him of the
charge then levelled against him: Sabellianism. To this, Constantius
responded: "He was present at the Council of Tyre and there judged,
and on that occasion all the bishops of the world condemned him. . . .
What part of the world are you, Liberius, that you should be alone to
vindicate that man and upset the peace of the whole world? . . . What
has been decided once should not now be rescinded. The sentence of
so many bishops should now be ratified." [21] The ever-present possibility that the emperor, even while scrupulously maintaining the principle that only episcopal synods can determine doctrine, might yet
support a doctrinally deviant assembly led a variety of churchmen to
essay the pruning back of the imperial prerogatives. Towards the end
of his life, Athanasius concluded that, when the emperor calls a council, he should not be seen near it, so as to avoid the slightest suggestion of imperial intervention. [22]

These anxieties, aroused during the Arian controversy, led, signifi-
cantly, to the making of a second, interpolated version of Eusebius'
Life of Constantine under Constantine's successor in both East and
West, Theodosius the Great. Eusebius, it will be remembered, had called

[19] *Historia Arianorum* 33.7.

[20] V. Twomey draws attention to Athanasius' use of fictional monologue and dialogue in the *Historia*, whose literary form he describes as "dramatic historiography".
Its object is "to interpret recent events by unveiling the motives of the chief protagonists . . . while these motives are themselves in turn X-rayed to discover their theological validity and relevance", *Apostolikos Thronos*, pp. 501–2.

[21] *Historia ecclesiastica* 2.16.7.

[22] A speech put on the lips of Pope Liberius in *Historia Arianorum* 36. Athanasius
seems to have arrived at an unambiguous distinction between ecclesial and imperial
authority by the time of writing his *Apologia secunda*.

Constantine *isapostolos*, "equal of the apostles", and Constantius, concerned to preserve his father's memory in its full glory, had built a church, dedicated to the twelve apostles, so as to house his father's mortal remains, as those of subsequent Christian emperors. The symbolism is obvious, but the interpolator of the *Vita Constantini* reduces Constantine's status, regarding him simply as *isepiskopos*, "the equal of a bishop". As he wrote: "He acted like a universal bishop appointed by God and convoked councils of the ministers of God. He did not disdain to be present at their meetings and to become one of the bishops. He sat in the midst of them ... surrounded by ... the friendliest of his faithful friends."[23] The interpolator stresses that Constantine deferred to the majority of the episcopate and, as universal bishop, carried out their decisions, not his own.

The Rôle of the Emperor in the West

And if, in a chastened East, the concept of the "universal bishop" was thus retained, it had its Western counterpart in the welcome accorded to the willingness of emperors to act against heretics and pagans, or at least to consider so acting. Ambrose, despite his hostility to a quasi-sacerdotal notion of the imperial office, never ceased to demand from the emperors the final destruction in Italy of the old Roman religion. Augustine, though of all the Latin fathers the least sympathetic to the Eusebian theology, eventually summoned the emperor to deal with the Donatist schism by the force of law once argument and persuasion had failed.

In the West, however, residual scepticism about the emperor's Church rôle persisted and, if relations between papacy and emperor deteriorated, could at any time become an active force. In the East, the conviction that, come what may, the Church must stay married to the empire endured till 1453.[24] It even survived the attempts of

---

[23] *Vita Constantini* 1.44.2.

[24] Indeed, one could push forward this date to 1917—via the assumption of Byzantine imperial traditions, titles, and ceremonial uses by the grand princes of Moscow. So J. Herrin, *The Formation of Christendom* (Oxford, 1987), p. 476.

the last emperors to enforce on the Greek church a reunion with Rome, their final interventions on the grand scale in matters ecclesiastical. We should not suppose, however, that the early popes saw themselves as the emperors' rivals. So long as the emperors left doctrine alone, the popes could accept the theory of *symphonia*. Only when they saw the emperors underwriting a particular synod, eyed dubiously by Rome, on Church-political grounds, did they object. If, in other words, the emperors followed orthodox doctrine, as understood at Rome, then the popes would allow them whatever privileges in the Church they asked—even to agreeing that papal elections be imperially ratified. But when the emperors failed to follow orthodox doctrine, as seen at Rome, the popes resisted, using language whose charge was to seem, in retrospect, weighty indeed. When, for instance, Pope Gelasius in the fifth century revived the imagery of the "two swords", or fashioned that of the "sun and moon", he meant to indicate that the *sacerdotium*, the episcopate, summed up in the person of the Roman pontiff, stands higher than does the *imperium*, the imperial power. For, according to the theory of papal theocracy that, by the year 1200, had emerged in the West in its full dress, the popes have the right to determine whether the emperor (or king) is carrying out his functions aright even within the temporal domain— since the peace and order of civil society are also moral realities of which the Church may judge. Moreover, in the view of that later, postpatristic, period, not only does the Roman bishop, as the highest representative of the *sacerdotium*, possess such a power of authoritative evaluation: in the case that he finds the ruler negligent, he also has the right to remove him from office by declaring that his subjects are no longer bound to obey him. Such a theory was not only unacceptable to the Byzantine monarchy: it was also alien to the Byzantine church.[25] But in the age of the fathers, all this lay years ahead.

[25] The *Dictatus papae* of Gregory VII, though a private document, expressed the thinking underlying his excommunication in 1078 of the Byzantine emperor Nicephorus III Botaneiates for deposing Michael VIII Palaeologos. Dvornik calls this "the first application of the stipulations of the *Dictatus papae*"; *Byzance et la primauté romaine* (Paris, 1964), p. 126.

The way in which papal attitudes to the imperial theology turned largely on imperial behaviour is well illustrated by the relations of Pope Felix III with the emperor Anastasius during the "Acacian" schism that followed the promulgation of Zeno's *Henotikon*. As we have seen, Zeno's Christological settlement had offered the proscription of both Nestorius and Eutyches but without the Chalcedonian definition, and the four Eastern patriarchates had bowed to this policy in the face of Roman disapproval. Pope Felix wrote to the emperor:

> Of a certainty it redounds to the prosperity of your affairs if, when the matter in hand concerns the things of God, you exert yourself according to his commandment to submit your imperial will to the bishops of Christ and not to assume leadership; to learn sacred matters from those who are set over them, not to teach them; to follow the prescription of the Church and not to prescribe to it laws to be followed after the fashion of men; nor to tyrannise over its ordinances, since it is in very deed God's will that you should bow yourself in humble obedience.[26]

But when he thought that the emperor was about to bring the schism to an end, the same pope wrote again, accepting the emperor's ecclesial mission—and even his right to depose bishops and to choose their successors.

The Holy Roman Empire created by the papacy in 800 differed *toto caelo* from the older Christian-Roman empire of the East. In principle, it was the Church's creation. The new Western emperors derived their authority from the divine realm but not, as in Byzantium, via the natural law. They received it via the authority of the church that had crowned them. To Eastern eyes, the new creation was distinctly *Ersatz*. It was the original, the traditional, Roman emperors whose rôle Providence had time and again confirmed. Those emperors had paved the way for the Messiah by the *pax augusta*; they had christianised the Roman world in becoming Christian themselves; they had used their power, diplomatic and

[26] Cited in T. G. Jalland, *The Church and the Papacy: An Historical Study* (London, 1944), p. 319.

military, to extend, or defend, the orthodox faith. Even in some
Western writers, the appeal of the East Roman ideology was strong.
Before the reunion council of Lyons (1274), a discussion took place
as to the fate of the empire in the event of ecumenical success. For
some Westerners, the best solution was to accept a Byzantine
emperor, married off to a Latin princess, as sole supreme ruler for
both East and West.[27]

Byzantium and Beyond

On the diminishment of Byzantine power in the course of the mediaeval period, no noticeable abatement of imperial claims ensued.
The imperial practice of presiding at the doctrinal debates of their
clergy continued under the Palaeologan dynasty, the last to sit on
the East Roman throne.[28] The comparison of the emperor to a bishop
was rendered more plausible by the adoption, inspired perhaps by
Western models, of the rite of anointing for a new emperor, in
the course of the thirteenth century. The Byzantine canonist Demetrios Chomatianos, defending the right of the emperor to translate
bishops, remarks that he does not only succeed the supreme pontiffs of antiquity. In the Christian dispensation, his powers are significantly increased. Thanks to his imperial chrism, he may be called
the Lord's anointed. Like Jesus Christ, the divine Messiah, he
receives the charisms proper to a high priest.[29] Accordingly, it verged
on the bathetic for the same author to add, "The emperor has all
the prerogatives of a priest except the right of administering the

[27] In "The Empire and the Schism in the *Opusculum tripartitum* of Humbert de
Romanis", *ECR* 5 (1973): 740, George Every ascribes to the Dominican master-
general some sympathy with "the idea put forward from Byzantium on more than
one occasion, that the schism might be healed if the unity of the empire were restored,
if the emperor who reigned in Constantinople was also emperor in Rome and Italy
and (Humbert might add) the Arelate [his home territory, in southeast France]. The
Germans would resent this, but the German part of the Holy Roman Empire had
now disintegrated."

[28] C. Walter, *L'iconographie des conciles dans la tradition byzantine* (Paris, 1970),
pp. 143–44.

[29] C. Walter, *Studies in Byzantine Iconography* (London, 1977), XIII., p. 69.

sacraments."[30] However, Father Christopher Walter of the Augustinians of the Assumption, whose study of the visual images produced by Byzantine society has greatly illuminated the understanding
of Byzantine attitudes, detects a certain ambivalence in the period
following the "eleventh-century watershed", with its precipitate
decline of Byzantine power. For the iconographic evidence points
to a strengthening of the sense of the significance of the episcopate, embodied in, for example, the new tendency, from the late
twelfth century onwards, to portray the bishops in the apses of
Byzantine churches (where hitherto only the apostles, or, at best, a
rare donor bishop, would have stood) and, from the thirteenth century, to place images of the ecumenical councils in the church's
narthex.[31] Certain texts confirm this. Nicetas Choniates' *History of
Manuel Comnenus* pours scorn on emperors who consider themselves to be so many Solomons in divinity. An encomium of the
patriarch Arsenius (died 1273) lauds the emperor Theodore II Lascaris' docility to his ghostly father, which is only as it should be,
since "the anointer is greater than the one anointed". A pastoral
instruction of the patriarch Matthew I (died 1410) encourages bishops to speak out, like the prophets, in the presence of kings. And
Walter's dossier concludes tellingly with a testimony to the views
of the fifteenth-century Macarius of Ancyra for whom, Gelasius-
like, the power of the priesthood stands higher than that of the
imperium. Other witnesses testify very differently—and occasionally
the same person will speak with a barely recognisable alternative
accent. Macarius in his treatise against the Latins reverts to the
more traditional Byzantine position that the emperor is "another
Christ", the first personage of Christendom, exalted above all patriarchs and councils.[32] As late as 1393, the patriarch Anthony IV
declared to Basil I of Moscow that the ecumenical Church postulates

---

[30] "Letter to Constantine Cabasilas", ed. J. B. Pitra, in *Analecta Sacra et classica spici-
legio solesmensi Parata* VI (Rome, 1891), cols. 631–32, cited in D. M. Nicol, *Church and
Society in the Last Centuries of Byzantium* (Cambridge, 1979), p. 3.

[31] C. Walter, "The Eleventh Century Watershed", in *Studies in Byzantine Iconography*, p. 249.

[32] Ibid., p. 247.

an ecumenical emperor: the one cannot exist without the other.[33] Walter's solution is elegant: *within* the Byzantine church, from the eleventh century onwards, the bishops stressed ever more emphatically the superiority of ecclesiastical authority over imperial power, but *outside* of it, in controversy with outsiders, the Byzantine clergy continued to exalt the imperial office.[34]

Is it proper, in the light of historical understanding, to call the Byzantine church "caesaropapist"? Is this why, *au fond*, it had insufficient room for the actual pope? The Byzantine Empire had no written constitution to which reference can be made for the adjudication of this question, yet it produced numerous legal collections that functioned as systematisations of custom and canon. Throughout the Byzantine centuries, the emperor could translate bishops, alter the relative status of dioceses, appoint the ecumenical patriarch from a list of three names provided by a synod, or even pick another name if the synod gave formal approval to this. He could convoke general councils of the Church, though in the developed Byzantine ecclesiology—the theory of the Pentarchy—no council might be considered ecumenical unless all four patriarchs and the pope attended or were represented, but despite this formidable panoply of powers, most Byzantinists are unwilling to call the Byzantine system a caesaropapist one, owing to the constancy of the tradition whereby the emperor is of himself impotent to determine the Church's faith. Indeed, some emperors with a high imperial ideology, such as Justinian, also held a high doctrine, at any rate in theory, of the pope's authority in matters of Christian believing. But if the Byzantine polity was not caesaropapist, then what should we call it? Hunting for a suitable word has become a scholars' pastime: caesaroprocuratorist? caesaropaternalist? even, with an anachronistically technocratic ring,

---

[33] Text in V. Grumel, V. Laurent, and J. Darrouzes, eds., *Les régestes des actes du Patriarcat de Constantinople*, vol. 1, *Les actes des patriarches* (Paris, 1972), no. 2931. For the idea of the "family of kings", used to preserve the notion of the all-embracing fatherhood of the emperor in the changed circumstances of Byzantine decline, see J. Dolger, *Byzanz und die europaische Staatenwelt* (Ettal, 1953), pp. 34–69, 159–96, 282, 369.

[34] Walter, "Eleventh Century Watershed", pp. 244–45.

caesarocybernetic?[35] The most common word used in Byzantium itself to describe the emperor was, perhaps, the more profound, if also optimistic, one, *christomimêtês*: the imitator of Christ. As Justinian had remarked in his laws, it is by imitating Christ's philanthropy and humility that the emperor will mirror God in the Christian commonwealth.

There is, then, a genuine if to us hardly recuperable element of ecclesiological feeling in the position of the emperor. We cannot understand the course of the Byzantine schism unless we take it into account. Nor in the wake of the eastern European revolutions and rumblings of 1989–1990 can we pronounce its day definitively over. Both in Russia and in Serbia, neotraditionalists seek once again an "Orthodox tsar", in the latter case to take responsibility for Bulgaria and Greece also. In the wake of a period when so little has been predicted aright, it would be foolish to rule out the possibility that the pope of Rome will yet have to face, in Moscow or Belgrade, figures for whom the ancient ideology of the emperor's rights and duties in the Church has again become reality.

[35] D. J. Geanakoplos, "Church and State in the Byzantine Empire: A Reconsideration of the Problem of Caesaropapism", *Church History* 34 (1965): 381–403.

Bibliography

Baynes, N. H. "The Byzantine State". In *Byzantine Studies and Other Essays*, pp. 47–50. London, 1955.

———. "Eusebius and the Christian Empire". In *Byzantine Studies*, pp. 168–72.

Dvornik, F. *Early Christian and Byzantine Political Philosophy: Origins and Background*. 2 vols. Washington, D.C., 1966.

———. "Emperors, Popes, and General Councils". *DOP* 6 (1951).

Greenslade, S. L. *Church and State from Constantine to Theodosius*. London, 1954.

Michel, A. *Die Kaisermacht in der Ostkirche, 843–1204*. Darmstadt, 1959.

Runciman, S. *The Byzantine Theocracy*. Cambridge, 1977.

Setton, K. M. *Christian Attitudes towards the Emperor in the Fourth Century, Especially as Shown in Addresses to the Emperor*. New York, 1941.

6

The Estrangement between Rome and Constantinople, III: The Growth of the Papal Claims

Catholics have come to believe that being in communion with the bishop of Rome is a necessary condition for being in communion with the Church of Christ herself—in anything other than a defective sense for the word "communion". Now this belief has a history, and that history played a major part in the making of the principal Eastern schism. Many Western Christians would not necessarily have followed the Western "line" on various issues had they not been concerned for fidelity to the papal tradition. Conversely, many Eastern Christians would hardly have allowed doctrinal disagreement to terminate in schism had they understood, and accepted, the claims of the Roman see in their full force.

New Testament Foundations

The "Roman claims" turn on an isomorphism between the position of Rome in the communion of the churches and the position of Peter (and, to a lesser extent, Paul) within the company of the apostles. The New Testament presents the special rôle of Peter as the will of both the Jesus of the historic ministry and the glorified, exalted Christ.[1] Among the Twelve, Simon is the first called (Mk 1:16), the

[1] R. Brown et al., *Peter in the New Testament* (London, 1973); S. Cipriani et al., *Pietro nella Sacra Scrittura* (Florence, 1975); R. Pesch, *Simon-Petrus: Geschichte und geschichtliche Bedeutung des ersten Jüngers Jesu* (Stuttgart, 1980).

first fisher of men (Mk 1:17), and the first witness of the Resurrection (1 Cor 15:5; Lk 24:34). He receives from the Lord the name of "Peter", the rock (Mk 3:16), and is thus designated as the cornerstone of the community of the final age, inaugurated in the fellowship of the Twelve. These foundations are further explored in the various Gospel traditions. In Luke, Peter is the steward of the future household (12:42), a missionary (5:1–11) who must "confirm his brethren" (22:32). In the Lucan Church history, the Acts of the Apostles, Peter appears not only as leader of the infant Church but as guide of her mission, vis-à-vis both Jews and Gentiles. In Matthew, Peter's confession of faith at Caesarea Philippi is expanded to show the full dimensions of Peter's mandate in relation to the Twelve and the whole Church: he is the bearer of special divine revelation, which guarantees the Jesus tradition transmitted in the Gospel. In John, it is Peter alone who lands the net filled with fish (21:11) without its tearing, and he alone who is solemnly invested with a pastoral charge that extends to the whole flock (21:15–17). The book of the Acts, and occasional other references, confirm the testimony of the Pauline letters that Paul of Tarsus acted as Peter's chief co-worker in the earthly establishment of the body of Christ. Paul's correspondence witnesses to the life of one who bore, by divine election, the "care of all the churches", notably in apostolic proclamation to the Gentiles, complementing Peter's primary involvement in mission to the Jews. Judging by the conclusion of the Acts of the Apostles, Luke was aware that Paul's career had come to its close in Rome. Likewise, in the First Letter of Peter, there are indications that this was the final scene of Peter's apostolate too.

Not surprisingly, then, the early Church held that the apostles Peter and Paul had sealed with their blood the faith of the church of the city of Rome—a church itself both Jewish-Christian and Gentile-Christian in composition.[2] Because the Roman church had been taught by these preeminent pastors of Jesus Christ, and notably by the first of the Twelve and chief of the apostles himself, and because it had been

---

[2] 1 Clem 5:2; Irenaeus, *Adversus haereses* 3.3.1. For the archaeological evidence regarding the death and burial of Peter, see J. M. C. Toynbee and J. B. Ward-Perkins, *The Shrine of St. Peter and the Vatican Excavations* (London, 1956).

privileged to see that faith confirmed by the witness of their martyrdom, this church of Rome enjoyed a correlative preeminence in the total network of communion of local churches that made up the Great Church of the early Christian period. Thus in the opening decade of the second century, we find Ignatius of Antioch lauding the Roman church as she who "presides in charity" among the churches,[3] and fifty years later Irenaeus of Lyons will ascribe to this same church a *principalitas*, which we might well translate "preeminence", such that all other churches must agree with the faith there held and taught.[4]

Such references to the Roman *church* necessarily applied also to the Roman *bishop*. A bishop is the guardian of the faith of his people and its principal teacher.[5] What is said about the rôle of the church of Rome in continuing the significance of Peter (and Paul) within the life of the Christian organism must therefore be applicable in some way to the bishop of Rome. The reference to Paul never disappears entirely in this context but is increasingly overshadowed by reference to Peter, to whom Christ had made promises that he would pastor the sheep of his community (John), confirm his brethren (Luke), and be the foundation stone of his Church (Matthew).

In the story of Roman relations with the Eastern churches, the calling into question of an (undefined) primacy for the bishop of Rome is relatively rare. More commonly disputed is how this primacy should be understood; its scope and limitations; how it should be exercised; and whether it is in the full sense of divine right or, alternatively, something that is of merely ecclesiastical creation, having emerged, and proved useful, in the Providence of God.[6]

---

[3] *To the Romans*, preface; see O. Perler, "Ignatius von Antiochien und die römische Christengemeinde", *Divus Thomas* 22 (1944): 413–51.

[4] *Adversus haereses* 3.3.3; see D. van den Eynde, *Les normes de l'enseignement chrétien dans la littérature patristique des trois premiers siècles* (Gembloux and Paris, 1933), pp. 171–79.

[5] Hence the importance of the connexion apostolicity–episcopate–primacy: M. Maccarrone, *Apostolicità, episcopate e primato di Pietro: Ricerche e testimoniante dal II. al V. secolo* (Rome, 1976).

[6] As Nilus Cabasilas (died c. 1363) wrote in his treatise *On the Causes of the Dogmatic Differences in the Church*: "We have never quarrelled with the Roman Church about primacy, and there is no question here about taking second place. We know the ancient

The Witness of the Early Fathers

Of the earliest writers who touch on the Roman primacy we can distinguish two kinds of commentator. First, there were those who saw the Roman church as the supreme example of a church that kept the rule of faith of the apostles. Characters like Irenaeus and Tertullian were chiefly preoccupied with the task of establishing the rôle of the Great Church as the accredited interpreter of the Bible—over against heretics, schismatics, and sectarians. Typically, they argue that Christ entrusted his Gospel to the apostles, and that the apostles founded churches and, in turn, entrusted that Gospel to bishops who succeeded them. In order to discover, therefore, what the Gospel contains, one should look to the apostolic churches (or those in communion with them), since they alone have the Christ-given right to interpret the words of the Redeemer. Among these churches, the Roman church has the clearest and weightiest apostolic origin, so it is supremely to the Roman church that one will go in seeking out the substance of the rule of faith.

Other writers, like Ignatius of Antioch and Clement of Rome, ascribe to the Roman church an authority, whether explicitly or implicitly, or rather, vis-à-vis other churches: an external, so to speak, as well as an internal, authority. Thus, as we have seen, Ignatius speaks of the church of Rome as "presiding in [the] charity", a phrase which almost certainly means taking the presidential rôle among the churches. Similarly, in the *Prima Clementis*, the Roman church addresses the church of Corinth as though she possessed the right to offer sibling correction to another church and with the legitimate expectation of being heard.[7]

Around the turn of the second and third centuries, these prerogatives, ascribed to the Roman church by figures representative of

practice of the Church and the decrees of the Fathers, who called the Roman Church the oldest of all the churches", PG 149: 685, cited G. Denzler, "Basic Ecclesiological Structures in the Byzantine Empire", *Conc.* 7, no. 7 (1971): 68; see 61–69.

[7] The Anglican scholar J.B. Lightfoot spoke of the letter's "urgent and almost imperious tone", *The Apostolic Fathers* (London, 1890), 1:69.

North Africa and Asia Minor as well as central Italy, come to be invoked by the Roman bishops themselves in their dealings with fellow bishops in the Great Church. Thus we find Pope Victor I proposing to cut off the churches of Asia Minor "from the common unity" (as Eusebius puts it in his *Church History*) on the grounds that they would not accept his ruling over the date of Easter—a point of some importance for those with a "realistic" concept of liturgical time.[8] Again, Pope Callistus I, directly invoking the authority of Peter, sought to impose upon other churches the Roman practice in matters of the discipline of penance. Although other Christians might argue that the Roman bishop was acting imprudently or ill-advisedly, none, so far as is known, disputed his fundamental right to intervene in the communion of the churches. Testimonies of a liturgical and archaeological kind to the primacy of Peter among the apostles, and a related primacy of Rome among the churches, can be found not only in Latin West and Greek East but also in places as far-flung as Arabia and Osrhoene (Eastern Syria).[9] Thus the great French savant Louis Duchesne could write of the situation of Rome in the Church of the first three centuries:

> In the ordinary course of events, the great Christian community of the metropolis of the world, founded at the very origin of the Church, consecrated by the presence and the martyrdom of the apostles Peter and Paul, kept its old place as the common centre of Christianity, and, if we may express it so, as the business centre of the Gospel. The

---

[8] *Historia ecclesiastica* 5.24.

[9] For the Byzantine liturgy, see T. Strotmann, O.S.B., "Les coryphées Pierre et Paul et les autres apôtres", *Irén.* (1963): 164–76. For the Slavonic liturgy, see C. Tondini de Quarenghi, *La primauté de s. Pierre prouvée par les titres que lui donne l'Eglise russe dans sa liturgie* (Paris, 1867). For the Syrian churches, both West Syrian and East Syrian, some liturgical material in B. Benni, *The Tradition of the Syriac Church of Antioch concerning Primacy and the Prerogatives of St. Peter, and of His Successors, the Roman Pontiffs* (Eng. trans., London, 1871). Additionally, Michel van Esbroeck, S.J., has stressed that one should not neglect the *legendary* sources, the "mass-media of the epoch": "Primauté, patriarcats, catholicossats, autocéphalies en Orient", in M. Maccarrone, ed., *Il primato del Vescovo di Roma nel primo millenio: Ricerche e testimonianze* (Vatican City, 1991), pp. 493–522.

pious curiosity of all the faithful and of their pastors, turned incessantly towards the Church in Rome. Everywhere people wanted to know what was being done and taught there; if necessary they found their way there. The founders of new religious movements tried to ingratiate themselves there, and even to get hold of the oecumenical authority by slipping in among the leaders. The charity of the Romans, kept up by a wealth already considerable, reached in times of persecution, or ordinary calamity, to the most distant provinces, such as Cappadocia and Arabia. Rome kept an eye on the doctrinal disputes which agitated other countries; it knew how to bring Origen to book for the eccentricities of his exegesis, and how to recall the powerful primate of Egypt to orthodoxy.[10]

Even pagans saw it. Yet the nature, as distinct from the fact, of this primacy was far from clear.

From Pope Stephen to Nicaea

The first distinct statement of a theory of primacy is provided by Pope Stephen I in the mid-third century. Stephen borrowed from Cyprian of Carthage the phrase *cathedra Petri*, Peter's chair.[11] In his letters and the first "edition" of the treatise *De unitate Ecclesiae*, Cyprian had used that phrase for the Petrine office, something that he saw as shared by all Catholic bishops. Cyprian's viewpoint was already somewhat innovatory because of his implicit claim that the rights and duties of the Church's bishops are those of the apostles themselves—and not simply the rights and duties of ministers appointed by the apostles. In a second "edition", Cyprian went on to say that the communion or solidarity of the episcopate must itself have a guardian. He found this guardianship rôle in the office of the bishop of Rome, where Peter had given the ultimate witness of his martyrdom.[12] Pope Stephen builds upon these proposals

[10] L. Duchesne, *Early History of the Christian Church: From Its Foundation to the End of the Third Century* (Eng. trans., London, 1910), pp. 390–91.

[11] M. Maccarrone, "*Cathedra Petri* und päpstlicher Primat vom 2. bis 4. Jahrhundert", *Saeculum* 13 (1962): 278–92.

[12] Cf. *Letter* 59; T. Camelot, "Saint Cyprien et la primauté", *Ist.* (1957): 421–34.

of Cyprian but concentrates everything that Cyprian has to say about the chair of Peter onto his own see. For Stephen, the episcopal chair of the Roman bishop simply *is* the *cathedra Petri*. On this foundation, Stephen claimed authority over, for instance, the bishops of North Africa and Asia Minor.

Although the founding of Constantinople in 324 tended to relativise the central position of the Roman bishop within the Christian world, it by no means pushed the popes altogether to the margins.[13] The First Ecumenical Council, Nicaea I, was summoned by the emperor Constantine, but it is at least possible that he consulted Pope Sylvester first. The *Liber pontificalis* states abruptly that the council was called at the pope's bidding, and while Rufinus, reporting on consultation with the bishops, does not mention the pope in particular, the Sixth Ecumenical Council, Constantinople III, meeting in 680, asserts that Constantine with Sylvester summoned the "great synod" of Nicaea—perhaps reflecting a memory of the actual situation. A possible explanation of why Sylvester of Rome did not attend Nicaea personally is contained in the counsel offered by Western bishops assembled at Arles in 315.[14] The Roman bishop, they advised, should stay put in his city: the city of the apostles who rule there always. In point of less disputed fact, the council was presided over by Sylvester's legate, Hosius of Cordova, and the Byzantine liturgy would interpret this as the moral presence of the pope: "Father Sylvester ... thou didst appear as a pillar of fire, snatching the faithful from the Egyptian error and continually leading them with unerring teaching to the divine light."[15] At Nicaea, the Roman primacy

---

[13] "[I]t is worth pausing at the very outset to remember that Constantine did not regard himself as having founded a new empire, let alone a new civilisation. Constantine was a Latin-speaker who came to the East as an outsider. He restored, he did not fracture, the unity of a Roman empire ruled by one man as *dominus orbis terrarum*—the 'Lord of the world'": thus P. Sarris, "The Eastern Roman Empire from Constantine to Heraclius (306–641)," in C. Mango, ed., *The Oxford History of Byzantium* (Oxford, 2002), p. 19.

[14] PL 8:818.

[15] Cited in S. H. Scott, *The Eastern Churches and the Papacy* (London, 1928), p. 85; cf. the letter addressed by the Council of Sardica to Pope Julius in 345: after quoting

was never made fully explicit, though what would later be termed the patriarchal rights of the pope were laid down in a canon, along with those of Alexandria and Antioch, and the legitimacy of the claim of the church of Jerusalem (Aelia Capitolina) to a special reverence.

Athanasius and the Council of Sardica

Some historians have concluded that, at the time of Nicaea, no Roman primacy relevant to the entire Church was admitted by Oriental Christians. They find this thesis confirmed by the behaviour of the Nicene hero Athanasius. Condemned by the semi-Arian Council of Tyre, Athanasius did not seek recourse at Rome but turned instead to the emperor. It is likely, however, that Athanasius saw himself as on trial not so much for heresy as for the civil crime of fomenting discord within the imperial church. As Father Vincent Twomey has written in his study of the contrasting attitudes of Athanasius and Eusebius, *Apostolikos Thronos*:

> It appears that he went to Constantine to procure a genuine eccle-
> siastical synod or, failing that, to secure at least a hearing from the
> emperor for his defence with regard to charges which included indict-
> ments of a civil nature. Since he had unwillingly travelled to Tyre
> only at the behest of the emperor, then he was forced by the logic of
> the circumstances to place his defence in the hands of the same, once
> a just hearing at Tyre turned out to be an impossibility.[16]

Athanasius' subsequent exile to Trier was itself followed by the attempt of the Arianising party led by Eusebius of Nicomedia to gain for their own candidate for the see of Alexandria, the blatantly Arian Pistos, letters of communion from Rome. In their 339 synod at Antioch, the Eusebians, recognising that Pistos' personal history was too

---

Paul's words in 2 Cor 13:3 about his presence in spirit at Corinth, the letter remarks that Julius' absence could be excused since he was mystically present with them in a harmony of thought and will.

[16] V. Twomey, *Apostolikos Thronos: The Primacy of Rome as Reflected in the "Church History" of Eusebius and the Historico-Apologetic Writings of St. Athanasius the Great* (Münster, 1982), pp. 254–55.

compromised for this ploy to succeed, prevailed upon the prefect of Egypt to secure Athanasius' replacement by the more presentable figure of Gregory of Cappadocia. In the same year, after dispatching an encyclical letter "to his fellow ministers everywhere", Athanasius fled to Rome, where a synod of 340 both admitted him to communion and restored him to his see. The resultant letter of protest penned by the Eusebian-controlled Synod of Antioch of 341 disprized the significance of the Roman church in the ecclesial *koinônia* to the point of eliciting a sharp retort from Pope Julius. In his *Apologia secunda*, Athanasius incorporates the crucial closing paragraph of this letter, where the pope asks, rhetorically: "Are you ignorant that the custom has been for word to be written first to us [in the cases of bishops under accusation, and notably in apostolic churches], and then for a just sentence to be passed from this place?" [17]

Though some historians consider that Athanasius' acceptance of Julius' help was merely tactical and that, with the poor show put up in his defence by Pope Liberius at the end of a two-year exile in 357, he lost interest in Rome, an alternative interpretation can also be sustained. In the light of his early recourse to Rome; the central rôle played by Julius' letter in his defence of the ecclesial wellfoundedness of his legal claim to his see; and his depiction, in the *Historia Arianorum ad monachos*, of the sufferings that led to Liberius' finally supporting Athanasius' condemnation as weighty confessions of the pope's *actual* belief, it may be that Athanasius' view of the "apostolic throne" was not significantly different from that of the Roman popes themselves.[18]

One especially important feature of this age of the Arian controversy for our purposes here is the 343 Council of Sardica (this placename is also spelled "Serdica"), which both exonerated Athanasius from the charge of unorthodoxy levelled against him by the Council of Tyre and also passed a number of canons relevant to the Roman claims.[19] These canons—and specifically 3, 4, and 7—remain today

[17] *Apologia* 35.4.
[18] Twomey, *Apostolikos Thronos*, p. 519.
[19] L. W. Barnard, *The Council of Serdica, 343 A.D.* (Sofia, 1983).

a matter of dispute between and among Catholic and Orthodox commentators.[20] According to canon 3 of Sardica, if a bishop whose
case has been submitted to the judgement of a provincial (ecclesiastical) court disputes that court's verdict, then those who have tried
the case may write to the bishop of Rome. If the pope agrees to a
review, he is to appoint judges to retry the candidate; if, on the
other hand, the Roman bishop refuses to reopen the case, then he is
to confirm the original sentence. The Latin text does not specify
the provenance of the retrial bishops, but the Greek version states
that they are to be chosen from among the bishops of neighbouring
provinces. In the Latin text, the appeal is directed to the Roman
bishop as such, whereas the Greek specifies Pope Julius by name.
This latter circumstance has allowed a number of commentators to
argue that this provision is a piece of "crisis ecclesiology", designed
to deal with a single limited, if dire, situation. It is, however, equally
possible to argue that the proposer of the canon, Hosius, took as
illustration the actions of the contemporary pope, who had heard
appeals from bishops deposed by the anti-Nicene party. Hosius did
not necessarily intend the operation of the canon to be restricted to
Julius' lifetime.

Canon 4 lays down that if a bishop has been deposed by a provincial council and disputes the sentence, a new bishop should not
be enthroned in his see until such time as the bishop of Rome gives
a decision. It is this canon that many Catholics (and occasional Orthodox) interpret as establishing in the person of the Roman bishop a
second formal court of appeal where alone final judgement can be
given. Against this interpretation it has been counterargued that, had
the makers of canon 4 intended to institute a further court of appeal,

[20] For the text, P.-P. Joannou, *Discipline générale antique*, vol. 1, pt. 2, *Les canons des
synodes particuliers, IVe–IXe siècles* (Rome, 1962), pp. 162–80. The founder of the modern Orthodox attempt to diminish the significance of these canons appears to have
been K. Rhalles, *Poinikon dikaion tês Orthodoxou Anatolikês Ekklêsias* (Athens, 1907),
pp. 48ff. A more generous view is taken by S. Troianos, *Hê ekklêsiastikê dikonomia
mechri tou thanatou tou Ioustinianou* (Athens 1964), pp. 144–46, itself criticised by B.
Pheidas, *Proüpotheseis dimorphôseôs tou thesmou tês pentarchias tôn patriarchôn* (Athens,
1969), pp. 105–11.

they would surely have stated this in explicit fashion. And once again, as with canon 3, it is possible to maintain that the canon's drafters had in mind a strictly limited contemporary situation—namely, the appointment of Gregory of Cappadocia as bishop of Alexandria at a time when, in Western eyes, Athanasius' case was not yet settled.

Canon 7 is the last that should detain us. In dealing with appeal to Rome, this canon provides for the possibility that a sentenced bishop may present his own case to the pope, moving him thereby to send Roman presbyters, vested with his own episcopal authority, to add their judgement to that of a provincial council. As with canons 3 and 4, some hold that canon 7 is simply a retrospective validation of what had actually happened in an emergency situation: in this case, at Sardica itself, where Julius' judgement vis-à-vis Athanasius was communicated and ratified by his legatine presbyters.

From Sardica to the "Latrocinium"

Since the fourth century, Sardica has become a bone of contention not only between East and West but also within the Western church, especially in the bitter and protracted dispute between Gallicans and Curialists in the seventeenth and eighteenth centuries. The Sardican canons acquired an especially august quality through the circumstances of their manuscript transmission in the Roman chancery, where they were added to the canons of Nicaea (in retrospect, an indisputably ecumenical gathering) without indication of source.[21] Gallican canonists argued that the right of appellate jurisdiction was something novel, conferred on Rome by a council so as to cope with a crisis. Their Curialist counterparts took a very different view: for them, the right to receive appeals from wherever in the Church inhered in the Roman primacy as a divinely originated institution, and Sardica merely gave expression to this. More recently, commentators have drawn attention, illuminatingly, to the parallel between the ecclesiastical appeal process envisaged by Sardica and its secular

---

[21] H. Chadwick, *East and West: The Making of a Rift in the Church: From Apostolic Times until the Council of Florence* (Oxford, 2003), p. 16.

equivalents. The force of this comparison is principally to suggest that the pope's appellate jurisdiction was modelled procedurally on that of the emperor—which would indicate, in the transferred context of Church communion, a high doctrine of Roman priority. Yet, unlike the emperor, in these canons the pope does not promulgate judgement by himself but rather entrusts it, in greater or lesser degree, to bishops of the provinces.

The rise of the Christian emperor was itself a threat to the prerogatives of the Roman popes, as the insecurity of Athanasius' position demonstrated. The popes reacted by defining their ecclesial position ever more sharply, a process already visible in the papal reaction to the Second Ecumenical Council, Constantinople I, which, in its third canon, had raised the church of the new imperial capital to the second place, immediately after Rome. While this move was mainly anti-Alexandrian, it also imperilled Roman primacy, since the ground for the promotion was that Constantinople was the New Rome. In the following year, 382, Pope Damasus held a synod that, inter alia, protested against the passing of this canon, stoutly maintaining that the Roman church owed her primacy to the decrees of no episcopal assembly but directly to Christ himself. For Damasus, indeed, Rome was the *sedes prima Petri apostoli*, the "first see of the apostle Peter".[22] More, the see of Rome is now spoken of as *sedes apostolica*, the apostolic see *simpliciter*—as though no others worth mentioning existed.[23] The pope begins to adopt in his public statements the "plural of majesty", speaking as "we" rather than "I", and to address his fellow bishops as sons rather than as brothers. On the other hand, considerable anger was caused in the East by Rome's not-very-happy attempt to interfere in the troubled affairs of the church of Antioch during a complicated schism there. As the East, secure in the framework of the Christian empire, found that it could do without Rome as a necessary *point de repère*, so Rome, by the

---

[22] H. Marot, "Les conciles romains des IVe et Ve siècles et le développement de la primauté", *Ist.* (1957): 458. However, F. Dvornik would date this Roman response to c. 500: *Byzance et la primauté romaine* (Paris, 1964), p. 41 and pp. 55–60.

[23] The theme of P. Battifol, *Cathedra Petri* (Paris, 1958), pp. 95–103.

same token, found it increasingly urgent to clarify its special position and to gain the adhesion of others to it. The claims of Constantinople compelled Rome to move further along the road to a fully efficacious primacy, gathering together her earlier titles into the compendious counterclaim to be the exclusive inheritor of all the New Testament tells us of the prerogatives of Peter.

In fact, it is in 354, less than half a century after the founding of New Rome, that we hear in the Old Rome on the Tiber of Peter as the first bishop of Rome—rather than the apostle who commissioned the first bishop.[24]

In the forty years after the First Council of Constantinople, we find Pope Siricius (384–399) claiming for papal decretals the same binding force as synodal decision; Pope Innocent I (401–417) asserting that all *causae maiores*, "major causes", should be reserved to the Roman see; and Pope Boniface I (418–422) affirming that the Roman church stands to "the churches throughout the world as the head to its members": the manifesto of a *caput* ecclesiology of the papacy. Though bishops everywhere hold one and the same episcopal office, they must "recognise those to whom, for the sake of ecclesiastical discipline, they should be subject".

That such claims were "received" by the Eastern churches in some degree seems clear from the events surrounding the Third Ecumenical Council, Ephesus, in 431. In 430, Pope Celestine convened a Roman synod to investigate the case of Nestorius, brought to his notice by Cyril of Alexandria. While Celestine believed that his own synod had dealt adequately with the matter, he consented nonetheless to a general Church council as "of benefit in manifesting the faith". At that council, the assembled bishops spoke of themselves as "necessarily impelled" to take action both by "the canons, and by the letter of our most holy father and colleague Celestine, bishop of the Roman church."[25] Not only did Cyril preside over the council in the pope's name, but Nestorius himself,

---

[24] In the Liberian "Catalogue", dated to that year. But Cyprian had already done much to elide the distinction between apostolic founder and bishop.
[25] DS 264.

when faced with the apparent victory of his bitterest opponents—
the extreme Alexandrians—at the subsequent *latrocinium* of 449 (for
Monophysites, the Second Council of Ephesus), also appealed to
Roman authority as an indispensable element in the determination
of doctrine. As he pointed out in criticism of the Ephesian synod:
"We did not find there the bishop of Rome, the see of Saint Peter,
the apostolic dignity, the beloved leader of the Romans."[26] Faced
with such texts, contemporary Orthodox spokesmen sometimes claim
that, in the patristic age, Easterners appealed to Rome only when
desperate, plying her with high-sounding titles in the hope of gaining her active support. And yet such appeals are made not only by
individuals in difficulties but also by councils themselves.[27]

The Contribution of Pope Leo

The efforts of the popes to express their sense of their own place in
the Church of God reached a patristic apogee in the pontificate of
Pope Leo I.[28] By background, Leo was a member of the old Roman
governing class; by training, he was an administrator. Accordingly,
he translated the papal claims into the language of law and public
policy. Since, as representative of Peter, the pope holds the power of
the keys, he must enjoy a *plenitudo potestatis*, "fulness of power", in
the congregation of all believers. At the same time, Leo did not
regard the pope as Peter's legal embodiment only. He also saw him
as Peter's mystical or sacramental embodiment—a theme especially
clear from his liturgical sermons on the feast of the chair of Peter.[29]

---

[26] In F. Loofs, *Nestoriana. Die Fragmente des Nestorius* (Halle 1905), p. 302.

[27] Scott, *Eastern Churches and the Papacy*, p. 148.

[28] W. Ullmann, "Leo I and the Theme of Papal Primacy", *JTS*, n.s., 11 (1960): 25–51.

[29] Notably *Sermo* 3.2–4; PL 54:145–47. For Leo's sacramental grasp of the Christian mystery, see M. B. de Soos, *Le mystère liturgique d'après S. Léon le Grand* (Paris,
1958). In Leo's claim that Peter is ever present *in sede sua*, ongoing serial time and the
special privileged time of the original revelation are mysteriously related. As Corne-
lius Ernst, O.P., sometime regent of Blackfriars, Oxford, expressed it: "It is primarily
because the time-horizons of Leo's anniversary sermons are the same as those of his

Leo had arrived, moreover, at a propitious moment. Various factors in the general situation of the Church conspired to make it more likely that Easterners might respond positively to Roman claims than had been the case hitherto. First, there was the consistently balanced and confident position that Leo adopted in matters of Christological doctrine. At the Fourth Ecumenical Council, Chalcedon, that would be acknowledged with the acclamation, "Peter has spoken through Leo." Such a cry of praise did not necessarily signify the acceptance of a unique authority for the Roman bishop in the sense that Leo himself would have maintained. The acclamation was inherently ambiguous. For some, it meant, simply enough, the acceptance of the *Tome* on its own merits—a singularity where the heavenly Peter and the earthly Leo for once spoke with one voice. As we have seen, the moderate majority at Chalcedon favoured the *Tome* as marrying moderate Cyrillianism with moderate Antiochenism in a way that promised doctrinal peace in the Church.

And here lay Leo's second strength. The mediating good offices of the see of Rome had never been more urgently needed. In the East, the Church was falling apart. The Nestorian and Monophysite controversies were tearing the patriarchates into factions. Any of these could turn to Rome if it felt it advantageous so to do, and a number did. Thus we suddenly find the Antiochene—and perhaps semi-Nestorian—theologian Theodoret of Cyr speaking of Rome's "hegemony over the churches of the world". Nor, if for different reasons, was Rome any less indispensable in the contemporary conjuncture in the West. There the barbarian invasions had disrupted the social process, and, with them, the organisation of regional synods was disabled. In this emergency, the Western emperors were willing to turn to whatever organ might help restore order, whether ecclesial

----

seasonal sermons that Leo can make that 'sacramental' identification of himself with Peter.... The 'event' of Leo's own ordination coincides sacramentally with the 'event' in which the Lord institutes Peter in his *honor*, his office of dignity in the Church, and can be re-presented each year, such that Peter's institution persists in and sustains Leo's": thus his "Primacy of Peter: Theology and Ideology", in *Multiple Echo* (London, 1981), pp. 176–77.

or civil, in a chaotic world. Thus four years after Chalcedon, we find the Western emperor Valentinus III ordering a provincial governor in Gaul to see to it that "if any bishop summoned to trial before the bishop of Rome neglect to come", he shall be compelled to go to the pope by the civil power. This decree of 455 conventionally marks the establishment of the pope's patriarchal jurisdiction throughout the empire of the West.

At Chalcedon, Leo's concern—apart, naturally, from the issue of Christology—was to persuade the Easterners that Rome's priority is not derived from the "principle of accommodation": the name given by modern historians to the habit, in the patristic Church, of evaluating the importance of local churches in terms of their position within the civil structure of the empire. The "accommodation" involved was to the administrative divisions of that empire.[30] Local churches were organised into provinces, with the bishop of the civil metropolis, the "metropolitan", at their head. Again, provinces were organised into dioceses, with a supermetropolitan, the bishop of the diocesan capital, at the head of those. From out of these dioceses there emerged the patriarchates: the diocese of Egypt became the patriarchate of Alexandria; that of Syria, Antioch; and so forth. Quite possibly, Ephesus and Caesarea, other diocesan capitals, each furnished with biblical connexions, would also have become patriarchates in due course had not Constantinople swallowed them up. (They sometimes appear as such in the deviant listing of sees preserved by the Assyrian and Oriental Orthodox churches.) Similarly, Italy, the Roman diocese, also became a patriarchate. But since the city of Rome was also the capital, and the traditional seat of the empire, it was not simply superprovincial: it was superdiocesan as well. It is sometimes alleged that this principle of accommodation to civil structures reflects a deterioration in the pristine sense of the Church—a secularisation, in the pejorative sense of that term. But here we must tread carefully. *Something* of the same idea is present in the New Testament, and notably in the Pauline Letters. For instance, the address that opens Second Corinthians shows Paul writing to the church of

---

[30] Dvornik, *Byzance et la primauté romaine*, pp. 23–25.

Corinth as the church of the capital of the province of Achaia (the Greek Peloponnese) and expecting the recipients—possibly the presbyterate of Corinth—to pass on the letter to the churches in the other cities of the province. By a direct development, when the Church began to hold councils, bishops—as already mentioned in connexion with the rôle of the emperor—would sign the conciliar *acta* in the order of precedence laid down by the civil authorities for their cities. Nor was the general principle involved rejected at Rome itself. Pope Boniface I decreed that every (civil) province should have its metropolitan and that metropolitans were not to exercise authority beyond their own province.[31] Moreover, when Diocletian—a pagan and, indeed, a persecuting emperor—reorganised Italy and made Milan the capital of the North, the Milanese bishop inherited jurisdiction over the churches there from his Roman brother, who accepted this transfer without demur.[32] In the East, where respect for imperial forms was stronger still, some of the prestige of Old Rome derived, inevitably, from that church's civil situation.

As already noted, the shifting of the capital to the East encouraged the Roman church to seek compensation by pressing further—over against such mundane factors—the importance of its unique apostolic foundation. Unfortunately for Leo, in whose pontificate this process comes to its first climax, the canons of Chalcedon—and notably numbers 9, 17, and 28—show an even more marked tendency to exalt Constantinople than do those of the Second Ecumenical Council. Canons 9 and 17 allow for appeals from anywhere in the East to the church of Constantinople, which they describe as "the [episcopal] Throne of the imperial city". To these, however, the pope made no objection. What he did find galling was canon 28, which includes these words:

> The fathers [that is, the bishops of Constantinople I] properly gave the primacy to the Throne of the elder Rome because that was the imperial city.... And [they], being moved with the same intention, gave equal privilege to the most holy Throne of New Rome, judging with reason that the city which was honoured with the sovereignty

[31] PL 20:773.
[32] Batiffol, *Cathedra Petri*, p. 43.

and Senate, and which enjoyed equal privileges with the elder royal
Rome, should also be magnified like her in ecclesiastical matters, being
the second after her.

This canon, evidently, ignores one (to Leo) crucial fact: Rome's priority depends fundamentally on her apostolic, and especially her Petrine, character.

Whether the Eastern bishops (and the emperor) understood this
point is a matter of debate. Letters from the East to Leo seem to
admit the notion of the apostolicity of the Roman see, but the absence
of all reference to the idea in the canon itself left the pope understandably unhappy. Canon 28 of Chalcedon was not received at Rome;
in the East, owing to the pope's protest, it remained officially
unrecorded until the sixth century. The papal legate advised his master to accept it but to accompany the acceptance with an unambiguous statement of the principle that Rome's primacy derives from
her foundation on Peter.[33] Such was the goodwill towards Leo's see,
or so the legate believed, that such a document would have found
ready response. If that were so, then a great opportunity was lost to
secure for Rome a clear conciliar statement that the Eastern churches
shared at root her understanding of her own claim. Perhaps the single most positive moment for the Roman side was a moment of
silence. When the papal legates read out to the assembly an inaccurate version of the canons of Nicaea, the Orientals appeared to find
nothing odd in the interpolated claim, *Romana ecclesia semper habuit
primatum*, "the Roman church has always had the primacy".[34]

From Leo to Justinian

Harmony between empire and papacy did not long outlast Chalcedon itself. As we have seen: to recover the lost Monophysite provinces,

[33] Dvornik, *Byzance et la primauté romaine*, p. 49; cf. A. Michel, "Der Kampf um
das politische oder Petrinische Prinzip der Kirchenführung", in *Das Konzil von Chalkedon: Geschichte und Gegenwart*, ed. A. Grillmeier and H. Bacht (Würzburg 1953–
1956), 1:491–562.

[34] Dvornik, *Byzance et la primauté romaine*, p. 47.

the emperors had to find a way of circumventing Chalcedon, and this was the very thing that the popes would not let them do. More widely, papal-imperial tension was in the nature of the case. The claims of Byzantine rulers were barely compatible with a papal claim to "plenitude of power" in spiritual government. And yet the Byzantine Empire seemed—even to Rome—the one chance of decent Christian administration in an otherwise largely anarchic temporal order. Furthermore, it contained all the apostolic sees aside from Rome herself; it was the mother of the councils, the home of monasticism, the seat of the best Christian learning. More negatively, it was able to strike at the city of the popes by sea, even after the incursions of the Slavic people cut off the land routes in the seventh century. Finally, the popes did not willingly surrender the hope that the emperors might be brought to a better mind in Christ and accept in their own episcopal persons the prerogatives of Peter—as indeed, towards the end of the story of Byzantium, they were to do. In the last chapters of that story, it would be the emperors who made the running in the cause of reunion between East and West, and the Oriental bishops—or many of them—who would no longer obey.

During the decades after Chalcedon, up to the year 800, the papacy's concerns are increasingly Western-facing. Often reluctantly, and with genuine regret, the popes extricate themselves from the East Roman Empire, a polity that was either too feeble to protect the Roman see or so powerful that it overshadowed it; neither state of affairs was welcome to the popes themselves.

In the early part of this period, from 461 (the death of Leo) to 527 (the accession of Justinian), the popes lacked effective control of most of their own patriarchate. Frankish bishops resisted papal authority, while Spain, North Africa, and northern Italy were officially Arian, since many of the Germanic tribes who now ruled in those territories had received the Gospel from Arian missionaries. In Byzantium the emperors did not possess the political will to help the pope recover his patriarchal authority. The period coincided, moreover, with the "Acacian" schism between Rome and the Eastern churches, sparked off, as we saw, by Zeno's *Henotikon*: an augury since, for the first time, West lines up against East in a clear-cut fashion. During this schism, the popes initiated an assault on the claim of the emperor to intervene in the affairs of the Church—a claim so thoroughly accepted by now within the Christian Hellenism of the Byzantine church that the papal attack on it was possibly not even registered there. In a letter to the emperor Anastasius I, Pope Gelasius put forward the idea of the "two powers": "There are two powers on earth: the sacred authority of the pontiff, and the imperial power. Of these two, the responsibility of the priest is the graver, since at the Last Judgement, priests must give an account not only for themselves but also for kings." [35]

At the same time, Eastern bishops, though accusing contemporary popes of arrogance and obstinacy, show further signs of understanding the peculiar position that the Roman see had in its own eyes as Peter's see par excellence. The schism of Acacius was terminated by Pope Hormisdas with the aid of the pro-Latin emperor Justin on terms entirely favourable to the papacy. The *Libellus Hormisdae*, which Byzantine bishops now signed, remained one of the clearest Eastern affirmations of the Roman primacy as an effective primacy of doctrinal authority—and not simply a "primacy of honour".

> We cannot pass over in silence the affirmations of our Lord Jesus Christ, "You are Peter, and upon this Rock I will build my Church." ... These words are verified by the facts. It is in the apostolic see that the Catholic religion has always been preserved without blemish.... This is why I hope that I shall remain in communion with the apostolic see in which is found the whole, true, and perfect stability of the Christian religion. [36]

[35] *Letter* 12.2–3, on which see F. Dvornik, "Pope Gelasius and Emperor Anastasius I", *Byzantinische Zeitschrift* 44 (1951): 111–16, and for an argument that Gelasius' pontificate, whose spirit is encapsulated in this text, constitutes the true turning point from the late antique world to that of the Middle Ages, W. Ullmann, *Gelasius I, 492–496: Das Papsttum an der Wende der Spätantike zum Mittelalter* (Stuttgart, 1981). For Ullmann, the papacy, by formulating and enacting the ancient *romanitas* in a Christian and ecclesial fashion, contributed in a crucial way to the "growth and physiognomy of the Latin West in contradistinction to the Greek East": E. Ullmann, *Walter Ullmann: A Tale of Two Cultures* (Cambridge, 1990), p. 66.

[36] PL 65:460.

These words do not recognise in the see of Rome a legal right to intervene in churches beyond the realm of her own patriarchate, but they do discern, in Rome's witness to the orthodox faith, a unique intrinsic authority. We should note, however, the preface that the Constantinopolitan patriarch John insisted on prefixing to the book. There he wrote: "I accept that the two most holy churches, that of your elder Rome and that of our new Rome, are one; I admit that the other see of Rome and that of the imperial city are one." [37] This preface qualifies the Byzantine acceptance of papal authority in the *Libellus Hormisdae*. It gives perfect expression to the Byzantine doctrine of the moral identity of the two Romes; it shows that Byzantine churchmen were seeking a compromise between, on the one hand, the principle of apostolic authority and, on the other, the principle of accommodation; and it leaves open the possibility that, should the Roman church—*per improbabile*—fall into heresy, its prerogatives could pass to the sister church, New Rome, Constantinople. We can also say that from this moment (519) onwards, the Roman see accepted tacitly or in practice the general primacy of Constantinople in the East, though in periods of tension Rome would revert to denying it in theory—as in the Photian crisis and the schism of Michael Kerullarios.[38] The popes of this period between Leo and Justinian felt bold enough to adopt policies unpopular in the East in part because they knew how little the empire could do whether for them or against them. This state of affairs did not long survive the accession of Justinian. Justinian's aim was nothing less than the restoration of the Roman Empire to its fullest ancient boundaries, and the refurbishment of its purest Christian traditions. He was vitally interested in the papacy, both because the goodwill of the popes was a major desideratum in restoring Byzantine government in Italy and

---

[37] PL 65:444A.

[38] The ecumenicity of the full text of Constantinople I was now effectively recognised: Y. J.-M. Congar, "La primauté des quatre premiers conciles oecuméniques", in *Le Concile et les conciles* (Paris and Chevetogne, 1960), pp. 75–109. But Rome remained ill disposed toward the title "ecumenical patriarch" taken by the bishop of Constantinople: S. Vailhé, "Saint Grégoire le Grand et le titre de patriarche oecuménique", *EO* (1908): 65–69, 161–71.

because the Roman church had been, after all, the original imperial church.[39] Justinian's comments on the papacy must rank among the "highest" that we find in Byzantine history: part of a (no doubt sincere) campaign to woo the popes to his side. Thus in a novella of 535 he wrote: "The ancient city of Rome has the honour of being the mother of our laws, and no one can doubt that in it the summit of the supreme pontificate lies. This is why we have also found it necessary to honour this cradle of the law, this source of priesthood, by a special decree of our sacred will."[40] And, in a letter to Pope John II, Justinian goes on to call the Roman church "the head of all the churches": the very title claimed by Pope Boniface I a century before.[41] Writing to his own patriarch, Epiphanius, Justinian had this to say:

> We have condemned Nestorius and Eutyches, prescribing that in everything the churches of God must keep unity with the most holy pope and patriarch of the elder Rome. . . . For we cannot tolerate that anything concerning the ecclesiastical order be left out of relation to the holiness of that church, since it is the head of all the most holy priests of God, and since, each time that heretics have arisen among us, it is by a sentence and right judgement of that venerable see that they have been condemned.[42]

Justinian continued, nevertheless, the policy of attempting to stabilise the ecclesiastical order by demarcating areas of competence for the two Romes: "Following the decisions of the councils, we decree that the most holy pope of Old Rome is the first of all the hierarchs and that the holy archbishop of Constantinople, the New Rome, occupies the second see, after the holy and apostolic see of Rome but with the right of precedence over all other sees."[43] The emperor's tributes to his two leading bishops were clearly respectful of patristic

---

[39] For Justinian's religious policy, see E. Stein, *Histoire du Bas-Empire* (Bruges, 1949), pp. 369–417, 423–690; and E. Schwarz, "Zur Kirchenpolitik Justinians", in *Gesammelte Schriften* (Berlin, 1938–1963), 4:276–328.

[40] *Novel* 9.

[41] PL 66:15.

[42] *Codex Justiniani* 1.1.7.

[43] *Novel* 131.

and conciliar tradition, but this does not imply abandonment of imperial pretensions to responsibility for the *pax Ecclesiae*. In the matter of the "Three Chapters", Justinian humiliated the papacy, forcing it to accept a series of posthumous condemnations that it did not believe right. The papal submission set off a burst of local schisms in the West, from Africa to Italy, lasting in some cases for a century.[44]

The "Byzantine Captivity" of the Papacy

Justinian's ruthlessness towards Pope Vigilius ushered in a period that has been termed the "Byzantine captivity" of the papacy. From Pelagius I (555–561) onwards, the papacy's dependence on the empire was expressed in a custom of seeking confirmation of the name of the elected pope from the exarch of Ravenna—the emperor's Italian representative—accompanying the petition for the same with a gift of money; in effect, tribute.[45] This practice continued for two hundred years, during which eleven popes were Greeks or Syrians by birth. Nevertheless, the nature of this dependence should not be exaggerated: it hardly impeded the pastoral outreach to the barbarian world of Gregory the Great. Moreover, the continuity of presentation of papal claims, coupled with Justinian's pro-Roman pronouncements, had done its work. The principle that Church authority derives primordially from apostolicity had impressed itself more deeply on the Eastern Christian mind.

To this period there belongs, therefore, the rise of the idea of the Pentarchy—the notion that major issues, both dogmatic and, more generally, religious, should be handled by the five patriarchal sees whose bishops would then represent the *sacerdotium* to the *imperium*.[46] The

---

[44] E. Amann, "Les Trois Chapitres", *DTC*, vol. 15, pt. 2 (Paris, 1950), cols. 1868–1924.

[45] It should be noted, however, that Pelagius I "found a text under Augustine's name saying that anyone separating himself from communion with the apostolic see defines himself as schismatic", Chadwick, *East and West*, p. 58: I take that to be an early sign of chafing under the yoke.

[46] M. Marella, "La pentarchia: Storia di un idea", *Nicolaus* 2 (1974): pp. 127–93; V. Peri, "La pentarchia: istituzione ecclesiale, IV–VII sec., e teoria canonico-teologico", in *Bisanzio, Roma e l'Italia nell'alto medioevo* (Spoleto, 1988), pp. 209–511.

pentarchic concept is already adumbrated in Justinian, for instance in novella 109. Constantinople, in order to keep her place among this privileged five, felt herself obliged to move beyond the claim that she partook, as New Rome, of the apostolic foundation of her elder sister. So, in the later sixth and seventh centuries, there is pieced together the legend of Constantinople's foundation by the apostle Andrew—who, after all, in the words of the Gospels, brought Simon (Peter) to Jesus.[47] So far as we know, relying on Eusebius, who got it from Origen, Andrew missionised in Scythia, the modern Crimea, where large Jewish colonies flourished. But a now lost "Acts of Andrew" of c. 300 spoke of him as visiting Thrace and Byzantium en route.[48]

The period during which the popes were in a condition of dependence on the emperors, expressed in the appeal for confirmation and the tribute money, lasted until the accession of Stephen II in 752. Enormous political changes were in the meantime convulsing Europe, and these brought to a head the cultural estrangement between Rome and the Greek East considered in the last chapter.

The chief source of these changes was the Arab invasion of the Mediterranean basin on the death of Muhammad in 632. Its effects were far-reaching. First, so far as Chalcedonian Christianity was concerned, the Muslim advance wiped off the map all the possible rivals of Rome and Constantinople, leaving them like two boxers in the ring at the end of a knockout competition: Alexandria, Antioch, and Jerusalem were reduced to pale shadows of their former selves, their patriarchs ever more frequently Greeks, sent out from Constantinople. Second, and as a direct result of this, the Byzantine church became a largely Greek church in the ethnic sense, almost a national church, which it would remain until the conversion of the Slavs. Third, and following the celebrated thesis of the Belgian historian Henri Pirenne in his *Mohammed and Charlemagne*, Arab control of

---

[47] F. Dvornik, *The Idea of Apostolicity in Byzantium and the Legend of the Apostle Andrew* (Cambridge, Mass., 1958).

[48] Present, however, within Gregory of Tours' *Liber de miraculis beati Andreae Apostoli* as the latter's chief source.

the Mediterranean seaways disrupted communication between Latin West and Greek East.[49]

Quite apart from the Arabs, other invaders were abroad as well. The descent of the Slavs and Avars into what is now Croatia, Serbia, and northern Greece swept away the main bridge-church between Rome and Byzantium, the church of Illyria, itself both Greek- and Latin-speaking yet under Roman jurisdiction.[50] The only Helleno-phone area now left to the Roman patriarchate was southern Italy and Sicily, where contact with Constantinople was diminishing thanks to the maritime disturbances. Finally, the entry of the Lombards into Italy destroyed Justinian's achievement in substituting orthodox Byz-antine government for Arian Gothic rule. Byzantine authority in Italy was so ended as never to be restored.

The popes now faced a dilemma. Before the unknown quantity of the Lombards, they could scarcely appeal to Constantinople— itself fighting for life on several fronts, and with a record of respect for the Roman see always qualified and occasionally nonexistent. The alternative was to look to one or more of the recently chris-tianised nations of the barbarian West for political support and pro-tection. They wavered, but finally and with the justification of imperial indifference, or incompetence, in the face of their appeals for help, under Stephen II (752–757) they turned definitively to the new peoples.

The involvement of the popes with the barbarian West had so far been purely missionary, not ecclesiopolitical. Gregory the Great had dispatched what proved a highly successful mission to England in 596, and the infant Anglo-Saxon church would soon turn to the evangelisation of the tribes of continental Germany under Saint Bon-iface of Crediton. These northern peoples came to have an extraor-dinary veneration for the Roman see as the mediating source of their own faith, and wherever their missionaries penetrated, they carried

[49] *Mahomet et Charlemagne*, 2nd ed. (Brussels, 1937). But see the criticisms of A. F. Havighurst, *The Pirenne Thesis: Analysis, Criticism and Revision* (Boston, Mass., 1958).

[50] F. Dvornik, *The Slavs: Their Early History and Civilization* (Boston, Mass., 1956), pp. 42–45, 118–22.

the same profound respect for Rome. The custom of making pilgrimages "to the threshold of the apostles", *ad limina apostolorum*, started in this period. But the Anglo-Saxon kingdoms were too far, and too fissiparous, to succour the pope militarily, while as yet the German people was only in the process of emergence from prehistory. The nation to whom the popes turned under Stephen II was the Franks.

Three events precipitated the final decision. First came the struggle with the imperially sponsored heresy of Monothelitism. In the mid-seventh century, the closing in of the Persian armies on Byzantium led the emperors in desperation to revive the temporising policies of Zeno vis-à-vis the Monophysites. In 638, the emperor Heraclius issued an *ekthesis* maintaining, as a sop to Monophysitism, that in Christ there is only one *energeia*—one stream of conscious, volitional activity: more simply, one will, a will that is "theandric", being at once human and divine. Resistance and, especially in the West, bitter opposition caused Heraclius' successor Constans II to withdraw this document and replace it with another, the *Tupos*, in which a veto was placed on all discussion of the question, "Does Christ have two wills, or one?" on pain of the direst civil penalties. When Pope Martin I refused to obey this directive, he was arrested and sentenced for high treason, dying in penal exile in the Crimea. His successor, Honorius I, whose case was much discussed at the First Vatican Council in connexion with papal infallibility, gave Constantinople deliberately evasive answers and would be condemned both at the Sixth Ecumenical Council and at Rome itself, in a formula preserved as an oath for newly elected pontiffs, for his culpable lack of vigilance.[51] However, the next three popes, up to Martin II, spoke out clearly enough against both the erstwhile imperial doctrine and the current imperial embargo on its public rejection. Interestingly, we have from this period a number of strongly pro-Roman

---

[51] G. Kreuzer, *Die Honoriusfrage im Mittelalter und die Neuzeit* (Stuttgart, 1975). On any plausible view of Honorius' beliefs or intention, it would scarcely be possible to maintain that he sought to dogmatise Monothelitism *ex cathedra* in the sense intended at Vatican I.

affirmations, emanating from Eastern churchmen who were themselves Dyothelites, believers in the two wills of the Word incarnate, and who could see no other place of recourse in this crisis save the see of Rome.[52] In Maximus the Confessor, the leading Byzantine theologian of the seventh century, we find quite categorical assertions of its unique priority. The Roman church, for Maximus, has received both from Christ and from the councils "the power to command all the holy churches of God in the entire world".[53] Maximus invites the Monothelites, therefore, to address themselves to that see, there to renounce erroneous doctrine and receive pardon. These remarks are echoed in the contemporary figure Sophronius of Jerusalem.[54]

The second happening that alienated the papacy from the empire but gained for it the admiration of many Byzantines was the imperially imposed Iconoclasm of the succeeding century. Not only did the emperor Leo III forbid the making and veneration of images of Christ, his Mother, and his saints, but he also tried to secure the acquiescence of the rest of Catholic Christendom in this ban. When the pope, Gregory III, refused to come to heel, Leo took the most drastic measures attempted by any emperor against Rome. He removed all of Greece, Dalmatia, southern Italy, and Sicily from the patriarchal jurisdiction of the pope, cutting off the Roman see, for all practical purposes, from the imperial church of whose body texts of Justinian, and others, had acclaimed it as head.[55] Not content with this, Leo also sent, unavailingly, a fleet to lay waste the city of Rome

[52] See especially the profession of Stephen of Dora, envoy of the patriarch Sophronius of Jerusalem, at the Roman synod of 649: Dvornik, *Byzance et la primauté romaine*, p. 79.

[53] PG 91:137–40; V. Croce, *Tradizione e ricerca: Il metodo teologico di San Massimo il Confessore* (Milan, 1974), pp. 115–31; some brief remarks in L. Thunberg, *Man and the Cosmos: The Vision of St. Maximus the Confessor* (Crestwood, N.Y., 1985), pp. 25–26.

[54] Mansi 10:896c. See C. von Schönborn, *Sophrone de Jérusalem: Vie monastique et confession dogmatique* (Paris, 1972), pp. 91–95.

[55] M. V. Anastos, "The Transfer of Illyricum, Calabria and Sicily to the Jurisdiction of the Patriarchate of Constantinople in 732–733", *Silloge bizantine in onore di S. G. Mercati* (Rome, 1957), pp. 14–31.

and encompass the death of the pope. During the Iconoclast crisis, which moved to an early climax at the 754 Iconoclast Synod of Hiereia, there were few places to which Iconophile churchmen might look for support other than the elder Rome.[56] Thus, such a defender of the images during the "First Iconoclasm" as Stephen the Faster challenged the assembled bishops at Hiereia by asking: "How can you call a council ecumenical when the bishop of Rome has not given his consent, and the canons forbid ecclesiastical affairs to be decided without the pope of Rome?"[57] But it was in the third phase of the Iconoclast crisis, the years of the "Second Iconoclasm", from 813 to 843, that Iconophile theologians like Nicephorus of Con-stantinople[58] and Theodore of Studios showed the most vivid papal-ist colours; in Theodore's case, at least, this belonged with a quite self-conscious defence of the Church *against* the emperor.[59] Admit-tedly, with the benefit of hindsight, we can say that Iconoclasm was the last attempt of a Byzantine emperor to modify the faith of the Church (unless we count the efforts of mediaeval emperors for reunion with the West as such!).[60] But such illumination was unavailable at the time, and it is not surprising that the popes were tiring of the imperial ideology.

Yet so time-hallowed was that ideology that the popes would doubt-less have endured its constraints and so kept contact with the official world of Byzantine Christianity had it not been for political devel-opments in Italy itself. And this was the third factor that precipi-tated their turning to the new peoples. In the early 750s, the Lombard tribes, who in 751 had captured Ravenna and terminated the rôle of

---

[56] E. Kaspar, "Papst Gregor II und der Bilderstreit", *Zeitschrift für Kirchengeschichte* 52 (1953): 72–89; E. Lanne, O.S.B., "Rome et les saintes images", *Irén.* (1986): 163–88.

[57] Cf. *Vita sancti Stephani Junioris*, PG 100:1144.

[58] P. O'Connell, *The Ecclesiology of St. Nicephorus I* (Rome, 1972).

[59] Cf. Theodore, *Letter* 2.86, PG 99:1332A: "If there is anything in the patriarch's reply about which Your Highness feels doubt or disbelief ... you may ask the elder Rome for clarification, as has been the past practice from the beginning, according to inherited tradition."

[60] J. Gill, "Eleven Emperors of Byzantium Seek Union with the Church of Rome", *ECR* 9 (1977): 72–84.

the Byzantine exarch, began to move against Rome, in all probability planning to incorporate the city into the Lombard kingdom. The threat to the popes' independence of action was acute. Since the collapse of the Western empire, they had functioned as governors of the city, more or less taking the position of the *prefectus urbis* of classical times.[61]

The Turn to the West

In 754, accordingly, Pope Stephen crossed the Alps and, in tears and on his knees, besought the Frankish king, Pippin, for protection. Thus began the chain of events that led to the moment, on Christmas Day, 800, when Pope Leo III crowned Pippin's son Charles the Great (Charlemagne) as emperor of the Romans. The significance of that action was complex, meaning differing things as it did to different parties.[62] From the side of the Franks, it marked the high point of Charlemagne's claim to have "renovated" the ancient empire of the West, and that in the context of increased rivalry, rather than diplomatic accommodation, with the empire of the East. For a millennium the idea of the Holy Roman Empire of the West would prove as tenacious as the imperial tradition in the East, if less credited. From the side of the papacy: although later popes, notably in the ninth century, kept one eye on the East, and contact between the papacy and the Byzantine capital was maintained well into the eleventh century, nevertheless Rome moved henceforth essentially in the orbit of western Europe.[63] Though keeping the Petrine tradition

[61] *Pace* the Donation of Constantine: there was nothing especially unusual about this development. Since city dwelling was a concept basically foreign to the new Germanic leadership, civic administration relied heavily on bishops.

[62] J. Herrin, *The Formation of Christendom* (Oxford, 1987), pp. 446–62. For the reaction of the Byzantines, see ibid., pp. 405–6; and, in more detail, W. Ohnsorge, "Das Kaisertum der Eirene und die Kaiserkrönung Karls des Grossen", *Saeculum* 14 (1963): 221–47.

[63] V. Peri argues, however, that contemporaries did not see the northward and (increasingly) missionary reorientation of the papacy as such an alternative policy. Insofar as it remained within the *ordinatio* or *taxis* of a great patriarchal church— namely, that of the West—it could still be interpreted within the ancient imperial

by which it claimed to be the first see and the touchstone of orthodoxy, it no longer troubled to struggle with New Rome on the
latter's home ground. Moreover, that Rome was now without rivals
in its chosen sphere of operation meant that it could begin to
realise in practice some of the large claims made in theory since at
least the pontificate of Damasus: it was a bigger fish in a smaller
pond. By the time that Photius had become patriarch of Constantinople in 858, the theory of the Pentarchy meant comparatively
little on the Tiber, whereas in the East the notion that the other
four patriarchs could do nothing without their elder brother represented the highest degree of papalism that Byzantine churchmen
were willing to accept.

The same period sees the beginning, for good or ill, of the temporal sovereignty of the bishops of Rome, something that heightened their prestige in the eyes of civilian *élites* but also undermined
the spirituality of the Roman Christian tradition. So far as we can
tell, the late-eighth-century popes conceived the plan of making themselves the effective rulers of Italy, or at any rate of central Italy, since
they could no longer count on the Byzantines to do it for them,
whereas the Franks, away across the Alps, were too distant to be of
immediate help in any new crisis situation. The Donation of Quierzy,
made by the Frankish monarchy, gave the popes a half share of the
Italian peninsula, to be ruled as a papal Roman republic: *sanctae Dei
ecclesiae respublica*, "the republic of the holy church of God".[64] Although
at the time the Franks were largely incapable of signing over these
territories, the statement of a pious hope came in due course to
fruition. Papal anxiety that, on the contrary, nothing would come of
this scheme is expressed in a contemporary document known as the
"Donation of Constantine". This claims, on the one hand, to confirm the popes' primacy over the four patriarchates of the East and,

conciliar picture, what Peri terms "l'ideologia costantiniano-giustinianea". Thus his
"La Chiesa di Roma e le missione 'ad Gentes', sec VIII–IX", in *Il primato del vescovo
di Roma nel primo millenio: Ricerche e testimonianze*, ed. M. Maccarrone, pp. 567–642.

[64] For the gradual emergence of an independent pontifical state, see T. F. X. Noble,
The Republic of St. Peter (Philadelphia, 1984).

on the other, to entrust the pope with dominion over the city of Rome and much of Italy besides. The Franks indeed succeeded in conquering and handing over, as their "patrimony", to the Roman bishops a large slice of central and northern Italy, stretching from south of Rome to Venice and beyond. Its effect was less to give the popes increased freedom of action and more to forge a halter for their necks.

Nor is it difficult to see why this was so and how it generated a certain contempt for the papacy in the informed East. The popes had got involved in politics, a somewhat dirty business. In the northern part of their patrimony, above Bologna, their power was barely more than nominal, and they expended a great deal of energy on trying to make it effective. In the south, around Rome, their government was more of a reality, but by this very fact they attracted the undesirable attentions of local landowners aware that control of the pope would be in future the key to power. Now begins the attempt of the Roman aristocracy to turn the papacy into a family possession. In the tenth century, the Petrine office would reach a nadir in terms of the personal qualities of its holders, and only a major reform movement, the Gregorian reform—itself an ambiguous blessing in the perspective of our study—would save it.

The incubus of the temporal power was not, however, the only papal inheritance of this period. For these were the years when the popes found themselves the spiritual patrons of the newly christianised areas of northern and central Europe. Whereas to the inhabitants of the cities of Italy, Spain, Greece, and Asia Minor the bishop of Rome was simply the highest dignitary in the ecclesiastical hierarchy, to the English and the Germans he was a quasi-transcendental figure in whom Peter lived again as the mediator of faith and the doorkeeper who one day would open the gates of the Kingdom to receive their immortal souls. When in 664, the kings of Northumbria were asked to decide between the Roman and the Celtic computations of the date of Easter, they opted for the method recommended in Rome since, in the words of King Oswiu: "Saint Peter is the doorkeeper, and I will not resist him but will follow him as best I can, so that, when I come to the gates of Heaven, there will be someone there to open them for me, and he who has the key will not turn me back."[65]

From this new, highly propapal Germanic Christian ambience, missionaries reached Scandinavia, Bohemia, and Poland, all of whose rulers accepted Latin Christianity in the tenth and eleventh centuries. These churches, stretching from Iceland to the western Slavs, remembered that they owed their faith, whether directly or indirectly, to the Roman see—something that could never be said of the churches of the East or even of the older churches in the West, such as Milan or Ravenna. The new communities looked to the papacy for spiritual leadership, and—though they did not find it in the dark days when a whole succession of unworthy popes reigned—in better times, with good and holy pastors on Peter's chair, their devotion to the Holy See was not only warm but also influential. For Rome listened to the enthusiasm of her adolescents, which was clear and distinct, compared with the calmer, subtler and more complicated interaction with her older, worldly-wise Mediterranean cousins.

Latin Christendom thus took shape as a spiritual and cultural unity, a Western counterpart to the Byzantine "commonwealth". By the start of the eleventh century, the popes, for their part, were ready to act out their rôle to the full. It is by no means a coincidence that within fifty years the most serious schism to date should have driven Rome and the Orthodox East apart when in 1054 churchmen at Rome and in Constantinople issued mutual anathemas, and, though lacking corporate ratification, the "Eastern Schism" began in earnest. It is an irony of Church history that the very same reforming movement whereby the popes became instruments of the purification of the Church of the West so forcefully contributed to the sundering from their communion of the Church of the East.

The Effect of the Gregorian Reform

The tenth and eleventh centuries were the greatest age of reform in the Latin church as a whole before the Catholic Reformation of the

---

[65] Bede, *Historia ecclesiastica gentis Anglorum* 3.25.

sixteenth century. This reform movement began in eastern France—in Burgundy and Lorraine—as a reaction to the corruption of society in general and the Church in particular. Unlike the sixteenth-century reform, its main centres were not bishops' palaces but monasteries: self-reformed, austere, fervent, whose abbots were consciously concerned with the revival of the whole Church. This reform movement was not minded, at first, to emancipate pastoral government from lay control, nor did it harbour great expectations of the papacy—family possession, as this had seemingly become, of the counts of Tusculum—in distant Rome. The reform went ahead in France, Germany, and northern Italy with the help of local rulers and without appeal to the pope. But gradually the reformers became aware that there was something anomalous about a situation where a lay ruler controlled, or even owned, dioceses, religious houses, parishes—the "*Eigenkirche* principle", as it is known.[66] Around 1000, Abbo of Fleury, a reforming abbot, could write: "Let him who wishes the health of his soul beware of believing that the Church belongs to any save God alone. For he said to Peter, the prince of the apostles, 'I will give thee my Church': 'mine', not 'thine'.... In truth, dear princes, we neither live nor speak as Catholics when I say, 'This church is mine', and some other says, 'That church is his'."[67] Some thirty years later, under the leadership of Guido of Arezzo, Italian reforming circles began to press for the branding of lay investiture of bishops as a practice involving heresy.

So far, the popes had scarcely noted the new wave. But in 1046 the Holy Roman emperor Henry III arranged for a synod that deposed all three rival candidates for the papal office, representatives as they were of aristocratic factions in the Latium; had himself declared "patrician" of Rome, a title meant to convey interested guardianship of papal elections; and placed a German reforming bishop on the Petrine chair. Thus began the sequence of reforming north European popes, of whom for our purposes the most important is Leo IX, an Alsatian who ruled the church of Rome from 1049 to 1054. These

[66] S. Wood, *The Proprietary Church in the Mediaeval West* (Oxford, 2006).
[67] Cited in G. Barraclough, *The Mediaeval Papacy* (London, 1968), p. 70.

popes filled the Lateran with advisers like unto themselves, virtually obliterating local Romans whose concerns had been indeed local, with the city and its surrounding countryside. The new men had been educated north of the Alps, where popes were seen as directing heads of the Christian community at large. In the words of Geoffrey Barraclough, "they had more belief in the papacy than the popes themselves".[68]

It was a sign of these new times that Leo IX spent scarcely six months of his pontificate in the city. At synod after synod, he issued decrees aimed at reforming the lives of clergy and laity and took energetic steps to see to their realisation. From this there emerged what is perhaps the single most important factor in the rupture between East and West. The servants of the papacy now sought the fullest scope for the reform by forging in the canon law an instrument for achieving the "universal jurisdiction" (as the First Vatican Council would term it), which, at least since Leo, had been ascribed to the Petrine office holder's pastoral supervision.[69] Around 1050, the first collection of canons fully to reflect the spirit of the reform made its appearance. The "Collection in Seventy-Four Titles" can be dated to within five years of the schism of Kerullarios. This new canon law was greatly exercised by the need to affirm the juridical prerogatives of the successor of Peter, and it selected its authoritative *loci* as much from the "decretals" or historic decisions of the popes themselves as it did from the Church fathers and the synodal decrees. The claims to universal ecclesial authority put forward by a newly self-confident papacy, confident that it constituted the God-inspired means of reforming the Church throughout the world, produced an intransigent reaction among the Byzantine churchmen. This turn of events we must consider in a subsequent chapter, but suffice it to say here that the papal legate who travelled to Constantinople to nego-

[68] Ibid., p. 74.

[69] J.J. Gilchrist, "Canon Law Aspects of the Eleventh Century Gregorian Reform Programme", *Journal of Ecclesiastical History* 13 (1962): 21–58; and, more widely, W. Ullmann, *Mediaeval Papalism: The Political Theories of the Mediaeval Canonists* (London, 1949); and idem, *The Growth of Papal Government in the Middle Ages: A Study in the Ideological Relation of Clerical to Lay Power*, 3rd ed. (London, 1970).

tiate with the patriarch Michael Kerullarios and who used his legatine powers to issue an anathema against him had himself been brought
to Rome by Leo IX for his reforming and propapal convictions.
Humbert of Moyenmoutier, made cardinal by Leo in 1050, was a
characteristic example of the vigorously evangelical Curialist that the
later stages of the reform threw up. To the mind of such a cleric, the
dignity and autonomy of local churches were mere vanity if they
stood in the way of the reform and sanctification of the people of
God. And to his mind, the chosen instrument for that reform and
sanctification was the see of Rome.

But here we are running ahead of our story—as accounts of background will tend to do. We must retrace our steps and begin to
examine the two crises in which the full-dress Catholic-Orthodox
schism of later centuries was rehearsed: the problem of Photius and
the *Filioque* and the case of Kerullarios and the azymes.

Bibliography

Barraclough, G. *The Mediaeval Papacy*. London, 1968.

Dvornik, F. *Byzantium and the Roman Primacy*. New York, 1966.

Grotz, H., S.J. "Die Stellung der römischen Kirche anhand früh-christlicher Quellen". *Archivum historiae pontificae* 13 (1975): 7–64.

Karrer, O. *Peter and the Church*. Eng. trans. London, 1970.

———. "Das Petrusamt in der Frühkirche". In *Festgabe Joseph Lortz*, edited by E. Iserloh and P. Mann, Baden-Baden, 1957.

Maccarrone, M., ed. *Il primato del Vescovo di Roma nel primo millennio: Ricerche e testimonianze*. Vatican City, 1991.

———. "Cathedra Petri und die Idee der Entwicklung des päpstlichen Primats von 2. bis 4. Jahrhundert". *Saeculum* 13 (1962): 278–92.

Meyendorff, J., et al. *The Primacy of Peter in the Orthodox Church*. Eng. trans. Leighton Buzzard, 1963.

Peri, V. "*Pro amore et cautela orthodoxae fidei*: Note sul ministero ecclesiale del Vescovo di Roma nella dottrina comune tra l'VIII e il IX secolo". *Rivista di storia e letteratura religiosa* 12 (1976): 341–63.

Scott, S. H. *The Eastern Churches and the Papacy*. London, 1928.

Tierney, B. *The Origins of Papal Infallibility, 1150–1350*. London, 1972.

Ullmann, W. *The Growth of Papal Government in the Middle Ages: A Study in the Ideological Relation of Clerical to Lay Power*. 3rd ed. London, 1970.

7

The Photian Schism and the "Filioque"

The Historical Background

The facts about the career of the controversial Byzantine patriarch Photius were enormously clarified by a single study, the work of the Czech Byzantinist Father Francis Dvornik, professor of Byzantine history at the Charles IV University in Prague. Dvornik fled to England on the German invasion of Czechoslovakia, carrying with him the manuscript published after the war as *The Photian Schism: History and Legend*. Dvornik had at first accepted the traditional account of Photius as a *parvenu* layman who had come to power by ousting the rightful patriarch from his throne and who, in his *prepotenza*, went on to deny the traditional primacy of the Roman Church and bishop. According to this received version, Photius, duly condemned by the Eighth Ecumenical Council of 869–870, proceeded to relapse into fresh misdemeanours, the so-called second Photian schism. During his research into the exactly contemporary missionary enterprise of Cyril and Methodius, the "apostles of the Slavs", Dvornik realised that a number of the documents which lay behind this reconstruction of the Photius story had been misconstrued. He concluded that the Latin church had accidentally obscured the true portrait of Photius and the real significance of the council of 869–870. In what follows I shall be indebted to Dvornik's painstaking rewriting of the narrative.[1]

[1] F. Dvornik, *The Photian Schism: History and Legend* (Cambridge, Mass., 1948); also, by the same author, "The Patriarch Photius in the Light of Recent Research", in *Berichte zum XI. Internationalen Byzantinistischen Kongress* (Munich, 1958), pp. 1–56;

Photius was born into a family already distinguished in the service of the church of Constantinople. His parents had supported Iconophilism, the movement in defence of images, so vocally as to be anathematised by a local synod and forced into exile. His uncle, Tarasius, was the patriarch who had presided over the formal restoration of the images in 787. Attracted for a while to the monastic life, Photius eventually chose a career in the Byzantine civil service, becoming in the process, like many of his colleagues, a considerable scholar.[2] Possibly the central figure of the Byzantine intellectual renaissance of the ninth century, he received the chair of philosophy at the University of Constantinople from the hand of the empress Theodora, under whom the final remnants of Iconoclasm had been snuffed out. When his brother married the empress' sister, Photius graduated to the further distinction of being head of the imperial chancery. To understand the circumstances of Photius' appointment to the see of Constantinople, one must bear in mind how recent the quarrel over the images had been. The Iconoclast crisis had been resolved by the victory of a moderate party within the Byzantine church. These moderates wanted the images restored, but they did not wish to penalise those who had opposed them. Nor did they intend to call into question the rights of the emperor in the Church, though they agreed that in the matter of the images the emperors of the reigning Macedonian dynasty had certainly abused those rights. Such moderates were defined over against a rigorist party that followed in the footsteps of the fiery monastic Iconophile and

reproduced in idem., *Photian and Byzantine Ecclesiastical Studies* (London, 1974), VI, 1–56. Dvornik himself, however, stressed the continuing value of the work of his predecessor, J. Hergenröther, in the latter's three-volume *Photius, Patriarch von Konstantinopel: Sein Leben, seine Schriften und das griechische Schisma* (Regensburg, 1867–1869).

  [2] See especially the evidence of his *Bibliotheca*, best studied now through the intermediary of J. Schamp, *Photios, historien des lettres: La "Bibliothèque" et ses notices biographiques* (Paris, 1987). Photius has been called the "inventor of the book-review": thus H. Chadwick, *East and West: The Making of a Rift in the Church: From Apostolic Times until the Council of Florence* (Oxford, 2003), p. 127. That many of the works Photius highlighted were by pagan authors has commended him to modern classical scholars, but not necessarily to Byzantine contemporaries, especially if monks.

anti-imperialist Theodore of Studios.[3] As Photius reached maturity, this rigorist school looked for support to two figures: the empress Theodora, who, strictly speaking, was only regent for her son Michael, and the patriarch Ignatius, Photius' predecessor. Tension between moderates and rigorists was expressed in hostility between the "demes" of the city of Constantinople, the two rival organisations of the urban populace. Theodora's brother Bardas favoured the moderate party, and when he took her place as regent, Ignatius sided openly with the rigorists—in part through fidelity to Theodora, by whose instrumentality he had become patriarch. In 858, fearing a resumption of hostilities between Church and government, the bishops of the patriarchate advised him to resign and, when he did so, agreed on the candidature of Photius, who was unattached to either party. Because of the imminence of the Christmas celebration, the patriarch-elect received all the major orders within a week, an action that was certainly unseemly and possibly uncanonical. Nevertheless, his consecrators were drawn from both the moderate and the rigorist parties.

Some few weeks later, however, followers of Ignatius began to demand the reinstallation of the previous patriarch, claiming that Photius had failed to honour certain undertakings about the treatment to be accorded the ex-archbishop. The precise nature of these undertakings remains in dispute. After a good deal of urban violence, Photius convened a synod that declared the entire patriarchate of Ignatius illegitimate on the grounds that he had been simply appointed by the empress without due canonical process. The aim of this statement was to remove the ground from beneath the feet of the Ignatian party, in the interests of peace in both Church and state. It was at this point that Photius sent to the Roman pope, Nicholas I (858–867), the customary notification of his election. At the same time, the emperor Michael, who alone in Byzantine law had the

---

[3] F. Dvornik, "The Patriarch Photius and Iconoclasm", *DOP* 7 (1953): 67–99. It seems likely that Photius played a major part in gaining the 787 Council of Nicaea its generally recognised status as an ecumenical council: thus C. Walter, A.A., "The Icon and the Image of Christ: The Second Council of Nicaea and Byzantine Tradition", *Sob.*, n.s., 10, no. 1 (1988): 23.

right to summon an ecumenical council, proposed that a general council should meet solemnly to confirm the ecumenicity of Nicaea II. This, it seems, sent the pope back to the *acta* of Nicaea II, where he discovered the demand of his predecessor Adrian I that the Balkans— what was then called "Illyricum"—which had been in years past a papal vicariate, based on Thessalonica, should be returned to the jurisdiction of Rome, from which they had been severed by the Iconoclast emperor Leo III as a reprisal for the papacy's support of the Iconophile party. As we shall see, this Balkan dimension became increasingly important as the affair of Photius wore on.

The pope's reaction to the letters from Byzantium was to declare himself thoroughly dissatisfied with the situation there, and notably with the direct elevation of a layman to a patriarchal see on the emperor's say-so.[4] He sent two Latin bishops to Constantinople with legatine authority to look into things, reserving to himself, how-ever, any final decision. The justification for this disposition in terms of Byzantine canon law are unclear. The canons of the anti-Arian Council of Sardica had, as we have seen, sanctioned appeal to the Roman church by any bishop. Though preserved in Byzantine legal collections, they may have been regarded as an "historic document" rather than a matter of *actualité*.[5] Byzantine appeals to Rome there had been,[6] but they did not cite Sardica. In any case, Pope Nicholas' action was a personal initiative and not a response to appeal. Dvornik suggests that both government and patriarch, being in a weak posi-tion at home, hoped to strengthen their hand by gaining a positive judgement from the papal legates. Though they laid down the pre-condition that the papal decision must be given on Byzantine soil and in the presence of the bishops of the patriarchate, the legates showed no disinclination to accept these terms, grateful, no doubt, for the implicit acceptance of the Roman primacy as including what

[4] For shifting attitudes in both West and East to the nomination of laymen to the episcopate, see Chadwick, *East and West*, pp. 128–32.

[5] The view of Louis Duchesne in his *Histoire ancienne de l'Eglise* (Paris, 1906–1910), 2:226–27.

[6] P. Bernadakis, "Les appels au pape dans l'Eglise grecque jusqu'à Photius", *EO* 6 (1903): 30–42, 118–25, 249–59.

Congar termed "a juridical right of intervention to determine major causes according to the holy canons." [7]

At this legatine synod of 861, the pope's representatives confirmed Photius' position. We do not know in detail how or why since the *acta* of this synod were destroyed by order of the anti-Photian council of 869. In any case, the pope, apparently irritated by the Greek insistence that a verdict must be given in the East itself, declared himself unconvinced by the documentary evidence, notably with reference to the part played in Photius' consecration by a suspended bishop, Gregory Asbestas of Syracuse. Encouraged by the efforts of rigorist Byzantine monastic clergy in Rome, he held a synod of his own in 863, condemning Photius and reinstating Ignatius, an act which provoked a bitter letter from Michael III and a reply from the pope setting forth a high doctrine of the Roman primacy. [8]

At this critical juncture, a fresh element suddenly entered in the shape of Bulgaria. The Bulgarians were a Eurasian people who had taken large areas of Thrace and Macedonia from the Byzantines in the eighth century and resettled them. The internal situation in these territories was of extreme concern to Byzantium, as the Bulgars were also a warlike people sitting on the Byzantine doorstep. The Bulgar khan, Boris, had expressed his willingness to accept baptism, but his policy was to play off the Greeks against the Latins in the hope of gaining the maximum ecclesiastical autonomy for the embryo Bulgarian church. The khan chose this moment to address himself to Rome, asking for Latin missionaries and offering to submit the Bulgarian church to the patriarchate of the West. [9]

---

[7] Y. M.-J. Congar, O.P., "1274–1974: Structures ecclésiales et conciles dans les relations entre Orient et Occident", *Revue des sciences philosophiques et théologiques* 58 (1974): 355–90.

[8] Nicholas based the Roman church's universal care for all other churches, that is, not on canon 6 of Nicaea I but on the person of Peter: see J. Meijer, *A Successful Council of Union: A Theological Analysis of the Photian Synod of 879–880* (Thessalonica, 1975), p. 28.

[9] R. E. Sullivan, "Khan Boris and the Conversion of the Bulgars: A Case-Study of the Impact of Christianity on a Barbarian Society", *Studies in Mediaeval and Renaissance History* 3 (1966): 55–139. Pope Nicholas' replies, enlightening on the Christianisation of a bellicose paganism, are also of interest for how Rome saw the patriarchal

The Latin missionaries who came to work in Bulgaria were chiefly Franks; that is, they came from the Germanic tribes evangelised in the seventh century, notably from England, and by now possessors of a considerable Latin Christian culture.[10] Through the Frankish monarchy they laid claim to the title of the Western Roman Empire, ostensibly restored in the person of Charlemagne in 800 and known to German-speaking historians even today as *das deutsche-römische Kaisertum*.[11] But, as we shall shortly see, it was the Franks who of all Western peoples had adopted the *Filioque* with most enthusiasm, believing, indeed, that it formed part of the original text of the ecumenical Creed. The Byzantine government was distinctly fearful of the pretensions and rising star of the Frankish monarchy. Its arrogation of the title "Emperor of the West" was seen by Byzantines as a denial of their chief political tenet, namely the claim that in principle there was only one Roman Empire, their own, which should be coterminous with the whole Christian world. The *Drang nach Osten* of the Franks by colonisation and evangelisation among the Slav peoples of central and eastern Europe filled the Byzantine authorities with dread. Accordingly in 867, Photius, with imperial concurrence, invited the other Eastern patriarchs— Alexandria, Antioch, Jerusalem—to come to Constantinople and pronounce on Latin "encroachments" in the East, as well as on the undesirability of the innovations introduced by them in Bulgaria, notably the addition of the *Filioque* to the Creed. In the isolation of the issue of the *Filioque*, the scholars see the theological hand of Photius.[12]

---

idea. Only the bishops of Rome, Antioch, and Alexandria were real patriarchs; Constantinople had a courtesy title from the emperor, while the true Jerusalem is above. Peter living in his Roman successor was in any case more important than the patriarchal principle. See Chadwick, *East and West*, pp. 114–17.

[10] See R. McKitterick, *The Frankish Church and the Carolingian Reform, 789–895* (London, 1977), pp. xv–xvi, on the impressive Frankish ecclesiastical programme for reform and expansion.

[11] See W. Ullmann, *The Carolingian Renaissance and the Idea of Kingship* (London, 1969).

[12] For this encyclical letter to the Oriental patriarchs, see PG 102:721–41.

The Genesis of the Filioque

At this point I must break off to consider the genesis of the *Filioque*, which lies in the Latin West of the fourth century. Let it be said at once that the *Filioque* is a Western interpolation into the text of the Creed of Nicaea-Constantinople. The Creed of the first two ecumenical councils does *not* say that the Spirit proceeds from the Father and the Son: it is not "Filioquist". However, neither does that Creed state that the Spirit proceeds from the Father alone: it is not "Monopatrist". Though Monopatrism was yet to find its champion, Filioquism was the de facto belief of a number of the Latin fathers,[13] and especially of Augustine. In various writings, but most notably in *De Trinitate*, Augustine had offered a number of reasons for holding that the Spirit proceeds eternally from the Son (as well as from the Father).[14] First, the Spirit is referred to by Scripture as the Spirit of the Son.[15] Second, according to the Last Supper discourse of Jesus in the Fourth Gospel, he is sent by the Son.[16] Third, after the resurrection of Christ in that same Gospel, he is "breathed" onto the disciples by the Son.[17] Fourth, he is the union of love between the Father and the Son and so must proceed from both; though not directly biblical, this claim represents Augustine's overall dogmatic interpretation of the place of the Spirit within the Trinity.[18] Finally,

---

[13] And notably of Tertullian, Hilary, Marius Victorinus, and Ambrose.

[14] See Augustine, *De Trinitate* 1.4.7, 1.5.8, 1.8.18.

[15] Gal 4:6; and, somewhat less clearly, Rom 8:15; Lk 6:19; Jn 14:26.

[16] Jn 15:26. The literal sense of this passage certainly concerns the *temporal* sending of the Spirit by the *incarnate* Word; yet, as the Anglican divine H. B. Swete remarked, an extrapolation here is not unreasonable. Since the Spirit belongs eternally to the divine essence, it is normal for the only Son, who as Word has been with God from the beginning, to enjoy a relationship with the Spirit of God that is beyond time: thus his *Holy Spirit in the New Testament* (London, 1909), pp. 304–5. Indeed, the Greek fathers themselves established the relation of the Word to the Father on the basis of the former's rôle in the economy: thus A. M. Dubarle, O.P., "Les fondements bibliques du *Filioque*", *Russie et chrétienté* 1 (1950): 227–44.

[17] Jn 20:22.

[18] *De Trinitate* 6.5.7, 15.19.36; *De fide et symbolo* 9.19. For a thoughtful defence of Augustine's teaching, see D. Coffey, S.J., "The Holy Spirit as the Mutual Love of the

if, as the New Testament insists, the Son has "all things" from the Father, will he not have the power, then, to bring the Spirit into being?[19]

> Augustine ... knew of no recent authoritative formula, stamped with the majesty of an ecumenical council recognized in the west, to which someone in the east might expect him to conform when he set out to state doctrine on the Trinity which excluded the possibility of Arian exegesis. To maintain the equality of Father, Son, and Spirit, he judged it wise to affirm that the Son participated in the Spirit's "proceeding from the Father".... Augustine thought the Arians could drive a coach and horses through a doctrine of the Trinity which excluded the Son from the coming forth of the Spirit from the Father.[20]

In the East, especially in the Cappadocian fathers who were Augustine's older contemporaries, a different triadology produced a very different view of the procession of the Spirit. The Cappadocians located God's unity in the fact that the Father is the single source and origin of the entire Godhead. The Son and Spirit proceed from him as from a single *aitia*, "cause", and are distinguished by their

---

Father and the Son", *Theological Studies* 51, no. 2 (1990): 193–229. Coffey sees the mutual-love theory as the only correct way of understanding and expressing, in the context of the Holy Trinity, the data of "ascending" theology, i.e., the return to the Father of Jesus, and of ourselves with him, and accordingly tends to disassociate it from Augustine's Filioquism since, as he points out, both Filioquism and its Eastern alternatives apply only to the data of "descending" theology, i.e., the outward movement from God that results in the mission of Christ and the offer of grace to us, p. 193. However, he adds: "This being said, it should be mentioned that the mutual-love theory affirms the Filioque, as it were in passing. The Holy Spirit proceeds from the Son inasmuch as the Son makes him his own and returns him to the Father as his own. The Father and the Son are therefore co-principles of the Holy Spirit, and since the Spirit is one, they must constitute a single principle": ibid., p. 220. Yet, as he writes in the same place, the theology of mutual love may perhaps presuppose the *Filioque* in a way that commends the *Filioque* to the East, for in it we clearly see that the Spirit issues ultimately from the Father alone, in that the Father's love for the Son has a priority of order (not of time) over the Son's love for the Father.

[19] *In Joannem evangelium, tractatus XCIX*, 8–9.

[20] Chadwick, *East and West*, p. 27.

mode of procession (filiation and spiration, respectively), not by their relations of origin. Neither of these views were dogmas. They were, rather, *theologoumena*, "theological opinions", and their authority lay in the strength of the arguments that could be marshalled in their favour.

In coming to terms with the Greek tradition in these matters, the Latins had two major problems. In the first place, they had an historical problem in that they were frequently unable to determine which of the texts ascribed to the Greek fathers were authentic. A number of spurious works were appealed to in all good faith, especially writings attributed to Athanasius, of which the most important was the *Quicunquevult*, or Athanasian Creed. That document is unashamedly Filioquist, and it followed that if the main author of the Nicene Creed had supported the *Filioque*, it was more likely that the Byzantines had suppressed a reference to the Spirit's procession from the Son in the original Creed than that the Latins had added one. But in the second place, Latin Christians *also* had a hermeneutical problem, a problem of interpretation, vis-à-vis the Greek East. Many Greek texts, once removed from the Eastern type of Trinitarian perspective, could be made to support the *Filioque*. Thus, for a Greek to say that the Spirit is the Spirit of the Son may well mean, within his picture of the Trinity, that the Spirit is consubstantial with the Son. In the Latin context, the same assertion would be taken as evidence that the Greek in question accepted the eternal procession of the Spirit from the Word. This hermeneutical problem was not so severe if one considers the case of the Greeks reading the Latins. That is because, at least until the fourteenth-century "Latinophrone" movement in the Byzantine church, the Greeks did not, by and large, read the Latins!

After Augustine, the West at large accepted the *Filioque*. This was so even for writers who were in other respects non-Augustinian.[21] Many regarded it as a teaching of the Church everywhere. Thus in the sixth century, Cassiodorus is able to refer to it

---

[21] Such as Leo, Boethius, Cassian, Gregory the Great, and Isidore of Seville.

in an unconditional way as doctrine taught "by Mother Church".[22]
Occasionally, a Roman pope such as Leo I is found expounding it,
though there was no Roman inclination to insert it into the Creed.
It was remembered that canon 7 of the Third Ecumenical Council
of Ephesus had been firm on this point: "The holy ecumenical
synod defines that no one shall be permitted to bring forward a
different faith, *hetera pistis*, nor to write, nor to ... teach it to
others. But such as dare to compose another faith or to bring
forward or to teach or to deliver a different Creed ... if they be
bishops or clerics, let them be deposed ... if they be monks or
laics, let them be anathematised."[23]

This canon, which refers to the Creed of Nicaea, was first unwittingly transgressed at a national council of the Spanish church held
in Toledo in 589.[24] In the late antique period, the Spanish Visigothic kingdom had been disturbed by various heresies, notably Arianism, the denial of the Godhead of the Son, and a peculiar
enthusiastic movement called Priscillianism, which in its Trinitarian
theology was somewhat Sabellian, tending to regard Son and Spirit
as forms of the Father. At Toledo III, the newly converted Spanish
king Reccared made a statement of Catholic faith that included the
phrase *a Patre Filioque*. Against Arianism, such a profession backed
up the Son's divinity: only One who is God can give the Spirit.
Against Sabellianism, it highlighted the Son's distinct identity as a
person: a Giver of the Spirit must be a true subject of activity. While
it is not certain that this council formally introduced the *Filioque*
into the Creed, it created the conditions for its dissemination by
advocating a common recitation of the Creed at the Eucharist before
the communion "according to the custom of the Eastern fathers".
(This practice had in fact been introduced at Antioch and Constantinople sometime around 500.) At once the *Filioque* began to enter

---

[22] See the important study by R. Haugh, *Photius and the Carolingians* (Belmont,
Mass., 1982), p. 24.

[23] J. Alberigo, ed., *Conciliorum oecumenicorum decreta*, 3rd ed. (Bologna, 1973), p. 65.

[24] J. A. de Aldama, *El símbolo Toledano I: Su texto, su origen, su posición en la historia
de los símbolos* (Rome, 1954).

the doctrinal formulae and liturgical books of local Western churches. Most fatefully of all, the interpolated Creed reached the court of Charlemagne perhaps through the Gaulish theologian Theodulf of Orleans or possibly via his English colleague Alcuin of York.[25]

In Italy, on the other hand, even those who accepted the *Filioque* as doctrine were opposed to any tampering with the Creed. Though the Roman church would not condemn the *Filioque*, it could and did condemn its insertion into the ecumenical Symbol. So much is clear from the dispute between Charlemagne and the Roman popes over the *Libri Carolini*, the "Caroline Books". Commissioned by the emperor as a kind of *Summa* of Carolingian Christian thought, these books were markedly anti-Byzantine. Charlemagne was always potentially hostile to the Byzantines because of their nonadmission of his claims to imperial status. Theologically, he had doubts about the manner in which the images were restored at Nicaea II, holding that while the making of images was legitimate, their liturgical veneration was not. The *Libri Carolini* were an apologia for the Franks to the papacy.[26] Charlemagne had objected to Pope Adrian I that the Byzantine patriarch Tarasius, in the course of the 787 council, had taught that the Spirit proceeds *per Filium*, rather than *Filioque*.[27] To this the pope replied that such was also the understanding of the church of Rome. The *Libri Carolini* maintain, by contrast, both the authenticity of the *Filioque* as an integral part of the Creed and the truth of its doctrinal claim. Through the Son, "all things were made", as the Prologue of the Fourth Gospel tells us. But the Spirit is not one of those things that are made. Therefore, he is not *through* the Son but *from* him. With the publication of the Caroline Books, the defence of the *Filioque* became the main preoccupation of Carolingian theologians who, in twenty years of feverish activity, produced an entire armoury of pro-*Filioque* argumentation.

[25] B. Capelle, "Alcuin et l'histoire du symbole de la Messe", *Travaux liturgiques de doctrine et d'histoire* (Louvain, 1962), 2:211–21.

[26] See Y.J.-M. Congar, *L'ecclésiologie du haut moyen âge* (Paris, 1968), p. 281: either Alcuin or Theodulf *may* be their chief author.

[27] Cf. Mansi, 12:1122.

The assertion that the *Filioque* belongs to the original text of the Creed was, however, dropped early, for in Paulinus of Aquileia, a contemporary of Charlemagne's, we find what has been called a "theology of interpolation". Just as the fathers of Constantinople I added in 381 to the primitive Creed of Nicaea, so when heresy requires further formulations the Church after them may add to their efforts. Paulinus laid down several conditions as to how this should be done. The addition must clarify the faith of the Church in opposition to heresy. It must accord with the intentions of the original council. It must be enacted by conciliar means. Paulinus evidently regarded the Carolingian councils as sufficiently authoritative for this purpose. In other writings of the early ninth century, the attempt is made to show that the ecumenical councils implicitly accepted the *Filioque* by formally accepting letters from doctors who supported it, notably Leo the Great and (more debatably) Cyril of Alexandria. The reaction of the papacy to this flurry of theological production is made clear in reports of a meeting between Frankish envoys and Pope Leo III in 810.

These envoys were dispatched in order to gain papal approval for the decision of the Frankish Council of Aachen in 809 to ratify the incorporation of the *Filioque* and seek theological assistance throughout the Western church for its justification.[21] The envoys argued that the addition of just four syllables, *et Filio*, could work wonders in giving the Christian people a right view of God. There is no point, they maintain, in objecting that the council fathers did not write it so if "by adding only four syllables we clarify such a necessary mystery of faith for all succeeding centuries." Pope Leo replied, however:

> I dare not say that what they did they did badly, since undoubtedly they omitted other matters of faith as well even though they knew them. . . . I dare not say that they understood less of this than we do. If they thought of it, why did they omit it? Or why, having admitted it, did they prohibit anything else from being added? See how I feel towards you and your people! I shall not say that I prefer myself to the fathers. Far be it from me to count myself their equal.

But the envoys brush this aside:

> If we presume to prefer ourselves to the fathers, and even to equate
> ourselves with them, this is only because of the needs of our times.
> Being patient and charitable towards our weaker brethren, we seek
> to work for one thing.... Since the end of the world is coming,
> when the times are dangerous, as predicted, we want to witness to
> our brethren as well as we can.... Many learned men, and men of
> all generations yet to come, need to be instructed in such a mystery
> if it is held by the Church. And some will not learn it unless it is
> sung.[28]

However, Leo was seemingly exasperated by this somewhat apoca-
lyptic zeal and required the *Filioque* to be removed at once from the
Carolingian creed.[29] He had two silver shields inscribed with the
original wording of the Creed, one in Greek, the other in Latin,
and placed them in Saint Peter's Basilica. This he did, according to
the main Greek scholar of the papal *familia*, Anastasius the Librarian,
"out of the love he bore for the orthodox faith and out of care for
its preservation".[30] As late as the twelfth century, writers like Peter
Lombard and Abelard refer to these shields, though they have since
disappeared. The Franks, however, took not the slightest notice of
the pope and continued to use the interpolated creed in their missions to the Slavs. And this brings us back again to the Bulgarians,
Pope Nicholas, and the patriarch Photius.

---

[28] For this discussion, see PL 102:971–76.

[29] The background was that Frankish monks on the Mount of Olives, having heard
the *Filioque* in the imperial chapel at Aachen, had introduced it in their own worship.
Accordingly, at Christmas 808, they were accused of heresy by a Greek monk of Mar
Sabas. They appealed to the pope, who wrote to the emperor, and the latter called
on Frankish divines to justify the Western teaching and practice over against the
Greeks: thus the synod of November 809. On this, see R. G. Heath, "The Schism of
the Franks and the Filioque", *JEH* 23 (1976): 97–113.

[30] John Romanides suggested that Leo believed the *Filioque* to be orthodox outside
the Creed and heretical within it—on the ground that, in the Creed, the term "procession" bore a different meaning: thus *Franks, Romans, Feudalism and Doctrine* (Brookline,
Mass., 1981), p. 16.

The Advent of the Crisis

We left the narrative of the career of Photius at the point where the emperor Michael III, in collusion with the patriarch, had summoned a council of the Eastern patriarchates to deal with Latin aggression in Bulgaria. It is just possible to make out a case for Pope Nicholas in this affair. On the issue of the condemnation of Photius, it may be said that the pope was within his rights to annul the decision of his legates, since after all they were only legates and he was the pope. On the issue of Bulgaria itself, part of Bulgaria was formerly Macedonia, and this had been, historically, a piece of the Roman patriarchate up until the eighth century.[31] On the other hand, an unbiased observer would surely have to say that the papal case was pretty flimsy. The papal legates had legatine authority to decide the case of Photius, otherwise they would not have been legates. It is hard to avoid the impression that Nicholas' aim was to humble the see of Constantinople, which he thought was too proud by half.[32] (Nicholas' pontificate represents a high point for papal claims in the patristic period; his letters "cherry-pick" passages from earlier documents so as to establish the principle that the Roman see, whose privileges derive from Peter, can be judged by no other.[33]) And as to Bulgaria, the overwhelming majority of Bulgarians were living in the ancient Thrace, which had always been part of the Byzantine patriarchate. Moreover, Bulgaria was so close to Constantinople that it was imperative to have the new state bound in ties of friendship to East Rome.

Be this as it may, Photius had already prepared the ground well for the council of 867. As already noted, he sent an encyclical letter to the other Eastern patriarchs in which he complained of the Latin missionaries' behaviour across the Bulgarian border. Many of

[31] V. Peri, "Gli *iura antiqua* sulla patria dei Bulgari: Un *topos* canonico per un risveglio missionario", in *Atti dell'8 Congresso internazionale di studi sull'Alto Medioevo* (Spoleto, 1983), pp. 255–68.

[32] One must also note Nicholas' sympathy with the Frankish church, e.g., Nicolaus I. Papa, *Epistolae* 100 (ed. Perels), Monumenta Germaniae historia 6, pp. 600–609.

[33] Chadwick, *East and West*, pp. 95–102. See also S. Vacca, *Primo sedes a nemine iudicatur: Genesi e sviluppo storico dell'assioma fino al decreto di Graziano* (Rome, 1993).

Photius' complaints were liturgical and disciplinary in character, probably reflecting mutual mud slinging between Greek and Latin clergy in Bulgaria. The Latins were attacked for treating Saturday as a fast day, for eating milk foods in Lent, and for insisting on a celibate priesthood. The Greeks were chided for their practice of presbyteral rather than episcopal confirmation. The canonical differences here derived from different attitudes to the canons of the Council *in Trullo* of 691, which were fully received in the East as the work of an extension of the Third Council of Constantinople of 680, while in the West they were accepted only selectively.[34] But the real bugbear was the *Filioque*, which, Photius remarks, would strike the Franks with the force of a thousand blasphemies "even if all the other charges did not exist". Although Photius is already clear that the *Filioque* is heresy, the encyclical represents his Trinitarian thinking in an embryonic stage. Essentially, he deals with what he sees as logical consequences of the *Filioque* idea and aims to show that since these consequences are repugnant to faith, so must the *Filioque* be. Thus he argues that if the *Filioque* is true, then the Spirit is more remote from the Father than is the Son. Again, he maintains that if the Spirit proceeds from both Father and Son, he is excluded from that common life from which he proceeds. Yet again he asks why, if there can be a procession of the third person from the second, why should there not be a procession of a fourth from the third and so on, *ad infinitum*? Notable by its absence is any reference to the notion that the Spirit might proceed from the Father through the Son—though this is by no means an unfamiliar thought, as we shall see, in the Greek tradition. At the close of his letter, Photius appeals to the other patriarchs to show solidarity and decide the matter in synod.[35]

The 867 synod, concurring in Photius' views, proceeded to the grave step of condemning Pope Nicholas, unheard, as a heretic and

[34] Chadwick, *East and West*, pp. 64–70.

[35] The status of the visitors from the other three Oriental patriarchal sees at Photius' synod is unclear: see Chadwick, *East and West*, p. 162. Photius should have been aware that a similar *dubium* had delayed the recognition at Rome of the authority of a far more sympathetic synodical event: the 787 Council of Nicaea. The problem would recur at the 869 council, Constantinople IV.

asked the Western emperor Louis II to depose him. Nicholas died without knowing precisely what had transpired, though he was aware that the Byzantines were up in arms. Papal legates in Bulgaria were refused entry into the East Roman Empire, and the khan Boris thoughtfully passed on to them Byzantine documents giving the Greek charges against the Franks for the pope's benefit. Had Nicholas been Leo III, he would presumably at once have distinguished the tradition of the Roman church from that of the Carolingians. But he did no such thing. Rather, he asked the Carolingian archbishop Hincmar of Rheims to find Carolingian divines willing to defend Western practice, and in so doing he gave the quite false impression that the papacy had accepted the introduction of the *Filioque* into the Creed. The result of this initiative was the first Western polemical treatises *Adversus Graecos*, "Against the Greeks".

The treatises that now began to pour forth from all corners of the Carolingian empire were very hostile to the East. Aeneas of Paris in his *Liber adversus Graecos*, for instance, remarks that the East is the mother of heretics, while no heretic has ever sat on the Roman chair.[36] A more impressive work is Ratramnus of Corbie's *Contra Graecorum opposita*.[37] Here Ratramnus claims that the Roman bishop has the same right to add to the Creed as does an ecumenical council itself. He holds, in other words, a high doctrine of the papacy equivalent to that of the thirteenth-century Latin papalists, an implicit doctrine of the infallibility not just of the *sedes*, the Roman see, but of the *sedens*, the person of the bishop who occupies it. Ratramnus interpreted John 15, where Jesus speaks of the sending of the Spirit, in a way that anticipates the later Latin defence of the *Filioque* at the reunion councils: "Just as the Son received his substance by birth from the Father, so likewise he receives from the Father his ability to send the Spirit of truth by having him proceed from him." It is not known whether any of these treatises ever actually reached Constantinople.[38]

---

[36] PL 121:685–762.

[37] PL 121:225–346.

[38] Cf. also the anonymous *Responsio de fide s. Trinitatis contra Graecorum haeresim* at PL 110:1201–12. Romanides draws attention to the possible political utility of this

At this point the whole situation was thrown into the melting pot by a coup d'état in Constantinople. The emperor Basil I, whom Michael III had promoted to be coemperor at his side, assassinated both the former regent Bardas and then Michael himself, thus bringing the Isaurian dynasty to an end and replacing it with the Macedonian, a royal family that would occupy the Byzantine throne for longer than any other. Technically, the throne was elective,[39] but methods of electioneering were not supposed to include the forcible removal of one's predecessors, and Basil's diplomatic position was naturally at first very weak. Anxious to win the support of conservative circles and the new pope, he deposed Photius and restored his predecessor Ignatius. Basil then invited the new pope, Adrian II (867–872), to send legates to his capital in a final effort to sort out the Byzantine patriarchal succession in a way acceptable to Rome.

But as as ill luck would have it, a preparatory mission to Rome, consisting of delegates from both parties, got off to a bad start in that the leader of the Photian delegation, Peter of Sardis, was drowned

---

polemical activity to the Frankish cause. Louis II would write to the emperor Basil I: "We have received the government of the Roman empire for our orthodoxy. The Greeks have ceased to be emperors of the Romans for their kakodoxy." *Franks, Romans, Feudalism and Doctrine,* p. 18, citing from B. Pullan, ed., *Sources for the History of Mediaeval Europe* (Oxford, 1971), p. 17.

[39] The nature of the act of imperial accession in Byzantium was complex. Father Christopher Walter, of the Augustinians of the Assumption, sums it up in this way: "In the first centuries the notion of dynastic legitimacy had little importance in the choice of a new emperor. In the case of Valentinian, for example (364), the choice was made jointly by the army and the Senate. Once the capital was firmly established at Constantinople, the approval of the people became increasingly important. When there was a stable dynasty, the emperor habitually designated his successor. To these active parties, who made known their choice by proclamation and acclamation, was added the Church. From 457 onwards the patriarch participates in the ceremonies, which by 602 had been transferred to a church, normally Saint Sophia. The patriarch blessed or crowned the new emperor, since he was the person most fitting to represent Christ, from whom the emperor's *basileia* derived. Finally, in the thirteenth century, the rite of unction was added to this complex of ceremonies." Thus C. Walter, *Studies in Byzantine Iconography* (London, 1977), X., p. 162. Walter refers his readers for fuller information to A. Christophilopoulos, *Eklogê, anagoreusis kai stepsis tou byzantinou autokratoros* (Athens, 1956).

during the crossing in a storm. Hence Pope Adrian came under the influence of Ignatian information alone. Early in 869 he held a synod in Rome that bitterly condemned Photius and the council of 867 for having dared to judge a pope. The decisions of this Roman synod were to be taken to Constantinople, where the Byzantine bishops were to redeem their great mistake of 867 by signing a *Libellus satisfactionis*. Thus, later that year, a council, later reckoned as the Eighth Ecumenical Council, Constantinople IV, met on the Bosphorus. Basil got his expected condemnation of Photius,[40] but so many of the patriarchal clergy supported the latter that Ignatius found it almost impossible to administer the church. As the council closed, the Eastern bishops took it upon themselves to decide that Bulgaria should be ecclesiastically Greek, and Ignatius took steps to implement this, in the face of papal disapproval. "Ignatius could profess strong belief in Roman primacy and supremacy at the council, but found his pastoral responsibilities impossible on the terms imposed by Rome."[41]

The only general statements by the council were in its canons, which, at least in their Latin version, finally laid aside all doubt as to the ecumenicity of Nicaea II. Of great interest to later churchmen in the West was the 869 canon forbidding laymen to install bishops. During the Investiture Contest of the period around 1100, Western canonists began to work to have the council raised, for just this reason, to fully ecumenical status.[42] On the Tiber, they were successful; from the Bosphorus, the view looked different.

The Byzantines never saw it as *that* important; for Basil it was a battle, not the whole war. In fact, he soon began to restore Photius to favour, realising that his gifts were irreplaceable. In a short while, Ignatius was dead and Photius was reinstated. A new council of 879, once again with papal legates in attendance, quashed the verdict of

---

[40] In effect, the council treated Photius as self-condemned, since in excommunicating Pope Nicholas he had himself become schismatic: Chadwick, *East and West*, p. 166.

[41] Ibid., p. 171.

[42] D. Stiernon, *Constantinople IV* (Paris, 1967).

the (to later Catholics) Eighth Ecumenical Council on Photius, with the approval of Pope John VIII—though just how enthusiastic that approval was is a matter of hot scholarly debate. The historians seem agreed that John was likely to be a peacemaker. For one thing, the political situation made an accommodation with the Byzantines highly desirable. Southern Italy was under attack from the Saracens, and Rome itself was threatened by an aggressive local aristocrat, the Count of Spoleto. For another, John seems to have had a genuine desire to do all he could to restore unity among Constantinopolitan Christians, where the Photian bishops, priests, and laity had been forced out of the official church. Everyone is agreed that John declared Photius absolved and recognised him as patriarch. But the precise terms in which he did so are in dispute. Two sets of the pope's letters exist, a Latin set, preserved at Monte Cassino, and a Greek set, preserved in the *acta* of the 879 synod. The two are notably different, the Greek letters being much milder than the Latin. One plausible thesis is that the Greek version is a recension prepared by Photius and the papal legates in consultation before the synod opened. In the Greek documents, the council of 869 is declared null and void, which reflects, no doubt, the Byzantine view; yet at the same time, they also ascribe to the pope the "care of all the churches", an affirmation that echoes the Roman standpoint. As Johan Meijer puts it: "The texts were adapted to Byzantine ears, but many typical Roman formulas were left untouched."[43]

Because the acts of this synod were lost to view in the West, Photius went down to Western posterity as an architect of schism and the sworn enemy of papal primacy. Anti-Roman Byzantine treatises of a later period were ascribed to him. Indeed, this accounts for much of his popularity in the church of Greece today. Returning, however, to the views of the pope, if we can accept the authenticity of a papal letter, known from its opening words as *Ouk agnoein* and preserved as a supplement to the council *acta*, John VIII promised Photius that, as far as was humanly possible, the *Filioque* would be removed from the Western Creed.

[43] Meijer, *A Successful Council of Union*, p. 49.

> We assure you concerning this issue, which has been such a scandal
> to the Church, that we [at Rome] not only recite the Creed [in its
> original form] but also condemn those foolish people who have had
> the presumption to act otherwise.... [We condemn them] as viola-
> tors of the divine words and distorters of the teachings of the Christ
> the Lord, and of the fathers who transmitted the holy Creed to us
> through the councils.

But the pope goes on to explain that getting the *Filioque* excised in
practice will not be done in an afternoon: "I think your wise holiness well knows how difficult it is to change immediately a custom
that has been entrenched for so many years."[44]

This was not quite the end of Photius' troubles. In 886 the emperor
Leo VI induced him to abdicate—probably because of a disagreement over some of his episcopal promotions. But Photius died in
full communion with the Roman church. The belief that the successors of John VIII broke a second time with Photius has been
shown to be a legend. There was no second schism. He was cano-
nised at Constantinople, and his feast was kept widely throughout
the Greek-speaking church from the end of the tenth century onwards,
i.e., in a period when the East was still in full communion with the
West.[45] However, John VIII's soothing but prudent letter—if his it
be—did not end the theological literature that the controversy brought
forth. Photius devoted a good deal of time in his last years to trying
to determine further what was wrong with the *Filioque*. Two further
treatises came from his pen.

First, sometime about 883, he wrote a lengthy letter on the *Filioque* to Bishop Walpert of Aquileia, the place at which a generation
earlier the theology of interpolation had been worked out.[46] This
letter does not add much to the encyclical to the Eastern bishops

[44] Mansi, 17:525; while Romanides accepts the authenticity of this letter unques-
tioningly, Dvornik holds that, in its present form at least, it derives from the fourteenth century.

[45] At any rate, he has an entry, for 6 February, in the tenth-century Synaxary of
the church of Constantinople. On his cultus, see M. Jugie, "Le culte de Photius dans
l'église byzantine", *Revue de l'Orient chrétien* 23 (1922–1923): 105–22.

[46] PG 102:793–821.

except that Photius comes to terms here with the fact that the Latin fathers on the whole believed the *Filioque* doctrine. We cannot prefer the words of the fathers to the word of our Lord, but in fact we are not called on to make a choice, as only a minority of the fathers of the whole Church took Augustine's view. But even of this minority we should not try to strip them of the title "father" since if in their lifetime they went unchallenged on some of the things they said, it is hardly their fault when occasionally they fell into error. As he writes: "If they spoke badly, or for some reason not known to us, deviated from the right path, but no question was put to them nor did anyone challenge them to learn the truth, we admit them to the list of fathers as if they had not said it—because of their righteousness of life and distinguished virtue and their faith, which was faultless in other respects." The eirenic tone of this letter is notable. But more theologically important is another essay, *De Sancti Spiritus mystagogia*, written after Photius had been succeeded in the patriarchal throne by Leo's brother Stephen, at some time, then, after 886.[47] In the *Mystagogia*, Photius is concerned with, first, Filioquist exegesis; second, the ecclesial status of the Latin fathers; and third, some arguments in systematic theology.[48] First, he comes to grips with the exegesis of the Fourth Gospel that Augustine had established and the Carolingians followed. The crucial text here was John 16:14, where Jesus declares of the Spirit, "He will glorify me, for he will take what is mine [*ek tou emou*] and declare it to you." Photius argues that "what is mine", i.e., the Son's, here is not the person of the Spirit but the person *of the Father*. So what would this mean in the context of the Fourth Gospel? In the previous verse, Jesus has spoken of the Spirit revealing to the disciples, after his crucifixion-exaltation, "all the truth". According to Photius, this truth is in fact the person of the Father, the Father of Jesus—"this Father of mine", as we might well say in English—and so the Father becomes the content of the apostolic proclamation, which the disciples are to make in Christ's name.

[47] PG, 102:263–400.
[48] PG, 102:301.

Photius seems to have been aware that Carolingian divines like Ratramnus conceded that if the Son gives the Spirit, he must receive the power to do so from the Father. So presumably they could go much of the way with Photian exegesis, simply adding that the revelation of the Father that Jesus promises is made through the Spirit whom he will send. But Photius rules out such a suggestion. It is, he says, "unjust" that the Son should have the privilege of sending the Spirit, while the Spirit, who originates with equal honour from the Godhead, is not privileged to give the Son.[49] The other main plank of Filioquist exegesis, after John, was Paul. On the Pauline references to the Spirit as "the Spirit of the Son", Photius regards the Latin interpretation here as somewhat question-begging. "Of the Son" does not necessarily mean "proceeding from the Son": and he draws attention to similar uses of the partitive elsewhere in Scripture where the Spirit is said to be, for instance, the "Spirit of wisdom".

There remained the problem, however, that doubtful as Filioquist exegesis of the New Testament might be, most of the Latin fathers taught it. Photius makes four points here, thereby developing his approach in the letter to Walpert of Aquileia. First, although the Latin fathers have taught the *Filioque*, they have not asked for it to be added to the Creed. Second, no one father or group of fathers can be opposed to the authority of the Lord's own teaching and the decrees of the councils. Photius writes: "[The fathers] were human and no one made of dust and ephemeral nature can preserve himself forever immune from every human error.... Though they by chance fell into something shameful and unbecoming, I for my part would imitate the good sons of Noah and hide my father's shame, using silence and gratitude for a covering."[50] Third, Photius points out that the Latin fathers do not necessarily appear to teach the *Filioque*

[49] This raises the important question whether the New Testament as a whole may be said to witness to an order (*taxis*) of the divine persons, of the kind that the Church, both Eastern and Western, has proposed liturgically in, for example, the doxology, where Father, Son and Spirit are always mentioned in that order. Is it random that the divine persons are so named, or is there an instinct of faith behind such doxological texts?

[50] PG 102:549, cited in Haugh, *Photius and the Carolingians*, p. 152.

as dogma but rather as their theological opinion. It is true that Augustine's theology of the Trinity, as developed speculatively in the latter part of *De Trinitate*, is specifically stated by Augustine to be in a genre distinct from dogmatic teaching. One has only to think of the prayer in book 15: "O Lord, the one God, God the Trinity, whatever I have said in these books that is of thine, may they acknowledge who are thine; if anything of my own, may it be pardoned both by thee and by those who are thine."[51] Last, Photius sets up against the Latin fathers the teaching of the Roman popes, and in this, at least insofar as the addition of the *Filioque* to the Creed is concerned, he had—as we have seen—the support of, at any rate, one and perhaps two contemporary popes.

Finally, Photius adds some systematic-dogmatic considerations that, he hopes, will clinch the matter. Above all, he stresses that, if the Spirit proceeds from the Son, then the distinctive hypostatic property of the Father, namely his being the source of the Godhead, would be emptied of sense. The Father and the Son would thus become confused. Principally, Photius' concern is to show that the processions, the internal differentiations, within the Holy Trinity are personal and not natural or essential in character. The Father is the cause of the Trinity not because this is implied by the concept of the divine nature as such but because we know it to be his hypostatic character—part of what makes him the unique person he is. Because the power to bring forth another person in the Godhead is the personal property of the Father, it cannot be common: it cannot be shared with the Son. To later Western theologians, however, it seems unclear that the *Filioque* cannot be restated in terms of a personalist view of the internal differentiation in God. Indeed, Ratramnus' idea that the Father, in generating the Son, gives him the privilege of spirating the Spirit with him is itself the best example of such a personalist version of the *Filioque* position.

The Photian crisis died away with its arguments unsolved. Neither side had convinced the other of the truth of its own position; worse still, neither side was convinced that the other position had a

---

[51] *De Trinitate* 15.28.51.

right to existence. The Greeks were not persuaded that Filioquism is a legitimate theological option; the Latins, and more especially the Franks, were not persuaded that Monopatrism was either. This was clearly an unstable state of affairs, and it would not take that much prescience to realise that the question would revive whenever tensions between Latin West and Greek East brought ecclesiastical tempers back to boiling point. Historically, Photius' error, as Dr. Richard Haugh has pointed out in his study, *Photius and the Carolingians*, was to underestimate the seriousness and potential influence of the Germanic north. If his spirit had been more ecumenical, more universal, it might have been possible to convoke a council including Frankish representatives to discuss and decide before positions became impossibly hardened. A letter to Pope Nicholas shows that, in theory, at least, Photius knew what attitudes were required. For there he writes:

> In reality nothing is more exalted and precious than love.... Through love, those who are separated are united.... Through love, the inner ecumenical bonds are more firmly knitted together; [through love] the entrance of discord and jealousy is shut off ... because love thinks no evil, it cherishes all things, it hopes all things, it endures all things; love never fades.... And for those who share the same religion, even though they live so far apart, even though they have never seen each other face to face, love binds them in unity and unites them in the same conviction.[52]

Père Congar is less eirenic. It cannot be denied, he wrote, that the theology of Photius narrowed down the teaching of the Greek fathers.[53] Though there is, as the twentieth-century Orthodox theologian Sergei N. Bulgakov admitted, no unamimous patristic doctrine of the procession of the Holy Spirit in the East,[54] there are openings in

[52] PG 102:593ff., cited in Haugh, *Photius and the Carolingians*, p. 174.

[53] Y. J.-M. Congar, *I Believe in the Holy Spirit* (Eng. trans., London, 1985), 3:59. For Filioquist sentiments in the Greek patristic tradition, see G. C. Berthold, "Cyril of Alexandria and the *Filioque*", *Studia patristica* 19 (1989): 143–47; M.-O. Boulnois, *Le paradoxe trinitaire chez Cyrille d'Alexandrie* (Paris, 1994), pp. 482–529; and G. C. Berthold, "Maximus Confessor and the *Filioque*", *Studia patristica* 18, no. 1 (1985): 113–17.

[54] Sergei N. Bulgakov, *Le Paraclet* (Paris, 1946), p. 110.

the direction of a *per Filium* or even a *Filioque*. Photius hardened pneumatology into a mould that made it impossible for the Orthodox to reach agreement with the West or even with those Latin fathers they accept as their own.

A Doctrinal Evaluation

How might a modern theologian, informed about the historical background, look at the *Filioque*? A full account of the *Filioque* as doctrine and problem would have to begin with the New Testament. Some commentators hold that in the light of New Testament scholarship, the Spirit should not be thought of as related to the Son simply as one sent by him. The Spirit also makes possible the work of the Son: a factor that Filioquist theology, it is claimed, has overlooked. In his conception, baptism, and ministry, and in his Resurrection and Ascension to the Father, the Son-made-man is indebted to the Spirit. At the same time, it is not denied that the Son also sends this Spirit whose subsequent work it is to make the Son present. But if the relations of Son and Spirit are ones of reciprocal dependence, a doctrine of the Trinity faithful to the New Testament evidence as a whole would speak not only of the *Filioque* but also of a *Spirituque*. Not only is the Spirit from the Father and the Son, but the Son is from the Father and the Spirit.[55] Unfortunately, this exegesis does not take into account a major hermeneutical point. Are statements of the Son's dependence on the Spirit made of the Son according to his Godhead or only according to his manhood? It is by ignoring the suggestion that such references are to the *homo assumptus* rather than to the Word that the authors of the World Council of Churches symposium on the *Filioque* issue came to their common conclusion that Filioquism is exegetically unbalanced. As they formulated their rhetorical question: "Is it possible that the *Filioque*, or certain understandings of it may have been understandable and indeed helpful in their essential intention in the context of particular

---

[55] Ibid., p. 142. See also a younger theologian of the Francophone Russian diaspora: P. Evdokimov, *L'Esprit Saint dans la tradition orthodoxe* (Paris, 1969), pp. 71–72.

theological debates, but yet inadequate as articulations of a full and balanced doctrine of the Trinity?" [56] But even if we were to agree here that the New Testament witness in its entirety cannot be simply described in Filioquist terms, this would not necessarily mean that there is a problem about the place of the *Filioque* in the Creed. The authors of the Geneva symposium seem to have lost sight of the fundamental difference here between a credal statement and a *summa theologiae*. A creed does not have to be the statement of a "full and balanced" theology. Historically, creeds have served two purposes. First, in their original baptismal context, they have served to specify the minimum content of the Church's faith that a candidate was about to accept. Second, in controversial contexts as expanded in the councils of the Church, the purpose of a creed is to defend the faith of the Church against some error. The Creed of Nicaea-Constantinople I is demonstrably *not* a balanced statement of Christian theology! A balanced statement of Christian theology would require, for instance, something about the life and ministry of Jesus; it would also require some reference to the *septenarium*, the seven sacraments. But the Creed has neither of these things. The expectation that a creed should say everything important about Christianity in a balanced way is not a legitimate expectation, nor is it in fact the basis of the hostility of the East to the Western position.

What is true is that in the patristic period Eastern and Western Christians differed in what they wanted the Creed to say, in what errors they wished it to intervene. Eastern Christians have never desired the Creed to say that the Spirit proceeds from the Son as well as from the Father; some Western Christians have, and their practice was finally sanctioned by Rome in the early eleventh century, probably in 1014 by Pope Benedict VIII. [57] But the fact that these two groups have sought different things from the Creed does not mean that their intentions were directly contradictory. I can "not want" something without wanting not to have it. Photius, and

---

[56] L. Vischer, ed., *Spirit of God, Spirit of Christ: Ecumenical Reflections on the Filioque Controversy* (Geneva, 1981), p. 10; cf. pp. 8–9.

[57] PL 142:1060f.

neo-Photian theology in modern Orthodoxy, hold that, by teaching the procession of the Spirit from the Father alone, they are simply clarifying the obvious intention of Constantinople I in its confession of faith that the Spirit proceeds from the Father. But there is a logical flaw here. As Pope Leo III pointed out to the Carolingians, as far as we know the fathers of 381 were not in a state of wanting the *Filioque* to be in the Creed. Yet this does not mean that they positively did not want it in, that they regarded the doctrine as superfluous or even wrongheaded. Evidently, the wording of the Creed is not in itself an adequate guide to the intentions of the council that produced it.

What *would* be an adequate guide? For many councils, the best of guides consists of the other documents, such as draft definitions, or records of council speeches, which accompany the dogmatic *horoi* in standard collections like those of Giovanni Domenico Mansi or Karl Joseph von Hefele. Unfortunately, we have no such extended *acta* either for the First Council of Constantinople or for any of the local Western synods that approved the *Filioque*—nor, indeed, anything analogous for the papal action in sanctioning its inclusion in the Creed after c. 1000. We must fall back, therefore, on our general historical knowledge of the period and its doctrinal problematic so as to reach a reasonable judgement about the conciliar (or papal) intention in each case.[58] So far as the council of 381 is concerned, that context indicates that its intention was not to teach about the origin of the Spirit but rather to declare the *homoousion* of the Spirit with the Father. Over against the Pneumatochian heresy, and completing the work of Nicaea: the Spirit is really God. The precise mode of the Spirit's coming forth from the Godhead was not directly at issue. As far as the Visigothic and Frankish councils are concerned, although we know less about the theological controversies

---

[58] So far as Constantinople I is concerned, Gregory Nazianzen's verse autobiography, the letters of Ambrose of Milan, and the chronicles of the fifth-century historians Socrates and Sozomen have to suffice as the equivalent of nonextant *acta*: thus Chadwick, *East and West*, p. 25. For fuller discussion, see A. M. Ritter, *Das Konzil von Konstantinopel und sein Symbol* (Göttingen, 1965), and, more recently, R. Staats, *Das Glaubensbekenntnis von Nizäa-Konstantinopel* (Darmstadt, 1996).

of the time and place, it is reasonably certain that the intention behind the addition of the *Filioque* was the defence of the divinity of the Son. If the Son gives the Spirit who completes our redemption, he must be God even as the Father is God. The Son has a rôle in the coming forth of the Spirit and so is truly God, but the precise nature of this rôle it was not the intention of at least the earliest Filioquist councils to specify. In this sense they teach the *Filioque* without teaching a developed Filioquist theology.

To this it might be objected that, though the intention of the fathers of 381 was not to teach Monopatrism as such, nevertheless the fathers of 431 clearly stated *their* intention that nobody afterwards should alter the form of the Creed. Yet the fathers of 451 evidently considered as quite justified the additions made to the Creed of Nicaea by the Council of Constantinople. In the Middle Ages, Latin theologians defended the Western form of the Creed by arguing that what was meant at Ephesus was not a ban on another form of words expressing the same truths but a veto on another form of words expressing a different, i.e., an incompatible, truth. The reference was, they thought, to Saint Paul's curse on those who preached any other gospel to the Galatians than that which he had preached (Gal 1:8–9). Again, one may ask, how are we to know what the intention of Ephesus was?

With the benefit of modern research, we can report that quotations of the Nicene Creed in the fathers of the fourth and fifth centuries are anything but verbally uniform. It looks, then, as though a variety of linguistic differences was acceptable as long as the sense was not changed. A surviving example is the phrase *Deum de Deo* in the Latin Creed, not found in the Greek. Originally, the introduction of the *Filioque* was just a large example of such a local modification in the Creed, called forth by a particular church situation vis-à-vis Spanish Arianism in the late sixth century, and not in any way meant to be a challenge to or a correction of the theology of the Greek fathers. Congar commented: "Both the Council of Ephesus and the later Councils of the Church up to the second council of Nicaea thought of *hetera pistis* as a teaching that was *contrary* to that of Nicaea. From the historical point of view, then, the Latins were right." [59] Nor is it simply Latin obstinacy to suppose that the same conclusion—the legitimacy of the addition of the *Filioque*—from the viewpoint of what it is to be a creed follows even if it be maintained that the Symbol of the Church of the fathers should have represented the teaching of the patristic Church in a balanced fashion. For, in that case, the Creed ought to have included the *Filioque*—or, at least, a *per Filium*—since the *Filioque* or *per Filium* doctrines were already being taught by the Latin fathers, presumably reflecting in some way the faith and piety of their communities, even before 381: for instance, Saint Ambrose's account of the procession of the Spirit *ab utroque*, from both the Father and the Son. In this perspective, as the Louvain patrologist André de Halleux wrote, the root problem is not so much the subsequent alteration of the Creed as the absence in the original Creed of an authentic ecumenical integration of two ways of confessing the mystery of the Holy Spirit in East and West. [60] As a matter of fact, the council of 381 was purely an Eastern council with no Western representation, the pope not even being invited, and it emerges as an ecumenical council in the thinking of the West not because the West shared in its making but because the West received its teaching.

The *Filioque* controversy is, in fact, a casualty of the theological pluralism of the patristic Church. The generally accepted view of this pluralism involves juxtaposing the Latin tradition against the Greek, but probably in matters of Trinitarian theology it is more correct to put the Latin and Alexandrian traditions in one basket [61] and the

[59] Congar, *I Believe in the Holy Spirit*, 3:205. The dispute was still continuing at Florence: see H.-J. Marx, S.D.B., *Filioque und Verbot eines anderen Glaubens auf dem Florentinum: Zum Pluralismus in dogmatischen Formeln* (Bonn, 1977).

[60] A. de Halleux, "Towards an Ecumenical Agreement on the Procession of the Holy Spirit and the Addition of the *Filioque* to the Creed", in Vischer, *Spirit of God, Spirit of Christ*, pp. 78–80.

[61] N.b. Cyril's concern with the divine unity: it is notable that he has at least one passage that appears to teach the *Filioque*, viz. *Thesaurus de Trinitate* 34. Concern to oppose Arianism was just as important to Cyril as were his disagreements with Nestorius and the exegetical school of Theodore. For discussion, see the works cited in note 53 above.

Cappadocian and later Byzantine tradition in another. However, the internal differences between the Alexandrians and the Cappadocians here are only now being fully studied by patristic scholars. Keeping then to the older analysis,[62] we can say that the Latin tradition has two aims in Trinitarian theology. First, it wanted to affirm that Father, Son, and Holy Spirit are one divine being; they are three personal ways of possessing the single divine essence. To this extent, the Latin tradition was less interested in the hypostatic particularity of the persons and more interested in how their distinctiveness does not prevent them from being one only God. The notion that the Spirit is spirated *by* and *as* the common love of Father and Son, and so is the bond of unity in the Trinity, was obviously attractive in this context. It showed how the unity of essence was (so to speak) reenacted in the relations of the persons. The second aim of the Latin tradition in this regard was to preserve what can be called the insight of Western piety that the Spirit is Christ's Spirit, the Spirit of the Son, spreading Christlikeness by his presence. Following the usual line of histories of doctrine, we can say that emboldened by this economic subordination of the Spirit to the Son in Western Christianity, Augustine in particular used the *Filioque* to think through a more unitary doctrine of the absolute Trinity, which he conceived as a dialectic of oneness-in-threeness and threeness-in-oneness. Later on, this crystallised into a formal system of a sophisticated logicometaphysical kind in the Scholastics of the High Middle Ages.

The Eastern tradition (once more on the customary view), has rather different emphases. From the time of the Cappadocians, the Greeks stressed two things. First, they emphasized the irreducible distinctiveness of the divine persons. Second, they underlined the uniqueness of the Father as the only "source" of the Godhead. Photian Monopatrism is an outcrop of the Cappadocian conviction that

---

[62] In his essay "De Régnon Reconsidered", *Augustinian Studies* 26 (1995): 237–50, Michael Barnes has shown how misleading can be the simple Latin versus Greek paradigm in Trinitarian theology, the classic statement of which is T. de Régnon, *Études sur la sainte Trinité* (Paris, 1892).

the specifying properties of the divine persons are not interchange-
able, not communicable, one to another. If they were, the whole
Godhead would, so to speak, collapse in anarchy, or, to put it more
sensibly, our names for the divine persons, Father, Son, and Holy
Spirit, would be just that: names, words. In the developed anti-
Filioquist Cappadocianism of Photius, Gregory of Cyprus, and Gregory Palamas, the distinguishing features of the Father are twofold.
First, the Father is he who derives his being from himself; second,
he is the One who gives being to the Son and the Spirit. According
to Photius, because these distinguishing features or hypostatic properties cannot be shared, given away, or exchanged without obliterating the distinction between the persons, we have to say that the
Father is the one cause of the being of the Spirit. This is why Photius could write that the double procession, the *Filioque*, makes the
Father a "simple name".[63] Although the West insisted that it accepted
the monarchy of the Father—his being the single *archê*, source, of
Son and Spirit, with the Son simply a "secondary cause" used by
the Father in bringing the Spirit forth—the Greeks would have none
of this defence. By treating the Son as in any sense the origin of the
Spirit, the Latins, they maintained, have obscured the difference
between the Father and the Son.

What modern scholarship can thus see as a regrettable side effect
of patristic pluralism confronts us with our two burning questions:
Was it legitimate for the Latin church to introduce the *Filioque* to
the Symbol (an ecclesiological question)? And, is the *Filioque* true (a
question in Trinitarian theology)? Though these questions have been
subterraneously present throughout this chapter, it is time now to
attempt an adjudication of them.

An Adjudication

To take first the ecclesiological side: something has already been said
in defence of the *Filioque* in terms of its introduction into the Creed.
On the debit side, it should be added, however, that it does obscure

---

[63] *De Sancti Spiritus mystagogia* 9; PG 102:289A.

the nature of an ecumenical creed to have it existing in sharply different local forms. Even within the Catholic Church it seems odd that a simple distinction of rite between Latin Catholics and (say) Syrian Catholics be expressed in saying or singing a different form of the Creed. When we extend the problem to the Orthodox, we have the massive fact of centuries of conviction in the East that the introduction of the *Filioque* was, in the words of a nineteenth-century Russian theologian, Alexei Khomiakov, "fratricidal". This is not how brothers behave, destroying the covenant of credal unity by a unilateral act. At the mediaeval union councils, the solution sought was to let the Greeks keep their form of the Creed and let the Latins keep the *Filioque*, with both affirming that neither disapproved of the Creed of the other. Today, emboldened by the guilt that many Westerners feel about the *Filioque* issue and also by a sense of the general doctrinal disarray of the Western churches, many Orthodox will now not be content until the churches of the West have agreed to remove the *Filioque* from the Western Creed. An early success is dated as long ago as 1875 when the Old Catholics, at a conference in Bonn, began to take steps to delete the *Filioque*.[64] The wheels of Old Catholicism must move slowly: not till 1969 did their bishops' conference finally let the axe fall. In 1978, the Lambeth Conference of Anglican bishops recommended the constituent churches of the Anglican communion to take it out.[65] As of 1981 it is the declared policy of the ecumenical patriarchate in its ecumenical outreach to remove the *Filioque* from the Creed of all the Western churches.[66]

The Catholic Church, however, will be a harder nut to crack. In Latin ecclesiology, as Thomas Aquinas remarks, *Editio symboli ad auctoritatem summi Pontificis pertinet*, "The bringing out of a creed belongs to the authority of the supreme pontiff."[67] In fact Saint Thomas,

[64] E. B. Pusey, *On the Clause "And Son" in Regard to the Eastern Church and the Bonn Conference* (Oxford, 1875).

[65] Congar, *I Believe in the Holy Spirit*, 3:195–96.

[66] See on this the report in "Chronique religieuse, I" in *Irén.* (1981): 230.

[67] *Summa theologiae* IIa IIae, q. 10.

who wrote before the struggles of the conciliar crisis, still assumes
that a creed will always be composed by a general council, not by an
individual pope. Nor do we have an example of a true creed composed by a pope, the last creed formulated by the Catholic Church
being that of the Council of Trent.[68] Nevertheless, for Thomas as
for the general tradition of Latin ecclesiology, a creed is not authoritative until promulgated or at least received by the Roman bishop—
and the *Filioque* as an article of the Creed has certainly been received
and promulgated by the popes since the eleventh century. Yet perhaps the Roman see could, nonetheless, acknowledge that the manner of introducing the *Filioque* was gravely imprudent, since it is the
nature of a creed to represent the concord of Catholic churches;
thus a distinction would be made between an action that was imprudent and an action that was *ultra vires*, beyond the competence of
the Roman bishop to sanction or licence. Thus, as an act of ecclesiastical charity and reconciliation, the Roman see could voluntarily
surrender the *Filioque* on behalf of its patriarchate. Such a voluntary
surrender would have to be accompanied by an affirmation that such
an action is not meant to call into question the truth of the *Filioque*
idea, which is not only the common teaching of Catholic theologians but defined doctrine in two general councils of the Church in
communion with Rome, Lyons II and Florence. Nevertheless, one
may doubt the ability of Church leaders to put across this distinction in a forceful way. In that case, the pastoral ill consequences of
removing an article from the Creed may be quite high.[69] It would
surely bring doubt into many people's minds as to whether the Roman
church really is, as Irenaeus stated, that church with which all other

[68] The 1564 Creed of Pius IV is more properly described as the *Professio fidei
tridentina*. Pope Paul VI's 1968 "Credo of the People of God" does not seem to be
intended to function canonically as a creed.

[69] Monsignor Franciscus Papamanolis, Latin bishop of Siros, Santorini, and Crete,
assured the present author, however, in a conversation on 15 August 1991 that no
adverse comment greeted the decision of the Holy See to remove the *Filioque* from
the vernacular Creed of the Latin church in Greece—on grounds of the nonidentity
of meaning of *ekporeusis* and *processio*. See for this text, Katholikê hierarchia tês Ella-
dos, *Diataxê theias Leitourgias* (Athens, 1990), p. 9.

churches must concur. At a less exalted but still not an unimportant level, there is also the question of the heritage of liturgical music in the Latin church. The settings of the Creed found in the masters of plainsong and polyphony—as well as such worthy contemporary versions as that of the Estonian (himself an Orthodox!) Arvo Pärt— would become unusable overnight. As the distinguished Anglican historian of theology Henry Chadwick once remarked to the present author, the main argument against removing the *Filioque* is that we would "no longer be able to sing Palestrina"; and our ability to express ourselves liturgically in classic and venerable ways is not something to be set aside lightly.

As this reference to the supreme Italian composer of the sacred music of the Catholic Reformation indicates, my discussion here concerns, of course, the Latin church alone. Though at some periods some Oriental Catholic churches have made use of the *Filioque* in the liturgical recitation of the Creed, by the twentieth century their official *typica* (standard editions of the liturgical books) increasingly placed the word or words in brackets, if indeed they appeared at all. That signified they could be used or omitted, according to the decision of the local bishop. With the decree *Orientalium Ecclesiarum* of the Second Vatican Council (1964), the promulgation of the Code of Canon Law for the Eastern Churches (1990), and—especially— the publication of the Roman Instruction for Applying the Liturgical Prescriptions of the Code of Canons of the Eastern Churches (1996), such decisions are likely to favour omission—as was determined by, for instance, the Ukrainian archeparchy of Philadelphia in 2004.[70] Since 1981, the fifteenth centenary after Constantinople I, the popes have themselves recited the Creed without the *Filioque* when presiding at ceremonies in the presence of the patriarch of Constantinople, or other representatives of the Ecumenical Throne.

Leaving the ecclesiological issue, what about the substantive issue of the *Filioque* itself as Trinitarian theology? Something more should be said in favour of the Latin position. In the first place, any Christian theology must make some attempt to relate the Spirit to the

---

[70] See D. L. Gurovitch, *The Creed and the Holy Trinity* (Philadelphia, 2004).

Son. From the New Testament what is clear is that the Father is essentially the Father of the Son. The very etymology of the word "Father" gives the game away! Since the Father can be thought of only as the Father of the Son, the Spirit cannot be thought of as proceeding from the Father except insofar as the Father is Father of the Son. The Spirit, then, must have *some sort* of relation to the generation of the Son from the Father. If he proceeds in total isolation from the Son, the Father's hypostatic particularity of being Father is called into question. And, moreover, on that hypothesis, the inner communion of life within the Holy Trinity becomes unthinkable. In the course of the later Middle Ages, Byzantine theologians implicitly admitted that the silence of the Creed on any possible relation between the Son and the Spirit was theologically unfortunate. In the middle Byzantine period, with Photius, the Greeks had simply taught a temporal relationship between the Spirit and the Son. In history, the Son as the Word incarnate, Jesus, sends the Spirit on his disciples. But to deny that this reflects anything at all in God's own eternal nature is unsatisfactory. Trinitarian theology is pointless unless God from all eternity is what he has shown himself to be in history. As the influential dogmatician Karl Rahner stoutly maintained, it should be axiomatic in all theology that the economic Trinity is the immanent (or absolute) Trinity.[71] The temporal relationship unfolds an eternal relationship. Recently, some writers in the West have started to dispute Rahner's principle here. They talk about too facile an extrapolation from the economy; too easy an assumption that God as he has shown himself to us is formally and directly the absolute God; they appeal for more restraint, more apophatic theology in attempting to describe what God must be in himself. Though such a criticism of Rahner's *Grundaxiom* can spring from a healthy respect for apophasis, it can also derive from the desire to tone down Christian claims to know the Absolute, the one only God in and of himself. Just because of this ambiguity, the

[71] K. Rahner, "Remarks on the Dogmatic Treatise *De Trinitate*", *Theological Investigations* 4 (Eng. trans., London, 1966): 77–102; idem, *The Trinity* (Eng. trans., London, 1970).

tendency to query the identification of the economic with the absolute Trinity should be treated with some caution.[72] Nor is it the position of Byzantine theology in its most developed phase, from which most modern Orthodox triadology descends. Writers like Gregory the Cypriot and his namesake Gregory Palamas, in the late thirteenth and mid-fourteenth centuries, felt a need to show what it is in the eternal Trinity that the temporal mission of the Spirit from the Son represents. These late Byzantine theologians argue that there can be an eternal manifestation of the Spirit through the Son, an *ekphansis*, which is not a procession or a matter of causality, an *ekporeusis*.[73] In effect, what this comes down to is a partial acceptance of the *Filioque*, in the form of a distinction between the *being* of the Spirit and the *manner* in which his being exists. The Spirit receives his existence from the Father alone. To this extent, the *Filioque* is heresy. But that existence of the Spirit in concrete terms is a relation not only to the Father but also to the Son. To this extent, the *Filioque* is a muddled reflection of a truth, although that truth is not expressed with any very great clarity or consistency by the Byzantines themselves. In Palamas' case, we hear of the energies or powers of the Spirit flowing forth from the Son as well as from the Father, but this way of putting things depends on his distinction between the divine essence and the divine energies, God's being and his self-manifestation. Gregory Palamas' attempt to come to terms with the

---

[72] But, for a very different attack on Rahner's *Grundaxiom*, see P. D. Molnar, "The Function of the Immanent Trinity in the Theology of Karl Barth: Implications for Today", *Scottish Journal of Theology* 42 (1989): 367–99; however, the author's real target appears to be, not Rahner, but the Lutheran Jürgen Moltmann, for whom "The economic Trinity not only reveals the immanent Trinity, it also has a retroactive effect on it." *The Trinity and the Kingdom of God* (Eng. trans., New York, 1981), p. 160. Such a *mutually conditioning* relationship of God and ourselves indeed compromises the sovereignty of God.

[73] For the later Byzantine theologians, see M. A. Orphanos, "The Procession of the Holy Spirit according to Certain Later Greek Fathers", in Vischer, *Spirit of God, Spirit of Christ*, pp. 21–45; for the important contribution to the theology of *ekphansis* of the ecumenical patriarch Gregory II of Cyprus, see A. Papadakis, *Crisis in Byzantium: The Filioque Controversy in the Patriarchate of Gregory II of Cyprus (1283–1289)* (Crestwood, N.Y., 1996).

problem showed that he recognised the strength of the Western case. Monopatrism can make the Spirit seem a stranger to the Son in its desire to exalt the monarchy of the Father, and this is a world away from the intimate account of the circumcession of the persons that we find in, say, the Gospel of Saint John. In some way consonant with its own theological genius, the East needs in fact to appropriate the Western insight, which is also Alexandrian, that the Spirit is not only the Spirit of the Father: from all eternity he is the Spirit of the Son insofar as the Son is one with and consubstantial with the Father.[74]

Second, the strength of the Latin position is also seen in connexion with the fact that in classical accounts of the Trinity, the persons are identified in terms of their origin, and if the origin of one person cannot be distinguished clearly from that of another, then the distinction between those two persons becomes unclear. The Greek fathers sometimes expressed their frustration at not being able to distinguish clearly the process or eternal act called "generation" in the Son and "spiration" in the Spirit. Both are processions of persons, but how do they differ? If they do not differ, then, because they are originating processions, telling us who someone is by saying where he comes from, it becomes impossible to distinguish the Son from the Spirit. And here the Latin doctrine's distinct advantage lies in its clarifying, in a fashion that is in keeping with the New Testament evidence, the differing origins of Spirit and Son. The Son is *e Patre*; the Spirit, *e Patre Filioque*. But this is at the cost, according to the Byzantines, and modern Orthodox, of throwing into confusion the distinction between Father and Son insofar as the Father now ceases to be the sole Originator.

---

[74] But cf. here A. Radović, "Le Filioque et l'énergie incrée de la Sainte Trinité selon la doctrine de s. Grégoire Palamas", *Messager de l'exarchat du patriarche russe en Europe occidentale* 89–90 (1975): 11–44. He argues that the Palamite distinction between essence and energies implies a distinction, or even a radical difference, between the existential origins of the persons and their economic manifestation. Contrariwise, the identification of the order of eternal existence of the hypostases with that of the economy is fundamental to the Latin position.

A third and last strength of the Latin view—underscored by the great Reformed dogmatician Karl Barth—is the way the *Filioque* helps preserve the essential kerygma of the New Testament, namely, the proclamation that there is no access to the Father, and no life in the Spirit, save through Jesus Christ.[75]

Perhaps at this point it would be helpful to sum up the positive requirements of Filioquists and Monopatrists and then ask whether there is any possible theology that can combine them all.

- Monopatrists insist that the unity of the Godhead is not to be found simply in the unity of the divine nature but at the level of the persons. However, the unity of the persons is itself not to be found simply in their relations of communion, in which, for instance, the Holy Spirit can be said to be the "bond of love" of the Father and the Son—what may be called the moral aspect of the Trinitarian relationships. The unity of the persons must also be found in their relations of origin, as all the classical theologies of East and West have insisted. Thus it is necessary to affirm that the one source of the being of Son and Spirit is the Father.
- Filioquists have insisted that (a) the Father's being the one source of Son and Spirit cannot mean that the Spirit comes forth as anyone *other* than the Spirit of the Father-of-the-Son; and also that (b) if the Son and the Spirit are not to be confused in *their* relations of origin, the Spirit must be from the Father and the Son, while the Son is simply from the Father.

The principal Catholic attempt to reconcile the two positions by meeting these two sets of demands is that of Jean-Miguel Garrigues, a Dominican who both left and returned to his Order but at the time of this eirenic theological venture was the cofounder of a new order of *moines apostoliques*, "apostolic monks", with a mother house at Aix-en-Provence. Garrigues published a number of articles on the *Filioque*, but his book on the topic draws his ideas together: this

[75] *Church Dogmatics*, 2nd ed., vol. 1, pt. 1, 3 (Eng. trans., Edinburgh, 1975), 12.2.5 p. 481.

is *L'Esprit qui dit "Père"*.[76] His central argument, laid out in chapter 3, runs as follows. The Father is, first, the fount or origin of the whole Godhead, but he is also, second, the source of the consubstantial communion of the divine persons. In this latter sense, which is that of the characteristic Latin emphasis, the divine nature "advances" (to use Garrigues' word) from the Father into the Son, and from the Father and the Son into the Holy Spirit. But there is no contradiction between asserting this on the one hand and asserting on the other that the Father is, third, the only origin of the hypostatic diversity of the Son and the Spirit, the characteristic Greek insistence. Thus we have three senses in which the Father is the source of the Godhead. He is (a) source of the divine nature, (b) source of the consubstantial communion of the persons, and (c) source of the hypostatic diversity of the Son and the Spirit. In sense (b) the Western form of the Creed is the better form; in sense (c) the Greek form is preferable. But these senses are not contradictory; rather, they are complementary.

This central argument is supported in Garrigues by a number of subsidiary arguments. Very importantly, he sets out to show that the Greek verb *ekporeuesthai*, as used in the Fourth Gospel and in the Greek Creed, does not have quite the same sense as the Latin verb *procedere*, used in the Latin Creed. *Ekporeuesthai* signifies a going forth in which the terminus B is really distinct from the starting point A; *procedere*, on the other hand, stresses the connexion between A and B: for instance, the stroke of a pencil proceeds from point A to point B on a piece of paper. The Greek verb suggests a principle from which a distinction arises; the Latin suggests the starting point of a continuous process. The *ekporeusis* of the Spirit is, then, his arising in his hypostatic particularity from the Father; the *processio* of the Spirit from the Father and the Son is the "last moment in the communication of the consubstantial divinity that proceeds according to the order of the divine persons", Father to Son, Father and Son to Spirit.

[76]J.-M. Garrigues, *L'Esprit qui dit "Père": L'Esprit-Saint dans la vie trinitaire et le problème du Filioque* (Paris, 1981).

The result of this difference is that in the West, *processio* comes to be used indifferently for both the generation of the Son and the spiration of the Spirit; as Saint Thomas remarks in this connexion, "Among verbs associated with any kind of origin, *procedere* is the broadest of all."[77] This was something that could never have been said, according to Garrigues, about *ekporeuesthai*; the equivalent Greek word would be *proinai*. Among the Latin fathers, it seems, Hilary was conscious of the special nuance of *ekporeuesthai* and distinguished between the Spirit's *processio* from the Father and his *receptio* of divinity in the Son. Why did the Latins use the word *procedere*, then? Simply because the Latin Bible used it in place of several Greek verbs in the Gospels at relevant points. Already at Florence, the Easterners had noted how few terms the Latins had for the relations of origin.

Having shown that the meaning of *ekporeuesthai* and the meaning of *procedere* are different, Garrigues has now got to show that they are complementary. In other words, he has to show that the *ekporeusis* of the Spirit from the Father in the East corresponds to something also believed in the West and that the *processio* from the Father and the Son in the West corresponds to something also believed in the East. To take the second problem first, what corresponds to the *Filioque* in the East? For Garrigues, the answer to this question is: the *perichôrêsis* or *circumincessio* of the divine persons. At first this seems a baffling suggestion. But we must remember that for Garrigues the *processio* of the Spirit from the Father and the Son is a procession in terms of the consubstantial communion of the persons. As he says,

> We speak of Trinitarian circumincession because the divine persons are not separated from one another, since the same consubstantial being proceeds in each from the person or persons to whom it remains linked in the Trinitarian order. We speak therefore of the procession of the Spirit because in him the divine nature advances from the Father and the Son, in relation to whom it maintains the Spirit in

[77] *Summa theologiae* Ia, q. 36, a. 2.

consubstantial communion according to the order of the Trinitarian *perichôrêsis* in which [the divine nature] is made manifest.[78]

Taking then the first problem, how can the West be said to accept the idea that the monarchy of the Father makes him in some unique sense the source of the Spirit? Here Garrigues relies heavily on a distinction of Augustine's in chapter 26 of the final book of *De Trinitate*, book 15. There Augustine says that the Spirit proceeds *principaliter* from the Father and *communiter* from the Father and the Son. For Garrigues, *procedere principaliter* is equivalent to *ekporeuesthai*: it does not mean that the Spirit proceeds "chiefly" from the Father, because Augustine's other adverb should then have been something like "secondarily" or "in a lesser way" and not *communiter*, "commonly". *Procedere principaliter* means coming from a source that makes one fundamentally what one is, according then to the order of the hypostatic diversity of the persons. In this case, *procedere communiter*, from the Father and the Son together, would be Augustine's opening up the other more usual Latin perspective: the consubstantial communion of the persons in which, as far as the Spirit is concerned, the Father is involved with the Son and not by himself alone.

Garrigues would have to admit, I think, that Augustine does not make very much of this distinction; but his point is that the presence of the distinction is enough to show that the West was aware of a sense of the Father's monarchy vis-à-vis the Spirit, which is his alone and not shared or communicated in any way to the Son.

Towards the end of the book, Garrigues offers his own formula for harmonising the two complementary explications, Cappadocian-Byzantine and Latin-Alexandrian, of the Creed:

Ek monou tou Patros ton Monogenê gennôntos ekporeuomenon kai ap'amphoin prôchorôn.

Ex unico Patre unicum Filium generante se exportans, ab utroque procedit.

---

[78] Garrigues, *L'Esprit qui dit "Père"*, pp. 97–98.

[We believe in the Holy Spirit, the Lord, the Giver of Life, who] going forth out of the only Father who begets the only Son, proceeds from both.[79]

In 1995, in a papal homily for the feasts of Saints Peter and Paul in the presence, in Saint Peter's Basilica, of the ecumenical patriarch Bartholomew I, John Paul II expressed a desire that

the traditional doctrine of the *Filioque*, present in the liturgical version of the Latin *Credo*, [be clarified] in order to highlight its full harmony with what the Ecumenical Creed of Constantinople [of 381] confesses in its Creed: the Father as the source of the whole Trinity, the one origin both of the Son and of the Holy Spirit.[80]

In responding to this request, the Pontifical Council for the Promotion of Christian Unity produced a neat summary of Garrigues' "solution", thus giving it a distinct Roman stamp of approval.[81]

The Incubus of the Filioque *Dispute*

Certainly, the *Filioque* issue has poisoned relations between West and East ever since. In the influential *Orthodox Confession* of Peter Moghila, approved by the four Eastern patriarchs in 1645, the *Filioque* and the papal primacy are described as *the* two "separating issues". In 1894 the Constantinopolitan patriarch Anthimos replied to Pope Leo XIII's appeal for the reunion of the Orthodox with Rome by remarking that such reunion is possible only if Rome can show her full doctrinal accord with the East up to the ninth century (to Photius!) and, more especially, if she can show that the *Filioque* was taught by the Greek fathers.

More recently, the influential Orthodox theologian Vladimir Lossky (who helped animate, at one point, a "Confraternité de Saint Photius"

[79] Ibid., p. 98.

[80] DC 92, no. 15 (1995), p. 371.

[81] "Les traditions grecque et latine concernant la procession du Saint-Esprit", *OR*, 13 September 1995; *The Greek and Latin Traditions about the Procession of the Holy Spirit* (Eng. trans., London, 1995).

in Paris) held persistently that, since all theology is essentially an application or further extension of Trinitarian theology, one error in Trinitarian theology can have untold consequences elsewhere. Lossky believed that the *Filioque* was responsible for all the deviations of the Roman Catholic Church. For instance, the subordination of the Spirit to the Son in the *Filioque* could account for the alleged authoritarianism of the Latin church, especially in its portrait of the Roman see. The free play of the Spirit in the Church is straitjacketed by a one-sided appeal to the teaching authority of the Son, through the vicar of Christ. This proposal has led to the extraordinary claim that the *Filioque* is "really" a doctrine about the papacy.[82] Other contemporary Orthodox divines, however, such as Sergei Bulgakov and Paul Evdokimov, believed that the *Filioque* had no impact on ecclesiology at all.[83] Yet others, such as the late nineteenth-century Vasily Bolotov, judged that the significance of the *Filioque* has been overplayed: at most, it symptomises a divergence in theological approach, not dogmatic faith.[84] But as we shall see, in the subsequent history of Roman-Byzantine relations, men showed, on the whole, less kindness. Photius and John VIII believed the wound healed. Events demonstrated that each new crisis could open it anew.

[82] V. Lossky, *The Mystical Theology of the Eastern Church* (Eng. trans., London, 1957), pp. 13, 191–92. See also O. Clément, "Vladimir Lossky, un théologien de la personne et du Saint-Esprit", *Messager de l'exarchat du patriarchat russe en Europe occidentale* (1959): 137–206, and idem, *L'Eglise orthodoxe* (Paris, 1961), p. 50.

[83] Bulgakov, *Le Paraclet*, pp. 124, 141; Cf. Evdokimov, *L'Esprit Saint dans la tradition orthodoxe*, p. 76.

[84] *Revue internationale de théologie* 6, no. 24 (1898): 681–712 (without indication of authorship); published in French trans. in *Ist.* 17 (1972): 261–89.

Bibliography

Dubarle, A.-M., O.P. "Les fondements bibliques du Filioque". *Russie et chrétienté* 1 (1950): 227–44.

Dvornik, F. *The Photian Schism: History and Legend*. Cambridge, Mass., 1948.

Garrigues, J.-M. *L'Esprit qui dit "Père": L'Esprit-Saint dans la vie trinitaire et le problème du Filioque*. Paris, 1981.

Haugh, R. *Photius and the Carolingians*. Belmont, Mass., 1982.

Hergenröther, J. *Photius, Patriarch von Konstantinopel: Sein Leben, seine Schriften und das griechische Schisma*. Regensburg, 1867–1869.

Meijer, J. *A Successful Council of Union: A Theological Analysis of the Photian Synod of 879–880*. Thessalonica, 1975.

Romanides, J. *Franks, Romans, Feudalism and Doctrine*. Brookline, Mass., 1981.

Vischer, L., ed. *Spirit of God, Spirit of Christ: Ecumenical Reflections on the Filioque Controversy*. London and Geneva, 1981.

8

Michael Kerullarios and the Issue of the Azymes

From Photius to Kerullarios

The settlement of the Photian crisis in the years 879–880 had its adversaries in both East and West. In the East, there remained as opponents of Photius the Studites and their allies, ever unwilling as these were to recognise patriarchs drawn from the civilian hierarchy. In the West stood the champions of the *Filioque*. But between the two oppositions, no filaments of connexion ran. True, the Studites held a high doctrine of Roman authority, maintaining that no matters affecting the whole Church should be determined without the bishop of the elder Rome. The *Filioque*, however, was not so much Roman as Frankish. At Rome, the growing influence of the Frankish church was eyed with suspicion. In the tenth century, relations between Old and New Rome were good. The dioceses of the Dalmatian coast were handed back to the Western patriarchate in 924, and the ecclesiastical shape of Bulgaria agreed in 927 under a new patriarchate.

Although the Roman family of Theophylact that dominated the tenth-century papacy had a black record for personal morality, they at least preserved the independence of the popes in an age of disorder in Italy. While the papal aim was "to have survived", that of the Byzantine patriarchate extended to the consolidation of an enormous ecclesiastical empire, acquired through a combination of missionary effort and political good fortune. In 944 the Byzantine armies retook the East Syrian city of Edessa, and twenty years later, Antioch. Georgia and Armenia fell within the Byzantine sphere of influence. The mission to Russia was well established, and envoys worked in Poland, Bohemia, and Hungary. The Greek-speaking dioceses of Sicily and southern Italy were recovered. In 962 the Byzantines occupied Bulgaria, whose empire (and patriarchate) had collapsed before a Russian invasion three years earlier.

These very East Roman advances aroused the concern of the German princely houses. In 962, Otto of Saxony came to Rome and induced Pope John XII to crown him emperor. Otto's north Italian friends urged him to defend southern Italy against Byzantine aggression. The papacy became a prize fought over by two groups: the Germans, acting mainly through Frankish candidates for the chair of Peter, and the Byzantines, acting through the old Roman families. The influence of the German emperors on relations between Rome and Constantinople was to be fateful for two reasons. First, the Ottonian rulers would convey to Rome the ideal of a reformed papacy with a universal divine mission for the remaking of the Church; second, the German emperors prevailed on the popes to introduce the *Filioque* into their liturgy and public doctrine. Thus in 1014 the *Filioque* was sung, as an integral part of the Creed, at pontifical Mass in Saint Peter's for the coronation of the emperor Henry II. There is a report that the Byzantine patriarch removed the name of the pope (Benedict VIII) from the diptychs of the church of Constantinople.[1] Modern historians take the view that, if so, the cause is more likely to be the pope's enthusiastic support for rebellions against Byzantine rule in southern Italy. In 1024, however, there *was* an incident with heavier implications for the future. Benedict VIII's successor, his brother John XIX, was approached by ambassadors from the Byzantine emperor Basil II asking that "with the consent of the Roman pontiff, the church of Constantinople in her sphere, as Rome in the world, might be called and accounted universal."[2] In other words: whereas, outside the Byzantine Empire, the Roman pope should be the final court of appeal for the many local churches, within it, the ecumenical patriarch should be a sufficient judge. Though as old as Justinian, the proposal aroused a tempest of protest

---

[1] Nicetas of Nicaea in PG 120:717–19.

[2] As reported by Raoul Glaber, *Historiarum libri quinque* 4.1, PL 142:671A.

from reforming circles north of the Alps. As one Burgundian abbot wrote to the pope:

> Although it may be that the power of the Roman Empire, which once upon a time flourished monarchically in the whole world, is now wielded in diverse places and lands by innumerable sceptres, the power to bind and loose in Heaven and on earth belongs to the magisterium of Peter. . . . As is fitting in a universal bishop, you should act with more vigour for the discipline and correction of the holy and apostolic Church.[3]

Evidently, the older patriarchal system was increasingly regarded as an infringement of the pope's liberty of action to purify and renew. The furore caused a German chronicler to record against the year 1028: "In this year, the Eastern church removed itself from obedience to the Holy See."[4] And while this date is conspicuous by its absence in general Church histories, it seems that after it no Roman pope was commemorated liturgically at Constantinople.

Humbert and Kerullarios

A fresh crisis erupted in 1053, and history would learn to call it the schism of Michael Kerullarios. The two sets of attitudes, Latin and Greek, are best viewed in the figures of the two main protagonists, the papal legate Humbert of Silva Candida, and the patriarch Michael himself.[5] Humbert we have already encountered as a characteristic representative of the Gregorian reform. All such reformers made the same analysis of the Church's ills and held out identical prescriptions for their remedy. Essentially, they extrapolated from the situation of the church in Germanic Europe. Germanic culture, lacking the notion of moral or juridical personality—a Roman law creation, common

[3] The protest of William of Cluny; see V. Grumel, "Les préliminaires du schisme de Michel Cérulaire ou la question romaine avant 1054", *REB* 10 (1952): 18–20.

[4] For the German chroniclers (perhaps influenced by a notion of the transfer of empire from Greeks to Germans between the death of Basil II and the accession, as an effective Holy Roman emperor, of Conrad II in 1028), see G. Every, *Misunderstandings between East and West* (London, 1965), p. 14.

[5] The approach of the classic study: A. Michel, *Humbert und Kerullarios* (Paderborn, 1925–1930).

to Mediterranean culture, whether Greek or Latin, but absent from the Teutonic north—tended to present churches and clerical or monastic foundations as the property of their founders: *Eigenkirchen*, a principle which also extended to bishoprics. Under the Ottonian emperors, and despite their sincere religious commitment to reform, the Church was a *Reichskirche*, at the marching orders of its temporal lord.[6] The pastoral ill effects may be imagined. The "Gregorian" solution was twofold. First, distinguish between kings, whose authority is for natural (civil) society, and churchmen, whose authority is for supernatural (ecclesial) society. Second, translate this distinction into actuality by the instrumentality of the Petrine office. These reformers stressed, therefore, that by Christ's express institution, papal jurisdiction is universal, and through the papacy the Church's authority is not only independent of the state's but superior to it. Thus the reform presented the Byzantines with those aspects of the Roman tradition that they least understood or approved. To make matters worse, such of their number as Bruno of Toul (uncle of the emperor Henry III and later pope as Leo IX), Hildebrand (eventually to be pope as Gregory VII), and Humbert himself came from the borderlands of France and Germany, where the Byzantine church—its customs, traditions, history, and distinctive ecclesiological ideas—seemed distant indeed.

On the other side of the Mediterranean, history had provided for Cardinal Humbert the perfect protagonist. Michael Kerullarios was fully aware of the Byzantine expansionism of the period: he had been himself a candidate for the imperial throne.[7] As a senior civil servant, prior to ordination, he participated in the tremendous efflorescence of culture brilliantly captured in the pen portraits of Michael Psellos. (Psellos also left an unflattering account of his namesake, written for the emperor Isaac Comnenus at Kerullarios' deposition trial.)[8] As patriarch, he harvested the fruits of the extension of

[6] F. Dvornik, *Byzance et la primauté romaine* (Paris, 1964), pp. 115–17.

[7] His niece, Eudokia Makrembolitissa, became the second wife of the emperor Constantine X Doukas (reigned 1059–1067).

[8] L. Bréhier, "Un discours inédit de Psellos", *Revue des études grecques* 16 (1903): 375–416; 17 (1904): 35–76.

Byzantine patriarchal authority and initiative, from Antioch to Russia, in the tenth century. He was unique in combining two ideas: the Studite concept of the independence, and superiority, of the episcopate with regard to the emperor in all matters religious (and not simply the definition of dogmas), and the notion (itself a reflection of the imperial theology) that the Byzantine patriarch had the right and duty to lead the rest.

It was characteristic that the immediate background of the crisis lay in Michael's insistence on uniformity of liturgical usage throughout his patriarchate. His first target was the Armenians, whose uses diverged from those of the Greeks in various respects. Some, such as the use of unleavened bread ("azymes") for the Eucharist, were paralleled in the Latin churches open for pilgrims and merchants in the Byzantine capital. Michael's ban was therefore extended to the Latin-rite churches, which, in 1052, on their refusal to abandon their eucharistic customs, he closed down. At the same time, he wrote a denunciation of Latin divergences, liturgical and canonical, for the benefit of the "most revered pope" and "all the bishops of the Franks". The pope was spending his leisure time in learning Greek, but his health was poor, which caused him to rely increasingly on his co-worker Humbert. A reply was drafted, setting forth, inter alia, the arguments for the Roman primacy, some of them drawn from the (pseudonymous) *Donation of Constantine*, that eighth-century document purporting to describe how the emperor Constantine, on leaving Rome for Constantinople, had given Pope Sylvester sovereignty over the whole Church (as well as a temporal papal state). A detailed defence of Latin usages accompanied this response. Soon after, however, a more eirenic communication arrived from Kerullarios. The pope, therefore, did not send his letter but commissioned three legates to travel east for a personal meeting with the patriarch. One of these was a south Italian bishop well acquainted with Greeks. But the other two were Humbert and the priest Frederick of Lorraine, chancellor of the Roman church. Humbert produced two more letters in the pope's name, one reproving Kerullarios for his use of the title "ecumenical patriarch" and casting doubts on the validity of his election, the other warning the East Roman emperor of Western reprisals if he failed to bring his patriarch into line. All three letters were to be carried but delivered only if discretion permitted.

Humbert had no doubt that it did. Handed the letters, Michael at first refused to believe them authentic. The pope was at the time a prisoner in Norman hands, so there was room for doubt. Kerullarios determined not to recognise the legatine authority of the Roman agents, a decision rendered justifiable with the death of Leo IX in April 1054. The emperor, who needed good relations with the papacy if he was ever to remove the Normans from southern Italy, was more accommodating. Unfortunately, Humbert queered his pitch by having the discretionary letters put into Greek and spread around the city. Tempers flared. Shortly after, Humbert took the action that became so famous. Before Vespers on 16 July 1054, he and his colleagues entered Hagia Sophia and laid upon the altar a bull excommunicating Kerullarios, the senior patriarchal clergy, and those who supported them. They would be known, in future, as "pro-zymite heretics".

The Issue of the Azymes

Because the issue of the azymes became such a serious part of the debate at this point and would constitute one of the four dividing issues debated at the first reunion council, we must pause to say a word about it. The controversy concerned chiefly the historical setting of the original Eucharist. The eucharistic consecration demands words and elements that make it possible for the Church to parallel, in the liturgical drama, the actions of Jesus on the night before he died. The seemingly conflicting chronologies of the Synoptics and the Gospel of John pose the question, Was the first Eucharist celebrated in the context of the Jewish passover, or not? The answer one gives has implications for how one conceives the relations of the two covenants, old and new.

Humbert defended the Latin custom of unleavened wafers, similar to the Jewish matzoth, by arguing that if Jesus were to remain sinless, he had to follow the provisions of the Torah, to "fulfil all righteousness".[9] But a Byzantine spokesman such as Leo of Ochrida counterargued that, while Jesus did indeed fulfil the Torah, he also terminated its ceremonial provisions by instituting his own sacramental order.[10]

The Byzantine position appears to reflect the thinking found in the early patristic Church order known as the *Didascalia Apostolorum*. There all aspects of the Torah, except for the Ten Commandments, are interpreted as punishments, or at least as restrictions, suffered by Israel for her idolatry in the wilderness. Jesus, in releasing human beings from the bonds of sin, abolished ipso facto this legislation. Thus the Christian is for all time obligated *not* to observe the Jewish passover. To observe it would be to join the majority of Israel in failing to recognise that Christ has freed man from the penalty of sin.

Similarly, Peter of Antioch, though chiding Kerullarios for his expostulation that the Latin practice was heretical, agreed with him that it must cease.[11] The azyme was expressly designated by the Old Testament for the commemoration of the Exodus, while the evangelists explicitly state that Jesus used bread, *artos*, as the efficacious sign of the sacrifice of his body. This was not an arbitrary decision. The physical properties of a loaf make it a fitting symbol of life and fulfilment, whereas a mere wafer, in its lack of yeast and salt, symbolises deprivation. Unleavened as they were, the azymes could not serve as the vehicle of man's daily "food of life", which is what the Logos offers the human race by giving man his flesh to eat. This explains why, at the reunion councils, the Byzantines would call on the Latins to abolish the "dead sacrifice"[12] and why Byzantine apologists connected the use of azymes with the defective Christology of Apollinaris of Laodicea, who had left out of his calculations the human soul of Jesus. But in the last analysis, we are dealing here—as

[9] PL 143:942–45.

[10] PG 120:89B: see M. H. Smith, *"And Taking Bread": The Development of the Azyme Controversy* (Paris, 1982), pp. 32–33.

[11] Ibid., p. 56. For the correspondence of Kerullarios with Peter, important for determining the local character of the schism of 1054, see PG 120:751–819.

[12] J. Gill, S.J., *The Council of Florence* (Cambridge, 1961), p. 114.

in the introduction of the *Filioque*—with a question of authority: the capacity of the Church to specify the symbolism of the sacraments (itself left to some degree undetermined by Christ), and that capacity's location.

The Consequences of the Crisis

Returning to the scene in Hagia Sophia: dramatically, a deacon ran out after the legates and begged them to take the bull back, but they refused. Brought to the patriarch, it was found to make three points. First, neither Michael nor any other bishop of Constantinople deserves patriarchal status. Second, the Greeks have removed from the Creed an original *Filioque*. Third, a catalogue of vitiated customs in Byzantine church practice is offered for perusal. Understandably, the Byzantinist Stephen Runciman found it "extraordinary" that a man of Humbert's learning could have "penned so lamentable a manifesto".[13] Publicly burnt by order of the emperor, its authors were anathematised by the church of Constantinople, but not in such a way as to involve the pope himself or the Western church in general.[14] A way was left open for any pope who would recognise that Humbert had acted *ultra vires*. As Runciman remarks, the situation in 1055 was no worse than in 1052, except for an increase of ill will. But why then did the incident come to take on such importance?

First of all, by the accident that, of the three legates, one, Frederick, became pope as Stephen IX, and another, Humbert, was the principal influence on the most effective of mediaeval popes, Gregory VII, the memory of their humiliation became institutionally internal to the papal tradition. Second, in the wake of the reform movement, the Roman see had acquired a much higher profile in the Western church,

[13] S. Runciman, *The Eastern Schism: A Study of the Papacy and the Eastern Churches during the Eleventh and Twelfth Centuries* (Oxford, 1955), p. 48. Martin Jugie is even sharper in his *Le schisme byzantin* (Paris, 1941), pp. 205–6.

[14] In this the response echoed the provocation. For, in the bull of excommunication, Humbert declared himself satisfied with "the honourable and wise men" of "this most orthodox and Christian city", cited in Every, *Misunderstandings between East and West*, p. 10.

and Greek attacks on not only Latin usage but Roman claims received accordingly greater publicity. Third, with the adroit exploitation of the affair by Michael at the courts of his fellow patriarchs in Antioch, Jerusalem, and Alexandria, Eastern churchmen willing to make anti-Romanism a way of life would not, for the future, be lacking. As the chief historical theologian to write on the crisis has commented on the terms of the bull: "Such an incautious use of theological tradition gave the leaders of the Byzantine church a good basis for rallying Eastern Orthodox churchmen against Rome." [15]

And yet, while the issue of the azymes had its wider sacramentological and even Christological dimensions, it has not stood the test of time as an ecclesiastical *casus belli* between East and West.[16] Most Orthodox theologians today are prepared to remove liturgical differences from the list of obstacles to reunion. As the late Alexander Schmemann wrote: "Almost all the Byzantine arguments against the Latin rites have long since become unimportant; and only the genuine dogmatic deviations of Rome have remained." [17]

What Humbert unwittingly did was more important: he reawakened the issue of the *Filioque*, slumbering peacefully as this had been for well nigh two hundred years.[18]

---

[15] Smith, *"And Taking Bread"*, p. 24.

[16] Not into the twentieth century, yet it was still of importance in the eighteenth: thus the lay theologian Eustratios Argenti of Chios in his *Syntagma kata azymōn* (Leipzig, 1760), who fitted the azyme controversy into his general thesis that the root of Western error is the attempt to make theology fit philosophy. As he wrote, ibid., pp. 171–72 (italics added): "From this source there arose in the Latin church so many heresies in the theology of the Holy Trinity, so many distortions of the words of the Gospels and the apostles, so many violations of the sacred canons and the divine councils, and finally so many *corruptions and adulterations of the holy sacraments.*"

[17] A. Schmemann, *The Historical Road of Eastern Orthodoxy* (New York, 1961), p. 248. It would now be generally recognised that the Church of the first few centuries was indifferent as to whether the bread used in the Eucharist was leavened or unleavened. The important thing is to maintain that form which expresses the emphasis of one's own rite. However, some Orthodox theologians still regard the matter of the eucharistic *epiklêsis*—and its rôle in the Consecration—as a "dividing issue": see below, chapter 10.

[18] Smith, *"And Taking Bread"*, p. 23.

The Kerullarian schism was, in effect, a sharpening of the estrangement situation between Rome and Constantinople, that basic tendency to go their separate ways apparent in some form since the fourth century. In this it may be compared to the Acacian schism of the fifth century and the schism of Photius in the ninth. But now the human and ecclesial difference between Rome and Constantinople was so great that goodwill was insufficiently forthcoming to repair the breach in a systematic way, as had been done by the emperor Justin and Pope Hormisdas in 518 and by the patriarch Photius and Pope John VIII in 879. While the principal reason for this further qualitative deterioration was the character of the claims put forth for the papacy by the Gregorian reformers, the ill consequences of their attitude were compounded by a new aggressiveness on the part of the Byzantine patriarchate of the eleventh century.

Nevertheless, as scholars seem agreed, there was no formal schism in 1054, nor was the Roman church condemned synodically.[19] The *Filioque*, the papal claims, the ragbag of supposed Latin deviations in discipline and liturgy—none of these had been condemned by a council. They could not in themselves, therefore, constitute a state of schism. How, then, did the schism come about, since the solemn convocation of reunion councils in 1274 and 1439 logically imply a conviction that schism existed—even if, as Père Congar writes, on this point contemporary testimonies are "not fully homogeneous"?[20]

[19] For discussion of various earlier accounts of the date of the schism, see Every, *Misunderstandings between East and West*, pp. 9–25. Every concludes that the most important architect of the customary modern view that the schism began with the events of 1054 was the Oratorian Jean Morin whose *De sacris ordinationibus* of 1655 considered, inter alia, the attitude of Church and popes to ordinations conferred in schismatic situations. Morin was followed by such influential writers as Du Pin, Mosheim, and Gibbon.

[20] Y. J.-M. Congar, O.P., "1274–1974: Structures ecclésiales et conciles dans les relations entre Orient et Occident", *Revue des sciences philosophiques et théologiques* 58, no. 3 (1974): 355. See also idem, "Quatre siècles de désunion et d'affrontement: Comment Grecs et Latins se sont appréciés réciproquement au point de vue ecclésiologique", *Ist.* 13 (1968): 131–52, and G. Denzler, "Das morgenländische Kirchenschismus im Verständnis von Päpsten und oekumenischen Konzilien des Mittelalters", *Münchener theologische Zeitschrift* 20 (1969): 104–17.

The Rôle of the Crusades

The answer that most historians would now accept is that the schism between Rome and the Orthodox East was the child of the Crusades.[21] Though never ratified by a council, it was formalised by the emergence of competing Greek and Latin hierarchies for three out of four of the Oriental patriarchal sees. (The Crusaders never took Alexandria, even if, early in the fourteenth century, Rome appointed a titular Latin patriarch in that city.) This was nothing to do with "Uniatism":[22] it concerned the replacement of Greek bishops, often in fragile communion, despite Kerullarios, with the pope, by Latin bishops more committed to the Crusaders and to the chief hierarch of the West.[23] But as few Greek bishops yielded without a struggle, rival lines of succession competed for dominance in Constantinople, Antioch, and Jerusalem. This fits perfectly the classical definitions of schism offered in the second and third centuries: the establishment of an alternative altar where an alternative bishop presides.

[21] A wealth of material in K. M. Setton, ed., *A History of the Crusades* (Madison, Wis., 1969–1977); for the later period, see idem, *The Papacy and the Levant, 1204–1571*, 4 vols. (Philadelphia, 1976–1981). For the interrelations of Rome, Constantinople, and the Crusaders, see P. Lemerle, *L'orthodoxie byzantine et l'oecuménisme médiéval: Les origines du "schisme" des Eglises* (Paris, 1965).

[22] In Crete, however, the popes did foster a kind of Uniate church alongside the Latin. For the most successful of the Crusader states, the Lusignan kingdom of Cyprus, see H. J. Magoulias, "A Study in Roman Catholic and Greek Orthodox Relations on the Island of Cyprus between the Years A.D. 1196 and 1360", in *Greek Orthodox Theological Review* 10 (1964): 75–106; J. Gill, S.J., "The Tribulations of the Greek Church in Cyprus, 1196–c. 1280", in *Church Union; Rome and Byzantium, 1204–1453* (London, 1979), pp. 73–93.

[23] The Normans must be blamed for much of this policy. In their principality at Antioch, when the Greek patriarch, John, refused to appoint more Latin bishops to important sees, they enlisted the aid of the new Jerusalemite patriarch, Daimbert of Pisa. When John retired in dudgeon to Constantinople, they replaced him with a Latin patriarch. Norman resistance to Greek demands for a restoration of their patriarch to Antioch sharpened Byzantine criticism of the Latin patriarch at Jerusalem, and, in general, increased Byzantine pressure on Latin churches in their own territory. Thus G. Every, *Understanding Eastern Christianity* (Bangalore, 1976; London, 1980), pp. 88–89. For the Latin patriarchate of Jerusalem see G. Fedalto, *La Chiesa latina in Oriente* (Verona, 1973).

The impact of the Crusades upon Byzantium cannot be explained without reference to the "peaking" of East Roman power in the period of Kerullarios. Within a generation, the Seljuk Turks, occupying much of Asia Minor by a staggering military victory in 1071, initiated four centuries of Byzantine decline that would end with the city's fall in 1453.[24] Ironically, the Crusades began as the brainchild of perhaps the most pro-Byzantine of all mediaeval popes, Urban II, and were charmed into being so as to aid the Byzantine Empire and church and to secure for the West, and Rome, a new benevolence from the East. But as Runciman wrote, the Crusaders brought not peace but a sword, and the sword was to sever Christendom.

Why did the Crusades have this disastrous impact? The same author points out that it is a liberal delusion to suppose that problems created by group antagonism would be solved if only people could get to know each other. With a touch of seigneurial disdain, he argues that, whereas educated people generally benefit from residence abroad, since their education gives them the imaginative ability to sympathise with foreigners and their different ways, the uneducated, when dropped into an alien situation, with a language they do not comprehend and customs that are strange to them, are more likely to experience passions of resentment and anger rather than benevolence. Similarly, it is fallacious to assume that if only people had the opportunity to thrash out their arguments in rational debate, everyone would be united. Debates between Latins and Byzantines rarely produced shared conviction. Each side looked for ever more arguments with which to bolster its own case, the more fervently if it felt its own side beginning to lose the day.[25] In the contemporary

[24] This was the period when the Byzantine state was strained by marked internal difficulties in the socioeconomic order, interpreted by modern historians either as economic problems generated by the development of feudal relations (thus G. Ostrogorsky, *History of the Byzantine State* [Eng. trans., Oxford, 1968]) or as economic successes engendered by feudal relations but themselves unleashing centrifugal tendencies (thus A. Harvey, *Economic Expansion in the Byzantine Empire* [Cambridge, 1989]).

[25] An important exception is explored by N. Russell in "Anselm of Havelberg and the Union of the Churches", *Sob.*, n.s., 1, no. 1 (1979): 19–41; 2, no. 1 (1980): 29–41.

ecumenical movement, it is a sign of the presence of the Holy Spirit that this agonistic mentality is largely absent—though at times a more economical explanation for such serenity may be the evaporation of distinctive conviction. In doctrinal debate, the two sides were, furthermore, at frequent cross-purposes. For the West, reunion meant the due subordination of the Eastern hierarchs to the pope; for the East, it meant the restoration of the Roman patriarch to his place as first among the five.

But if these were chronic features of East-West relations in the Middle Ages—in the term of the French *Annales* school of historiography, *conjunctures*—things were made immeasurably worse by the incidental history created by certain Crusading acts (*les événements*). The antipathy that the Crusading host eventually aroused at Antioch and Jerusalem was something new in the history of those sees, for they had no quarrel of precedence with Rome as did Constantinople. Still, the key event was the sack of Constantinople in 1204: one of those traumatising events in the life of a people that leaves behind a new and negative sensibility.[26] Comparable to the Cromwellian settlement in Ireland, the Nazi invasion of Soviet Russia, or the expulsion of the Palestinians from the Holy Land by the state of Israel, it was not simply a question of the forcible imposition of an alien government and church. Nor was it simply a question of the sheer volume of sacrilegious actions.[27] It was, above all, a body blow to the whole mystique of Byzantium as the city chosen by God, a mystique integral to the cultural and religious identity of Christian Hellenism.[28]

The alienating effect of the Crusades can be traced in a new rigour of tone when Byzantine people wrote of the Latin Church, and especially of the papacy. Examples range from canon law to political history. Two such may stand for others. In the twelfth century, the

[26] Runciman, *Eastern Schism*, pp. 145–58, and more fully in *A History of the Crusades* (Cambridge, 1951–1954), vol. 3.

[27] See on this the eyewitness account of Nicetas Choniates, cited in J.J. Norwich, *A History of Venice* (London, 1982), p. 139.

[28] For a beautiful attempt at a literary recreation of this mystique, see P. Sherrard, *Iconography of a Sacred City* (Oxford, 1964).

Greek church produced a crop of brilliant canonists, of whom three
tower above the rest: Alexis Aristenes, John Zonaras, and Theodore
Balsamon. Around 1190—after the displacement of the Greek patriarch at Antioch, and perhaps after too, that of his brother of
Jerusalem—Balsamon replied to a request from the patriarch Mark
of Alexandria for an opinion about the propriety of giving communion to Latins.

> For many years ... [we note the lack of a precise date], the Western
> church has been divided in spiritual communion from the other four
> patriarchates and has become alien to the Orthodox ... and therefore
> the pope is not mentioned in commemoration in the diptychs. So no
> Latin should be communicated unless he first declares that he will
> abstain from the doctrines and customs that separate him from us and
> that he will be subject to the canons of the Church, in union with
> the Orthodox.[29]

Gradually, the very idea of the Roman primacy began to fade in Byzantine minds. Though, at the reunion councils, the official view might
be that Rome rightly enjoyed primacy until she forfeited it by her own
act—exaggerating her claims and tampering with the ecumenical
Creed[30]—for many educated Byzantine men and women, hostility to
Rome drove out earlier memories of her place as the first in the *taxis*,
the ordering of the churches. Anna Comnena, in her *Alexiad*, a biog-
raphy of the emperor Alexius I, her father, a work completed in 1148,
the achievement of a gifted and well-informed woman, had this to say
about an action of Pope Gregory VII of which she disapproved:

> This was the deed of a pontiff, yes, of the supreme pontiff, the deed
> of the man who claims to preside over the whole world, or so the
> Latins say and believe, so great is their arrogance. But really when the
> seat of empire was transferred from over there to our country and
> our imperial city, together with the senate and all the administration,
> the chief rank in the episcopal hierarchy was transferred at the same
> time. Ever since that time the emperors have given precedence to the
> see of Constantinople, and above all the Council of Chalcedon raised

---

[29] PG 138:968, cited in Runciman, *Eastern Schism*, p. 139.
[30] J. Spiteris, *La critica bizantina del primato romano nel secolo XII* (Rome, 1979).

the bishopric of Constantinople to the highest place, and subordinated to it all the bishoprics in the *oikoumenê*.[31]

Only if large segments of Byzantine opinion credited this could such a writer produce, surely, such an inaccurate account.[32] Greek Christian historiography from the eighteenth century onwards reflects these opinions. Consistently it ascribes the schism to the innovations, and despotic pretensions, of the bishops of Rome. The so-called unions brought only trouble and scandal, for they were founded not on truth but on expediency and as such were gravely displeasing to God.[33] Whether the reunion councils *were* founded on expediency alone we must consider in the chapters that follow. Meanwhile, we can note the continuing trauma in the corporate memory caused by the sins and transgressions of the mediaeval Church. In May 1971, when the cardinal president of the Secretariat for Promoting Christian Unity, Jan Willebrands, visited the Holy Synod of the Church of Greece, Archbishop Hieronymos of Athens, in the course of an otherwise cordial welcome, had these hard words to say:

> The faithful of our Church have, over the centuries, grown accustomed to discerning in actions of your Church intentions which were anything else but fraternal, and as a rule now find it difficult to convince themselves that the fervent attempts towards Christian unity being exerted today by the Holy See are free from past tendencies. Hence the necessary time must be given to our faithful to realise from the events themselves that hands which are now being extended are in truth brotherly.[34]

[31] *Alexiad* 1.12, cited in Runciman, *Eastern Schism*, pp. 112–13. Runciman remarks, however, of Anna's silence in regard to Urban II: "One almost has the impression that she could not bear to speak well of any pope but was too scrupulous to speak ill of Urban"; ibid., p. 111.

[32] For the eminent late twelfth-century canonist Theodore Balsamon, who credited the authenticity of the Donation of Constantine, there *was* a universally primatial see, but, by the imperial will, it was at New Rome, not Old. See Chadwick, *East and West*, p. 236.

[33] J. Anastasiou, "Greek Church History", *Conc.* 7, no. 7 (1971): 139–44.

[34] [H. Giorgiadis], "A Decisive Turning Point: Official Visit of Cardinal Willebrands to the Church of Greece", *Chrysostom* 3, no. 3 (Winter 1971–1972): 50.

Bibliography

Dvornik, F. "Les origines du schisme de Michael Cérulaire". *Conc.* I, no. 7 (1966): 137–49.

Fedalto, G. *La Chiesa latina in Oriente*. Verona, 1973.

Grumel, V. "Les préliminaires du schisme de Michel Cérulaire et la question romaine avant 1054", *REB* 10 (1953): 1–23.

Michel, A. *Humbert und Kerullarios*. Paderborn, 1925–1930.

Runciman, S. *The Eastern Schism: A Study of the Papacy and the Eastern Churches during the Eleventh and Twelfth Centuries*. Oxford, 1955.

Smith, M. H. *"And Taking Bread": The Development of the Azyme Controversy*. Paris, 1982.

9

The Second Council of Lyons and
the Notion of Purgatory

From Lateran IV to Lyons II

The policy of the Latin Church in the fifty years following the Fourth Crusade was so incompetent as to beggar belief. Pope Innocent III, in recognising as a *fait accompli* the Latin emperor and patriarch at Constantinople, was right to think that many Greeks were so demoralised by the fall of the city as to accept both an emperor of Western birth and the restoration of communion with the Church of Rome—a case, to the papal mind, of Providence writing straight with crooked lines.[1] Other Byzantines were willing to accept a duality of bishops in the great sees: a Latin bishop and a Greek, each recognising the other. This would have been an arrangement of the kind practised today by both the Catholic and the Orthodox churches in places where numerous faithful of different rites (Catholicism) or jurisdictions (Orthodoxy) live cheek by jowl. Admittedly, both then and now such a policy goes counter to the best ecclesiology. The bishop unites the faithful of a given place in one body: hence in no place should there be more than one bishop. Nevertheless, by an exercise of "economy" (in the Greek canonical term) or "dispensation" (in its Latin equivalent), such a measure might have found widespread

[1] For the pope's vigorous condemnation of the plan to seize Constantinople, see J. Gill, S.J., "Franks, Venetians and Pope Innocent III", in *Church Union: Rome and Byzantium, 1204–1453* (London, 1979), pp. 85–106, and idem, "Innocent III and the Greeks: Aggressor or Apostle?" ibid., pp. 95–108. But cf. *Regata Innocentii III* 6.154, his *post factum* letter to the ecclesiastics of the city, with its curt application of the prophecy of Daniel, "He [God] changes times and transfers kingdoms."

acceptance in those regions of the Greek East where the Crusader host had settled in decent numbers.[2]

But the Fourth Lateran Council, summoned by Innocent III in 1215, put an end to all such eirenic hopes. It decreed that the pope was the head of all the patriarchs of the East. It provided that in each see there must be but one bishop, regarding the alternative solution as an ecclesial monstrosity, a body with two heads.[3] In practice, then, it determined that the bishops of the empire should be Latins, for nearly all the Greek bishops had fled to the shadow states of Nicaea and Epirus, there to await better times. As for the Greek liturgy, that, the council found, might be tolerated "insofar as this is possible in the Lord". In the council's wake, many Latin bishops took possession of their sees but suffered ejection if that possession were not underwritten by force. Gradually, the Byzantine will to survive reasserted itself. In 1261, Constantinople was retaken by Michael Palaeologos, a Greek claimant to the imperial throne who had bided his time across the Bosphorus at Nicaea. The Latin Empire, and its patriarchate, had lasted a little over half a century.

It might be thought that, after this sorry tale, the Byzantines would have wanted nothing more to do with the Latin Church. And indeed, as George Every wrote of the aftermath of the sack of the city:

> Commemoration of the pope in the diptychs came to be a mark of collaboration with the invaders, indeed of treason. It also became a mark of submission to the local Latin authorities, political and ecclesiastical alike, to be deleted when any locality was liberated. In subsequent negotiations between the Greeks of the empire of Nicaea and the papacy, the heart of the difficulty was that a patriarch of Constantinople in communion with Rome, who consented to acknowledge the pope as primate of the whole Church and to commemorate him in the diptychs could not hope to recover possession of Sancta Sophia, or authority over the Greeks in the Latin principalities.[4]

---

[2] See R. Janin, "Au lendemain de la conquête de Constantinople: Les tentatives d'union des Eglises, 1204–1208, 1208–1214", *EO* 32 (1933), pp. 5–21, 195–202.

[3] *Concilium Lateratense IV*, capitulum 9.

[4] Every, *Understanding Eastern Christianity*, p. 95.

And yet, within fifteen years of the recapture by the Greeks, a reunion council had met at Lyons, and communion was officially restored between Rome and the East. How can one explain this turn of events? To a considerable degree, as early modern Greek Orthodox historiography was right to assert, it must be explained by political and even military considerations.[5] The Byzantine Empire was not only weakened but territorially diminished. Most of Greece remained in Western hands. At Trebizond on the coast of the Black Sea sat a rival claimant to the imperial inheritance. Most seriously, the Angevins, who had inherited, from their base in Naples and Sicily, the Norman rôle of chief Western aggressors in the East, were planning a fresh Latin expedition to recover Constantinople. Nor were the Angevins without ability to bring pressure on the papacy, whom they were shielding against the imperialist pretensions, in Italy, of the Hohenstaufen Conradin.

In 1267, accordingly, the Paleologan emperor Michael VIII initiated contacts with Pope Clement IV to discuss reunion, in the hope of strengthening his hand by support from some of the Western states, perhaps Hungary or Genoa.[6] Clement's successor, Gregory X, used all diplomatic means to prevent the Angevin crusade from embarking but in effect laid the Byzantine delegation under threat that, should reunion conversations break down, a different sort of reunion might be established by other means. It will readily be seen that, to the rest of the Byzantine church, a settlement arrived at in such a context could be repudiated with equanimity.

Yet the picture must not be painted in too dark colours. Evidence of a more generous, indeed a truly ecumenical, approach, is furnished by the reports that Gregory commissioned from various Western bishops and heads of religious Orders, intending that they should be used in preparing the council's agenda. Responding to this invitation, Humbert of Romans, the fifth Master of the Dominicans,

---

[5] D. M. Nicol, "The Greeks and the Union of the Churches: The Preliminaries of the Second Council of Lyons, 1261–1274", in *Mediaeval Studies Presented to Aubrey Gwynn* (Dublin, 1961), pp. 454–80.

[6] For his policies, see D. J. Geanakoplos, *Emperor Michael Palaeologus and the West, 1256–1282: A Study in Byzantine-Latin Relations* (Cambridge, Mass., 1958).

composed an *Opus tripartitum*, whose central section concerns the relations between the Greek and Roman churches.[7] Classifying the Byzantines as schismatics rather than heretics, Humbert ascribes partial responsibility for the division to Westerners. Differences, both ritual and cultural, were exacerbated by unfraternal conduct; when at last the Latins added the *Filioque* to the Creed without consulting the Eastern church, the stage was set for a schism that has disabled the mission of Christendom at large. Humbert considered the pope duty bound to take a lead in the work of reconciliation, perhaps by travelling to Greece in person: "Christ came down from Heaven in order to make both one [that is, Jews and Gentiles], and therefore his vicar ought not to refuse, if it is necessary, to travel into Greece if there is hope that in so doing he might be able to unite the Greeks and the Latins. He is the father not only of the latter but of the former as well, although they are less devoted sons."[8] Humbert recommended great discretion in the choice of nuncios to the Byzantines, correction of overzealous Latins in the Western colonies of the Peloponnese, encouragement of Greek scholars to live and study with their Latin counterparts, and the development of Greek letters in the West. He also advised the pope to content himself with confirming, merely, the election of the Byzantine patriarch and with asking that his legates be received honourably by Greek clergy and officials.[9]

In Byzantium itself, the chief concern of churchmen was undoubtedly the ecclesiological issue of the primacy. In his "chrysobull" announcing the commitment to reunion, the emperor expounded the concrete content of his unionist policy. The sincerity of its preamble can still be sensed: "I set myself with all seriousness to see how the broken body of the Church may be fitted together to become one and be given back again its union with God himself, who is the head of a single body with all its members, as the apostle conceives

---

[7] In P. Crabbe, *Concilia omnia tam generalia quam particularia*, vol. 2 (Cologne, 1551), pp. 967–1103.

[8] *Opus tripartitum* 2.16.

[9] E. T. Brett, *Humbert of Romans: His Life and Views of Thirteenth-Century Society* (Toronto, 1984), pp. 186–91.

it." [10] Michael VIII presents the union as a twofold affair. On the one hand, all the dogmas and customs of the Byzantine church will remain in full vigour; on the other hand, that church will recognise the Roman bishop, "ecumenical pope and successor on the apostolic throne", as "the supreme and first bishop", *akron . . . kai prôton archierea.* "Our holy church" will "conserve and accord to the apostolic throne those innumerable prerogatives in accordance with the jurisdiction observed from the beginning, which the piety of emperors and the laws and canons of the divine fathers sanctioned and, one receiving them from the hands of another, held them with common approval to the end, right up to the time of the division." [11]

For their part, the bishops, commenting on the chrysobull, agreed to regard the pope as first bishop, to admit a right of appeal to Rome from any ecclesiastic who felt himself unjustly treated by the Byzantine tribunals, and to commemorate his name in the liturgy "as was the ancient and patristic custom that prevailed from of old". The *Filioque*, contrast, received remarkably little notice in these preliminaries of the council. The patriarch, John Bekkos, had become personally convinced that, in accounts of the Spirit's coming forth, the Greek *dia*, the *per Filium*, was convertible in meaning with the *Filioque*. On the basis of his reading of the fathers (he was struck especially by Saint John Damascene's assertion that the Father is the "producer through the Word of the illuminating Spirit") [12] as of certain Byzantine treatises sympathetic to the Western theology of the procession (by Nicephorus Blemmydes and Nicetas of Maroneia), the patriarch swept aside the *Filioque* issue as mere *logomachia*, fighting about words, and in so doing swept it under the carpet—with unfortunate effects.

At the Second Council of Lyons, the Greek delegation was small. [13] Owing, in part, to the military situation, the reunion agreement

[10] Cited in J. Gill, S.J., "The Church Union of the Council of Lyons (1274) Portrayed in Greek Documents", in *Church Union*, p. 13.

[11] Cited ibid., p. 15.

[12] *De fide orthodoxa* 13, PG 94:849B. See also *Communio* 36 (2009): 259–94.

[13] For the council itself, see B. Roberg, *Die Union zwischen der griechischen und der lateinischen Kirchen auf dem II. Konzil von Lyon, 1274* (Bonn, 1964), and H. Wolter and H. Holstein, *Lyon I et Lyon II* (Paris, 1966).

was reached in haste, with little in the way of theological negotiation. Four points were at issue: first, the nature of the Roman primacy; second, the *Filioque*; third, the validity of a Eucharist celebrated with unleavened bread—and of these three none should surprise us, for the first had been at stake since the fourth century, the second since the ninth, and the third since the quarrel of Humbert and Kerullarios—but the fourth issue was a newcomer, and this was the notion of Purgatory.

The topic of Purgatory had surfaced only quite recently in Latin-Byzantine polemic, probably around 1230.[14] The earliest known debate on the subject between Greeks and Latins took place in southern Italy, with a Franciscan friar and a visiting Greek bishop, Bardanes of Corfu, as protagonists. The friar was anxious to know what the Greeks thought of the state of Christians who died with their penance for sin uncompleted. In the Western church, penance is regarded as an essential aspect of the sacrament of second repentance or, as it is known in modern times, reconciliation, and indeed has long lent that sacrament its own name. Traditionally, the sacrament's components are auricular confession, absolution, and the setting of a penance. In the Greek church, however, the giving of a penance, *epitimia*, by the confessor was (and is) regarded as something optional that is often omitted. The Greek bishop was alarmed by the Franciscan's statement that those who die with their penance for sin unfinished must submit to a purifying fire. To the Greek, such a notion of the intermediate state seemed alien.

And indeed, the Western distinction between the everlasting guilt of sin, removed in the contrite sinner by God himself, and the temporal punishment still due for the repairing of the (in the widest sense) moral order, was by no means so clearly present in the Greek tradition. Moreover, the idea of the *fire* of Purgatory was wholly absent. To the Greek, it sounded like Origenism: in other words, that, for the Latins, even those in Hell may ultimately be saved. The bishop wrote quickly to the Constantinopolitan patriarch,

[14] R. Ombres, O.P., "Latins and Greeks in Debate over Purgatory, 1250–1459", *JEH* 55 (1984): 1–14; idem, *The Theology of Purgatory* (Dublin, 1978).

Germanus II, exiled at Nicaea, warning him that the Latins were distorting the quite traditional doctrine that prayer and almsgiving can assist the departed into a new teaching that there is a part of Hell from which—so to speak—escape is possible. Within a short time, the issue would reach the highest ecclesiastical levels.

As we have seen, relations, of an exploratory kind, between the emperor Michael VIII and the papacy were established in the course of 1267. In that year, Pope Clement IV issued a lengthy profession of faith for imperial consideration.[15] It included the topic of Purgatory. This profession was to remain the basis for subsequent negotiations and was adopted in 1274 at Lyons II (and reappeared in 1439 at Florence). So far as Purgatory is concerned, the "Clementine formula" abstains from any reference to fire, though it does use the term "purgatorial", in its Greek form (*pourgatorios*). Those who die in charity, truly repentant but without as yet making satisfaction for their sins, whether of commission or omission, by worthy fruits of repentance, will, so the formula maintains, be purged after death, *poenis purgatoriis seu cathartiis*, "by purifying or cathartic pains". Despite the attempt at eirenicism—the restrained tone of the formula—it was not "received" by the Byzantine church when the Greek delegates, with their emperor, returned home. Along with the affirmation of the papal *plenitudo potestatis*, of the *Filioque*, and of the liceity of using unleavened bread for the Eucharist, it was repudiated by a well-attended Byzantine synod of 1277, which proceeded to excommunicate the emperor and the "unionist" party.

The Birth of the Doctrine of Purgatory

Before considering the causes of this breakdown, it seems suitable to add a little on the issue of Purgatory itself. The background to the doctrine of the intermediate state is the "realistic" or "intrinsicist" view of justification common to both Eastern and Western tradition. Although justification is gratuitous, coming about as it does through the free grace of God, this does not render it merely a legal

---

[15] For the Clementine formula, see DS 851–61.

fiction—a divine decision to regard us as other than we are. The grace of justification is not something extrinsic, in the sense of something that remains abidingly external to our own being. On the contrary, just as each sinner is responsible for his sins (else wrong-doing would not be his), so the forgiveness of those sins must affect every part of him. The New Testament speaks of the transformation of the person into a new creature, who is the friend of God. For Saint Paul, the Christian presses on to make salvation his own, as Philippians 3 testifies, and if the Christian life is seriously lived, then, for the same apostle, writing in his second extant letter to the Church at Corinth, our inner nature is being renewed every day. There must be, in other words, a thorough and progressive appropriation of grace at all levels of our existence.

It is true that, in principle, we cannot lay down a priori limits to what the moment of death may be able to achieve in us. Nevertheless, it contradicts everything that we know of God's "methods", and of our own nature, to suppose that, in the dread moment, some instantaneous transformation takes place. Our freedom must play some rôle in our final purification. Thus the early nineteenth-century Tübingen doctor Johann Adam Möhler regarded the doctrine of Purgatory as inseparable from the doctrine of justification.

Of this postmortem purification, the New Testament has little to say. Its concern is with the general resurrection and the final consummation of all things more than with the destiny of individuals. But its canon furnished images that could be developed in the direction of an application to the individual person: what, in contemporary exegesis, are sometimes termed "trajectories", trains of thought, not followed up yet pointing along a path that postbiblical dogmatic development proceeds to realise. One such image is found in the third chapter of the First Letter to the Corinthians: in less sophisticated times, the clinching "proof text" for the Latin doctrine of Purgatory.

> According to the commission of God given to me, like a skilled master builder I laid a foundation, and another man is building upon it. Let each man take care how he builds upon it. For no other foundation can any one lay than that which is laid, which is Jesus Christ.

Now if any one builds on the foundation with gold, silver, precious stones, wood, hay, stubble—each man's work will become manifest; for the Day will disclose it, because it will be revealed with fire, and the fire will test what sort of work each one has done. If the work which any man has built on the foundation survives, he will receive a reward. If any man's work is burned up, he will suffer loss, though he himself will be saved, but only as through fire.[16]

The imagery of this purifying fire belongs to the Old Testament symbolism of the "Day of the Lord", the terrible, yet wonderful, final epiphany of God to Israel. Modern Catholic Christians, if their grasp of doctrine is classical, are so used to linking this passage to the developed doctrine of Purgatory that it is worth noting of the first use of the word *purgatorium* that it occurs in the writings of Hildebert of Lavardin, whose dates are 1056–1135—in other words, hardly more than a century before the opening of the Latin-Byzantine debate on the topic. This in no way impugns the authoritativeness of the Western doctrine as a rendering of a New Testament insight—yet it helps to explain the Byzantine hesitation.

The elements of the later doctrine—apart, perhaps, from the distinction between *peccatum* and *poena*—are all clearly present in the Latin fathers, and notably in the anonymous author of the *Passion of Saint Felicity and Saint Perpetua*, Saint Augustine, and Saint Bede. It is instructive that cognate passages in Greek fathers are to be found chiefly in those writers who espoused a thoroughgoing soteriological universalism—Clement of Alexandria, Origen, and Saint Gregory of Nyssa. For all of these latter writers, Hell was, almost certainly, not an everlasting condition but, rather, an opportunity for repentance, expiation, and growth. We might hazard a statement, then, that whereas the Latin fathers had a clear-cut view of the intermediate state, Greek writers tended to make one single continuous spectrum of Hell, Purgatory, and Heaven. After the Fifth Ecumenical Council, Constantinople II, there was, however, a strong reaction against such Origenistic speculativeness in the presentation of eschatological doctrine by the Byzantine church. One result was reserve

---

[16] 1 Cor 3:10–15.

in developing a full-blown doctrine of Purgatory, out of fear for the reintroduction of Origenism by the back door. The Greek church, as a consequence, prayed for the dead in its public liturgy, as well as in private, yet it did not attempt to describe the distinct state—neither hellish nor heavenly—to which those so prayed for belonged.

In the West, the liturgical development of the sacrament of penance accentuated the reparatory aspect of the doctrine of Purgatory. Originally, canonical penance had been carried out prior to absolution, usually in the form of so many days' exclusion from holy communion, fasting, and the wearing of penitential clothes ("sackcloth and ashes"). The absolution, once given, therefore entailed the complete sacramental communication of forgiveness, with no loose ends attached. Satisfaction had been offered in the penance done. When these two elements were reversed, so that absolution preceded penance, the aspect of satisfaction was projected into the future. Temporal reparation would be made later, hopefully on earth, but if not, then in the intermediate state. Thus the distinctively Western doctrine of Purgatory was born. Building on the Latin patristic notion of a purifying fire beyond death, it contributed the nuance that one, at any rate, of the chief aims of this transformation was the forgiveness of the temporal punishment owing to sin. In the East, the comparatively undeveloped character of the doctrine of Purgatory should be accounted for, not only by fear of Origenism but also in terms of the different liturgical-canonical development of the sacrament of penance. Noteworthy in the West, by contrast, is the fact that in 1215, at the Fourth Lateran Council, the Catholic faithful were obliged to confess all serious sins once a year. This must have thrust the issue of Purgatory uppermost in many minds. Only fifteen years afterwards there took place the conversation of the Franciscan with Bishop Bardanes.

One beneficial effect of the debate with the Greek East was the toning down, by the Latins, of the image of purgatorial fire. Or, rather, they understood more clearly that this was an image and not a literal reality. A contemporary theology of Purgatory, drawing on the resources of tradition at large, would wish to utilise other symbols to complement the symbolism of fire that once so alarmed the

Greeks. It will wish to make use of more "models" in the understanding of doctrine than simply the penal model: punishment and its performance. At its most fundamental, the doctrine of Purgatory affirms that, for those who die with their wills set towards charity, further transformation is possible beyond death as preparation for Heaven. And stated thus, the doctrine is an ecumenical doctrine, which belongs equally to the Greek and Latin churches, no matter what the terminology used.[17]

The readiness of some twentieth-century Orthodox dogmaticians to concede as much is exemplified in the work of George Florovsky (1893–1979). Florovsky's essay "The Last Things and the Last Events" contained a spirited defence of the doctrine of Purgatory as that emerges from such writers as Dante, Catherine of Genoa, and Cardinal Newman.[18] Florovsky has been commenting, in the essay's course, on the eschatology of Emil Brunner, the Reformed theologian contemporary with Barth, and he criticises Brunner, and by implication, the Protestant tradition at large, for speaking of all men as sinners in the same sense. Brunner deals only with two factors, mankind as a sinful man and the forgiving grace of God. He does not ask how sin and forgiveness may affect in varying degrees the inner, intimate structure of the human person. And this criticism brings Florovsky to the topic of Purgatory.

Florovsky's apologia for Purgatory (it is hardly less!) harmonises with the best Catholic theology on the topic—namely, to stress not so much the punitive as the transformative nature of Purgatory. If one regards justification as something that actually changes the person and not merely as a legal fiction on the part of a God who declares just (thanks to Christ's merits) a sinner who will never in fact be just at all, then, for Florovsky, something like the doctrine of Purgatory imposes itself. As Florovsky writes: "It is not enough to acknowledge by faith the deed of the divine redemption—one has

[17] For a fine statement of the Orthodox understanding of the sacrament of confession, within a more general account of *metanoia*, see K. Ware, "The Orthodox Experience of Repentance", *Sob.*, n.s. 2, no. 1 (1980): 18–28.

[18] G. Florovsky, *Creation and Redemption*, vol. 3 of *Collected Works* (Belmont, Mass., 1976), pp. 243–68.

to be born anew. The whole personality must be cleansed and healed.... Paradoxically, nobody can be saved by love divine alone, unless it is responded to by grateful love of human persons." [19] And the Russian theologian goes on to explain that Purgatory is, like Heaven, for those who are pledged to Christ, who have already made plain a fundamental orientation towards God. It is for such people if they are at the same time "deficient in growth and achievement". Assisted by Florovsky's characteristic emphasis on the rôle of ascetic effort, *podvig*, in the formation of the Christian, this is, in effect, a contemporary presentation of that modest doctrine of Purgatory agreed at Florence—the mediaeval Latin doctrine shorn of its judicial aspect and its imagery of fire. In this sense, Florovsky's doctrine represents the kind of grasp of the intermediate state that the Latin unionists of the later Middle Ages hoped the Greeks could acquire.

The Failure of the Union of Lyons

Returning to the story line: Why was it that the union of Lyons II lasted no more than a bare three years? The unionists were always a tiny—if influential—handful. More precisely, they consisted of two groups: one, around the emperor, that saw the political and military value of the union; the other, around the Byzantine patriarch John Bekkos, that consisted of theologically convinced supporters of reunion with Rome, on terms largely favourable to Rome.

If the great English Byzantinist Joseph Gill of the Society of Jesus was correct, then the mistake of emperor and patriarch lay in their failure to engage directly the issue of the *Filioque* and so to win minds for the dogmatic peace: "It seems that the bishops and ecclesiastics, having agreed to the union on a canonical basis, deliberately closed their minds—or at least their mouths—on the theologically controversial Filioque. But it peeped up." [20] Considering that two of the greatest Latin mediaeval divines, Albert of Cologne and Bonaventure, had attended the Second Council of Lyons (Thomas Aquinas

---

[19] Ibid., p. 262.
[20] Gill, "The Church Union of the Council of Lyons", p. 43.

was meant to join them but died on the way), it seems extraordinary how meagre was the theological diet served. The conciliar constitution published in November 1274 was nonetheless useful in answering a charge dating back to Photius when it professed the Spirit's procession from Father and Son "not as from two first principles but as from one, not by two spirations but by one single spiration which has always been believed by the holy Roman church, mother and mistress, and is also the faith of both Latin and Greek fathers." (Chadwick is inclined to think this statement may have been fine-tuned in the papal chancery after the council concluded.)[21]

In the council's wake, theological polemic on the *Filioque* was resumed, and to the bishops' chagrin, Bekkos, having first kept a discreet silence, determined to answer it on its own ground. Thus began the union's unravelling, for, according to the contemporary historian George Pachymeres, the bishops "had with very great difficulty accepted the peace and had barely yielded and were unionist only in appearance, pacifying their consciences not from Scripture (for there was no occasion for that) but by economy usual in the Church for the attainment of a greater good."[22] The short years of the union became known as the "time of scandal" or the "period of ecclesiastical confusion". Gill called the opposition "strong and general". Understandable in political terms was the resistance of the "Arsenite" monks, so called because of their rallying to the deposed patriarch Arsenius, whom Michael had removed from office on the ground of his continued support for the young son of his predecessor Theodore II Lascaris, blinded to bar his succession. But they were not the only opponents of the union, for the ranks of the latter extended to the imperial family, the senate, and officials of all ranks in both Church and state. The patriarch and his synod responded by asking for loyalty oaths, a condition of perseverance in office.

Meanwhile, at Rome, the impotence of the emperor to secure the union's future looked like treachery. The pope, Nicholas III, sent envoys to Constantinople to seek proof of the emperor's efforts

---

[21] Chadwick, *East and West*, p. 250.
[22] G. Pachymeres, *De Michaele Palaeologo*, ed. I. Bekker (Bonn, 1835), p. 480.

to gain his people's concurrence in the union agreement. In fact, amid the growing uncertainty and political instability, Michael Palaeologos had become only too violent and tyrannical in his unionist endeavours. To no avail: in 1281 Pope Martin IV excommunicated the emperor and his entourage for simulating return to communion and, by a secret treaty, agreed to support Philip of Courtenay (the last Latin emperor of Constantinople), Charles of Anjou, and the doge of Venice in an expedition to reconstitute the Latin Empire. Michael responded by forbidding the naming of Martin at the liturgy, but he was not to be forgiven by the Byzantine church. Dying on campaign in Thrace, his body was buried by night. His coemperor, who succeeded him as Andronicus II, renounced the union; Bekkos was exiled; Hagia Sophia was liturgically purified after its pollution; unionists were fined; and the dead emperor's wife was made to forgo the consolation of religious rites for the repose of her husband's soul.[23] By 1283 no see was in union with Rome. The papacy, soon to be transferred to Avignon, now fell prey to the temptation of *Realpolitik*: *force majeure* might succeed where conciliar suasion had so manifestly failed. The revolt of Sicily against the house of Anjou ("the Sicilian Vespers"), however, crippled the only pugilist willing for the fight.

For such a policy was increasingly anachronistic, since the states of the West were too preoccupied with their own affairs to go on such adventures: one thinks especially of the Hundred Years' War between France and England and the increasingly commercial, rather than colonial, ambitions of Venice. But wilder spirits in the Latin Church did not abandon the idea. The Italian humanist and poet Petrarch encouraged Urban V to organise a reconquest, writing: "The existence of Constantinople is as great an evil as the loss of Jerusalem. For to honour Christ in the way the Greeks do is to wound him.... These rascals call the Roman church their mother, but they treat our Latin rite with contempt and purify their churches if one of us enters.... I leave others to decide if we should call it patience

---

[23] J. Gill, S.J., "John Beccus, Patriarch of Constantinople", in *Church Union*, p. 256.

or torpor that makes us bear with them so long".[24] In 1332 a Dominican, William of Adam, sent a memorandum on the Greek question to the French king Philip IV. He proposed, inter alia, Latin education for every second or subsequent son born to a Greek family, tax incentives to encourage Greeks to profess the Catholic faith, and the redesigning of church buildings to fit Latin customs![25]

In the later fourteenth century, such attitudes became less common. The extension of the Ottoman threat to all Europe (and not just Byzantium) led to a refocussing of corporate hostility elsewhere. (As early as 1332, a Turkish fleet had appeared off Rome.) Moreover, Byzantine diplomacy was successful in its aim of presenting the empire as a necessary bulwark of the West, a defence of the security, and freedom of faith, of the Church in western Europe. The promise of the sultan, that his horses would yet eat off the altar of Saint Peter's Basilica, is not irrelevant to the background of the Council of Florence.

---

[24] *Senilium rerum libri* 2.1.

[25] Writing under the sobriquet "Brocardus", in *Directorum ad passagium faciendum* 8; see A.-D. von Brincken, *Die "Nationes Christianorum Orientalium" im Verständnis der lateinischen Historiographie von der Mitte des 12. bis in die zweite Hälfte des 14. Jahrhunderts* (Cologne and Vienna, 1975), pp. 64–65.

Bibliography

Geanakoplos, D. J. *Emperor Michael Palaeologus and the West, 1256–1282: A Study in Latin-Byzantine Relations.* Cambridge, Mass., 1958.

Gill, J., S.J. *Church Union: Rome and Byzantium, 1204–1453.* London, 1979.

Holstein, H. *Lyon I et Lyon II.* Paris, 1966.

Nicol, D. M. "The Greeks and the Union of the Churches: The Preliminaries of the Second Council of Lyons, 1261–1274". In *Mediaeval Studies Presented to Aubrey Gwynn,* pp. 454–80. Dublin, 1961.

Ombres, R., O.P. "Latins and Greeks in Debate over Purgatory, 1230–1439". *JEH* 35 (1984).

———. *The Theology of Purgatory.* Dublin, 1978.

Rees, H. *The Catholic Church and Corporate Reunion: A Study of the Relations between East and West from the Schism of 1054 to the Council of Florence.* London, 1940.

Roberg, B. *Die Union zwischen der griechischen und der lateinischen Kirchen auf dem II. Konzil von Lyon, 1274.* Bonn, 1964.

10

The Council of Florence and the Stumbling Block of Rome

The Making of the Council of Florence

The negotiations that eventually led to the second reunion council, that of Ferrara-Florence in 1438–1439, were, as with their predecessor of the late thirteenth century, partly political in inspiration, at least from the Byzantine side. The Eastern emperors now dealt with the popes not so much as first patriarchs, as had emperors in patristic times, but more as the natural leaders of the Western Christian polities. Yet many politically aware Greeks were conscious of the limited usefulness of such overtures. They knew of the increasing *étatisme* of the Western monarchies and republics of the early Renaissance and also of the attack mounted against papal authority by the Conciliar movement. They doubted the ability of the Latin West to come to their rescue by means of a fresh papal initiative.

Yet these negotiations were far from exclusively secular in inspiration. The popes were genuinely committed to the ecumenical cause. They regarded the political aspect as the work of Providence, using the Turkish menace to throw divided Christians together. Wherever they thought the Greek world might offer them a hearing, they sent letters full of zeal for reunion. Not all such letters fell on deaf ears. In educated circles, Byzantine people were becoming interested in Augustine and Aquinas.[1] Such "Latinophrones" might well have Italian

---

[1] For the outstanding Latinophrone writer Demetrios Kydones, see J. Likoudis, *Ending the Byzantine Greek Schism: The Fourteenth-Century Apology of Demetrios Kydones for Unity with Rome* (New Rochelle, 1983), and T. Tyn, "Prochoros und Demetrios

friends, humanists, come to Constantinople to study Greek. Or again, they might themselves have lived for a while in an Italian city, generally Venice, where their scholarship was reckoned a valuable commodity.[2] Moreover, Westerners, for their part, were beginning to think that not all the wrongs must be laid to the Byzantine account. About 1411, the general of the Carthusians, Boniface Ferrier (brother of the Dominican saint whose name is customarily given in English as Vincent Ferrer), ascribed the schism to the ambition of the French and the avarice of the Italians. Some years earlier, the Latin patriarch of Alexandria, Simon de Cramaud, had placed responsibility for the schism squarely on the pope who "wanted to demand from the Greeks more than his duty allowed him, and more than was necessary". At the Council of Pisa in 1409, the scholar-theologian Jean Gerson, chancellor of the University of Paris, noting that many Greeks preferred the turban to the tiara, concluded that the Latin Church must find out why.[3] One difficulty for the Latins was that, in strict terms, the whole issue had, in theory, been resolved at Lyons II. Up until the pope of Florence, Eugenius IV, popes insisted that reunion meant getting the Greeks to put into practice what they had agreed in 1274.[4]

Kydones: Der byzantinische Thomismus des 14. Jahrhunderts", in W. P. Eckert, O.P., ed., *Thomas von Aquino: Interpretation und Reception* (Mainz, 1974), pp. 857–912. Also, more widely, D. M. Nicol, *Church and Society in the Last Centuries of Byzantium* (Cambridge, 1979), pp. 76–84. A prudent caveat has been, however, entered here by K. T. Ware, who writes: "If we try to range the Greek intellectuals of the fourteenth–fifteenth centuries into two opposed 'teams'—on the one side, the Platonists, the Palamites and the anti-Unionists; on the other, the Aristoteleans, the Thomists and the Unionists, we quickly discover that the real situation is far more complicated." Thus his "Scholasticism and Orthodoxy: Theological Method as a Factor in the Schism", *ECR* 4 (1972–1973): 26.

[2] D. J. Geanakoplos, *Greek Scholars in Venice: Studies in the Dissemination of Greek Learning from Byzantium to Western Europe* (Cambridge, Mass., 1962).

[3] For these references to Ferrier, Cramaud, and Gerson, see M. Viller, "La question de l'union des églises entre Grecs et Latins depuis le Concile de Lyons jusqu'à celui de Florence", *RHE* 17 (1921): 260–305, 515–32; 18 (1922): 20–60.

[4] A. Leidl, *Die Einheit der Kirchen auf den spätmittelalterlichen Konzilien von Konstanz bis Florenz* (Paderborn, 1986).

In Byzantium itself, the chief obstacle to union was undoubtedly the *vox populi*: ever since the disastrous experiment of the Latin Empire, the very idea of union with Westerners repelled popular feeling. At the theological level, the great issue was the *Filioque*. In the fourteenth century, all Catholics who became Orthodox had to abjure the *Filioque* explicitly, other Latin errors (if such existed) only by a general formula. On the papal claims, two schools of thought can be discerned. One inclined to allow a very high doctrine of the Roman primacy, in the line of the Studites. This was always on the understanding, however, that the pope would return to the faith of Peter; that is, would cease to be heterodox on the *Filioque*.[5] The other school adopted a position not unlike that of Western Conciliarism: for its members, the pope was subject, as any other bishop, to a general council. Could he define doctrine alone, general councils would be superfluous; but we know from tradition that they are not. Less reasoned was the position of those for whom the inventory of Roman sins and offences grew daily: the veneration of three-dimensional figures as well as, or rather than, icons; the multiplication of the forms of monastic life; the use of round, not square, patens for the Mass, though the square is the shape of perfection.[6] It would be a complex and ambitious project that the Venetian pope Eugenius IV took on when he determined to begin anew with the reunion and, in the winter of 1437, invited the Byzantine church to send representatives for a great and holy council.

In the light of this general background, we shall not be surprised to learn that the council's origins lay in a happy marriage between the pope's ecumenical fervour and the political necessities of the emperor John VIII Palaeologos, for, at Constantinople, the Turks were nearing the gates. Nevertheless, the sheer number of Eastern churchmen present (probably 700 Orientals as compared with only 360 Latins), together with the exhaustive nature of the conciliar

[5] A view shared, it may be noted, by Philoxenus of Mabboug in his (early sixth-century) letter to Maro, although in this case Rome's "heresy" was not, of course, the *Filioque* but the alleged Nestorianism of Chalcedon.

[6] As M. Viller wrote, "La liste s'allonge interminablement": "La question de l'union", p. 524.

debates, means that one cannot reasonably regard Florence as a mere political device or a body unrepresentative of the Byzantine church and tradition (as had been, at any rate in a quantitative sense, Lyons II).[7] Indicative of the partial thaw in Greek-Latin relations were distinguished converts to the idea of union in the Byzantine ranks, notably Bessarion of Nicaea and Isidore of Kiev (both to be cardinals of the Roman Church).[8] The four topics discussed at Lyons were again aired, but this time much more thoroughly. To the eucharistic debate on the azymes was added, from the Greek side, the objection that the Roman liturgy (as then constituted) lacks an explicit *epiklêsis*, or consecratory prayer to the Holy Spirit over the bread and wine, something that the Greeks had noticed only in the course of the previous century.[9]

However, Orthodox and Catholic accounts of what transpired at Florence often differ wildly, the former tending to stress everything that might lead to the conclusion that the Greek delegates, when they signed the council's decrees, were not genuinely free. Joseph

[7] J. Gill, *The Council of Florence* (Cambridge, 1959).

[8] The fullest study of Bessarion is L. Mohler, *Kardinal Bessarion als Theologe, Humanist und Staatsmann* (Paderborn, 1923); for Isidore, see A. W. Ziegler, "Isidore de Kiev, apôtre de l'union florentine", *Irén.* 13 (1956): 393–410.

[9] The Roman rite has *traces* of a preconsecratory epiclesis: the prayer *Quam oblationem* includes the words (from the time of Pope Gregory I), when speaking of the offered gifts, *Ut nobis fiat Corpus et Sanguis dilectissimi Filii tui, Domini nostri Jesu Christi*—and this "May it be to us ..." is regarded by liturgical historians as a result of Alexandrian influence on the development of the Roman Canon. There is also a postconsecratory invocation, the *Supplices te rogamus*, which, while not mentioning the Holy Spirit (for it asks, rather, that the Holy Sacrifice be carried to the heavenly altar by the hand of "your angel" or "angels"), resembles the primitive forms of the epiclesis of the Syrian tradition in having as its object the filling of the communicants with blessing and grace. However, the fundamental Western tradition, that the consecration is achieved through the recital of the institution account, is clearly stated as early as Saint Ambrose, *De sacramentis* 4.22–23. The earliest Eastern anaphoras, moreover, lack a true consecratory epiclesis themselves. The earliest testimony to such a prayer we have is the late fourth-century *Mystagogical Catecheses* of Jerusalem (5.7), probably a reflection of the developing pneumatology of the Greek fathers. A. G. Martimort, ed., *The Eucharist* (Eng. trans., Shannon, 1973), pp. 153–55 and 161–63.

Gill established the basis of this discrepancy in terms of the historical sources for the council's unfolding.

Fundamentally, there are three sources.[10] First come the Greek
acts or *praktika*, now known to be a multiple compilation whose
basic document is, however, fully trustworthy.[11] This basic document consists in a transcription of the public speeches made by three
Greek notaries who checked each other's accounts and also compared them with a Latin version. Second are the so-called Latin *acta*:
"so-called" since the original Latin acts are lost, and all that remains
is a personal transcription of the speeches by a papal notary, Andrea
da Santa Croce. But comparison with the Greek sources shows
Andrea's recording habits to be reliable also. Into third place fall the
memoirs of Sylvester Syropoulos, a deacon of the church of Hagia
Sophia. Sylvester attended the council as a member of the entourage
of the patriarch Joseph II and wrote his behind-the-scenes account
of the Greek experience around 1444. To Sylvester, whose version
has fed the dominant account in Greek Orthodox historiography,
the Greeks gave their signatures to the council's determinations only
under duress. The Latins wore them out with interminable debates
and extracted concessions by serving up atrocious food. They made
agreement to the union a necessary condition for permitting the
Byzantine delegates to leave Italy. The emperor stage-managed the
Greek side, allowing no freedom of speech, by turns threatening
and cajoling to get the union, the only chance of saving Constantinople. Comparison with a similar diarylike source, the "Description" of John Plousiademos, suggests that Sylvester's account is highly
partial. Pointing out that Sylvester was himself a signatory to the
council, Gill suggests that "his dissatisfaction with himself caused
him to forget the light and remember only the shadow in the picture, the weariness, the want, the homesickness." Of course, Florence was subject to pressure from groups within, and forces without,

---

[10] Conveniently collected in G. Hofmann, S.J., et al., *Concilium Florentinum: Doc-
umenta et scriptores* (Rome, 1940–1955).

[11] J. Gill, "The Sources of the *Acta* of the Council of Florence", in *Personalities of
the Council of Florence* (Oxford, 1964), pp. 131–43; idem, "The *Acta* and the Memoirs
of Syropoulos as History", ibid., pp. 144–77.

but in this it in no way differed from any other accredited council of the Church.

From the Greek acts, our most reliable source, what emerges is the centrality, at Florence, of the *Filioque*. It was, as Gill remarks, the undoubted centre of concern. The dogmatic decree affirms the liceity of introducing the *Filioque* clause to the Creed and offers, in miniature, an exposé of the doctrine's foundations in terms of what, with Garrigues' assistance, we have learnt to call the "substantial communion" view of the Spirit's procession. The Spirit proceeds, for Florence, from both the Father and the Son *ab uno principio et unica spiratione*, "by a single procession and spiration". While insisting that all Christians must recognise the *Filioque*'s truth, it leaves open two ways of understanding what the truth involves. For the Greeks, the Son is simply *quidem causa*, some sort of cause of the Holy Spirit's being. For the Latins, he is, for the Spirit, *vere principium subsistentiae*, that being's very source. The council allows, therefore, a certain pluralism of understanding that mirrors the patristic pluralism at the root of the *Filioque* problem.

On the azymes and Purgatory, the statements of Florence reflect those of the Second Council of Lyons. On the intermediate state the language of temporal punishment due to sin, despite its pervasiveness in the Latin tradition, was carefully avoided. In its place, the decree speaks of the need to bring forth fruits of penitence, *paenitentiae fructus*. To the issue of azymes, however, there had been added, as already mentioned, a problematic liturgical sibling. The rôle of the *epiklêsis* prayer, in calling upon the Holy Spirit to consecrate the eucharistic bread (whether leavened or unleavened) and wine, has proved a sufficiently troublesome issue to warrant treatment here in its own right.

The Problem of the Epiclesis

Where the eucharistic consecration is concerned, patristic theology, like its liturgical texts, is somewhat ambivalent: Is the agent of that consecration God the Son, or God the Spirit? Symptomatically, the fathers may refer the transformation of the elements sometimes to

the words of the institution narrative, stemming from the Son, sometimes to the prayer for the descent of the Spirit. Historians of doctrine, however, have noted a tendency for the Eastern fathers, whether
Greek or Syriac, to treat the *epiklêsis* as in the fullest sense consecratory and to mention the institution narrative only by way of complement, while the Western fathers—whose liturgies did not, in any
case, always include a sharply defined *epiklêsis*, or one concerned
explicitly with the coming of the Spirit—privilege the institution
narrative, the words of the great High Priest, and treat the *epiklêsis*
as, by and large, "postconsecratory" in significance. For the fathers
at large, or so it seems, the anaphora (the Eucharistic Prayer) was
consecratory in its entirety, though with its sanctifying force concentrated at two high points. Accordingly, for them, both Son and
Spirit are coinvolved, and that with and from the Father—the Fount
of the Godhead—in the eucharistic transformation.[12] In the West,
by the time of the high Scholastics, this more fluid position had set
in crystal. Saint Thomas, for instance, identified the moment when
the real presence comes to be with that of the institution narrative:
when the original words of consecration, as given in the Gospels
from the lips of Christ, are repeated in the liturgical drama by the
celebrating priest.[13]

For some students of the history of the liturgy, Thomas' clear-cut
position on this point (he remarks that the rest of the Canon of the
Mass is unnecessary for the consecration, though a celebrant who
omitted all else would sin gravely in failing to observe the rite of the
Church) derives from the internal demands of the doctrine of transubstantiation, which had entered the Western conciliar tradition at
the Fourth Lateran Council in 1215. Transubstantiation seems to
entail an instantaneous transformation of the gifts.[14] On the other
hand, Aquinas may well have been reacting to the somewhat confused and implausible alternative positions taken up by a number of

[12] J. H. McKenna, *Eucharist and Holy Spirit: The Epiclesis in Twentieth Century Theology, 1900–1966* (London, 1975), pp. 48–71.
[13] *Summa theologiae* IIIa, q. 78, a. 1 and 3.
[14] McKenna, *Eucharist and Holy Spirit*, pp. 72–75.

his predecessors. Amalarius of Metz, for example, seems to have considered that the Our Father could consecrate, while the prayer of the Roman liturgy at the fraction of the Host ("This commingling *and consecration*") may have given rise to misunderstanding in others. Still, though Thomas did not advert to the importance of the *epiklêsis*, or of the *epiklêsis*-like prayers in the Western liturgies of his day, he by no means neglected the rôle of the Holy Spirit in the consecration.[15]

Latin-Byzantine debate on this topic was initiated by Western ecclesiastics active in the Levant at the beginning of the fourteenth century.[16] While the Latins regarded ascribing a consecratory value to the *epiklêsis* as wrongheaded, or even heretical, such Byzantine theologians as Symeon of Thessalonica and the great liturgical commentator Nicholas Cabasilas came to the defence of the Greek position, the latter in a way both assured and also eirenic. Though Cabasilas, with the Latins, regarded the words of consecration as the basic instrument of the eucharistic conversion, he also held that they need to be applied by the Church's prayer for the Spirit.[17]

At Florence, while the *epiklêsis* issue did not enter the final decree of union, it was made the subject of an oral profession of faith. Bessarion, in the name of the Greek bishops, declared that, following Chrysostom, the Byzantine church indeed held the words of institution, "the divine words of the Saviour", to "contain all the power of transubstantiation"—a statement that left open, or so it would seem, the prevailing view of the East that, nonetheless, it is the *epiklêsis* that renders the words of consecration effective here and now. After the council's repudiation, both Latin and Greek positions hardened. The influential Confession of Peter Moghila of Kiev, given authoritative sanction by the Orthodox patriarchs, in its Greek translation, in 1643, ascribes the eucharistic conversion, *metousiôsis*, to

[15] R. F. Buxton, *Eucharist and Institution Narrative: A Study in the Roman and Anglican Traditions of the Consecration of the Eucharist from the Eighth to the Twentieth Centuries* (Great Wakering, 1967), pp. 39–40.

[16] S. Salaville, "Epiclèse eucharistique", *DTC*, vol. 5, pt. 1 (Paris, 1913), pp. 303–18.

[17] Nicolas Cabasilas, *Explication de la divine liturgie*, ed. S. Salaville, 2nd ed. (Paris, 1967), p. 182.

the *epiklêsis* alone, a view echoed by patriarch and synod of the church of Constantinople in their response to a unionist initiative of Pope Leo XIII in 1894. On the Catholic side, a similar exclusivity was written into the reunion agreements with Armenian and Syrian Monophysites in the immediate wake of Florence, while in 1822, Pope Pius VII required of the (Catholic) Melchite patriarch of Antioch, under obedience, that no one support, publicly or privately, the teaching that "the form, by which the life-giving sacrament is realised, does not consist in the words of Jesus Christ alone." An interesting survival of an alternative subtradition in the West was the view of the rather maverick Dominican *peritus* at Trent, Ambrosius Catherinus (Lancelot Politi): he regarded the consecration as achieved through the *conjunction* of institution narrative and *epiklêsis*, taking the Roman prayer *Quam oblationem* to be, in fact, a "preconsecratory" invocation of the Spirit.[18]

The chronicle of twentieth-century Catholic theology records two especially notable attempts to reach out to the Orthodox position without abandoning that of the Latin church. The royal Orientalist Maximilian of Saxony, writing on the eve of the First World War, proposed that, in consonance with the Latin view, the "words of our Lord ... cause the sacrament" yet produce their effect in relation to the Church's intention in using them in her prayer. Maximilian continued:

> Since, then, in the Roman liturgy the consecration consists solely of our Lord's words, these produce their effect immediately, as soon as they are pronounced. Since, on the other hand, in the Oriental church, and according to her intentions, the *epiklêsis*, which follows our Lord's words, is the principal part of the consecration and its completion, it follows that in the East the words produce their effect through the *epiklêsis* and that our Lord is present only when the *epiklêsis* is concluded.[19]

Pope Pius X, however, expressed himself dissatisfied with this attempt at eirenicism, considering that Christ himself intended the words of institution as a liturgical consecration formula by which, accordingly,

---

[18] For references, see McKenna, *Eucharist and Holy Spirit*, pp. 77–85.

[19] Maximilien de Saxe, "Pensées sur la question de l'union des Eglises", *Roma e l'Oriente* 1 (1910): 13–29, and here at p. 25.

the whole Church was bound.[20] Writing in the course of the Second World War, the Roman Benedictine Anselm Stolz proposed, therefore, that the entire Eucharistic Prayer should be regarded as, in a fundamental sense, epicletic in character—and the words of institution certainly cannot be divorced from this wider context of the Church's praying action and yet retain their force as the "form" of this sacrament.[21]

The Roman Primacy at Florence—and After

Finally, after the matter of the *epiklêsis*, the bishops of the Council of Florence had to deal with the question of the primacy.[22] Here the decree ascribes to the Roman bishops the main features of the papal profile in the Latin patristic tradition. The Roman bishop is universal primate; he is the successor of blessed Peter; Christ gave to the Roman bishop, in Peter, the full authority, *plena potestas*, to shepherd and govern the universal Church. So much is pure Leo the Great. Certain other offices or titles are added that have a more mediaeval ring. The pope is also "vicar of Christ", a name first used by Saint Bernard;[23] "head of the whole Church"—earlier, it would have been more usual to call the Roman *see* "head" rather than its occupant;[24] and father and doctor of all Christians. To many who signed these titles were, doubtless, largely honorific compliments to the first patriarch, especially as this portion of the decree takes care, in connexion with the other four patriarchal figures, to say that the privileges and rights of all will be guarded, *salvis privilegiis omnibus et iuribus eorum*. Today, both Orthodox and Catholics will wish for a fuller and more nuanced account of what

[20] DS 3556.

[21] A. Stolz, O.S.B., *Manuale theologiae dogmaticae VI: De sacramentis* (Freiburg, 1943), pp. 143–44. For other contemporary liturgiologists and theologians, chiefly in the Catholic and Orthodox traditions, see McKenna, *Eucharist and Holy Spirit*, pp. 91–172.

[22] J. Gill, "The Definition of the Primacy of the Pope in the Council of Florence", *Personalities of the Council of Florence*, pp. 264–86.

[23] For the history of this title, see M. Maccarrone, *Vicarius Christi: Storia del titolo papale* (Rome, 1952).

[24] *Kephalê pasôn (tôn) tou Theou ekklêsiôn* is not unknown as a Greek formula for reference to the Roman see.

it is that the Roman pontiff, by Christ's dispensation, does for the whole Church. At root, only one issue of substance divides the Orthodox and Catholic churches, and that is the issue of the primacy. How so? At the level of theological doctrine: until some sufficiently authoritative source proclaims otherwise, we know of four dogmatic problems in Orthodox-Catholic relations, the four points of the Clementine formula. Of these, the azymes and Purgatory are scarcely any longer in dispute, and the *Filioque* question is on the way to resolution. There are, it is true, further objections lodged by many, or even most, Orthodox theologians to other aspects of the Catholic tradition: the structure of sacramental initiation, for instance, in the Latin rite (where confirmation is generally delayed until after a child's first holy communion),[25] or Mary's original righteousness: the "Immaculate Conception".[26] Then there is also the disputed metaphysical divinity of the "essence-energies" distinction pioneered, or at least highlighted, by the fourteenth-century archbishop of Thessalonica, Gregory Palamas.[27] Nor can we forget the divergent traditions on divorce.[28] Yet on none of these issues has disagreement been articulated at conciliar level.

The statement that, *au fond*, only the papacy divides the Orthodox and Catholic churches can also be defended in terms of history. The Roman patriarchate developed in a different way from the rest (though we may note that the regional primacy of Alexandria in her patriarchate was and is far more directive an affair than that of Rome

[25] See below, pp. 363–64, on the contemporary discussion of initiation.

[26] On the disputed Marian dogma, see M. Jugie, A.A., *L'Immaculée Conception dans l'Ecriture sainte et dans la tradition orientale* (Rome, 1952), who concludes that the modern Orthodox view that Mary's purification took place at the Incarnation is a predominantly sixteenth-century creation.

[27] With a huge literature: Daniel Stiernon's "Bulletin sur le palamisme", in *REB* 30 (1972): 231–541, contains 303 titles for the period 1959–1972 alone. It is interesting to note that Rome did not object to the (re)introduction of a liturgical feast of Saint Gregory Palamas into the Melchite calendar in 1971: see *Irén.* 45 (1972): 104.

[28] Compare K. T. Ware, "The Sacrament of Love: The Orthodox Understanding of Marriage and Its Breakdown", *Downside Review* 109, no. 375 (April 1991): 79–93; P. L. Reynolds, "Marriage, Sacramental and Indissoluble: Sources of the Catholic Doctrine", ibid., pp. 105–50.

among the Latins). So far as Chalcedonian Christendom, at any rate, is concerned, the institutions and the thought forms found within the Western patriarchate are comparatively *sui generis*. To the explanation of why Latin theology and Church practice followed their separate path, cultural, political, and even economic historians have much to contribute. Yet no such account could be complete unless it explained why this one patriarchate felt able to insist on the abiding validity of certain of its own distinctive features vis-à-vis the shared features of the others to the East. The process is inexplicable without the conviction of the Latin Church that the Roman patriarch was also the whole Church's universal primate: the vicar of Peter, prince of the apostles.[29] Policies and beliefs found in his patriarchate, if given his full sanction, drew from that sanction an authority that they could not possess simply in their own right. Augustine and Ambrose are fathers, just as are Basil and Chrysostom. But in ecclesial arithmetic, the sum of the first pair and the pope exceeds that of the second and any Eastern patriarch. It was because of the papacy that the peculiarities of the Latin Church could be perceived as a threat to the unity of Chalcedonian Christendom.

The affirmations of the Second Council of Lyons, and of Florence, on the Roman primacy were couched in terms too thoroughly Latin in origin to carry lasting conviction to the Greek mind. The Latin ecclesiology that the reunion councils largely presupposed is, as we have seen, predominantly a universalist ecclesiology, which considers the Church, in the first instance, as a single society spread throughout the world. The question that came to exercise this ecclesiology in its mature form was: Who is to unify this worldwide society? In other words, where does its supreme authority lie? The description of the primacy at Florence, even more than that of the first *Vaticanum*, is a Roman answer to a Latin question.[30]

---

[29] On this more modest title, see G. Conti, *Il papa, vicario di Pietro: Contributo alla storia dell'idea papale* (Brescia, 1966).

[30] The First Vatican Council, in its dogmatic constitution *Pastor aeternus*, repeats verbatim the definition of Florence, yet its own prologue to that constitution contains important elements of an older ecclesiology of communion.

In the East the universalist ecclesiology was by no means unknown, yet by and large it belonged more to the political than to the strictly theological side of the Greek Christian mind. When the Byzantine Christian thought of the rôle of the emperor in the Church, he was indeed thinking of the Church as the *oikoumenê*, a universal society needing a focus of unity and practical decision making. But when he did his ecclesiology from Scripture and tradition, he worked, generally speaking, with a different picture. For the Greek East, the Church is, in the first place, a network of local churches, each ontologically equal with the others yet ordered in a hierarchy of function. The local churches, the bishoprics, are arranged in terms of a *taxis*, "order", deriving in its fundamental relationships from apostolic times and having as its goal the upbuilding of the members of the series in faith and charity. Is it possible to express the papal primacy in terms of this ecclesiology—which is still the fundamental ecclesiology of the Orthodox today? Can there be a Roman answer to a Greek question?

How can the pope be seen in Orthodox perspective and yet remain the pope in Catholic eyes? A "Greek" ecclesiology of the Petrine office must set out from the premise that the pope is the first patriarch and as such occupies the first place in the *taxis*, the ordering, of bishops. This title of patriarch is, in the West, a largely forgotten name for the papal office.[31] The new Code of Canon Law of the Latin church never draws on it, even though only that title can make sense of the Code's own opening canon, "The canons of this Code concern only the Latin church." As long ago as 1927, however, the Greek Catholic bishop of Athens remarked to his Greek Orthodox counterpart that 99 percent of the decisions of Rome belong to the power of the pope as Latin patriarch and concern, therefore, only those within his patriarchal juridiction.[32]

---

[31] Y. J.-M. Congar, "Le pape comme patriarche d'Occident: Approche d'une réalité trop négligée", *Ist.* 28 (1983–1984): 374–90.

[32] Hiéromoine Pierre, "L'union de l'Orient avec Rome: Une controverse récente; correspondence échangée entre S. B. Chrysostome Papadopoulos et Mgr. Georges Calavassy", *Orientalia Christiana* 18, no. 1 (1930).

It is true that, from early times, the Western patriarchs, conscious that they were more than patriarchs (and I shall return to this), tried to distance themselves from the title and its implications.[33] To the notion of the Pentarchy, Rome preferred the idea of three Petrine sees: herself, Antioch, and Alexandria.[34] In her struggle with the pretensions of metropolitan sees in the West, she rarely, if ever, invoked her patriarchal status, preferring to rely instead on more exalted claims. When, in the course of the Crusades, she created the Latin patriarchates, she gave the impression that she saw herself as the origin of the rights of the patriarchal sees. The statement made at Lyons II, and repeated later, that those sees owe such rights and privileges to papal concession is, when understood as a thesis about historic origins, not defensible.[35] It is because Rome has never managed to distinguish adequately in her own mind her administrative functions as a patriarchal see from her apostolic charge as the Petrine see (remarked Father Joseph Ratzinger, now Pope Benedict XVI, in 1964) that she has presented the image of centralising, omnicompetent governmental force—something which, in that form, the East could never accept. Nevertheless, there were Latin Christians who never forgot, when practising ecclesiology, that the pope is a patriarch and that what he appropriately does patriarchally is both more than what he does as bishop and less than what he may do as successor of Peter: thus Nicholas of Cusa and John Stoyković of Ragusa, both figures of the early fifteenth century.[36] And the title has been there in the *Annuario*

---

[33] A process assisted by the fact that "patriarch" was not originally a Western title. Apparently, the imperial chancery avoided it even for the supreme sees of the East so long as the Jewish patriarchate existed (until 429); Leo the Great was the first pope to be called patriarch. Thus A. Garuti, "Il papa patriarca d'Occidente? Riflessioni sull'origine del titolo", *Antonianum* (1985): 42–85.

[34] On the idea of "petrinity", see J. Richards, *Consul of God: The Life and Times of Gregory the Great* (London, 1980), p. 65.

[35] Congar, "Le pape comme patriarche d'Occident", p. 381; W. de Vries, *Rom und die Patriarchaten des Ostens* (Freiburg and Munich, 1963), pp. 347–53.

[36] Nicholas of Cusa, *De concordia catholica* 2.7; John Stoyković, *Tractatus de ecclesia*, ed. F. Sanjek et al. (Zagreb, 1983), 1.2, pp. 18–19; 3.3, p. 222.

pontificio, the papal yearbook, for all to see. The abandonment of
the title in the 2000 yearbook, for which reasons—by no means
fully persuasive, not least to the Orthodox—were subsequently offered
by the Pontifical Council for Promoting Christian Unity, does not
obliterate the obvious ecclesial fact: the Roman bishop enjoys a
special form of primacy in the context of the Latin church (as
distinct from his rôle in the Catholic Church generally). In Latin
Christianity the pope has, at the very least, a "patriarch-like" rôle.[37]

This is where we must begin: as first patriarch, the bishop of Rome
is the first bishop in the Church's *taxis*. Primacy of honour, here,
however, is a red herring; there can be no honour in the Church of
the Servant, Jesus Christ, that is not based on service—and therefore
on ministerial function. The first bishop of the *taxis* has a primacy
of function, of rôle, within the episcopal order, and so within the
communion of churches over which the bishops preside.

But then is the pope *only* a patriarch, albeit the first? The chafing
of the Western patriarchs against the limitations of their patriarchal
status expresses an enduring factor in the self-consciousness of the
Roman see: the sense, sometimes feeble and obscure, sometimes acute
and precise, that the Roman patriarch is also more than a patriarch.
Can this "plus factor" find expression in terms of Orthodox ecclesiology too? We can say that, as first patriarch, the Roman bishop is
not simply within the *taxis*, though he is indeed within it for many
purposes. Nevertheless, as the bishop responsible for maintaining the
entire *taxis* in its integrity, for assuring the rights and duties of its
members (and in particular of its patriarchal members), the Roman

---

[37] A. A. J. DeVille, "On the Patriarchate of the West", *Ecumenical Trends* 35, no. 6
(2006): 1–7. It seems likely that Benedict XVI was, as Cardinal Ratzinger, impressed
by the study of Adriano Garuti, O.F.M., *Il papa patriarca d'Occidente? Studio storico-
dottrinale* (Bologna, 1990). It is, presumably, not coincidental that Garuti collaborated
with him in the course of the Franciscan's long years of service, 1975–2003, to the
Congregation for the Doctrine of the Faith. But question marks are set against Garuti's findings in J. Nedungatt, S.J., "The Patriarchal Ministry in the Church of the
Third Millennium", *Jurist* 61 (2001): 1–89, and Monsignor Michael Magee's Gregorian University dissertation "*In unum conspirans varietas*: The Patriarchal Institution in
the Catholic Church" (2006).

patriarch cannot be said to be just one member of the *taxis*. Insofar as he has responsibility for the whole *taxis*, he also stands above it. He is not, in the words of Florence, "universal primate" in the sense of being every suffragan's surrogate metropolitan or every metropolitan's surrogate patriarch. He is universal primate in the sense that he is entrusted (by Christ through Peter) with responsibility for the right functioning of the entire episcopal—and so patriarchal—order throughout the world.

This is, evidently, more than a patriarchal task, more, even, than the task of a first patriarch. And yet, since it can be defined in terms of the episcopal *taxis*, it cannot be regarded as a notion alien to the Eastern tradition and mentality.

So far I have been concerned with the pastoral rôle of the pope in jurisdiction. What of his prophetic rôle as teacher? At one level, as one bishop among many, the pope stands within the corporate realm of the *magisterium* (in Greek, *didaskalia*) of the Church's bishops. In this sense he stands among equals, with all those who, through the grace of the sacrament of orders in its plenary form, have inherited the promise of Christ to the apostles, "He who hears you, hears me" (Lk 10:16). But, just as the ecclesial *taxis* has a first bishop, *primus*, *prôtos*, with a special function or rôle of leadership, a "first" who is also entrusted with the defence of its total corporate integrity, so too here the *didaskalia* or teaching activity of the episcopate has a first teacher and one who is responsible for the authenticity of the bishops' teaching as a whole.

In normal times, the rôle of the universal primate as teacher is simply to be the mouthpiece of the corporate episcopate in their teaching activity, articulating for all what each is saying. But, in cases where the episcopate is too divided to speak with one voice (and this book has charted numerous such occasions), the universal primate can speak for it in the heightened sense of speaking in place of it—speaking because it cannot speak. In some such way, the teaching of Florence can thus be "re-received" in terms more congenial to the East and, thus recontextualised, have its own authoritative meaning illuminated and confirmed, not obscured and weakened.

The Failure of Florence

Before leaving Florence, we must note the greatness of its conception and the manner of its failure. The council was conceived on a grandiose scale. It envisaged union not only with the Byzantine-Slav churches but with the Copts, Ethiopians, and Armenians among the Oriental Orthodox and with the Nestorians, as well as confirming the union with the Maronites: an erstwhile Monothelite portion of the Antiochene patriarchate, stranded by the tides of history on Mount Lebanon, encountered by Westerners in the Crusading period, and the prototype of all "Uniate" churches of the post-Florence period. For a while, the council succeeded with each and every one of these parties. Since its day, its decrees have served as a basis for reunion with various Oriental groups seeking peace and communion with Rome: for instance, in the union achieved with the Ruthenians (Slavs of the Subcarpathian Galicia) in 1596 and with the Romanians of Transylvania in 1700.

The council's eventual failure may be attributed to three factors. First, the failure of the military aid sent in its wake by the West to the newly Catholic East marked a setback in its fortunes. At the battle of Varna in 1444, the Crusade to save Byzantium led by the Jagellon king of Hungary-Poland, Vladislav III, was destroyed by the Ottomans at a blow. Second, the overwhelming majority, so it is thought, of the population of Constantinople (and by now the empire was essentially the city) would not rally to it. Third, though only one bishop, Mark Eugenicus of Ephesus, had refused to sign the conciliar decrees, that bishop was a truly formidable opponent of union.[38] On his early return from Florence, he was successful in arousing resistance among the influential. When in 1453 Byzantium finally passed away, the patriarch, Gennadius II,

---

[38] For a spirited defence of Eugenicus, see N. P. Vasileiadis, *Markos ho Evgenikos kai hê henôsis tês Ekklêsias* (Athens, 1972): the author compares those Easterners who accepted the Florentine definition to modern ecumenists, whom he regards as dominated by extratheological considerations. More restrained is C. N. Tsirpanlis, *Mark Eugenicus and the Council of Florence* (Thessalonica, 1974).

would judge the city's fall as punishment for its Florentine betrayal of its Saviour.[39]

The council was not formally repealed by the Greeks until 1484. In that year, a Byzantine synod drew up a rite for the reception of Latin converts.[40] They must recite the Creed without the *Filioque*; they must also abjure the *Filioque* doctrine and denounce its addition to the Creed. They must renounce the Council of Florence and its teachings. They must declare their formal rejection of communion with the Latin church. At this point, they were to be received by chrismation (confirmation). In 1755 the Greeks realised that to deny the validity of Latin confirmation but accept that of Latin baptism was inconsistent. On a thoroughgoing "Cyprianic" view of the sacraments, which their theology largely implied, there can be no sacraments outside the visibility of the one true Church.[41] In that year, accordingly, the patriarch Cyril V declared Western baptism to be null and void. Since then, at least in principle, the Greek church has insisted on the need for the rebaptism of Catholic converts.[42] Today, although the ecumenical patriarchate neither practices nor sanctions such extreme measures, the church of Greece itself finds in them nothing that is necessarily objectionable—at least in the sense of not inhibiting their occasional application. Is this not a glaring example of how, in the Orthodox family of churches, the lack

---

[39] He had been a signatory at Florence! The sharp disjunction between his early pro-Latin writings and his later antiunion declarations have led the author of the massive study *Gennarios B' Scolarios: Bios, syngrammata, didaskalia* (Thessalonica, 1980) to postulate that the former are spurious works, composed to discredit Scholarios by John Plousiademos at the instigation of Bessarion.

[40] The text of this service is found in I. N. Karmiris, *Ta dogmatika kai sumbolika mnêmeia tês Orthodoxou Katholikês Ekklêsias*, vol. 2 (Athens, 1953), pp. 987–89.

[41] Owing to the use of Western theological sources! As George Every puts it: "The attitude of the Greeks to schism in and from the Church was deeply influenced by Western ecclesiastical ideas, since most Eastern teachers of theology had received part of their education in Western schools, Roman Catholic and Protestant", *Misunderstandings between East and West* (London, 1965), p. 24.

[42] [K.] T. Ware, *Eustratios Argenti: A Study of the Greek Church under Turkish Rule* (Oxford, 1964), pp. 65–78. The Church of Russia had rebaptised Catholic converts earlier but abandoned the practice in 1666–1667.

of a centre of doctrinal and practical unity makes for confusion and contradiction? Is this not a lacuna to which the Petrine ministry of the Roman bishop corresponds—though needing, doubtless, suitable recalibrations in its mode of exercise?[43] This was, in part, the message of Pope John Paul II's 1995 encyclical letter *Ut unum sint*, whose last words read:

> I, John Paul, *servus servorum Dei*, venture to make my own the words of the Apostle Paul, whose martyrdom, together with that of the Apostle Peter, has bequeathed to this See of Rome the splendour of its witness, and I say to you, the faithful of the Catholic Church, and to you, my brothers and sisters of the other Churches and Ecclesial Communities: *"Mend your ways, encourage one another, live in harmony, and the God of love and peace will be with you ... The grace of the Lord Jesus Christ and the love of God and the fellowship of the Holy Spirit be with you all."*[44]

It is to the halting steps on the road to resumption of a "dialogue of love" with the church that "presides in the Charity" that we must now turn.

[43] There are Orthodox who recognise as much: see, for example, Bishop Vsevolod of Scopelos, "What about the Roman Primacy?" *ECJ* 4, no. 3 (1997): 9–54.

[44] John Paul II, *Ut unum sint* (Vatican City, 1995), 103, p. 115. There is an internal citation of 2 Cor 13:11, 13.

Bibliography

Alberigo, G., ed., *Christian Unity: The Council of Ferrara-Florence, 1438/ 9–1989.* Leuven, 1991.

Gill, J. *Byzantium and the Papacy, 1198–1400.* New Brunswick, N.J., 1979.

————. *The Council of Florence.* Cambridge, 1959.

————. *Personalities of the Council of Florence.* Oxford, 1964.

Lanne, E., O.S.B. "To What Extent Is Roman Primacy Unacceptable to the Eastern Churches?" *Conc.* 4, no. 7 (1971): 62–67.

Likoudis, J. *Ending the Byzantine Greek Schism: The Fourteenth-Century Apology of Demetrios Kydones for Unity with Rome.* New Rochelle, 1983.

Mapelli, E. "L'epiclesi al concilio di Firenze". *Scuola cattolica* 67 (1939): 326–59.

Mohler, L. *Kardinal Bessarion als Theologe, Humanist und Staatsmann.* Paderborn, 1923.

Nicol, D. M. *Church and Society in the Last Centuries of Byzantium.* Cambridge, 1979.

Peri, V. "Sul ruolo ecclesiale del Vescovo di Roma: Il problema attuale nella luce del passato unitaro". In *Papato e istanze ecumeniche*, pp. 61–118. Bologna, 1984.

Tsirpanlis, C. N. *Mark Eugenicus and the Council of Florence.* Thessalonica, 1974.

Viller, M. "La question de l'union des Eglises entre Grecs et Latins depuis le Concile de Lyon jusqu'à celui de Florence". *RHE* 17 (1921): 260–305 and 515–32; 18 (1922): 20–60.

11

After Florence: The Way of the Uniates

Despite the unravelling of the Union of Florence in the course of the later fifteenth century, it should by no means be assumed that an iron wall of division separated the Catholic and Orthodox communities in the subsequent period. Speaking of the years from 1600 to 1700 in particular, Bishop Kallistos Ware has remarked that both educated clergy and simple believers, in considerable numbers, acted as though no schism existed. Yet the phrase "as though" must be taken with full seriousness. Pointing out that the instances of intercommunion all come from the Greek sphere, as distinct from the Slav, Ware continues:

> The official theology of the Greek church throughout the seventeenth century remained fiercely polemical: though influenced by the thought-forms and terminology of Latin Scholasticism, it never ceased to chastise the Latins for their doctrinal deviations, treating them not just as schismatics but as heretics. If the Greek bishops acted differently in practice, this was not because of any special theory concerning the incomplete nature of the schism, but because of urgent pastoral necessity. They and their flocks were fighting for survival under the rule of a non-Christian government; their own clergy were almost entirely simple and ill-educated; in desperate need of qualified preachers, catechists and confessors, they turned naturally to the Latin missionaries.[1]

[1] K. T. Ware, "Orthodox and Catholics in the Seventeenth Century: Schism or Intercommunion?" in *Schism, Heresy and Religious Protest*, ed. D. Baker, Studies in Church History 9 (Cambridge, 1972), p. 259.

The Latin position vis-à-vis the Greeks was somewhat different. In part, at least, their policy was one of opportunism. Striving to win the confidence of Greek Christians, Latin priests—above all, members of the Society of Jesus—adopted what Ware has called a "Trojan horse policy". They aimed not so much to create Uniate churches (that lay largely in the future) as to foster "a Catholic nucleus inside the canonical boundaries of the Orthodox communion".[2] Jesuitical as this indeed sounds, Catholic theologians could be found to defend it with legitimising reasons. Ware draws attention to two works in particular. The Theatine Angelo Maria Verricelli's *Quaestiones morales ... de apostolicis missionibus*, published in Venice in 1656, argued for the policy in terms of canon law; Leo Allatius' *De ecclesiae occidentalis atque orientalis perpetua consensione*, which saw the light of day at Cologne in 1648, argued for the policy in terms of Church history and ecclesiology proper. Verricelli's view is that *communicatio in sacris* (the sharing of the sacraments) with heretics and schismatics is permissible, provided that the persons in question have not been excommunicated "publicly and by name". It seems likely that his treatise, which appeared at Venice where the Inquisition had no effective jurisdiction, would not have passed the hoops of Church censorship in the papal state. Allatius' position, contrastingly, had it that the Greek church, as such, is neither heretical nor schismatic, though some of her members may be.

> Individual persons, although holding office in the Greek church, do not constitute the Greek church. Nor, because various heresies have arisen and spread within that church is she herself to be considered heretical.... The Greek church as a whole, whether in her professions of faith or in the service books read continually in her public worship, has never professed any heresy condemned by the councils and the church of Rome.... Because certain individual Greeks have endeavoured to spread some ancient or freshly invested heresy, and have inveighed against the papacy in their published writings, it does not therefore follow that the Greek church is separated from the church of Rome: this would only be the case if the heresy in question were

[2] Ibid., p. 65.

universally adopted and outwardly professed by all alike; and this, you will find, has never happened on the occasions when certain individuals have launched attacks against the Roman church.[3]

Although Allatius was not alone in his opinion, and the much-disseminated *Manuale missionariorum orientalium* of Carlo Francesco da Breno faithfully reproduced his predecessor in the doubtless more influential genre of a missionary handbook,[4] an attractive alternative lay close at hand. This was the creation of Uniate churches—Oriental in rite and canon but Roman in ecclesial allegiance—through preaching and diplomatic suasion among particular Orthodox communities. We have already had occasion to touch on the formation of such "Catholic Eastern Churches" in the context of Nestorianism and Monophysitism. Their archetype, and their most successful empirical realisation, was the Maronite church, a body beginning from an uncertain position on the doctrinal spectrum of patristic Christianity but whose members, by the time of Florence, had entered on communion with Rome not as *pars pro toto* but *en bloc*. In no other case was an Eastern church thus united, leaving no hurt schismatic mother behind. In all other instances, the Uniates constituted alternative Orthodoxies, living side by side with the original schismatic community and to a considerable extent in rivalry with it. Where the Chalcedonian Orthodox were concerned, the most enthusiastic apostles of Uniatism were often enough Catholic rulers mindful of the principle laid down by the Peace of Westphalia of 1648 in its attempt to pacify the warring Europe of the post-Reformation epoch: *cujus regio, eius religio*, "religion follows rule".

The ending to the age of flexibility in Catholic-Orthodox relations for, at any rate, the Greek-speaking sphere of the Church after Florence came with the attempted export of Uniatism to the lands of the Ottoman Empire. More specifically, it was the 1724 schism

---

[3] Cited from another work of Allatius', the curiously named *Joannis Henricus Hottingerus fraudis, et imposturae manifestae convictus* (Rome, 1661), pp. 6–7, by Ware, ibid., p. 273.

[4] Carlo Francesco da Breno, *Manuale missionariorum orientalium* (Venice, 1726), 1:83, cited by Ware, ibid.

within the patriarchate of Antioch, bringing into existence as this did the Greco-Arab church of the (Catholic) Melchites, that convinced the Orthodox of the perils awaiting them in the Trojan horse. At the same time, Rome herself began to look askance at Jesuit leniency and in 1729 issued a directive that excluded all common worship with the Orthodox "in terms of the utmost strictness". While civil cooperation was not excluded, *communicatio in sacris* was pronounced an abuse and a snare. We may take this decree of the Congregation Propaganda fide as marking the definitive attachment of the Holy See to the Uniate idea as the only viable way to reunion at a time when Chalcedonian Orthodoxy as a whole held fast to its rejection of the council of union, the abominated Florence.[5]

Let us look, then, more closely at the emergence of the (Chalcedonian) Uniate churches, which at the present time play so large a part in the complicating of Rome's relations with her Orthodox sisters.

The Maronites

The obvious place to begin is what I have termed the archetype of successful *unia*: the Maronites. The name "Maronite" derives from the monastery of Saint Maro (a hermit from Theodoret's city, Cyr, who died around 410) in the valley of the Orontes near Apamea (the modern Qalat al Mudiq). The monastic community distinguished itself in the struggle against Monophysitism—though scholarly opinion is divided as to whether the grounds of their opposition were full-bloodedly Chalcedonian or simply Monothelite.[6] In the confusion that followed the Arab invasion of 636, the Antiochene patriarchate either remained unfilled, or its occupant resided at Constantinople; the monks of Saint Maro, together with some neighbouring bishops, took steps, accordingly, to obtain a patriarch of

---

[5] Ware, "Orthodox and Catholics in the Seventeenth Century", pp. 274–75; see also idem., *Eustratios Argenti: A Study of the Greek Church under Turkish Rule* (Oxford, 1964), pp. 28–30.

[6] P. Naaman, *Théodoret de Cyr et le monastère du Saint Maroun: Les origines des Maronites; Essai d'histoire et de géographie* (Kaslik, 1971).

their own devising. Although the exact date of creation of the Maronite patriarchate of Antioch is unclear, the Maronites were recognised as an autocephalous community by the caliph Marwan II (died 748). Under Muslim pressure, the Maronites migrated in the course of the ninth century from Syria to Mount Lebanon, whose less accessible, thickly wooded countryside provided them with refuge. Civilly semiautonomous, under their own leadership, the *muqaddamin*, their ecclesiastical government was curious. The patriarch was the sole diocesan of a local church with no geographically fixed *cathedra*; he enjoyed the assistance, however, of a number of assistant bishops. With the arrival of the Crusaders in Syria, the Maronites at once made common cause with the Catholic Westerners, an alliance that survived the collapse of the Latin kingdoms of Outremer. The patriarch Jeremiah II attended the Fourth Lateran Council of 1215 and was confirmed in his office by Pope Innocent III in the bull *Quia divinae sapientiae* of the following year.[7] Relations with the Holy See have flowed interrupted since that time and produced such fruits as the seventeenth-century publication at Rome of their liturgical books,[8] the encouragement provided by the papacy in the establishment of a more classically episcopal (rather than patriarchal-vicarial) church system at the Synod of Luwazyeh in 1736, and the special protection of the "Governate of the Lebanon" allowed by the Ottoman Empire to the Catholic powers from 1861 onwards. Robert Betts wrote of them in his survey of the Christians of the Arab East: "Solidly Lebanese nationalist in politics, exclusively Catholic in religion, decidedly pro-French in culture, prosperous, educated, dedicated to their community, acting as a majority when in fact they are

---

[7] K. Salibi, "The Maronite Church in the Middle Ages and Its Union with Rome", *Oriens Christianus* 42 (1958): 92–104. More widely: the outstanding historian of the Maronites was Pierre Dib, whose two-volume *L'Eglise maronite* (vol. 1, *L'Eglise maronite jusqu'à la fin du moyen age* [Paris, 1930]; vol. 2, *Les Maronites sous les Ottomans: Histoire civile* [Beirut, 1962]) was anticipated in his article "Maronite (Eglise)" in the *DTC*, vol. 10, pt. (Paris, 1928), cols. 1–142, and condensed in his *Histoire de l'Eglise maronite* (Beirut, 1962).

[8] P. Raphael, *Le rôle du Collège maronite romain dans l'orientalisme aux XVII et XVIII siècles* (Beirut, 1950).

not, the Maronites of Lebanon are today very much what Charles Malik half-jokingly called them a few years ago: the Christian answer to Islam." [9] Unfortunately, this description throws light on the comparative short-livedness of peace in the Lebanese Republic, proclaimed in 1943 but effectively independent only in 1946, surrounded as it is by Muslim neighbours except to the south, where lies the tinderbox of the state of Israel. Despite the fearful death toll of the Lebanese civil war (itself in part a war by proxy of other powers, and notably of Syria, which has used the Palestinian minority to further its plans for a "Grande Syrie" stretching to the highly useful Mediterranean ports), the Maronite patriarch still presides over a religious community of over a million within Lebanon itself, from his seat at Bikerka on the Bay of Juniyah some miles north of Beirut. The Maronite diaspora may now add as much as another two million to this total. (Perhaps two million practise overall.) The eparchies of Saint Maro in Detroit, Our Lady of the Lebanon at Sao Paulo, and Saint Maro in Sydney account for the majority of these and, though sited in the territory of Latin bishops, are "aggregated" to the patriarchate by action of the Holy See. [10] In 1992 the Maronite church published a revised missal that seeks to recover the original Syrian liturgical form in its eucharistic celebration, prior to the onset of Latinisation. The patriarch, Nasrallah Peter Sfeir, took the opportunity to appeal for return likewise to the vestments and architectural style proper to the Syrian tradition.

Greek Catholics and Byzantine Slavs of the Balkans

From the Maronites, we turn to Eastern Catholics of the Byzantine rite. Here the situation is much more complex. In the first place, there are the Italo-Greeks, or, more properly, Italo-Albanians, of the

---

[9] R. B. Betts, *Christians in the Arab East: A Political Study* (London, 1979), pp. 49–50.

[10] Sacra congregazione per le Chiese orientali, *Oriente cattolico* (Vatican City, 1974), p. 154. It is noteworthy that the resources of Western historical scholarship available to the Maronite diaspora have encouraged them to take a livelier interest in their Syriac origins: as in S. G. Beggiani, *Early Syriac Theology with Special Reference to the Maronite Tradition* (Lanham, Md., 1983).

Italian peninsula itself.[11] Southern Italy (and, until the tenth century, Sicily) historically included numerous Greek dioceses of the
Roman patriarchate. Their existence was flagging by the sixteenth
century, and in the eighteenth they disappeared, though the Greek
language, much corrupted, survived in pockets.[12] Those Greeks,
attracted by commerce, who settled in Naples, Venice, and the ports
of the south after the fall of Constantinople had as pastors emissaries
of the (Orthodox) patriarch of Constantinople or the archbishop of
Ochrid in Macedonia, but such exarchs, anxious not to be disturbed
in their jurisdiction, sometimes made profession of the Catholic faith
and received privileges from a grateful Rome. The number of faithful who adhered to such agreements, however, diminished after the
Council of Trent, and by the close of the nineteenth century, the
most important parochial community of the "nuovi Italo-Greci",
that of Naples, had passed definitively to the Orthodox.[13] Today, the
three Byzantine-rite circumscriptions in Italy—the eparchies of Lungo
in Calabria and of Piana in Sicily, together with the "exarchal" monastery of Grottaferrata—owe their popular support to Albanians who,
after the Turkish conquest of their country and the death of their
last prince, George Castriota ("Skanderbeg"), migrated to Italy and
Sicily.[14] Some arrived as Catholics, yet others accepted the Union
of Florence in the course of time; others again were Latins, from the
north of Albania, whose fate does not concern us here. In 1742
Pope Benedict XIV provided them with a code of canons of their
own, though their (independent) eparchies are of early twentieth-
century creation. They number today around seventy thousand. This
is a church that "has continued to bear witness that in Italy, within

[11] They are, in effect, the subject of A. Fortescue's *Uniate Eastern Churches: The
Byzantine Rite in Italy, Sicily, Syria and Egypt* (London, 1925), since the author died
after completing his section on the Italo-Greeks (and some few pages on the Melchites).

[12] For the history of the original Italo-Greeks, see auctores varii, *La Chiesa greca in
Italia, dall'VIII al XVI secolo* (Padua, 1973).

[13] *Oriente cattolico*, pp. 212–13.

[14] The Centro internazionale de studi albanesi presso l'Università di Palermo is in
process of publishing a vast collection of documents connected with Skanderbeg
("Alexander-bey").

the jurisdiction of the Primate of Italy, the two traditions, the Roman and the Byzantine, have always continued to exist."[15]

Small communities of Byzantine rite exist also in Greece itself, as in the Slav nations of the Balkans. Alongside Greeks of the Latin rite, descended from the merchant adventurers of Venice, Genoa, and Amalfi, sufficient individuals among the Orthodox Greeks of the Ottoman Empire embraced Catholicism in the course of the seventeenth and eighteenth centuries to justify the existence of the Collegio Greco founded at Rome in 1576 by Pope Gregory XIII. The removal of Eastern-rite Catholics from the *filet* of the Orthodox patriarch by the sultan Mahmud II in 1829 opened the way to some kind of corporate life for those so minded. In 1895, after various local initiatives had faltered, Pope Leo XIII mandated the Augustinians of the Assumption to found at Constantinople a Greek Catholic seminary on a generous scale, as well as two Byzantine-rite parishes, at Istanbul and, across the Bosphorus, the neighbouring Kadiköy (the erstwhile Chalcedon).[16] The learned Byzantine review *Echos d'Orient* was a fruit of these beginnings.[17] In 1911 Leo's successor Saint Pius X created an exarchate at Constantinople for all Greek-rite Catholics in Turkey, but the disastrous attempt by the Greek government to profit from the collapse of the Ottoman Porte in 1919 by seizing not only the city but also Asia Minor brought down the wrath of the Turks on not just Greek Orthodox but Greek Catholics too. The exarch and the great majority of his community transferred to Athens, where his successor rules today a community of some three thousand souls. (A separate exarchate for the handful of Greek Catholics left in Turkey was established in 1932.) Within a sympathetic circle, the pure Byzantine quality of the worshipping life of this small church is much admired. But it will not be the

[15] E. Fortino and G. Gallaro, "The Byzantine Church in Italy: Tensions and Communion", *ECJ* 7, no. 3 (2000): 63.

[16] *Oriente cattolico*, pp. 202–3; C. J. Walter, *The Assumptionists and Their Eastern Apostolate, 1863–1980* (Rome, 1980).

[17] Also the series *Les régestes des actes du patriarcat de Constantinople, 381–1206* (Kadiköy and Bucharest, 1952–1947); ibid., *1208–1309* (Paris, 1971), originally edited by Venance Grumel, A.A.

work of a day to gain for it brotherly relations from the Orthodox side. The visit in 2001 of Pope John Paul II to Greece, as a pilgrim in the steps of the apostle Paul, included, to the surprise of many, a meeting with the holy synod of its church. Though its primate Christodoulos of Athens spoke plainly, and even harshly, of historical animosities, the sheer fact of the encounter, which went ahead despite well-supported petitions to the contrary from Orthodox clergy and monastics, gives some hope for the future. Still, for many Greek Orthodox, a Byzantine Catholicism is of all pills the most bitter to the taste.

In Bulgaria, Uniatism was somewhat more successful. To begin with, it had pre-Florentine precedents. In 1019 the Byzantine emperor Basil II, "the Bulgar-slayer", as part of his campaign to eliminate from Constantinople's doorstep an overmighty Bulgarian neighbour, suppressed the autonomous patriarchate (based originally at Preslav, but later at Ochrid) since the reign of the czar Simeon the Great (893–927).[18] Although Ochrid remained a highly influential archdiocese, whose metropolitan was a name to be conjured with not only in the Balkans but as far as Kiev,[19] a new patriarchal see, Tirnovo, was created in the throes of the twelfth-century independence movement. Unable to look for a patriarch to the ancestral (and very recent) enemy, Byzantium, the Bulgarians turned to Rome, and in 1204 Pope Innocent III gave Basil of Tirnovo primatial rights of a patriarchal kind. In 1233, however, for political reasons the Bulgarians entered into alliance with the Byzantine successor state of Nicaea; two years later the patriarch Germanus II of Constantinople recognised in the Tirnovo archbishop a brother patriarch. Although the Ottoman conquest of 1393 ended its life, this second Bulgarian patriarchate was sufficiently expansionist to have introduced Slavonic into the liturgy and public life of limitrophe Romania: a fact not without

---

[18] The most comprehensive study of mediaeval Bulgaria is V. N. Zlatarski, *Istorija na blgarskata država prez srednite vekove*, 3 vols. in 4 (Sofia, 1918–1940). The same author's earlier single volume history was translated into German during the First World War as *Geschichte der Bulgaren: Von der Gründung des bulgarischen Reiches bis zur Türkenzeit*, 679–1296 (Leipzig, 1917).

[19] I. Snegarov, *Istorija na Ochridskata Archiepiskopija*, 2 vols. (Sofia, 1924–1932).

relevance, as we shall see, to the story of Romanian Uniatism in later centuries.[20] The beginnings of the modern Catholic exarchate in Bulgaria cannot be disassociated from the nineteenth-century nationalism that took as its simultaneous aims civil emancipation from the Ottomans and ecclesiastical freedom from the Phanariot Greeks.[21] At Easter 1860, the Bulgarian churches ceased to commemorate the ecumenical patriarch in the liturgy. At the same time, a delegation of Bulgarian churchmen, with the approval of the Porte, sought to enter into Catholic communion, and Pius IX welcomed their initiative to the extent of personally consecrating the archimandrite Joseph Sokolski as archbishop in 1861. Kidnapped by Russians at Constantinople and interned at Kiev, Sokolski's career came to a dramatic full stop.[22] Despite this setback, the community persisted and, under a succession of further bishops, enjoyed a late nineteenth-century springtime, thanks especially to the inspirational monastic figure of Panteleimon Zhelov. At the turn of the century, however, the unionist movement lost momentum, owing to the lack of Catholic clergy, the counteroffensive of the pan-Slav-minded Orthodox Church–state of Russia, and the return to the church of his baptism of the formerly Orthodox exarch Nilus Izvorov. In the course of the Balkan Wars and the First World War, many of the Bulgarian Catholics of Thrace and Macedonia were displaced from their homelands. There remain today some fifty thousand Bulgarian Catholics of the Byzantine rite, whether at home or abroad. Since the fall of Communism, it proved possible to recreate an apostolic exarchate: their greatest strength is in Plovdiv, Bulgaria's second-largest city. Bulgaria is another country where a pilgrimage by the ailing Pope John Paul II, in 2002, made some impact on the condition of

[20] *Oriente cattolico*, p. 182.

[21] I. Sofranov, *Histoire du mouvement bulgare vers l'Eglise catholique au XIXe siècle* (Rome, 1960).

[22] See A. Slavov, *Kievskijat zatvornik Archiepiskop Iosif Sokolski* (Sofia, 1930) for the story of this "prisoner of Kiev". The wider context is sketched in M. Arnaudov, *Ekzarch Josif i blgarskata kulturna borba* (Sofia, 1940), an incomplete study of which (for, one supposes, political reasons) only the first volume was published. The prolific historian of Bulgarian literature lived until 1978.

Catholic-Orthodox relations, though his reception by the hierarchs—who look principally for inspiration to the patriarch of Moscow—was notably cooler than the welcome he had from the people.

In the former Yugoslavia, a Uniate population of some sixty thousand is chiefly Ukrainian in origin and derives from movement of labour in the Austro-Hungarian Empire—which ruled both the western Ukraine and the south Slav provinces of Slovenia, Croatia-Dalmatia, and Bosnia-Herzegovina until 1919. Yet attempts at union with the native Orthodox were not unknown. When exactly the Serbian church accepted the Byzantine schism is difficult to say.[23] Stephen II (1195–1228), son of the real founder of the Serb monarchy, Stephen Nemanja, received his royal crown and the title of *prvovenčani*, "primus coronatus", from Pope Honorius III. The attitude of his brother Saint Sava, the first archbishop of Serbia, was more ambivalent.[24] Although the patriarchal see of Peć survived the Ottomans, at least intermittently—being suppressed in 1459 by Mehmet II after his final destruction of the vestiges of Serbian independence, restored by the Janissary grand vizier Mehmet Sokolović in 1557 in favour of his brother the priest-monk Makarii, and abolished once again by Mustafa III in 1766—unionist initiatives made a dislocated appearance in the western parts of the country. Serbs fleeing from Turks necessarily encountered Croats, and it was in the borderlands of Serbia, Croatia, and Slovenia that unionist centres arose—for instance, in the monastery of Marca and the mountainous terrain of Žumberak, the *Uskočke gore*—in the course of the early seventeenth century.[25] To these may be added the Ruthenians who, as early as the reign of Maria Theresa, established colonies among their south Slav cousins. That empress, aware of the unattractiveness to the Orthodox of the older

---

[23] For the history of the Serbian church, see especially D. Slijepčevič, *Istoria srpske pravoslavna Crkva*, 3 vols. (Munich, 1962–1966).

[24] R. Rogošić, "Prvi srpski arhiepiskop Sava i Petrova Stolica", *Nova Revija* 7 (1929): 144–65.

[25] J. Simrak, *De relationibus Slavorium meridionalium cum sancta Romana sede apostolica saeculis XVII et XVIIII* (Zagreb, 1926); J. H. Schwicker, *Zur Geschichte der kirchlichen Union in der croatischen Militärgrenze* (Vienna, 1874).

Austrian policy with Uniates—their placing under the jurisdiction of Latin bishops but with a "ritual vicar" of their own in episcopal orders—sought and obtained from Pope Pius VI an eparchy for the Uniates of Croatia and adjacent parts, with its seat at Križevci, northeast of Zagreb.[26]

Before leaving the western Balkans, it remains to touch briefly on the topic of Albania—which is, however, neither Greek nor Slav. Though part of the historic Roman patriarchate, Albania was evangelised from both Latin West and Greek East, a circumstance that favoured the attempts of the Byzantine emperors to attach it ecclesiastically to Constantinople.[27] Its submission to Ochrid by Basil II in 1019 marks the consummation of this process. From 1628 to 1765, however, the mountainous district of Cimarra on the coast of Epirus housed a Byzantine-rite Catholic presence, which included for a period the archbishop of Ochrid Athanasius II, who had declared for union in 1660. The twentieth-century Eastern-rite church derives from the decision of a group of villages of the Mali Shpatit, southeast of Elbasan, to enter ecclesiastical union with Rome. Though their desire for a bishop was frustrated by the consular representations of Russia and Montenegro, they received pastoral help, after the First World War, from the (Italo-Albanian) monks of Grottaferrata.[28] The "apostolic administration" created for them in 1939 was swept away, along with the rest of public Christianity, by the coming of the Marxist-Leninist state in its virulently atheistic form in 1945. Some hundreds of Byzantine-rite Albanians live abroad.[29] At the time of writing (2009), their co-religionists at home are grouped with Latin Catholics in an "apostolic administration of Southern Albania", although the bishop chosen by Rome to govern it, in 1996, was a Croatian born Franciscan of the Byzantine rite.

[26] J. Šimrak, *Graeco-catholica Ecclesia in Jugoslavia: Diocesis Crisiensis* [i.e., Križevci], *olim Marčensis, historia et hodiernus status* (Zagreb, 1931).

[27] G. Petrotta, *Il cattolicesimo nei Balcani, I: L'Albania*, La tradizione I (Rome, 1928), fascicules 3–4.

[28] N. Borgia, *I monaci basiliani d'Italia in Albania*, 2 vols. (Rome, 1935–1942).

[29] *Oriente cattolico*, pp. 170–71.

Byzantine Catholics in Romania

A much more substantial Uniate community is that of Romania. Concessions of land to veteran legionaries in the frontier province of Dacia, prior to its abandonment by Aurelian in 270, constitute the origin of the "neo-Latin" people of Romania, as well as cognate ethnic groups, known as "Arumens" or "Vlachs" in the Pindus Mountains of northern Greece, Macedonia, and elsewhere. In the Middle Ages, Romania was made up of two principalities under native rulers, Wallachia and Moldavia, while its remaining territory, Transylvania, was occupied by the Magyars in 1004. With the Muslim advance into Europe, the two principalities became vassals of the Ottoman Porte (with the exception of a brief period of independence under Michael the Brave, 1593–1601), while Transylvania, though acknowledging for a while Ottoman overlordship of its Hungarian princes, passed under the Hapsburg sceptre in the closing years of the seventeenth century.[30] As we have seen, the ecclesiastical dominion of the see of Ochrid extended to the Turco-Romanian lands, a relic of Bulgar rule in the heyday of the two Bulgarian empires. But the markedly Latinate nature of all theological vocabulary in Romanian testifies to the original Westward orientation of the Romanian church.[31] Modern criticism ascribes to one of its early bishops, Nicetas of Remesiana, authorship of the ode of thanksgiving of Latin Christendom, the *Te Deum*.[32] No direct relations with Rome are known, however, before the fifteenth century. In 1418 an embassy from the princes of Wallachia and Moldavia, comprising representatives of eighteen cities, and reaching Constance during the closing sessions of the council there, opened the reunion negotiations that would be resumed on a wider scale at Florence. Although Damian,

[30] A. D. Xenopol, *Histoire des Roumains de la Dacie Trajane jusqu'à l'union des principautés en 1859* (Paris, 1896).

[31] J. Zeiller, *Les origines chrétiennes dans les provinces danubiennes de l'Europe romaine* (Paris, 1918).

[32] This attribution is, however, described as "assai incerta" by M. G. Mara, "Niceta di Remesiana", in *Dizionario patristico e di antichità cristiane*, ed. A. di Berardino (Casale Monferrato, 1983), vol. 2, col. 2398.

metropolitan of Moldavia, signed the union agreement, his successor Joachim was forced to abandon his see, taking refuge in Rome. The Moldavians eventually acquired a new archbishop from Ochrid in the shape of a certain Teoctist, formerly archdeacon to the formidable antiunionist Mark of Ephesus. Some years later, the sponsoring of Lutheran and Calvinist doctrines by the Magyar princes in Transylvania led to a lively reaction. In Moldavia this took the form of Orthodox synods—of 1642, against the confession of faith of Cyril Lukaris, the "Calvinist patriarch" (of Constantinople), and of 1645, in condemnation of the Protestantising catechism of Prince Rákóczy. In Transylvania, however, it led Oriental Christians to seek support from the church of Rome. At the Synod of Alba Julia of October 1698, under the auspices of the bishop of the see, Athanasius Anghel, they accepted a union that promised not only liberation from the unwelcome attention of the Calvinist superintendents but also civic immunities and privileges from the hands of the Hapsburg emperor.[33] One curiosity of the Protestantising efforts of the Magyars had been the new consciousness of both traditional doctrine and Romanian identity furnished by a liturgy that, they decreed, must henceforth be celebrated not in Old Slavonic but the vernacular tongue.[34] The Uniate bishops proved not unworthy of this inheritance, well placed as they were to reappropriate a Romance inheritance neglected by their Slavicised and Hellenicised Orthodox neighbours. When the eparchy of the Romanian Uniates created by Pope Innocent XIII was transferred from Fagaras to Blaj in 1737, under the aegis of the great scholar-bishop John Innocent Micu-Klein, the richness of the cultural and ecclesiastical institutions that proliferated in the latter city gained for it the name of "Little Rome". After the collapse of Austria-Hungary, the Uniate bishops welcomed the union of Transylvania (and the Banat) with the Romanian kingdom, and in the interwar years, the Holy See took the opportunity to increase the number of eparchies so that their pastoral care

[33] O. Barlea, "Die Union der Rumänen", in *Rom und die Patriarchaten des Ostens*, ed. W. de Vries (Freiburg, 1963), pp. 152–80, 394–423.

[34] A. S. Prundus, *Introductio linguae romanae in sacram liturgiam* (Rome, 1943).

could take in the faithful of the whole country, including Bessarabia. In law, however, the union did not long survive the advent of Communism. On the night of 29–30 October 1948, the six Uniate bishops were arrested and incarcerated in the summer residence of the Orthodox patriarch at Dragoslavele. Some three weeks earlier, the patriarchate had itself signalled its desire for the suppression of the *unia* by a synodal act formally abrogating the historic decisions of Alba Julia, taken exactly 250 years before.[35] The bishop of Cluj, still alive in prison in 1969 when Paul VI created him a cardinal *in pectore*, was the last of a hierarchy created for the service of some 1.5 million Uniates—until, that is, the revolution that toppled the Ceaucescu regime in 1990 enabled Romanian Catholics of the Byzantine rite, in Transylvania above all, to come out of the shadows. Their numbers today are estimated at 2 million, of whom three-quarters are practising.

Despite the interchurch tension caused by the emergence of Eastern-rite Romanian Catholics from the underground, Pope John Paul II was able to visit Romania in the spring of 1999. The journey was perhaps more at the invitation of state than church. The pope was specifically prohibited from including in his itinerary Transylvania, where the very numerous Uniates—"Greek Catholics"—were engaged in legal if not physical struggle with the Orthodox for the return of their church buildings. Nonetheless, he was able to establish warm relations with the Romanian Orthodox patriarch, Teoctist: a somewhat beleaguered figure, owing to political involvements or compromises. As the first papal visit to a predominantly Orthodox country, the event, in the words of the French Orthodox lay theologian Olivier Clément, marked "the destruction

---

[35] For the history of the Uniate church from 1700 to 1950, see auctores varii, *Biserica Română Unita* (Madrid, 1952). Its travails in the Communist period are described in C. Vasile, *Intre Vatican si Kremlin: Biserica Greco-Catolica in timpul regmului comunist* (Bucharest, 2003). The failure of the Orthodox Church to absorb the Byzantine-rite Catholics led it to seek the state's aid, an action it justified by appeal to Romanian patriotism. See O. Gillet, *Religion et nationalisme: L'idéologie de l'Eglise orthodoxe roumaine sous le régime communiste* (Brussels, 1997).

of a taboo".[36] The new amity seems set to continue between Benedict XVI and Teoctist's successor, Patriarch Daniel, an intellectual and ecumenist, who was enthroned at Bucharest in 2007. By that date Pope Benedict had raised the see of Fagaras and Alba Julia to the quasi-patriarchal dignity of a Major Archiepiscopal church, a sign of the flourishing of Romania's Catholics of the Byzantine rite.

Byzantine Catholics in the Russias (and Near Neighbours)

The Russias provide a comparable example of a Uniate community of a size sufficient to constitute something of a threat to its Orthodox brethren. So far as Great (or Muscovite) Russia is concerned, the abortive attempt by Isidore of Kiev, faithful to the Florentine union, to gain the adhesion of the grand ducal church of Moscow was followed by his retirement, as a fugitive, to Rome, where he died in 1463; the election of the antiunionist metropolitan Jonah as presiding bishop in Isidore's place; and the divisive appointment of a rival, Gregory, a companion of Isidore, by Pope Callistus III in 1458.[37] From that time on, the ancient metropolitanate of Kiev was split in two. The areas governed civilly by the Polish-Lithuanian state preserved ecclesiastically a reference to Kiev, while Jonah's successors (from 1589 until Peter the Great with the title of patriarch) used the style of "Metropolitan of Moscow and All Russia". Under the influence of the Society of Jesus (maintained in the Polish lands of the Romanov dynasty even after its formal suppression by the papacy) and of emigrés from the French Revolution of 1789, a number of

[36] Cited in "Chronicle of the Eastern Churches: The Visit of Pope John Paul II to Romania", *ECJ* 6, no. 2 (1999): 144.

[37] For Russia's church history, see, inter alia, A. V. Kartašev, *Očerki po istorij russko Cerkvi* (Paris, 1959). Ideas of ecclesiology in the Russian theological tradition are charted in chap. 1 of my *Theology in the Russian Diaspora: Church, Fathers, Eucharist in Nikolay Afanas'ev, 1893–1966* (Cambridge, 1989). For Russia's relations with Rome, see P. Pierling, S.J., *La Russie et le Saint-Siège* (Paris, 1896–1912), and J. B. Koncevicius, *Russia's Attitude towards Rome, 9th to 16th Centuries* (Cleveland, Ohio, 1927; rpt., 1983).

individual Russians from the noble estate became Westernisers, embracing the Latin rite at least as enthusiastically as they did Roman communion. But from the late nineteenth century onwards, such changes of ecclesial allegiance, now more frequently on the part of members of the intelligentsia and the more educated clergy, produced a desire for a Catholic community of the Russian rite. Formed in Saint Petersburg in 1905, this body took advantage of the liberalisation of the laws relative to religion, in the period after the "revolution" of 1905, and, with the coming of the short-lived constitutional republic of February 1917, obtained an exarch in the person of Father Leonid Feodorov.[38] Imprisoned soon after the Bolshevik revolution of that October, Feodorov died in 1935, whereupon the Polish-based Byzantine-rite metropolitan of Halič (Galicia), the charismatic Andrew Szeptyckyj, consecrated his own brother Clement as Feodorov's successor. This second exarch died in prison at Vladimir in 1952. The fate of the small Russian Catholic church has been chronicled by James Zatko under the suitable title *Descent into Darkness*,[39] but there survive a few thousand or so Russian-rite Catholics in the diaspora, with pastoral and sacramental care provided most often by priests trained at the Roman Collegium Russicum, founded by Pope Pius XI as part of a grand scheme for the conversion of Russia in the event of an imminent collapse of the Leninist state. The appeal of the last visitator of the Russian Catholics of the Byzantine rite, Georgiy Roshko (1915–2003), to the Congregation for the Eastern Churches for a renewal of the Russian exarchate after the fall of Communism in 1989 fell on ears rendered deaf by a combination of anxiety for the ecumenical consequences and informational knowledge about just how limited the fruitfulness of that enterprise had been. However, parishes of that rite do appear to exist, for example, at Omsk, where an attempt to re-create the exarchate in 2005 was deemed uncanonical by the Holy See, which instead

---

[38] P. Mailleux, S.J., *Exarch Leonid Feodorov: Bridgebuilder between Rome and Moscow* (Eng. trans., New York, 1964).

[39] J. Zatko, *Descent into Darkness: The Destruction of the Roman Catholic Church in Russia, 1917–1923* (Notre Dame, Ind., 1965).

informed the Moscow patriarchate it had made administrator of such
entities in Russia the Latin rite bishop of the diocese of the Trans-
figuration at Novosibirsk. Any significant public revival of Byzantine Catholicism in Great Russia, while demographically justified—
there are said to be at least ten thousand Eastern Catholics in Moscow
alone—would no doubt arouse the Moscow patriarchate's undying
hostility. It must be said that its hostility is easily aroused. The naming in 2001 of four Latin Catholic bishops for Russian territory drew
from it protests that were distinctly unfair given not only Orthodox
practice in the West (twelve bishops in Germany, for example) but
also the sheer size of the Catholic population involved. Several hundred thousand Latin Catholics live in European Russia, and the even
more substantial Catholic population in Siberia—a country of sects
and stubbornly surviving traditional paganism—derives from forced
migrations ordered by the Soviet state. But in the psychology of
many in the patriarchate, everyone born on the soil of Holy Rus' is
Orthodox *in potentia*.

To the southwest, the Uniates of Ukraine are a major bulwark of
national autonomy in a republic whose economic resources readily
draw to it the envy of its close neighbour, the Russian Federation.
If the baptism of the first Christian princes of the Kievan Rus, and
notably of Saint Vladimir (978–1015), took place in an age of full
communion between the Catholic and Orthodox churches, the schism
of Michael Kerullarios and the rivalry of Greek and Latin in the
Crusading period did not impair that communion in a day.[40] In
1075 Prince Izjaslav of Kiev placed his lands under the protection of
Pope Gregory VII, and, further west, Danylo of Halič (with Vladimir
or Volynia, the most important of the polities of western Russia)
entered into relation with Pope Innocent IV so late as 1243, receiving from him a royal crown ten years later. In the course of the
fourteenth century, however, these lands were conquered by the Polish king (Galicia) or the Lithuanian grand dukes (Volynia, right up

[40] For the Ukrainian (and Byelorussian) churches, see J. Madey, *Kirche zwischen Ost und West. Beiträge zur Geschichte der ukrainischen und weissruthenischen Kirche* (Munich, 1969).

to the Dnieper River, including, then, Kiev itself). With the union
of Poland and Lithuania in 1386, rendered definitive by the pact of
Lublin of 1569, this Catholic power came to exert a major influence
on the fortunes of the churches traditionally subject to Kiev. In 1458,
as we have seen above, the anti-Florentine metropolitan Jonah took
the title of "Moscow and all Russia", while his pro-Florentine rival
Gregory confined himself to the territories of Poland-Lithuania, albeit
with the more traditional title "of Kiev". Both Gregory and his successor, Misail Prucki, were in peace and communion with Rome,
but on the latter's death in 1480 the union lapsed for a hundred
years. A fresh union, the true beginning of the Ukrainian Catholic
Church, was decided upon by the Kievan metropolitan Michael
Rahoza and his bishops in 1594, accepted by the papacy in 1595,
and ratified by the Synod of Brest-Litovsk in 1596.[41] But its subsequent story differs greatly in the western Ukraine compared to the
eastern Ukraine. In the east, the potent Cossack element in the population resisted the union and obtained an Orthodox bishop for the
"mother" of Russian cities in 1620. With the waning of the Cossack power in the later seventeenth century, Kiev and the eastern
Ukraine passed into the hands of Muscovy (henceforth, "Russia"),
and in 1685 Bishop Gideon Četvertynskyj accepted nomination to
the see of Kiev on condition of its outright submission to the patriarchal church of Moscow. In the Polish-ruled western Ukraine, however, the union held; at the time of the First Partition of Poland
(1772), it is reckoned that some twelve million faithful of the Byzantine rite lived as civil subjects of the Polish crown. When, with
the Second and Third Partitions (1793, 1795), the Ukrainian lands,
except Galicia, were assigned to Russian rule, the hostility of the
tsardom to Uniatism decreed a lingering death for the Eastern Catholic Church and in 1839 the eparchies of Byelorussia ("White Russia")

[41] An exhaustive account is offered in J. Pelesz, *Geschichte der Union der ruthenischen Kirche mit Rom* (Würzburg and Vienna, 1881); see also O. Halecki, *From Florence to Brest* (Rome, 1958). A more recent study, with particularly rich documentation, is B. A. Guziak, *Crisis and Reform: The Kyivan Metropolitanate, the Patriarchate of Constantinople, and the Genesis of the Union of Brest* (Cambridge, Mass., 1998).

and Volynia were finally suppressed. The eparchy of Cholm, given
to Austria in 1795, found itself incorporated in the Romanov-ruled
"Kingdom of Poland" by the Vienna Congress of 1815. Both clergy
and faithful suffered considerably at the hands of the nineteenth-
century Russian empire and only in the period between 1918 and
1938 could they declare themselves Catholics of the Eastern rite with
safety—a state of affairs which came to an end, except for the city
of Cholm itself, which remained Polish, with the ad hoc territorial
redistributions of 1945. Under the less predatory eagle of the Hapsburgs, however, the Ukrainian Catholic church flourished. In 1807
the Holy See, responding to the Russian government's declaration
of nullity of the Uniate metropolitanate of Kiev in the previous year,
created for its people a new primatial church at Leopolis (Lviv).
Ukrainian ("Ruthenian") studies became a specialty of the University of Leopolis. In 1856 Pius IX named its archbishop, Michael Levy-
ckyj, the first Oriental cardinal since the time of Florence. Particularly
renowned among his successors was Andrew Szeptyckyj (1900–
1944), whose efforts for theological and monastic life, Ukrainian history and archaeology, and tireless zeal for the union idea gained him
the sobriquet (among Ukranian Orthodox as well as Catholics) "father
of the Ukrainian people".[42] But with the conquest of Polish Galicia
by the Soviet Union in 1944, the truth of the maxim that Soviet
Communism was often enough tsarist despotism rendered techno-
logically efficient was put to the test. As in Romania, the Communist authorities used the desire of the Orthodox Church for an
abrogation of the *unia*, signalled in the "Synod of Lvov" of 1946, as
a pretext for the deportation of its leaders. The driving underground of Ukrainian Catholicism was made especially bitter by the
charges of wartime collaboration with Germany—and indeed both
Ukrainian Catholics and those Orthodox who took the opportunity
to reconstitute the short-lived autocephalous Ukrainian Orthodox
church of 1919–1930 had at first regarded the German invasion as a

---

[42] C. Korolevskij, *Métropolite André Szeptyckyj, 1865–1954* (Rome, 1964). An English
translation of this work, as revised by Archimandrite Serge Keleher, was published as
Metropolitan Andrew, 1865–1944 (L'viv, 1993).

providential liberation. Until the liberalisation of the Soviet Union in 1989–1991, the public life of Ukrainian Catholicism was confined to its emigration—which was, however, numerically considerable in its two main waves of 1880–1914 and 1945 onwards. In 1974, by the only official figures that could be provided, there were reckoned to be somewhat over eight hundred thousand faithful in the diaspora.[43] Now, after an ecclesial "passion and resurrection", there are an estimated 4.2 million Ukrainian Catholics of the Byzantine rite.[44] Some 3.5 million are deemed, on recent showing, to practise worldwide. The fragmentation of the Orthodox in Ukraine into several competing jurisdictions suggested to some in the 1990s that, with lubricating oil from the ecumenical patriarchate, Byzantine Catholics there might be brought into a new "Kievan church" that would, in effect, mediate the intercommunion of Constantinople and Rome. These hopes of the "Kievan Church Study Group", initiated in Oxford (of all places!) in 1992, proved less than realistic. The existing commitments of other Orthodox (most pertinently the Moscow patriarchate) and the demands of a developed Catholic ecclesiology, in which the concept of mediate communion has no obvious place, were too strong. The topic of a Catholic patriarchate has been aired in the foreword to the second edition of this book. The title was asserted in 1975 by the major archbishop in exile, Joseph Slipyi, in the face of disapproval from Pope Paul VI. Since the return of his successors to Lviv and subsequently Kiev, they have, under pressure from their flocks, allowed its use de facto. Roman concern with Orthodox sensibilities has so far impeded its adoption de jure.

Before leaving western Russia, something more must be said of two groups whose names have been mentioned in passing above: the Byelorussians and Ruthenians. The approximate area of the mediaeval principate of Polotsk became part of Lithuania in the thirteenth century. With the adhesion of White Russians to the union, around 1700, the Lithuanian cities of Novahradak and Vilnius became

[43] Details and bibliography in *Oriente cattolico*, pp. 333–38, 339–40.
[44] S. Keleher, *Passion and Resurrection—the Greek Catholic Church in Soviet Ukraine, 1939–1989* (L'viv, 1993).

major centres of Uniate activity.[45] Under the rule of Moscow, from 1795 onwards, the dioceses of Byelorussia were reduced—by the tsar, without consultation of the Holy See—to two only, one "Lithuanian", with its seat in the monastery of Žyrovicy, and the other "Byelorussian", based at Polotsk. In 1839 the phil-Orthodox and Russophile bishops of these sees, together with twenty priests, separated from the union but failed to win the hearts of their people.[46] In 1905 almost a quarter million Byelorussian Orthodox returned to the Catholic Church but, by the religious laws then enacted, might worship only in the Latin rite. After the First World War, some thirty thousand others joined them but were now able to preserve their Slav-Byzantine tradition in Catholic communion. This tiny church was forced underground, with its Latin coreligionists, during the Soviet annexation of eastern Poland. In 1990 at Minsk, following Byelorussia's emergence as an independent state, "four hundred people solemnly proclaimed the rebirth of the Byelorussian Eastern Rite Catholic Church."[47] In 1995 its practising members were estimated at thirty-three thousand. Ten years later the Byelorussian Byzantine Church had re-established some twenty parishes in its homeland and a small monastery at Polotsk. Some few thousand Uniate Byelorussians in exile had, since 1960, an episcopal visitor resident in London.[48] For lack of parishes and churches, it is hard for the diaspora to keep a sense of identity alive.

The name "Ruthenian" originally signified Uniate Catholics, ethnically Slav and ritually Byzantine, in the kingdoms of Poland and Hungary. However, the name is retained by numerous "Ruthenes" now in America and elsewhere and is conventionally attached to the inhabitants of Subcarpathian Russia (Podkarpatska Rus) and, more exactly, to the erstwhile "lordship of Mukačevo", created by the fourteenth-century Hungarian monarchy for its Podolian feudatory,

[45] N. P. Vakar, *Belorussia: The Making of a Nation* (Cambridge, Mass., 1956), gives the background.

[46] W. Chotkowski, *Dzieje zniwoczenia sw. Unii na Bialorusi i Litwie w świetle pamiętników Siemaszki* (Cracow, 1890).

[47] J. Broun, "The Byelorussian Church", *Month* (March 1992): 94.

[48] *Oriente cattolico*, p. 177.

Theodore Koriatovič (1396–1414). Passing through various noble hands, the seigneurial authority was taken by the Hapsburgs from its last Magyar holders, the Calvinist Rákóczy family, and entrusted to the counts von Schönborn, who held it until 1918. Thereafter Subcarpathian Ruthenia became part of the Czecho-Slovak Republic. In 1939 it was proclaimed an independent republic of the Carpathian Ukraine. Transferred to Hungarian rule by the victorious Germans, it finished in 1945 as an *oblast* of the Soviet Union. In the wake of the sixteenth-century Protestant reform, the Orthodox bishops of Mukačevo, fearful of enforced Protestantisation at the hands of the Rákóczy, had made tentative approaches to the Catholic Church for support. The "Union of Užhorod" of 1646 was entered into by presbyters and layfolk.[49] To obtain a bishop, the unionists, anxious to avoid the strongly Orthodox candidate about to be wished upon them by the princess Rákóczy, sent their episcopal candidate, Parthenios Petrovič, to Transylvania, to the mercies of a pro-Catholic Orthodox bishop of Alba-Julia who consecrated him while deliberately omitting the oath of allegiance to Orthodoxy. The Holy See, vexed at the irregularity, delayed its acceptance of the new union until 1655. Only in 1771, at Maria Theresa's request, was the eparchy of Mukačevo fully established. During the uncertainties of the First World War, many Uniates of Subcarpathian Ruthenia rallied once again to Orthodoxy. By 1937 Rome had decided upon the creation of a Byzantine-rite metropolitanate for the Ruthenes, now in Czechoslovakia, but the advent of the Second World War delayed the matter— fatally, as it transpired, since in 1944 the Soviet armies occupied the region that was incorporated into the USSR, as part and parcel of Soviet Ukraine. An ecclesiastical assembly in the monastery of Saint Nicholas of Mukačevo declared the Union of Užhorod at an end, whereupon a Russian bishop, dispatched from the patriarch of Moscow, took over the episcopal residence and administration.[50] After

---

[49] M. Lacko, S.J., "The Union of Uzhorod", *Slovak Studies* 6 (1966): 7–190.
[50] M. Lacko, S.J., "The Forced Liquidation of the Union of Uzhorod, I: The Destruction of the Diocese of Mukačevo", *Slovak Studies* 1 (1961): 145–57; B. Boysak, *The Fate of the Holy Union in Carpatho-Ukraine* (Toronto and New York, 1963).

the collapse of Communism, a popular petition led to the recreation of the Byzantine Catholic diocese of Užhorod in 1991. In his 1996 letter commemorating the 350th anniversary of the Union of Užhorod, Pope John Paul II went out of his way to commend the churches of the union for their courage under trial, noting how by divine aid they were enabled "to preserve the wealth of their Eastern tradition and to remain at the same time in full communion with the Bishop of Rome".[51]

By these words the pope included in his sweep of reference the similar fate that befell the Uniate church in the present-day Slovak Republic. As a distinct body, that church dates from a division of the too-extensive eparchy of Mukačevo in 1787, in which year its western district was erected into the eparchy of Prešov (in eastern Slovakia).[52] By the 1950 synod of the same name—a somewhat bizarre affair at which five antiunionist priests presided over a lay gathering, a number of whose members were atheists—this church was reabsorbed into Orthodoxy.[53] The new schism never met with popular approval: in the opportunity provided by Alexander Dubček's attempted "democratisation" of Communism in 1968, the "Greek-Catholic" church of Prešov was recreated.[54] Although the post-Dubček years brought new difficulties, under the presidency of Vaclav Havel the Uniates of Slovakia have been able to reclaim their ecclesiastical property, though not without some litigation from the Orthodox. Some three hundred thousand Ruthene Catholics belong to their American metropola, while Slovak Catholics of the Byzantine rite are

[51] Cited from the nuanced account of the union and its recreation found in D. M. Petras, "An Ecumenical Commentary: The Union of Užhorod", *ECJ* 4, no. 3 (1997): 65.

[52] A. Duchnovič, *The History of the Eparchy of Prjasśev* (Rome, 1971: the translation of a Latin study of 1846).

[53] M. Lacko, S.J., "The Forced Liquidation of the Union of Uzhorod, II: The Destruction of the Diocese of Presov", *Slovak Studies* 1 (1961): 158–85.

[54] For an account of the revived Greek Catholic church, against the background of its past and with a description of its present conditions and future prospects, see J. Pavlovic, "The Byzantine Catholic Church in Slovakia", *ECJ* 5, no. 3 (1998): 61–84.

estimated at a quarter of a million, of whom 175,000 are said to practise.

The immigration of these groups (and others) into Hungary in the middle ages has left traces in a fairly sizeable Uniate population in what remains of the "lands of Saint Stephen" also.[55] In 1912 Saint Pius X established for these Christians the eparchy of Hajdudorog, a suffragan see of the Hungarian primate at Estzergom; in the 1920s, by a remarkable translating achievement, almost all the liturgical books of the Byzantine rite were put into Magyar.[56] In 1924, as a consequence of the massive relocation of borders after the First World War, a new exarchate of Miskole gathered to itself the parishes remaining in the reconfigured Hungary. In 1980, Pope John Paul II extended the exarch's jurisdiction to the whole Hungarian Republic. As with the Ruthene Catholics in Slovak Subcarpathia, their numbers are likely to be in the region of a few hundred thousand.

The Melchites

It remains to consider the (Arab) Melchites, whose appearance on the historical stage was, in the judgement of Bishop Kallistos Ware, the cause of a new coldness in Catholic-Orthodox relations in the early eighteenth century, putting an end to the Greek-Latin collaboration in the Mediterranean world and the relatively easy way in which many of the Byzantine Orthodox in east-central Europe could, as we have seen, pass to (and from) Catholicism in the sixteenth and seventeenth centuries.

Strictly speaking, the term "Melchite" signifies Byzantine-rite Christians, whether Catholic or Orthodox, of the Chalcedonian patriarchates of Alexandria, Antioch, and Jerusalem. "Melchites" followed the *malka* (Syriac) or *malek* (Arabic), the *emperor's* faith. Popularly, however, the word has become confined to Catholics of Arabic speech. In Syria, the Union of Florence lasted slightly longer than at

---

[55] L. Tautu, "Residui di rito bizantino nelle regione balcano-danubiane nell'Alto Medioevo", *Orientalia christiana periodica* 15 (1939): 41–70.

[56] G. Patacsi, "Die ungarischen Ostchristen", *Ostkirchliche Studien* 11 (1962): 273–505.

Constantinople. Renewed by the Antiochene patriarch in 1457, and in 1460, through a legation to the humanist pope Pius II (Aeneas Sylvius Piccolomini) at Siena by his brother patriarchs of Jerusalem and Alexandria, it survived until the conquest of Syria by the Ottomans in 1517. Thereafter, it fell into oblivion—hastened, no doubt, by the growing influence with the Porte of the Phanariots, the Greeks of Constantinople. Between 1587 and 1724, a number of Arab Orthodox bishops of the Antiochene patriarchate made profession of the Catholic faith, sometimes on retirement (as with the patriarch Michael VII in 1587) or clandestinely (as in the case of Macarius III in 1664).[57] By 1724 the Catholicising party was sufficiently strong to have elected to the patriarchal throne an openly Catholic Melchite, Euthimios Saifi, who took the name of Cyril VI. The Phanariots reacted by putting forward their own candidate, a Cypriot, as Jeremiah III, and the resultant struggle for control of the patriarchal church was bitter. The two patriarchal lines have continued since, providing leadership for two communities of roughly equal size.[58] The Melchite patriarch of Antioch, with some 450,000 practising adherents out of a total body of perhaps 1.2 million in his patriarchal territory, carries as well the personal titles of Alexandria and Jerusalem, where Melchite eparchies are entrusted to the care of patriarchal vicars. His community in Egypt is small, but in Palestine the faithful of the rite are more numerous though ever threatened by the pressures making for emigration in the present conflictual condition of the state of Israel. The Melchite diaspora counts some quarter of a million members. In its home territories, this is a church of islands floating in an Islamic ocean, concerned to recover the Arab identity necessary for its political survival but without surrender of its evangelical mission.[59]

---

[57] J. Nasrallah, *Notes et documents pour servir à l'histoire du patriarcat melchite d'Antioche*, vol. 1 (Jerusalem, 1965).

[58] C. Korolevskij, "Antioche", in *Dictionnaire d'histoire et de géographie ecclésiastique*, vol. 3 (Paris, 1924), cols. 563–703, provides lists of both Catholic and Orthodox lines of succession. The wider context is usefully sketched in S. Descy, *The Melkite Church: An Historical and Ecclesiological Approach* (Eng. trans., Newton, Mass., 1993).

[59] J. Corbon, *L'Eglise des Arabes*, 2nd ed. (Paris, 2007).

Melchite churchmen frequently see themselves as bridge builders between Orthodoxy and Rome, interpreting the concerns of each communion to the other, and played a notable rôle in this sense at the Second Vatican Council.[60] In 1995 the former Melchite archbishop of Baalbek, Elias Zoghby, with the concurrence of his successor Cyril Boustros, and the latter's Orthodox equivalent, Georges Khord, metropolitan of Byblos and Batrun, produced a profession of faith intended to bring about a state of full communion between the Melchites and the Orthodox in the Antiochene patriachate. Meeting in synod, twenty-four out of twenty-six of the Melchite bishops signed. The document was centred on two affirmations: "I believe all that Eastern Orthodoxy teaches. I am in communion with the Bishop of Rome, within the limits recognised by the holy Fathers of the East in the first millennium and before the separation to the first of bishops." This was taken to mean that the teachings of councils held in the West after 1054 would in future be regarded as theological opinions held by the Western church. The response of Rome and the Orthodox were equally negative. The Antiochene patriarchal synod averred that such an instrument of union would require the consent of all the other Orthodox churches. Rome for its part answered diplomatically, counselling the Melchites to wait on any conclusions to be reached by the international Catholic-Orthodox dialogue, the "mixed commission" appointed in the wake of the Second Vatican Council.[61]

It is to the changing attitudes of the Roman see in the hundred years before that council, and to the fruits of its new openness to the Chalcedonian Orthodox, that we must now turn.

---

[60] See *L'Eglise grecque melkite au Concile: Discours et notes du Patriarche Maximos IV et des prélats de son Eglise au Concile oecuménique Vatican II* (Beirut, 1967).

[61] For an account of this episode, see *Irén*. 68, no. 3 (1995): 369–71. The "ecclesiological approach" advanced by Serge Descy in his study (see footnote 58) is indebted to the Zoghby initiative.

Bibliography

Ware, [K.] T. *Eustratios Argenti: A Study of the Greek Church under Turkish Rule*. Oxford, 1964.

————. "Orthodox and Catholics in the Seventeenth Century: Schism or Intercommunion?" In *Schism, Heresy and Religious Protest*, edited by D. Baker, pp. 259–76. Studies in Church History 10. Cambridge, 1972.

Various *Unia*

Congregazione per le Chiese orientali, *Oriente cattolico: Cenni storici e statistiche*. 4th ed. Vatican City, 1974. (Full bibliography.)

Roberson, R. *The Eastern Christian Churches: A Brief Survey*. 6th ed. Rome, 1999. (Full bibliography and updated information.)

Uniatism as an Ecumenical Issue

Attwater, D. *The Catholic Eastern Churches*. 2nd ed. London, 1937.

Dumont, C.-J., O.P. "L'Eglise orientale catholique et le problème de l'unité". *Ist.* 7 (1960): 409–32.

Rousseau, O. *Les fractions d'Eglises orientales unies à Rome et l'unité*. Paris, 1961.

Suttner, E. C. *Church Unity—Union or Uniatism? Catholic-Orthodox Ecumenical Perspectives*. Bangalore, 1991.

Zoghby, E. *Uniatisme et oecuménisme*. Cairo, 1963.

12

The Second Vatican Council and
the Dialogue of Charity

Initiatives and Setbacks

By the nineteenth century, acts of shared worship had become little more than a dim and distant memory for both Catholics and Orthodox. In 1862, the monk of Solesmes and future curial cardinal Jean-Baptiste Pitra reported to the Holy See on the issue of *communio in sacris* with separated Eastern Christians.[1] Well aware of the evidence for intercommunion from two centuries previously, he considered that these precedents now possessed only a "speculative value". Such practices were out of the question in the mid-nineteenth-century world. The reason was, surely, the modern development of the Ultramontane movement (itself with deep roots, certainly, in the early modern, mediaeval, and even patristic periods), for which acknowledged communion with the Roman see figured as an *articulus stantis aut cadentis Ecclesiae*, an "article whereby the Church stands or falls", a necessary condition of the being of the Church. Yet even in Pitra's day the sacramental severance was not total, for Latin canon law never ceased to permit a Catholic to receive the Orthodox sacraments if in danger of death or cut off from his own church.

Pius IX's pontificate, moreover, was characterised not only by the advances of Ultramontanism, which would reach at once their climax and their limit in the decree *Pastor aeternus* of the First Vatican Council of 1869–1870, but also by a papal concern for the Christian

---

[1] A. Battandier, *Le cardinal Jean-Baptiste Pitra* (Paris, 1893), pp. 435–39.

East of a depth and urgency not seen since Florence. In 1847 there was founded at Rome the "Society for the Union of All the Christians of the East". In the following year, by way of response to appeals that he should direct an encyclical to the Orthodox, the pope produced the first "unionist" encyclical of the modern papacy, *In suprema Petri apostoli sede*. This document offered the careful maintenance of the Eastern liturgies as a quid pro quo for the acceptance of all Catholic doctrine. But with an extraordinary tactlessness, which was to hamper all Pius' relations with the Orthodox, the text was dispatched not to their bishops but, in thousands upon thousands of free copies, to their faithful and elicited an extremely negative response from the four Oriental patriarchs later that year.[2] By the end of the 1850s, the pope had lost confidence in the optimism of his entourage about the prospects of Uniatism. But he did not lose interest in the Orthodox as such.

In 1865 Pius IX became preoccupied with the idea of summoning a general council. He welcomed the suggestion of various prelates—and especially of Uniate bishops—that he should use the council to try once more for renewed contact with separated Eastern Christians. The council's preparatory commission encharged a Church historian at the Sapienza (the university of the Papal States) with the task of drawing up a series of argued recommendations, which they accepted. The bishops of the Orthodox were not to be invited to the council, but each individually was to receive a letter urging him, on the occasion of the council, to return to Roman unity. Undiplomatically, the commission further proposed that the suitable person for approaching the Orthodox patriarchs, the better to prepare the ground, was their Catholic brother, the Latin patriarch of Jerusalem. In September 1868, the papal letter *Arcano divinae providentiae* was sent out. Unfortunately, as its episcopal recipients were not slow to protest, its contents had been made known beforehand in the Roman newspapers, and the offending article itself reached

[2] *Lettre encyclique de sa sainteté le pape Pie IX aux chrétiens d'Orient et encyclique responsive des patriarches et des synodes de l'Eglise d'Orient*, trans. D. Dallas (Paris 1850); R. Aubert, *Le Saint-Siège et l'union des Eglises* (Brussels, 1947), pp. 20–22.

their hands nonceremonially, indeed unceremoniously—frequently through the mediation of missionaries.

The ecumenical patriarch, Grigorios VI, explained to the Roman delegation the three reasons why he felt unable to accept his copy. First, the pope had called the council without consulting his brother patriarchs; second, the patriarch had already encountered the communication in the press; and third, and most significant for the future, the patriarch complained of the known personal attachment of the pope to extreme theories of both primacy and infallibility. The First *Vaticanum* led inevitably, therefore, to an even more marked deterioration of relations.[3]

In 1902 the newly enthroned Constantinopolitan patriarch Joachim III, in the course of an encyclical letter to the Orthodox churches on, inter alia, the question of Christian unity, lumped together on one side the Catholic Church with the "church of the Protestants" while bracketing more graciously on the other Old Catholics and Anglicans. Of the former, the patriarch wrote:

> Of course, the union of them and of all who believe in Christ with us in the Orthodox faith is the pious and heartfelt desire of our Church and of all genuine Christians who stand firm in the evangelical doctrine of unity, and ... the subject of constant prayer and supplication; but at the same time we are not unaware that this pious desire comes up against the unbroken persistence of these churches in doctrines on which, having taken their stand as on a base hardened by the passage of time, they seem quite disinclined to join a road to union, such as is pointed out by evangelical and historical truth; nor do they evince any readiness to do so, except on terms and bases on which the desired dogmatic unity and fellowship is unacceptable to us.[4]

---

[3] Cf. C. G. Patelot, *Vatican I et les évêques uniates: Une étape éclairante de la politique romaine à l'égard des Orientaux, 1867–1870* (Louvain, 1981).

[4] "Patriarchal and Synodical Encyclical of 1902", text in C. G. Patelot, ed., *The Orthodox Church in the Ecumenical Movement: Documents and Statements, 1902–1975* (Geneva, 1978), p. 30. For Orthodox relations with Protestantism, see *The Orthodox Church and the Churches of the Reformation: A Survey of Orthodox-Protestant Dialogues*, Faith and Order Paper 76 (Geneva, 1975).

However, by 1920, the tone of the ecumenical patriarchate had notably softened. In the encyclical to all the "Churches of Christ" issued by Germanos V in January of that year, Constantinople spoke of the desirability of a "League (*proseggisis, koinônia*) of Churches" to complement the newly founded League of Nations and, while renewing its protests against proselytisation, placed its emphasis on mutual interest and help, in no way excluding the church of Rome from the latter.[5] To this more eirenic spirit one might perhaps link the new uncertainty faced by the patriarchate with the collapse of the Ottoman Porte, as also the loss of Orthodoxy's chief political arm, the tsardom, in the revolution of February 1917. Not until after the Second World War, however, was a "League of Churches" created, in the shape of the World Council of Churches, inaugurated in Amsterdam in 1948. The internal debate within Orthodoxy about the appropriateness of Orthodox participation in the council led to the 1952 encyclical of Athenagoras I, which ratified such participation within clearly defined limits. Orthodox delegates were not to be compromised doctrinally by co-option onto the "Faith and Order" commission of the council, nor were they to share indiscriminately in non-Orthodox acts of worship: "They should aim at celebrating, if possible, purely Orthodox liturgical services and rites, that they may thereby manifest, before the eyes of the heterodox, the splendour and majesty of Orthodox adoration."[6] Since the papacy, still looking askance at the ecumenical movement as both the effect and the cause of religious indifferentism, an attitude given forthright expression in Pius XI's letter *Mortalium animos* of 1928, did not propose that the Catholic Church should become a member of the council, or even an observer at its assemblies, the acts of commission and omission enjoined at Constantinople meant nothing at Rome.[7]

Not that, with the collapse of Pius IX's unionistic hopes, Rome had become careless of the fate of the separated East: far from it.

---

[5] Patelos, *Orthodox Church in the Ecumenical Movement*, pp. 40–45.

[6] Ibid., p. 46.

[7] For a Greek view of the development of ecumenism, see B. Stavridis, *Historia tês Oikoumenikês kinêseôs* (Athens, 1964).

In 1894, Pius' successor Leo XIII restated the prioritarian character of relations with Orthodoxy in his letters *Praeclara* and *Orientalium dignitas*; in the following year, this pope established a permanent cardinalatial commission to consider ways and means for the furtherance of unity.[8] In 1917, Benedict XV transformed this into the full-scale "Congregation for the Eastern Churches", whose responsibilities embraced not only Uniates but all questions touching the Christian East.[9] Simultaneously, the pope created a pontifical institute for the study of the Christian East as a whole, based at Rome. In 1928, Pius XI, in the very year of his fulmination against the liberal and indifferentist tendencies of the wider ecumenical movement (as then established), produced the encyclical *Rerum orientalium*, which sought to stimulate all kinds of initiatives—movements, associations, publications—with a view to reunion. Meanwhile, historic anniversaries provided occasions for popes to look with longing eyes to the mother church of the Eastern doctors: Pius X in 1908, on the fifteenth centenary of the death of Chrysostom; Pius XII in 1944, on the same anniversary of the demise of Cyril.

Nevertheless, the prevailing ecclesiology, with its insistence on the all-or-nothing character of schism, together with an understandable reserve towards the potent establishmentarian attitudes of the Orthodox in some of their traditional homelands, rendered these signals ambiguous. For example, in 1951 the church of Greece, then engaged in celebrating the nineteenth centenary of the arrival of the apostle Paul on Greek territory, invited the Catholic Church to participate in the festivities. The letter of decline studiously avoided giving its addressee, Spiridion of Athens and All Greece, his ecclesiastical title. Indeed, it managed not to refer to the Orthodox Church at all, confining itself to references to the celebrations taking place "in the nation". Its signatory was the then assistant (*sostituto*) to the papal secretary of state: his name was Giovanni Battista Montini.

---

[8] See R. Esposito, *Leone XIII e l'Oriente cristiano* (Rome, 1960), for Leo's work.

[9] For the background in the canonical relations of the *unia* with Rome, see V. Peri, "L'unione della Chiesa orientale con Roma: Il moderno régime canonico occidentale nel suo sviluppo storico", *Aevum* 58 (1984): 439–98.

The Dialogue of Charity

What made possible a change of heart was of course the development of a principled Catholic ecumenism under the inspiration of such men as Lambert Beauduin and Yves Congar, a development that issued in the invitation to the Orthodox churches to send observers to the Second Vatican Council (1962–1965).[10] In September 1963, *papa* Montini, Paul VI, initiated an exchange of letters with the ecumenical patriarch Athenagoras I, letters in which he drew attention to the shared faith and sacramental life already partially uniting the two communions. In 1964, the pope met the ecumenical patriarch at Jerusalem while on pilgrimage to the Holy Land, a venue chosen so as not to embarrass Athenagoras who, in some difficulty with anti-Roman segments of his own flock, could present the encounter, if need be, as a personal, even a private, gesture. In December 1965, at the close of the Second *Vaticanum*, parallel ceremonies in Rome and Constantinople (certainly of a public nature this time) lifted the mutual anathemas of 1054. From the Orthodox side, this was the deed of the local church of Constantinople acting through its patriarchal bishop and did not as such engage the totality of the Orthodox churches. Nevertheless, it was a more significant gesture for Constantinople than for Rome in that, by Latin canon law, excommunication is a therapeutic measure that lapses with the death of the excommunated person, whereas in the Eastern tradition it is regarded as a definitive privation of ecclesial communion, of its privileges, and of its graces. The mutual lifting of anathemas was so worded that it made sense in either context, as an act of forgiveness ordered to the healing of memories. Naturally, since the anathemas involved were (as we have seen) placed on individuals, not communities, this action was no more

[10] S. A. Quitslund, *Beauduin: A Prophet Vindicated* (New York and Toronto, 1975); A. Nichols, O.P., *Yves Congar* (London, 1989), pp. 96–140. For the development of Catholic ecumenism in the French-speaking world (the pivotal case), see E. Fouilloux, *Les catholiques et l'unité chrétienne du XIXe siècle au XXe siècle: Itinéraires européens d'expression française* (Paris, 1982).

(but no less) than a symbol of the intention to restore full communion when time was ripe.[11]

The phase of the dialogue that runs from 1963 to 1979 has been called, very reasonably, the "dialogue of charity": the idea being that, in a schismatic situation where, historically, so much rancour and bitterness exist, the restoration of fraternal relations in the spiritual and moral realm must precede any attempt at theological dialogue if the latter is to have any hope of success. This dialogue was sustained by the regular exchange of liturgical greetings—from the Phanar to Rome via episcopal representatives on the feast of Saints Peter and Paul, and from Rome to the Phanar via an embassy, always headed by a cardinal, on the feast of Saint Andrew.[12] On the tenth anniversary of the lifting of the anathemas, in December 1975, a beautiful event took place that nicely signified the intimate connexion of the dialogue of charity with its subsequent phase, the dialogue of (doctrinal) truth. On receiving a delegation from the Phanar bearing the news that the ecumenical patriarchate had agreed to establish a commission for the preparation of a theological dialogue, Paul VI, in an unprecedented reversal of custom, knelt and kissed the foot of the patriarch's representative, metropolitan Meliton of Chalcedon.

The Dialogue of Doctrine

Four years passed, however, before the beginning of the dialogue proper, a delay to be explained, in part, by the efforts required of the ecumenical patriarchate to convince the rest of the Orthodox churches—or at least the more recalcitrant of them, such as the church of Greece—of the value and prudence of such a step. Additionally, the preparatory commission had much work to do in determining the goals and methods of the dialogue. The overarching

[11] C. J. Dumont, O.P., "La levée des anathèmes de 1054 (7 décembre 1965) et sa signification dans la conjuncture oecuménique contemporaine", in A. Blane, ed., *The Ecumenical World of Orthodox Civilisation* (The Hague and Paris, 1974), pp. 193–214.

[12] J. E. Desseaux, ed., *Le livre de la charité* (Paris, 1984), gathers together the relevant documents.

goal would be, not surprisingly, the restoration of full communion between the two churches, but, in an important formula, this prospective full communion was described as founded on a unity of faith that would follow the lines of (*suivant*) the common experience and tradition of the ancient Church. In other words, Church history was to offer a model for the future relations sought, though at the same time, as the term *suivant* indicates, this pattern from the past was not to be recreated in an antiquarian fashion but in a way that bore in mind subsequent development in the story of the two communions. As to the method of the dialogue, this was to be exploration of what the two churches possess in common of the apostolic and patristic patrimony—though without attempting to avoid or obscure the divergences between them. The choice of a theological axis for the coming dialogue fell on the sacraments— but seen in the perspective of the unity of the Church. As the preparatory commission explained: "The sacraments must be chiefly understood as ... an expression and realisation of the unique sacrament of the Church, which comes to be in history and, par excellence, in the Holy Eucharist."

In November 1979 these preliminary discussions appeared to have reached a sufficient ripeness. Pope John Paul II, returning to Europe from his first pastoral journey to the United States, paid a surprise visit to Istanbul. On the eve of that visit, the pope declared:

> By this visit I wish to show the importance the Catholic Church attaches to this dialogue. I want to express my respect, the deep brotherly love, towards all these churches and their patriarchs, but above all towards the ecumenical patriarch to whom the church of Rome is linked by so many age-old bonds [*tanti vincoli secolari*], which in these last years have recovered new force and actuality.[13]

The announcement of the mixed (Catholic-Orthodox) commission of sixty members was made jointly by pope and patriarch in the Phanar on 30 November 1979.[14]

---

[13] *OR*, 22 November 1979.
[14] *OR*, 1 December 1979.

So far the commission has produced four documents.[15] The first, the "Munich Statement" of 1982, took as its title "The Mystery of the Church and of the Eucharist in the Light of the Mystery of the Holy Trinity".[16] This work is a little masterpiece of the ecclesiology of communion, which may itself be described as a eucharistic ecclesiology extended so as to reveal its own Christological and Trinitarian foundations. The eucharistic ecclesiology subjacent to the document—and called for, as we have seen, in the recommendations of the dialogue's preparatory commission—lives from roots that sink deep in both the Latin and the Greek traditions, as perusal of the liturgical prayers of West and East would show. Yet, *qua* systematic theology, it is a modern reinvention, owed chiefly to two Orthodox writers, the Russian secular priest Nikolai Nikolayevič Afanas'ev, who died in 1966, and the Greek lay theologian John Zizioulas, now a bishop of the Holy Synod of the Ecumenical Patriarchate.[17] Important fragments thereof are also lodged in the writings of such Catholic divines as Henri de Lubac and Joseph Ratzinger.[18] The value of a eucharistic ecclesiology is that it derives the ministerial, and therefore governmental, structure of the Church from the pattern of her eucharistic life and in so doing suggests how we should understand the relation

[15] For the events and declarations up to 1986, see D. Salachas, *Il dialogo teologico ufficiale tra la Chiesa cattolico-romana e la Chiesa ortodossa: Iter e documentazione*, Quaderni di o odigos 2 (Bari, 1986).

[16] Along with the two succeeding doctrinal agreements, the Munich Statement is conveniently reproduced in *One in 2000? Towards Catholic-Orthodox Unity*, ed. P. McPartlan (Slough, 1993), pp. 37–52.

[17] N. Afanasieff, *L'Eglise du Saint-Esprit* (Paris, 1975); on this writer's work, the interested reader might consult my *Theology in the Russian Diaspora: Church, Fathers, Eucharist in Nikolai Afanas'ev 1893–1966* (Cambridge, 1989). Zizioulas' chef d'oeuvre is *L'être ecclésial* (Chambésy, 1980).

[18] For de Lubac, see P. McPartlan, "Eucharist and Church: The Contribution of Henri de Lubac", *Month* (August–September 1988); idem, *The Eucharist Makes the Church: Henri de Lubac and John Zizioulas in Dialogue* (Edinburgh, 1993); and idem, *Sacrament of Salvation: An Introduction to Eucharistic Ecclesiology* (Edinburgh, 1995). For Ratzinger, see A. Nichols, O.P., *The Theology of Joseph Ratzinger: An Introductory Study* (Edinburgh, 1988), pp. 136–39, also published in idem, *The Thought of Pope Benedict XVI: An Introduction to the Theology of Joseph Ratzinger* (London, 2007), pp. 96–99.

of the local church, which celebrates the Eucharist in a particular place, to the universal Church, the *Catholica*. The Eucharist is always celebrated by a particular group, yet that which is so celebrated is, in fact, the Eucharist of the whole Church. The local church, therefore, manifests the plenitude of the Church—yet only in the measure of its communion with all the other churches. Each church is responsible for the others, "receiving" their testimony of faith and sharing with them its own experience. The eucharistic consubstantiality of the churches is conditioned by the identity, then, of their faith.[19]

The Munich document deals in three chapters with three questions. First, the commission was asked, how is the sacramental nature of the Church and Eucharist to be understood in relation to Christ and the Holy Spirit? Second, how does the local church's celebration of the Eucharist, centred on the bishop, relate to the mystery of the one God in three persons? Third, what is the relationship between this Eucharistic celebration of the local church and the communion of all local churches in the one holy Church of the one God in three persons?

In answering the first of the inquiries, the text holds together in an admirable fashion the economies of the Spirit and the Son.

> The Incarnation of the Son of God, his death and Resurrection were realised from the beginning, according to the will of the Father, in the Holy Spirit. The Spirit, who proceeds eternally from the Father and manifests himself through the Son, prepared the Christ-event and realised it fully in the Resurrection. Christ, who is the Sacrament *par excellence*, given by the Father for the world, continues to give himself for the many in the Spirit, who alone gives life.[20]

And applying this to the Holy Eucharist, the signatories maintain:

---

[19] For an analysis of this document, see R. Barringer, C.S.B., "Catholic-Orthodox Dialogue: The Present Position", in *Rome and Constantinople: Essays in the Dialogue of Love*, ed. R. Barringer (Brookline, Mass., 1984), pp. 136–39. The text of the Munich and Bari Statements, cited here is as given in *One in 2000?*

[20] Munich Statement 1, 3.

That is why the eucharistic mystery is accomplished in the prayer which joins together the words by which the Word-made-flesh instituted the sacrament and the *epiclesis* in which the Church, moved by faith, entreats the Father, through the Son, to send the Spirit so that in the unique offering of the incarnate Son, everything may be consummated in unity.[21]

In dealing with the second question of the trio, the commission proposed what Father Robert Barringer, of the Congregation of Saint Basil, has termed "a certain mystical identity/analogy" between the life of the Church, understood as "the sacrament of Christ", and the mystery of the Trinity itself. The origin of the Church in a given place is not interpreted sociologically but as the novel presence of the "Jerusalem from on high ... coming down from God", the Trinitarian *koinônia* itself, which makes of the Church, compared to the world, a "new creation": "This mystery of the unity in love of many persons constitutes the real newness of the Trinitarian *koinônia* communicated to men in the Church through the Eucharist.... This is why the Church finds its model, its origin and its purpose in the mystery of God, one in three persons." [22] And the text situates the ministry of the bishop, the leader of the local church, in this context, insisting that the community's union with him is "first of all of the order of *mysterion* and not first and foremost in the juridical order". For the bishop's authority is sacramental—"the authority of servant, which the Son received from the Father and which he received in a human way by his acceptance of the passion"—and charismatic, for "the bishop stands at the heart of the local church as minister of the Spirit to discern the charisms and take care that they are exercised in harmony, for the good of all, in faithfulness to the apostolic tradition." [23] Finally, the Munich document speaks of the many bonds of communion that, through the Spirit of Christ, conjoin local churches in the single Church: "*communion* in faith, hope, and love; *communion* in the sacraments, communion in the diversity of charisms,

[21] Ibid., 1, 6.
[22] Ibid., 2, 1.
[23] Ibid., 2, 3.

communion in reconciliation, *communion* in the ministry." And, in keeping with this affirmation, the commission spoke of the worldwide episcopate in these terms: "The *episkope* for the universal Church is entrusted by the Spirit to the totality of local bishops in *communion* with one another. This *communion* is expressed traditionally through conciliar practice. We shall have to examine further the way in which the latter is conceived and realised in the perspective of what we have just explained." [24]

The natural second step after the Munich document would have been a consideration of the canonical structure of the Church. For in this total exchange between local churches—an exchange based both on sacramental reality and a common faith—certain particular churches enjoy a privileged position. They are, in the words of the French Orthodox lay theologian Olivier Clément, "centres d'accord". [25] In such centres of accord, a bishop with primacy exercises a special concern for the unity, in life and faith, of the surrounding local churches, presiding in love among them, notably by actualising on certain specially weighty occasions—synods and councils—the "conciliarity" of the episcopal body as a whole. Though the authors of the Munich Statement did not find it opportune to move immediately to a common exploration of the interrelation of conciliarity with the authority of such churches in priority, one sees how the Petrine office of the pope might fit into the picture—a centre of accord for all the churches, a presidency in love that crowns a hierarchy of lesser, regional presidencies of an analogous kind.

Realising, however, the peculiarly delicate character of such an undertaking, the commission preferred to devote its attentions, in the second place, to the sacraments of initiation whereby the Church, at its most basic level of being, is constituted in faith as a unity.

[24] Ibid., 3, 4.

[25] O. Clément, "L'ecclésiologie orthodoxe comme ecclésiologie de communion", *Contacts* 61 (1968). For his generous response to Pope John Paul II's plea for ecumenical advice on the concrete exercise of the Petrine office, see idem, *You Are Peter: An Orthodox Theologian's Reflection on the Exercise of the Papal Primacy*, Eng. trans. (Hyde Park, N.Y., 2000).

Meanwhile, its own work was faced with a number of criticisms—mild from the Catholic side, sometimes severe from that of the Orthodox. From Catholics, the text was seen by some as excessively idealistic—without adequate reference to the sin-marked "people of God" on painful pilgrimage through history. Again, where the document had touched on the issues of the Spirit's procession, and his rôle in the eucharistic consecration, its language was occasionally felt to be too weighted towards the Orthodox position. More technical criticism focussed on the perhaps insufficiently differentiated language whereby the eucharistic body and ecclesial body of Christ were treated as identical, and on the somewhat bare paradox by which the unity of the Godhead was deemed to consist in the diversity of the Trinitarian persons. From Orthodox, more drastic censures could be heard, bearing, however, more on the advisability of the dialogue as a whole than on the shortcomings of the Munich Statement in itself. An "Extraordinary Joint Conference of the Sacred Community of the Holy Mount Athos", for example, expressed the need for the greatest caution. Its declaration ascribed the Catholic desire for dialogue to a wish to "annex" Orthodoxy, as a counterbalance to the powerful internal disturbances and crises now shaking traditional faith in Latin Christendom, as well as to anxiety at the number of Catholics becoming members of the Orthodox Church.

The wisdom of hurrying slowly was demonstrated by the serious obstacles encountered in preparing the Bari Statement of 1987, entitled "Faith, Sacraments and the Unity of the Church".[26] In this text, whose formulation had been bedevilled by a controversy surrounding a display in the Vatican of Macedonian icons (an exhibition thought by some Orthodox to constitute papal support for the as-yet-unrecognised declaration of autocephaly by the church of Macedonia), the commission looked at the sacramental life as an expression of faith. More particularly, it investigated the way in which believers are initiated into that life. Problematic was the order of the sacraments of initiation, given the fact that, at a certain point in its history, the Latin church has altered the original sequence,

[26] See McPartlan, *One in 2000?* pp. 53–70.

producing the order: baptism, Eucharist, confirmation, for infants and children, rather than that universal in Orthodoxy: baptism, chrismation, Eucharist.[27] The commission declared on the point: "This inversion, which provokes objections or understandable reservations both by Orthodox and Roman Catholics calls for deep theological and pastoral reflection because pastoral practice should never lose sight of the meaning of the early tradition and its doctrinal importance."[28] That some Orthodox members of the commission could regard this as an heretical practice, sufficient in itself to justify the continuance of the schism, speaks eloquently of their ambivalence towards the dialogue—though their negative attitude can be explained in part by frustration at the commission's alleged deficiencies in its manner of working.[29]

In 1988, meeting at the Orthodox monastery of Valamo in Finland, the commission moved closer to the neuralgic point of the primacy by turning its attention to "the rôle of the ordained ministry in the sacramental structure of the Church".[30] The Valamo document signals complete agreement on the place of the ministerial priesthood in the economy of salvation. It offers an enlightened concept of the apostolic succession as "succession in a church, which testifies to the apostolic faith, in communion with other churches testifying to that same faith", leaning here on the Munich document of eight years previously, and thus identifies the bishop as the

[27] D. Salachas, *Il dialogo teologico ufficiale tra la Chiesa cattolica-romana e la Chiesa ortodossa: La quarta assemblea plenaria di Bari, 1986–1987*, Quaderni di o odigos 4 (Bari, 1988).

[28] Bari Statement 51. It is not often noticed that as late as 1897, Pope Leo XIII, in a letter to the bishop of Marseilles, declared the practice of communicating the unconfirmed to be "neither congruent with the constant practice of the Church nor useful to the faithful" and laid down that the abuse can be tolerated only on the assumption in each case that confirmation will follow. See D. Stone, "Confirmation a Prerequisite for Holy Communion", *Papers IX* in *Darwell Stone: Churchman and Counsellor*, by F. L. Cross (Westminster, 1943), p. 422.

[29] [Metropolitan] Chrysostomos di Peristeria, "Il dialogo teologico tra le Chiese ortodossa e cattolica-romana", *Il regno* 31, no. 560 (1986); original in *Teologia* (1986), pp. 529–42.

[30] For the Valamo Statement, see McPartlan, *One in 2000?* pp. 71–86.

living link between his own church and others' in professing an identical faith and manifesting that faith in eucharistic celebration. The drafters of the Valamo declaration point out that the Church has known diverse forms in the exercise of interepiscopal communion and trace, in brief compass, the story of many of the Church polities we have had occasion to consider in this book: metropolitanates, the ancient patriarchates, the Pentarchy, and the new patriarchates of later Orthodoxy. So far as the synodal element in the life of the Church is concerned, it cannot be conceived without reference to the notion of presidency. Here the document cites the thirty-fourth of the so-called Apostolic Canons (third century), which call for the recognition in every synodal gathering of a *prôtos*, or "first", among the rest. The Valamo text does not grasp this nettle, merely noting that "the theme of primacy in the Church as a whole, and notably that of the primacy of Rome, constitutes a grave divergence between us and will be discussed further."

At Freising (Munich) in 1990, the commission at last confronted the interrelation of conciliarity (the Eastern equivalent of the more juridical term "collegiality" in the West) and (primatial) authority. Meanwhile, however, the collapse of Communism as the form of the state throughout eastern Europe had liberated not only the Orthodox churches from state interventionism there but also the suppressed Uniate churches of the Ukraine and Romania, which resurfaced, sometimes tremblingly, sometimes triumphantly, after their dark night underground. The decision of the Holy See to recognise the clandestinely created bishops of the former, and to appoint bishops for the latter in the confused aftermath of the Romanian revolution was an inevitable response to the needs of Oriental Catholics, who had suffered much, not least for their fidelity to Rome. But it could not be swallowed easily by the Orthodox, whose dislike of Uniatism and distrust of Rome's onetime predilection for such "parallel churches" are dogs who sleep only too lightly.[31] The timing

---

[31] R. G. Roberson, "Catholic-Orthodox Relations in Post-Communist Europe: Ghosts from the Past and Challenges for the Future", *Centro pro unione Bulletin* 43 (1993): 17–31.

was unfortunate—and yet it confronts the Orthodox with a question they should ponder. Why have millions of Christians of Byzantine tradition seen in the Elder Rome something so precious that forty years of enforced reabsorption into Orthodoxy has not shaken their conviction? In some cases, a nationalist answer to this question may be forthcoming, but by no means in all. What may be true in the fields of the western Ukraine rings false on the hills of Transylvania. Those benevolently inclined to the dialogue could only hope that the desire for reconciliation between estranged members of what was once one family, the passion for unity, will prove stronger than the memory of past animosities and the divisive tendencies of nationalisms, both old and new—not least in the face of that other "West" and other "East" that both Rome and Constantinople must look on with equal foreboding, the advance of consumer materialism and the renaissance of Islam.

In point of fact, the commission had to sidetrack. Rather than following through the logic of its expected agenda, it halted to produce an "emergency" document on, precisely, Catholic Uniatism in the East. This document was the 1993 Balamand Statement, named for a Lebanese monastery (originally a Benedictine abbey of the Crusader period) in the patriarchate of Antioch. This text, entitled "Uniatism, Method of Union of the Past and the Present Search for Full Communion", was well intentioned but underwent the unfortunate fate of pleasing no one.[32] Remarkably, it created a united front between Eastern Catholics on the one hand and hardline Orthodox on the other.[33] Needless to say, each rejected it for diametrically opposed

[32] For the text, see "The Balamand Statement", *ECJ* 1, no. 1 (1993–1994): 17–25.
[33] The entirely negative response of the Romanian Uniate hierarchy, published in *ECJ* 1, no. 2 (1994): 49–53, as "Romanian Greek-Catholic Comments on Balamand", is balanced by the more eirenic response of their Ukrainian brethren, who endured at the hands of the Orthodox (and not only a Communist state) duress almost as severe: see D. Petras, "The Balamand Statement and Hierarchial Reception", ibid., pp. 69–88, and R. G. Roberson, C.S.P., "Catholic Reactions to the Balamand Document", *ECJ* 4, no. 1 (1997): 53–74. On the Orthodox side, one should note the (presumably not fortuitous) absence at Balamand of such weighty bodies as the churches of Greece, Serbia, and Bulgaria, as well as the Jerusalem patriarchate. What has drawn the ire of many, not least

reasons: Eastern Catholics because it seemed to imply they should never have existed in the first place, the more rigorous Orthodox because while saying "Never again!" it did not actually call on Rome to abolish them.

The "fallout" of the crisis that the Balamand document in different senses at once reflected and created produced a marked lowering of tone in Catholic-Orthodox relations at the highest level. The ecumenical patriarch, Bartholomew I, arriving in Rome for a fraternal visit for the feast of Saints Peter and Paul in 1995, addressed the pope in words so extraordinary that the Vatican "newspaper of record", *L'osservatore romano*, found it more judicious not to publish them. Insinuating that the "Vatican state" might be behind the resurgence of the Eastern Catholic churches, the patriarch apparently denied them the name of "churches": they should be regarded as irregular communities that must find their way back to Orthodoxy as quickly as possible. He did not spare John Paul's eirenicon, *Orientale lumen*, with its repeated praises of the Christian East, since the pope had committed the sin of treating Eastern Orthodox and Eastern Catholics as though they were at parity.[34] Equally painfully, and in clear contradiction of the Balamand provisions, the Orthodox copresident of the Joint International Commission for the Theological Dialogue between the Roman Catholic Church and the Orthodox Church, Archbishop Stylianos of Australia, gave Uniates a choice: either to sever the connexion with Rome and revert to their mother churches or to become Latin-rite Roman Catholics.[35] Despite efforts in the United States to relaunch the dialogue, it was not until 2005 that the commission resumed its normal course, with a meeting at Belgrade, in Serbia, on the "ecclesiological and canonical consequences

in the church of Greece, is what Lewis Patsavos terms the implied abandonment, in the name of the Orthodox, of their "ecclesiological and soteriological exclusivity": thus his "An Orthodox Response to Balamand", *ECJ* 1, no. 3 (1994): 22–29.

[34] For details of publication of the patriarch's speech in at least one Greek journal, see "The 'Final Solution'? Reflections on Recent Orthodox Statements concerning Eastern Catholics", *ECJ* 4, no. 3 (1997): 107–32, note 10.

[35] "Comment on the Papal Encyclical *Orientale lumen*", *Phronema* 10 (1995): 51–60.

of the sacramental nature of the Church: ecclesial communion, conciliarity, and authority".

That document, which in 2005 was simply a draft, had lain on
the drawing board since a 1990 meeting of the Joint Coordinating
Committee of the dialogue. The passage of time, and such positive
ventures as the visit of Pope John Paul II to Archbishop Christodoulos of Athens in 2001, had eased the way. But the decision was
taken at the meeting not to refer again for the time being to the
issue of Uniatism.[36] Evidently, more brambles may lie across the
path ahead. In October 2006, the commission resumed its discussions at Ravenna, though the event was marred by a "walkout" on
the part of the Moscow patriarchate's representative. Bishop Hilarion's protest was caused not for once by the wrongdoings, real or
imagined, of the Catholic Church but by the presence of a delegation from the Estonian Orthodox church, whose autocephaly,
underwritten by Constantinople, is still denied in Russia. His action
demonstrated, of course, the need precisely for a strong universal
primacy so as to balance synodality in the Church. A year after the
Ravenna gathering, Bishop Hilarion maintained that the non-
representation of the Moscow patriarchate, the Church of Bulgaria
and the former Russian metropolia in North America meant that
the Ravenna document—which thus lacked the backing of a numer-
ical preponderance of Orthodox—could be considered only an accord
between representatives of Rome and those of "certain Orthodox
churches". He also expressed a doubt as to whether "Orthodox
consciousness" would accept the text's conclusions about a universal primacy, even in the case of those churches that actually
participated.[37]

That the Orthodox Church is not a unitary communion but a
polycephalic one (it has a plurality of patriarchal and archiepiscopal

---

[36] As reported by C. Sabbatos, "Dialogo teologico cattolico-ortodosso: Assemblea
plenaria di Belgrado (18–24 settembre); Testimonianza di un membro ortodosso rap-
presentante della Chiesa di Grecia", *O odigos* 25 (2006): 25–26.

[37] For the bishop's words, see "Chronique religieuse, I: Relations entre les Communions. I Catholiques et autre chretiens", *Irén* 81, no. 1 (2008): 53–55.

heads) does of course mean it is not easy for it to speak on all issues with one voice. The spectrum of attitudes to dialogue with Rome is marked. The patriarchate of Moscow would seem to prefer a collaboration that is not so much theological and ecclesiological as cultural and ethical, by way of a common front against secularization, for the defence of Christian values in Europe. That is certainly worthwhile and may be the best that can be obtained, especially when the patriarchate has to consider the virulently antiecumenical attitudes of not only Russian supernationalists but also the "Russian Orthodox Church Abroad", with which it is in the process of uniting. But the church of Cyprus, in a common declaration made by Chrysostomos II, archbishop of Nea Justiniana and All Cyprus, with Pope Benedict XVI, in June 2007, came much closer to seeing things in what is surely the pope's own perspective.

> We desire that the Catholic and Orthodox faithful of Cyprus live a fraternal life in full solidarity, based on our common faith in the risen Christ. We also wish to sustain and encourage the theological dialogue that is preparing, through the competent international commission, to address the most demanding issues that marked the historical event of the division. For full communion in the faith, the sacramental life, and the exercise of the pastoral ministry, it is necessary to reach substantial agreement. To this end, we assure our faithful of our fervent prayers as pastors in the Church and ask them to join us in a unanimous invocation "that they may all be one ... so that the world may believe" (Jn 17: 21).[38]

The decision of the Moscow patriarchate in October 2007 to withdraw its representatives from the Ravenna meeting of the International Catholic-Orthodox Theological Commission in protest against the presence there of the "Apostolic Church of Estonia"—an Orthodox body whose "autonomy", granted by the ecumenical patriarchate, the Russians did not recognise—was not only an irritating impediment to that dialogue; it was precisely the sort of happening that makes Catholics think the Orthodox need the pope as much as the pope needs them. On 15 November following, the Ravenna

[38] For their exchange, see *Acta Apostolicae Sedis* 99 (2007): 689–91.

Statement was made public under the title "Ecclesiological and Canonical Consequences of the Sacramental Nature of the Church: Ecclesial Communion, Conciliarity and Authority".[39] Revisiting the
Munich, Bari and Valamo documents, the Commission registered
how on all three levels—local, regional and universal—"primacy and
conciliarity are mutually dependent."[40] Its signatories agreed that
from ancient times the Church at large had recognised the primacy
of the bishop of Rome. But as to what his prerogatives were, and on
which foundations, biblical and theological, they rest, the commission could reach no common mind. Like the historic Ravenna, it
remained suspended midway between Rome and Constantinople. Pru-
dently, it asked for scholars to report on the modes of exercise of the
primacy and attitudes thereto in the two millennia of the Church's
life so far. Any more concrete embodiment of aspiration to unity
was deferred, left to the ecumenical future. That need not prevent
individuals from making proposals of their own here and now.

A Proposal for Reunion

What form would an eventual (hypothetical) reunion with Rome of
the separated Eastern churches properly take? Consonant with Tradition, both Eastern and Western, it would be achieved by a conciliar assembly of the episcopate. But how would such an assembly
proceed? As indicated in chapters 2 and 3 of this book, when dealing with the doctrinal obstacles to union in the cases of the Assyrian
and Oriental Orthodox churches, the assembly should proceed by
some form of "re-reception" of the doctrines of the Catholic Church
in the new context created by their juxtaposition with the Christian
patrimonies of the separated East. (The principles now to be set
forth vis-à-vis the Orthodox will also apply, therefore, *mutatis mutan-
dis*, to the Nestorian and Monophysite traditions.)

[39] Joint International Commission for the Theological Dialogue between the Roman
Catholic Church and the Orthodox Church, "The Ravenna Statement, October 2007",
Pontifical Council for Promoting Christian Unity Information Service, no. 126 (2007),
pp. 178–84.
[40] Ibid., para. 43.

The possibility of overcoming the Eastern Schism lies in the ability of the Catholic Church to extract the positive teaching of those mediaeval and modern councils that follow on the patristic age of the seven councils and to reexpress this teaching in a new context, with complementary supplementation from the Eastern tradition, presenting the whole in the forum of a fresh ecumenical council to which the Orthodox bishops would be invited (as they were, *qua* equal participants, to Florence). The grounds for such a possibility in terms of fundamental ecclesiology and, more specifically, in terms of a theology of the councils, have been identified in an admirable way by the French historical and dogmatic theologian Père Bertrand de Margerie of the Society of Jesus.[41]

De Margerie sets out from the question: Is the ecumenicity of a council susceptible of diverse and unequal realisations? He suggests that, implicitly present in traditional discussion of the councils, has been the idea that ecumenicity is analogical. It admits of degrees of realisation, whether minimal, average (*moyen*), or perfect. At any rate, there is no reason to think that such a distinction has ever been *denied* in a way that is theologically compelling—either on argumentative or authoritative grounds. De Margerie thus proposes a principle: "By analogy we ascribe unequally [*inégalement*] the self-same ecumenicity to different councils whose multiplicity is unified … in their common participation in the being of the Word incarnate."[42] De Margerie points out that, in his *Summa de ecclesia*, John of Turrecremata (Torquemada) distinguished between two levels of ecumenicity.[43] Those ecumenical councils that reunite all the successors of the apostles are at once *plenary* and *universal*, owing this fulness to—in particular—the presence of the five patriarchs. By contrast, those councils that comprise only a certain number of bishops (and notably lack one or more of the patriarchs) are not plenary, yet they can be universal if, at their assembly, the Roman bishop, the

---

[41] B. de Margerie, S.J., "L'analogie dans l'oecuménicité des Conciles: Notion clef pour l'avenir de l'oecuménisme", *Revue Thomiste* 84, no. 3 (1984): 425–46.

[42] Ibid., p. 427.

[43] See V. Peri, *I concile e le chiese* (Rome, 1965), pp. 100ff.

successor of Peter, is present, whether personally or via his legates. Similarly, Robert Bellarmine (the chief author of the list of ecumenical councils currently in use in the Roman Church) regarded the presence of all the patriarchs as of the *bene esse*, though not the *esse*, of a council: another testimony to "analogicity".[44]

Turning from history to ecclesiology, de Margerie picks up a suggestion of Dom Adrien Gréa that, at an ecumenical council, both pope and bishops render the whole Church present, and that in a manner at once differentiated and unified.[45] The pope, being head of the episcopal college, represents the whole college, including, then, its potential and its absent members. Thus, at Chalcedon, all the bishops of the West were present in the persons of the legates of Pope Leo. At Trent, one must say, correspondingly, the Eastern bishops in imperfect communion with the Roman see were, though physically absent, in some sense present in the representatives of the popes. And yet the pope is not the *exclusive* bearer of representation of the whole Church. Every bishop, as member of the college, represents to a degree the whole Church. To explain this requires recourse to what, in the opening chapter of this study, on the nature of schism, we found reason to call the "universalist" model of the Church. Because the universal Church precedes the particular churches in the divine plan and gives them whatever they have, so Jesus Christ, in sending the apostles to the entire world, made them doctors of the whole Church before they had even begun to form particular churches. It is because of this that the episcopal college, in succeeding centuries, can teach the faith at ecumenical councils. And so de Margerie concludes: "The ecumenical councils of the first millenium, held in the East, represented and engaged the churches of the West as well; and the ecumenical councils of the second millenium, held in the West, represented and engaged the churches of the East. For in both cases the ecumenical councils represented the universal Church."[46]

[44] R. Bellarmine, *De controversiis christianae fidei adversus hujus temporis haereticos* 1.17, cited in de Margerie, "L'analogie," p. 430.

[45] A. Gréa, *L'Eglise et sa divine constitution* (Paris, 1965).

[46] De Margerie, "L'analogie", p. 431.

But, so de Margerie argues, this conclusion does not suppress the "concrete consequences" of unequal ecumenicity. For some commentators we need, at this point, to introduce a distinction between an ecumenical council and one that is (merely) "general". In 1974, on the seventh centenary of the Second Council of Lyons, Paul VI, in a public letter to Cardinal Jan Willebrands, described Lyons II as "the sixth of those general councils celebrated in the Western world". On the other hand, Innocent III, in convoking Lateran IV, expressly termed it an ecumenical council. De Margerie proposes to synthesise these two "givens" by saying that, whereas the will of the Roman pope to summon a council so as to present "the one and universal doctrine of the whole Church" or to "legislate for [that Church] in its totality" suffices to render a council both ecumenical and universal, it does not suffice to render it plenary. The Roman see can give a council ecumenical *esse* but not ecumenical *bene esse*.[47]

Thus de Margerie finds that there are three levels of council. First, there are councils convoked without doctrinal aim but simply to reform the Church—such as Lateran I, Lateran II, Lateran III, and Lyons I. Here the universality of the reforming intention safeguards the essence of ecumenicity, but, in the nature of the case, there can be nothing definitive about the work of these councils: "It does not seem that, at the present time, there is any necessity of receiving the decisions [*actes*] of these councils, or of agreeing to them, or of making them one's own."[48] Second, there are councils convoked with the doctrinal aim of expounding the faith of the Church in a solemn fashion yet where the doctrinal presentation is limited by a certain absence. The physical absence of representatives of whole regions of the Church signalises the absence of "the contributions of different traditions theologically rooted in the New Testament". Examples would be Constantinople I, Lateran IV, Lyons II, Vienne, Constance, Lateran V, Trent, Vatican I, and, to a degree, Nicaea and Chalcedon. Third, there are councils that best manifest the Church's catholicity and exhibit the highest degree of ecumenicity. This they

[47] Ibid., p. 433.
[48] Ibid., p. 434.

do since, at them, "East and West converged morally and physically in elaborating and presenting the teaching of the one and universal Church." [49] Instances cited by de Margerie are Nicaea and Chalcedon (again), Florence, and Vatican II. The occurrence of the names of Nicaea and Chalcedon in both lists shows the difficulty that attaches to judgements about particular cases. Yet the general principle is clear.

What, in the light of this discussion, the preparation of a reunion council requires is a *double relecture*, a "twofold rereading", of tradition. The West must reread the ecumenical councils held in the East during the first millenium, and the East must reread the ecumenical councils held in the West during the second. This rereading would be characterised by *ressourcement* and reformulation: it would at once recapitulate and unify. Exploring the "substantial" harmony found in and beyond the "accidental" differences of expression in East and West, it would situate this method within a recognition of a hierarchy of councils (as well as of a hierarchy of truths).

If, on the basis of this preparatory work, such a council of reunion were held, it might well be appropriate, de Margerie thinks, for it to define solemnly the concept of episcopal collegiality, since such a definition (which would of course include an account of the pope as the head of the college) would create "a richer and more balanced understanding of the rôle of the pope in any and every ecumenical council." [50] For the pope's task is not simply to convoke and confirm. In the language of *Lumen gentium*, it is also "to assemble in charity the traditions proper to the particular churches, thus allowing them to deploy their universal virtualities." [51] In this way, the "partially" separated bishops of the East would "accede to a perfect communion with the chair of Peter, recognising with Peter the imperfectly ecumenical councils of the second millennium." [52] And de Margerie concludes that such recognition, consequent on a profound *relecture* of the content of these councils, might be expressed

[49] Ibid., pp. 434–435.
[50] Ibid., p. 439.
[51] Ibid., p. 440; cf. *Lumen gentium* 13.
[52] De Margerie, "L'analogie", p. 440.

either explicitly or by a simple "global recognition" of the rôle of the Roman bishop as *doctor omnium Christianorum*, "teacher of all Christians". We live, however, not in a world constructed by theological doctrine, though, for the orthodox Christian, only theological doctrine can construe the world in which we live. The world is shaped by a variety of human forces, and it is to these that we must attend if, in conclusion, we attempt to estimate the likely fortunes of this proposal or the wider chances of reunion between Rome and the Eastern churches, in the play of human history.

Bibliography

Barringer, R., C.S.B., *Rome and Constantinople: Essays in the Dialogue of Love*. Brookline, Mass., 1984.

Borelli, J., and J. H. Erickson. *The Quest for Unity: Orthodox and Catholics in Dialogue; Documents of the Joint International Commission and Official Dialogues in the United States, 1965–1995*. Crestwood, N.Y., and Washington, D.C., 1996.

Bria, I. *The Sense of Ecumenical Tradition: The Ecumenical Witness and Vision of the Orthodox*. Geneva, 1991.

Brunello, A. *Le Chiese orientali e l'unione*. Milan, 1966.

Desseaux, J. E., ed. *Le livre de la charité*. Paris, 1984.

Esposito, R. *Leone XIII e l'oriente cristiano*. Rome, 1960.

Lopetegui, L. S. *El Concilio Vaticano primero y la unión de los Orientales*. Berriz, 1961.

Orthodoxie et mouvement oecuménique. Chambésy and Geneva, 1986.

McPartlan, P., ed. *One in 2000? Towards Catholic-Orthodox Unity*. Slough, 1993.

Patelos, C. G. *Vatican I et les évêques uniates: Une étape éclairante de la politique romaine à l'égard des Orientaux, 1867–1870*. Louvain, 1981.

Salachas, D. *Il dialogo teologico ufficiale tra la Chiesa cattolica-romana a la Chiesa ortodossa: Iter e documentazione*. Bari, 1986.

Stiernon, E. J., ed. *Towards the Healing of Schism: The Sees of Rome and Constantinople; Public Statements and Correspondence of the Holy See and the Ecumenical Patriarchate, 1958–1984*. New York, 1987.

Conclusion

The present study has not been intended simply as an historical excursus—though without historical study there can be no illumination of existing reality. It is also meant as a contribution to the overcoming of the various schisms described—through an eirenic, yet confessionally responsible, adjudication of the chief "separating issues" involved. This is not to say, however, that the author is especially optimistic about the possibility of a positive outcome for the various bilateral negotiations, whether formal or informal, currently taking place. Quite apart from the dogmatic investment of the different churches in their own interpretations of the apostolic deposit and the relative intractability of a number of the questions involved (especially, perhaps, the matter of the status of doctors regarded as heretical by opposing traditions and, at the heart of it all, the Roman claims themselves), the Catholic theologian must face the fact that the present and future of the separated Eastern churches are not and will not be shaped by doctrinal considerations alone. These churches, considered as human communities with a given history, and determinate hopes and anxieties vis-à-vis other communities whose living space they share, will be obliged to give due weight to nontheological factors relevant to their survival and flourishing.

It is obvious that the operation of these nontheological factors— which are basically political, whether in a broad or a narrow sense of that word—will vary from country to country, from church to church.[1] The Copts of Egypt, for instance, an exposed island buffeted by the winds of an Arab ocean, may be expected to welcome

[1] For a brief overview, see S. Runciman, *The Orthodox Churches and the Secular State* (Auckland, 1971). There are useful essays in P. Ramet, ed., *Eastern Christianity and Politics in the Twentieth Century* (Durham, N.C., 1988); see also the same editor's *Catholicism and Politics in Communist Societies* (Durham, N.C., 1990), and, as author,

sympathy and solidarity from the Christian West, although working against this will be the corporate mystique of the Coptic church as the "true" Egyptian nation and the guardian of Athanasian and Cyrilline orthodoxy when all the world was Arian (or semi-Arian) and "Nestorian" (or Chalcedonian). In India, by contrast, the Syrian Orthodox, self-governing (with the exception of the small minority still dependent on the Jacobite patriarch of Antioch) and proudly aware both of their Palestinian origins and centuries of Indian domicile, will not find it notably politic to create links with a Rome associated in the minds of Indian nationalists, whether secularising or Hindu, with the territorial aggression of the Portuguese or the spiritual "aggression" of the later European missionaries.

The issue of nationalism—the greatest political conundrum of the twentieth century—is also highly relevant to the position of the Chalcedonian Orthodox.[2] If the Byzantine church came to function as a church of the Hellenes, it nevertheless retained some sense of "Pan-Orthodoxy" thanks to the intricate relations that bound the East Roman *basileus* to other Orthodox princes and peoples in what Dimitri Obolensky called the "Byzantine commonwealth".[3] But the particularist lesson of Byzantine Hellenism was only too well learned by the Orthodox nations in the course of time. An emerging state apparatus naturally wishes to utilise, and dominate, the religious organs of its territory—a phenomenon as well known in the Catholic West as in the Orthodox East. But the existence of a supranational common centre in the see of Rome, endowed with a primacy not merely decorative but functional, has prevented the crystallisation in the West of truly national churches that operate as the religious arm of their *ethnos*, with scant regard to the needs, desires, or values of a wider communion. The failure of the ecumenical patriarchate to maintain

---

Nihil Obstat: Religion, Politics and Social Change in East-Central Europe and Russia (Durham, N.C., 1998).

[2] L. Duchesne, *Autonomies ecclésiastiques: Eglises séparées*, 3rd ed. (Paris, 1904); F. Dvornik, *National Churches and the Church Universal* (Westminster, 1944).

[3] D. Obolensky, *The Byzantine Commonwealth: Eastern Europe, 500–1453* (London, 1971).

at any rate an effective *analogy* with the church of Rome in this regard has—to the eye of the outside observer—cost Orthodoxy dearly.

Although at the present time there are signs that the see of Constantinople may try to regain a Pan-Orthodox significance largely obscured in modern times, it may be doubted whether it will find the resources to overcome the tendency of many of its sister churches to become vehicles for cultural and political nationalism. For the factors that led to the partial eclipse of the ecumenical throne of New Rome are still potent today. The Ottoman Empire, it is true, lies beyond any conceivable possibility of historical reconstruction. But the Turkish state, though still committed to a secular ideology, takes as its long-term policy goal the achievement of an ethnically homogenous Turkey of the Turks, while recent governments have shown themselves not averse to significant concessions to a newly renascent Islam. In these circumstances, the partriarchate's freedom of initiative is obviously limited. Again, whereas the attempt of the Russian church to unite all Orthodox under its own aegis largely collapsed with the tsardom, that church remained, and remains, a formidable competitor to Constantinople. Used by the Soviet state for its own foreign policy ends,[4] it is in the process of becoming the (officially or unofficially) established church of the Russian Federation, post-Communist and thirsty for the slaking of historical memories, passions, and dreams. Since the Russian church will, on any reckoning, remain numerically the single most important Orthodox community, it is clearly possible that it may regain something of the position of dominance that it achieved through the Romanov dynasty before the Great War of 1914–1918. Once again, the spectre of ecclesiastical nationalism rears its head. The third factor that maintains the wings of the ecumenical patriarchate in a state of clippedness derives from the circumstance that the emancipation of the Orthodox Church in the lands of the former Ottoman Empire coincided with the arrival in those territories of the ideological packhorse of nineteenth-century nationalism. The new patriarchates of Serbia,

---

[4] For the period from the end of the Second World War to 1970, see W. C. Fletcher, *Religion and Soviet Foreign Policy* (London, 1975).

Romania, and Bulgaria, as well as the autocephalous churches that orbit as planets these minor stars, are too firmly wedded to the national idea to be divorced therefrom at Constantinople's say-so—as the ineffective late nineteenth-century condemnation of "Filetism" by the Phanar demonstrates.[5] Finally, owing to a mixture of insouciance towards temporary schism and an attitude of "pick and choose" towards the canons, both aided and abetted by the lack of a clearly recognised and effectively functioning universal primacy, there is, in much Orthodox church life, a wilfulness that lends itself only too easily to the free play of corporate egoisms.

Rome must reckon, then, with the probable continuance and even accentuation, within Orthodoxy, of a vigorous ecclesiastical nationalism, and, from her viewpoint, little seems more depressing. If the movement in the church of Greece known as "Neo-Orthodoxy" (essentially an Orthodox nationalism of Christian Hellenism, opposed not only to the Latin West but also to the non-Greek churches of the Orthodox world) plays a major part in the continuing resistance of many Greek Orthodox to the ecumenical movement, the hostility of the Moscow patriarchate to the Ukrainian church[6] and that of the Romanian patriarchate to the Uniates of Transylvania is no less founded on the national church idea.[7] If the ploys of the Moscow patriarchate and the harshness of its hierarchs have earned well-merited strictures from such an admirer of Orthodoxy as the Anglican Russianist Michael Bordeaux,[8] it is at least encouraging to find that among the Greek monastic clergy there are stern critics of the gains made in recent times by religious nationalism.[9] Until those

[5] For this 1872 Orthodox synod of Constantinople, see Mansi, 45:417–546; also M. Zyzykine, "L'Eglise orthodoxe et la nation", *Irén.* 13 (1936): 265–77.

[6] M. Tataryn, "Russian Orthodox Attitudes towards the Ukrainian Catholic Church", *Religion in Communist Lands* 17, no. 4 (Winter 1989): 313–31.

[7] See, for instance, I. Ratiu, "The Uniates in Romania", *Tablet*, 27 February 1982, pp. 198–99.

[8] M. Bordeaux, *Gorbachev, Glasnost and the Gospel* (London, 1990), pp. 167–70, 181–87.

[9] Father Maximos [Lavriotis], *Human Rights on Mount Athos: An Appeal to the Civilized World* (Welshpool, 1990), pp. 8–9. For the background, see K. Ware, "Catholicity

attitudes are purified and replaced by an internationalism, a catho-licity, better befitting the pattern of the Christian *koinônia*, there can be no place within Orthodoxy for a Roman see embodying the universal pastorate of Peter and the apostolate to the Gentiles of Paul.

Rome looks at this important aspect of contemporary Ortho-doxy with such dismay because she not only desires but *needs* reunion with the Orthodox East. In the face of her own numerous theo-logical liberals and the innovationist tendencies of churchmen (and churchwomen) in various portions of her far-flung "Western" patri-archate, from Santiago de Chile to Manila, from Melbourne to Detroit, Catholicism's grasp of the historic Christian tradition can only be strengthened by the accession of Orthodoxy to commu-nion with Rome. In such matters as the upholding of the tran-scendentality of revelation vis-à-vis human understanding; the defence of the Trinitarian and Christological doctrine of the first seven councils; a perception of the nature of salvation as more than tem-poral alone; the maintenance of a classical liturgical life; the nour-ishment of group and personal devotion to Mary and the saints; the preservation of the threefold apostolic ministry of bishops, pres-byters, and deacons (in that same gender in which the incarnate Word exercised his own high priesthood); the encouragement of the consecrated life, especially in its most basic form, monasticism; and the preservation of the ascetic dimension in spirituality, in all of these the present struggle of the papacy to uphold Catholic faith and practice in a worldwide communion exposed to a variety of intellectual and cultural influences often baleful, if sometimes also beneficent, can only benefit from Orthodox aid. The energies of authentic Catholicism can only be increased by the inflow of

---

and Nationalism. A Recent Debate in Athens", *ECR* 10 (1978): 10–16. Dr. Richard Clogg, of the School of Eastern European and Slavonic Studies, London, in the course of reviewing C. Frazee, *The Orthodox Church and Independent Greece, 1821–1852* (Lon-don, 1969), in the same journal, called the book—one of whose main themes is the creation of the autocephalous church of Greece by the constitution of 1833—"an object lesson in the perils inherent in Erastianism": *ECR* 3 (1970–1971): 351.

Orthodox faith and holiness: the precious liquid contained within the not seldom unattractive phial of Orthodoxy's canonical form. Can this greatest of all ecclesiastical reunions be brought off? The auguries are not good, yet the Christian lives from hope in the unseen.

General Bibliography

Assfalg, J., and P. Krüger. *Kleines Wörterbuch des christlichen Orients.* Wiesbaden, 1975.

Atiya, A. S. *A History of Eastern Christianity.* London, 1968; repr., Millwood, N.Y., 1991.

Attwater, D. *The Catholic Eastern Churches.* 2nd ed. London, 1937.

————. *The Christian Churches of the East.* Vol. 2. *Churches Not in communion with Rome.* 2nd ed. London, 1962.

Barrett, D. B., G. T. Kurian, and T. M. Johnson, eds. *World Christian Encyclopaedia: A Comparative Survey of Churches and Religions in the Modern World.* Oxford, 2001. (For statistics and the present-day situation.)

Brunello, A. *Le Chiese orientali e l'unione.* Milan, 1966.

Centro Franciscano di Studi Orientali cristiani. *Il primato e l'unione delle chiese nel Medio Oriente.* Studia orientalia christiana collectanea 5. Cairo, 1960. (On Copts, Syrians, Armenians, and Chaldaeans.)

Chadwick, H. *East and West: The Making of a Rift in the Church; From Apostolic Times until the Council of Florence.* Oxford, 2003.

Detlef, C., and G. Müller. *Geschichte der orientalischen Nationalkirchen.* Göttingen, 1981.

Fortescue, A. *The Lesser Eastern Churches.* London, 1913.

————. *The Orthodox Eastern Church.* London, 1907.

————. *The Uniate Eastern Churches.* London, 1923.

Ivánka, E. von, et al. *Handbuch der Ostkirchlichenkunde.* Düsseldorf, 1971.

Janin, R. *Les Eglises orientales et les rites orientaux.* 3rd ed. Paris, 1935.

Kidd, B. J. *The Churches of Eastern Christendom, from A.D. 451 to the Present Time.* London, 1927.

Neale, J. M. *A History of the Holy Eastern Church.* London, 1896.

Parry, K. et al. *The Blackwell Dictionary of Eastern Christianity.* Oxford 1999.

Roberson, R. G., C.S.P. *The Eastern Catholic Churches: A Brief Survey.* 6th ed. Rome, 1999.

Vries, W. de. *Oriente cristiano ieri e oggi.* Rome, 1950.

———. *Rom und die Patriarchate des Ostens.* Freiburg and Munich, 1963.

Index